# TM 9-710

## WAR DEPARTMENT TECHNICAL MANUAL

# BASIC HALF-TRACK VEHICLES M2, M3 TECHNICAL MANUAL

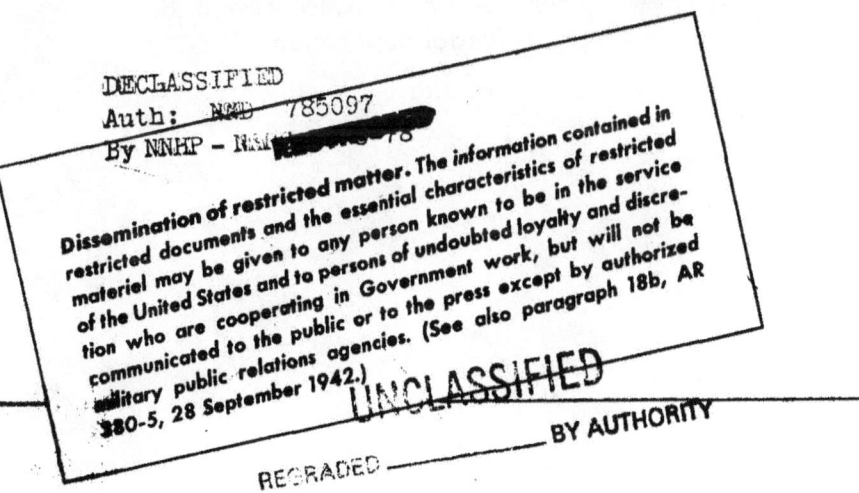

**WAR DEPARTMENT**　　　　　　　　　23 FEBRUARY 1944

©2011 Periscope Film LLC
All Rights Reserved
ISBN# 978-1-937684-97-6

This book has been digitally watermarked by
Periscope Film LLC to prevent
illegal duplication.

WAR DEPARTMENT TECHNICAL MANUAL

*TM 9-710 — RESTRICTED

# ASIC HALF-TRACK VEHICLES (WHITE, AUTOCAR, AND DIAMOND T)

WAR DEPARTMENT
23 February 1944

**RESTRICTED**

Dissemination of restricted matter. The information contained in restricted documents and the essential characteristics of restricted material may be given to any person known to be in the service of the United States and to persons of undoubted loyalty and discretion who are cooperating in Government work, but will not be communicated to the public or to the press except by authorized military public relations agencies. (See also paragraph 18b, AR 380-5, 28 September 1942.)

*This manual supersedes TM 9-710A, 16 Sept 1943; TM 9-708, 9 Feb 1943; TB 710-10, 1 Jul 1942; TB 710-17, 2 Sept 1942; TB 710A-19, 12 Nov 1942; TB 712-1, 1 Jul 1942; TB 712-2, 25 Jun 1942; TB 715-2, 1 Jul 1942; TB 715-3, 25 Jun 1942. This manual also supersedes pertinent information from TB 700-26, 12 Dec 1942; TB 700-47, 12 Apr 1943; TB 700-63, 10 Jun 1943; TB 700-65, 10 Jun 1943; TB 700-74, 1 Jul 1943; TB 700-82, 21 Jul 1943; TB 700-83, 23 Jul 1943; TB 700-88, 6 Aug 1943.

WAR DEPARTMENT
Washington 25, D. C., 23 February 1944

TM 9-710, Basic Half-track Vehicles (White, Autocar, and Diamond T), is published for the information and guidance of all concerned.

[A.G. 300.7 (21 Aug. 43)]

BY ORDER OF THE SECRETARY OF WAR:

G. C. MARSHALL,
*Chief of Staff.*

OFFICIAL:

J. A. ULIO,
*Major General,*
*The Adjutant General.*

DISTRIBUTION: D (5); B 2 (3); R 2, 5, 17, and 18 (3); Bn 9 (2 IBn 2, 5, 6, 7, 17, 18, and 44 (3); C 9 (8); IC 2, 5, 6, 7, 17, 18, and 44 (5).

(For explanation of symbols, see **FM 21-6**.)

TM 9-710

## CONTENTS

### PART ONE—VEHICLE OPERATING INSTRUCTIONS

|  |  |  | Paragraphs | Pages |
|---|---|---|---|---|
| Section | I | Introduction ............... | 1 | 5 |
|  | II | Description and tabulated data | 2–4 | 6–22 |
|  | III | Driving controls and operation | 5–7 | 23–31 |
|  | IV | Auxiliary equipment controls and operation........... | 8–9 | 32–33 |
|  | V | Operation under unusual conditions ............. | 10–16 | 34–43 |
|  | VI | Inspection and preventive maintenance services..... | 17–21 | 44–53 |
|  | VII | Lubrication ............... | 22–23 | 54–66 |
|  | VIII | Tools and equipment stowage on the vehicle........... | 24–33 | 67–94 |

### PART TWO—VEHICLE MAINTENANCE INSTRUCTIONS

| | | | |
|---|---|---|---|
| IX | Record of modifications and new vehicle run-in tests.... | 34–37 | 95–99 |
| X | Organization tools and equipment ............. | 38–39 | 100 |
| XI | Organizational preventive maintenance services..... | 40 | 101–117 |
| XII | Trouble shooting........... | 41–57 | 118–132 |
| XIII | Engine data, maintenance, and adjustment in vehicle..... | 58–66 | 133–147 |
| XIV | Engine removal and installation .............. | 67–68 | 148–156 |
| XV | Clutch ................... | 69–72 | 157–159 |
| XVI | Fuel system............... | 73–78 | 160–169 |
| XVII | Intake and exhaust system... | 79–82 | 170–173 |
| XVIII | Cooling system............. | 83–89 | 174–186 |
| XIX | Ignition system............ | 90–96 | 187–199 |
| XX | Starting and generating system | 97–100 | 200–206 |
| XXI | Transmission, transfer case, and power take-off....... | 101–103 | 207–213 |
| XXII | Propeller shafts and universal joints ................... | 104–106 | 214–217 |
| XXIII | Front axle................. | 107–111 | 218–224 |
| XXIV | Rear axle (jackshaft)....... | 112–115 | 225–228 |
| XXV | Bogie suspension and track.. | 116–120 | 229–250 |
| XXVI | Brake system.............. | 121–134 | 251–285 |

3

# TM 9-710
## BASIC HALF-TRACK VEHICLES (WHITE, AUTOCAR, and DIAMOND T)

|  |  |  | Paragraphs | Pages |
|---|---|---|---|---|
| Section | XXVII | Wheels, sprockets, hubs and bearings, tires, and chains | 135–138 | 286–292 |
|  | XXVIII | Springs and shock absorbers | 139–140 | 293–295 |
|  | XXIX | Steering gear and drag link | 141–142 | 296–302 |
|  | XXX | Body and frame......... | 143–151 | 303–309 |
|  | XXXI | Battery and lighting system | 152–159 | 310–319 |
|  | XXXII | Instruments and gages.... | 160–165 | 320–325 |
|  | XXXIII | Winch ................ | 166–170 | 326–330 |
|  | XXXIV | Shipment and temporary storage ............. | 171–173 | 331–335 |

### PART THREE—VEHICLE ARMAMENT

|  |  |  |  |  |
|---|---|---|---|---|
|  | XXXV | Armament ............. | 174–185 | 336–347 |
| References | | | | 348–351 |
| Index | | | | 352– |

TM 9-710

# PART ONE—VEHICLE OPERATING INSTRUCTIONS

Section I

## INTRODUCTION

|  | Paragraph |
|---|---|
| Scope | 1 |

**1. SCOPE.**

a. This technical manual is published for the information and guidance of the using arm personnel charged with the operation, maintenance, and minor repair of this materiel.

b. The specific vehicles derived from the basic half-track which is covered by this manual are designated:

(1) Car M2 and M2A1.
(2) Personnel Carrier M3 and M3A1.
(3) 81-mm Mortar Carriers M4 and M4A1.
(4) 75-mm Gun Motor Carriage M3 and M3A1.
(5) 75-mm Howitzer Motor Carriage T30.
(6) 105-mm Howitzer Motor Carriage T19.
(7) Multiple Gun Motor Carriage M13.
(8) Multiple Gun Motor Carriage M15 and M15A1.
(9) Multiple Gun Motor Carriage M16.
(10) 81-mm Mortar Carrier M21.

c. In addition to a description of the basic half-track vehicle, this manual contains technical information required for the identification, use, and care of the specific vehicles listed in subparagraph b above, and similar vehicles. This manual is divided into three parts. Part One, Section I through Section VIII, gives vehicle operating instructions. Part Two, Section IX through Section XXXIV, gives vehicle maintenance instructions to using arm personnel charged with the responsibility of doing maintenance work within their jurisdiction. Part Two also includes instructions for preparing the vehicles for shipment and temporary storage. Part Three, Section XXXV, gives armament data.

d. In all cases where the nature of the repair, modifications, or adjustment is beyond the scope or facilities of the unit, the responsible Ordnance Service should be informed so that trained personnel with suitable tools and equipment may be provided, or proper instructions issued.

# TM 9-710

## BASIC HALF-TRACK VEHICLES (WHITE, AUTOCAR, and DIAMOND T)

Section II

## DESCRIPTION AND TABULATED DATA

|  | Paragraph |
|---|---|
| Description | 2 |
| Differences among models | 3 |
| Tabulated data | 4 |

### 2. DESCRIPTION.

*a.* The armored vehicles covered in this manual are the half-track type, consisting of a wheel suspension in the front, and a bogie and track suspension in the rear. The chassis is essentially the same on all the models with the main differences being in the armor plated body, converting the vehicle to best advantage for its specific duty. The chassis equipped with heavier armament are reinforced with extra frame members to carry the additional load. A roller or winch is mounted on the front end of the frame. The vehicles have doors located at advantageous positions, or side panels which fold down to gain gun depression. The vehicle has front and rear drive and is powered by a six cylinder gasoline engine.

### 3. DIFFERENCES AMONG MODELS.

*a.* **Car M2** (figs. 1 and 2). This vehicle has a seating arrangement for a crew of ten. A driver's seat, commander's seat, and one other seat are in the driver's compartment. Arrangement of all seats is shown in figure 39. A gun rail extends throughout the inside of the body allowing the movement of the guns mounted on skates to command full 360 degrees rotation. There is no rear door on this model, but it has two large ammunition storage compartments with outside doors, located just behind the driver's compartment. A lid on each stowage chest opens from inside the vehicle, allowing removal of ammunition boxes from the top shelf. Access to the remaining shelves is reached from outside the vehicle. The gas tanks are located inside the vehicle body at the rear sides. A radio mast is located at the side of the rear center seat. There are no rifle scabbards or gun pedestals on this model and it comes equipped with a roller or a winch at the front end of the vehicle. The M2 armament consists of one caliber .30 and one caliber .50 machine gun and a caliber .45 submachine gun. A top view may be seen by referring to figure 39.

*b.* **Car M2A1** (figs. 3 and 4). This vehicle is the same as the Car M2 with the addition of a ring mount on the front side of the driver's compartment. It has one caliber .50 machine gun in ring mount. There are also three pintles for caliber .30 machine guns, located one on each side, and one in rear.

*c.* **Personnel Carrier M3** (figs. 5 and 6). This vehicle has a seating arrangement for a crew of 13 men. There are three seats in the driver's compartment and the other ten are arranged in two rows of five each, backed up against the fuel tanks and body sides. The fuel tanks are

# TM 9-710

## DESCRIPTION AND TABULATED DATA

Figure 1—Car M2 (Right Front)

RA PD 313982

RA PD 313983

# TM 9-710
3

## BASIC HALF-TRACK VEHICLES (WHITE, AUTOCAR, and DIAMOND T)

RA PD 313984

*Figure 3—Car M2A1 (Right Rear)*

RA PD 313985

## DESCRIPTION AND TABULATED DATA

RA PD 313986

**Figure 5—Personnel Carrier M3 (Right Front)**

RA PD 313987

**Figure 6—Personnel Carrier M3 (Left Rear)**

# TM 9-710
3

## BASIC HALF-TRACK VEHICLES (WHITE, AUTOCAR, and DIAMOND T)

Figure 7—Personnel Carrier M3A1 (Left Front)

Figure 8—Personnel Carrier M3A1 (Right Rear)

**TM 9-710**
3

## DESCRIPTION AND TABULATED DATA

Figure 9—Personnel Carrier M3A1 (Front)

Figure 10—81-mm Mortar Carrier M4A1 (Right Side)

**TM 9-710**
**3**

## BASIC HALF-TRACK VEHICLES (WHITE, AUTOCAR, and DIAMOND T)

RA PD 313990

*Figure 11—75-mm Gun Motor Carriage M3 (Right Front)*

RA PD 31399

*Figure 12—75-mm Gun Motor Carriage M3 (Left Front)*

TM 9-710
3

## DESCRIPTION AND TABULATED DATA

RA PD 313992

*Figure 13—75-mm Howitzer Motor Carriage T30 (Right Front)*

RA PD 313993

*Figure 14—75-mm Howitzer Motor Carriage T30 (Left Rear)*

# TM 9-710

## BASIC HALF-TRACK VEHICLES (WHITE, AUTOCAR, and DIAMOND T)

located just behind the driver's compartment at the sides of the vehicle. There is no gun rail or radio mast inside the body of this vehicle, but it has one pedestal, mounting a caliber .30 machine gun, located just behind the center seat of the driver's compartment (fig. 40). A door is located at the rear of this model, and it also has rifle scabbard mounts, six on each side, along the sides in the space at the back of the side seats. A top view may be seen by referring to figure 40.

RA PD 313994

*Figure 15—105-mm Howitzer Motor Carriage T19 (Left Front)*

d. **Personnel Carrier M3A1** (figs. 7 and 8). This vehicle is the same as the Personnel Carrier M3 with the addition of a gun ring mount on the top right side of the driver's compartment.

e. **81-mm Mortar Carriers M4 and M4A1** (fig. 9). These vehicles carry a crew of eight men with the usual seating arrangement for three in the driver's compartment. Each vehicle has a gun ring running completely around the inside of the body, mounting one caliber .50 machine gun on a skate mount. A caliber .45 submachine gun and one 81-mm mortar complete the armament. There is an extra door at the rear of the vehicle and two extra doors for the stowage compartments at the front sides of the body. The gas tanks are located at the rear sides of the body.

## DESCRIPTION AND TABULATED DATA

f. **75-mm Gun Motor Carriage M3 and M3A1** (figs. 11 and 12). These vehicles carry a crew of five men, seating two in the driver's compartment, one on each side of the body at breech of gun, and one against rear door. The armament consists of one 75-mm gun with an armor plate hood which covers the breech of the gun and moves with the pointing of the gun. The gas tanks are mounted in the rear at each side of vehicle body. A top view may be seen by referring to figure 42.

RA PD 313995

*Figure 16—105-mm Howitzer Motor Carriage T19 (Left Rear)*

g. **75-mm Howitzer Motor Carriage T30** (figs. 13 and 14). This vehicle has a rear door and a gun pedestal mount at the rear center which carries a machine gun. There is no gun rail inside the body and the gas tanks are mounted in the rear at the sides. An armor plate hood covers the breech of the 75-mm howitzer. A crew of five men is carried.

h. **105-mm Howitzer Motor Carriage T19** (figs. 15 and 16). This vehicle has a rear door and a gun pedestal mount at the rear center which carries a machine gun. There is no gun rail inside the body and the gas tanks are mounted in the rear at the sides. An armor plate hood covers the breech of the 105-mm howitzer. A crew of six men is carried.

**TM 9-710**
3

**BASIC HALF-TRACK VEHICLES (WHITE, AUTOCAR, and DIAMOND T)**

RA PD 313996

*Figure 17—Multiple Gun Motor Carriage M13 (Right Front)*

RA PD 31399

*Figure 18—Multiple Gun Motor Carriage M15 (Right Front)*

TM 9-710

## DESCRIPTION AND TABULATED DATA

*Figure 19—Multiple Gun Motor Carriage M15 (Left Rear)*

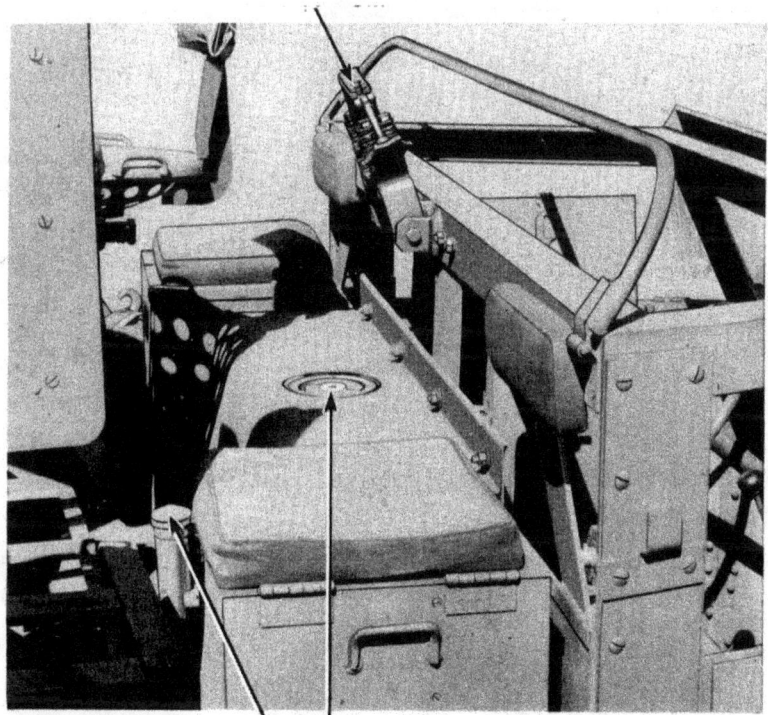

*Figure 20—Gun Support and Fuel Tank Filler Caps M15*

## BASIC HALF-TRACK VEHICLES (WHITE, AUTOCAR, and DIAMOND T)

i. **Multiple Gun Motor Carriage M13** (fig. 17). This vehicle has an electrically operated gun turret, carrying its own battery charging unit. The turret mounts two caliber .50 machine guns and turns a full 360 degrees. There is no gun rail, pedestal mount, or rear door on this model. There are folding panels at the two sides and rear end of the body. The gas tanks are mounted just to the rear of the driver's compartment on each side of the body. This vehicle carries a crew of five men.

j. **Multiple Gun Motor Carriage M15 and M15A1** (figs. 18 and 19). This vehicle has a manually operated gun turret mounting three synchronized guns. The turret turns a full 360 degrees, mounting one .37-mm automatic cannon and two caliber .50 machine guns. The driver's compartment and gun turret are separate units on this model. Two gas tanks are located at the center of the vehicle, the upper tank just behind the driver's compartment, and the lower tank is below the level of the floor just to the rear of the upper tank. The filler spout of the lower tank rises at the left-hand rear corner of the upper tank (fig. 20). A gun support (fig. 20), located on the rear of the driver's compartment, and two turret locks (fig. 21), lock the turret and cannon in position while traveling. This vehicle carries a crew of seven men. The M15A1 is a later model; the main difference is a change in mounting the cannon and two machine guns at a common level (the cannon is below the level of the machine guns in the M15). A top view of the M15 may be seen by referring to figure 43.

k. **Multiple Gun Motor Carriage M16** (figs. 22 and 23). This vehicle resembles the M13 Multiple Gun Motor Carriage. It has an electrically operated gun turret with four caliber .50 machine guns in place of two as on the M13. The folding side and rear panels have a dip or section cut out of their top edge to permit more gun depression. The M13 becomes an M16 with the above changes incorporated. A top view may be seen by referring to figure 44.

l. **81-mm Mortar Carrier M21 (Forward Firing)** (fig. 24). This vehicle carries a crew of six men. Its armament consists of an 81-mm mortar which fires forward only; one caliber .50 machine gun and pedestal mounting; one caliber .45 submachine gun.

## DESCRIPTION AND TABULATED DATA

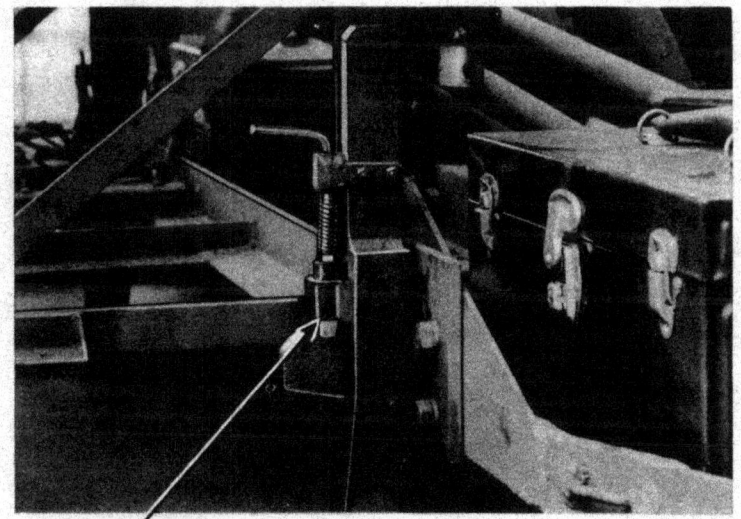

Figure 21—Turret Lock M15

Figure 22—Multiple Gun Motor Carriage M16 (Right Front)

# TM 9-710

## BASIC HALF-TRACK VEHICLES (WHITE, AUTOCAR, and DIAMOND T)

### 4. TABULATED DATA.

#### a. Vehicle Specifications.

| | Car M2 | Car M2A1 | Personnel Carrier M3 | Personnel Carrier M3A1 | 81-mm Mortar Carrier M4 | 81-mm Mortar Carrier M4A1 |
|---|---|---|---|---|---|---|
| Wheelbase...in. | 135½ | 135½ | 135½ | 135½ | 135½ | 135½ |
| Length (Roller)...in. | 234 | 234¾ | 242⅝ | 242⅝ | 243⅞ | 243⅞ |
| (Winch)...in. | 241 | 241⅝ | 249⅝ | 249⅝ | 250⅝ | 250⅝ |
| Width...in. | 87 | 87½ | 87½ | 87½ | 77½ | 87½ |
| Height...in. | 89 | 95⅛ | 89 | 95⅛ | 89⅜ | 89⅜ |
| Wheel size...in. | 20x7 | 20x7 | 20x7 | 20x7 | 20x7 | 20x7 |
| Tire size (front)...in. | 8.25x20 | 8.25x20 | 8.25x20 | 8.25x20 | 8.25x20 | 8.25x20 |
| Tire type... | Combat | Combat | Combat | Combat | Combat | Combat |
| Tread...in. | 63¹³⁄₁₆ | 63¹³⁄₁₆ | 63¹³⁄₁₆ | 63¹³⁄₁₆ | 63¹³⁄₁₆ | 63¹³⁄₁₆ |
| Crew... | 10 | 10 | 13 | 13 | 6 | 6 |
| Weight (gross)... | 19,195 | 19,600 | 17,650 | 20,500 | 17,350 | 18,000 |
| Ground press. (unit) 16 per sq in. | 45 | | | | | |
| Ground clearance...in. | 17⅛ | 11³⁄₁₆ | 17⅛ | 11³⁄₁₆ | 17⅛ | 17⅛ |
| Pintle height...in. | 28 | 28 | 28 | 28 | 28 | 28 |
| Octane rating of fuel (gasoline).. | 72 | 72 | 72 | 72 | 72 | 72 |
| Approach angle (Roller)...deg | 37 | 37 | 37 | 37 | 37 | 37 |
| (Winch)...deg | 32 | 32 | 32 | 32 | 32 | 32 |
| Departure angle...deg | 35 | 35 | 35 | 35 | 35 | 35 |

#### b. Performance.

| | Mph | | | | | |
|---|---|---|---|---|---|---|
| Speeds allowable (1st gear) | 9.15 | 9.15 | 9.15 | 9.15 | 9.15 | 9.15 |
| without front wheels (2nd gear) | 17.3 | 17.3 | 17.3 | 17.3 | 17.3 | 17.3 |
| driving (transfer case (3rd gear) | 26.2 | 26.2 | 26.2 | 26.2 | 26.2 | 26.2 |
| in high range) (4th gear) | 45 | 45 | 45 | 45 | 45 | 45 |
| Speeds allowable (1st gear) | 3.68 | 3.68 | 3.68 | 3.68 | 3.68 | 3.68 |
| with front wheels (2nd gear) | 6.96 | 6.96 | 6.96 | 6.96 | 6.96 | 6.96 |
| driving (transfer case (3rd gear) | 10.45 | 10.45 | 10.45 | 10.45 | 10.45 | 10.45 |
| in low range) (4th gear) | 18.05 | 18.05 | 18.05 | 18.05 | 18.05 | 18.05 |
| Min. turning circle (diam.)...ft | 59 | 59 | 59 | 59 | 60 | 60 |
| Maximum fording depth...in. | 32 | 32 | 32 | 32 | 32 | 32 |
| Towing facilities (front)... | Two tow hooks | Two tow hooks | Two tow hooks | Two tow hooks | Two tow hooks | Two tow hooks |
| (rear)... | Pintle | Pintle | Pintle | Pintle | Pintle | Pintle |
| Max. grade ascend. ability..pct | 60 | 60 | 60 | 60 | 60 | 60 |
| Max. governed engine speed rpm | 3,000 | | | | | |
| Miles per gallon (approx.)... | 3½ | 3½ | 3½ | 3½ | 3½ | 3½ |
| Cruising range (approx.)...mi | 200 | 220 | 200 | 220 | 200 | 200 |

#### c. Capacities.

| | | | | | | |
|---|---|---|---|---|---|---|
| Trans. cap. (less P.T.O.)...qt | 7½ | 7½ | 7½ | 7½ | 7½ | 7½ |
| Trans. case cap. (with P.T.O.)qt | 9 | 9 | 9 | 9 | 9 | 9 |
| Front axle capacity...qt | 3½ | 3½ | 3½ | 3½ | 3½ | 3½ |
| Rear axle capacity...qt | 9 | 9 | 9 | 9 | 9 | 9 |
| Fuel capacity...gal | 60 | 60 | 60 | 60 | 60 | 60 |
| Cooling system capacity...gal | 6½ | 6½ | 6½ | 6½ | 6½ | 6½ |
| Crankcase capacity...qt | 12 | 12 | 12 | 12 | 12 | 12 |

# DESCRIPTION AND TABULATED DATA

| 57-mm Gun Motor Carriage T48 | 75-mm Gun Motor Carriage M3 | 75-mm Gun Motor Carriage M3A1 | 75-mm Howitzer Motor Carriage T30 | 105-mm Howitzer Motor Carriage T19 | Multiple Gun Motor Carriage M13 | Multiple Gun Motor Carriage M15 | Multiple Gun Motor Carriage M15A1 | Multiple Gun Motor Carriage M16 | 81-mm Mortar Carrier M21 |
|---|---|---|---|---|---|---|---|---|---|
| 135½ | 135½ | 135½ | 135½ | 135½ | 135½ | 135½ | 135½ | 135½ | 135½ |
| ..... | 249⅞ | 249⅞ | 240⅛ | ..... | ..... | 236½ | 236½ | ..... | ..... |
| 252⅝ | ..... | ..... | ..... | 241¾ | 256 | ..... | ..... | 256 | 244⅞ |
| 83 | 77⅞ | 77⅞ | 77¼ | 84 13/16 | 77⅞ | 98 | 98 | 77⅞ | 87¼ |
| 84 | 92 | 92 | 83¼ | 88 | 88 | 104 | 104 | 88 | 87 |
| 20x7 | 20x7 | 20x7 | 20x7 | 20x7 | 20x7 | 20x7 | 20x7 | 20x7 | 20x7 |
| 8.25x20 | 8.25x20 | 8.25x20 | 8.25x20 | 8.25x20 | 8.25x20 | 8.25x20 | 8.25x20 | 8.25x20 | 8.25x20 |
| Combat | Combat | Combat | Combat | Combat | Combat | Combat | Combat | Combat | Combat |
| 63 13/16 | 63 13/16 | 63 13/16 | 63 13/16 | 63 13/16 | 63 13/16 | 63 13/16 | 63 13/16 | 63 13/16 | 63 13/16 |
| 5 | 5 | 5 | 5 | 6 | 5 | 7 | 7 | 5 | 6 |
| 19,000 | 20,000 | 20,000 | 20,500 | 19,240 | 18,500 | 20,000 | 20,000 | 19,000 | 20,000 |
| ..... | 33.5 | 33.5 | ..... | ..... | 29.5 | 33.5 | 33.5 | 29.6 | ..... |
| 17⅛ | 17⅛ | 17⅛ | 17⅛ | 17⅛ | 17⅛ | 17⅛ | 17⅛ | 17⅛ | 17⅛ |
| 28 | 28 | 28 | 28 | 28 | 28 | 28 | 28 | 28 | 28 |
| 72 | 72 | 72 | 72 | 72 | 72 | 72 | 72 | 72 | 72 |
| 37 | 37 | 37 | 37 | 37 | 37 | 37 | 37 | 37 | 37 |
| 32 | 32 | 32 | 32 | 32 | 32 | 32 | 32 | 32 | 32 |
| 35 | 35 | 35 | 35 | 35 | 35 | 35 | 35 | 35 | 35 |
| 9.15 | 9.15 | 9.15 | 9.15 | 9.15 | 9.15 | 9.15 | 9.15 | 9.15 | 9.15 |
| 17.3 | 17.3 | 17.3 | 17.3 | 17.3 | 17.3 | 17.3 | 17.3 | 17.3 | 17.3 |
| 26.2 | 26.2 | 26.2 | 26.2 | 26.2 | 26.2 | 26.2 | 26.2 | 26.2 | 26.2 |
| 45 | 45 | 45 | 45 | 45 | 45 | 45 | 45 | 45 | 45 |
| 3.68 | 3.68 | 3.68 | 3.68 | 3.68 | 3.68 | 3.68 | 3.68 | 3.68 | 3.68 |
| 6.96 | 6.96 | 6.96 | 6.96 | 6.96 | 6.96 | 6.96 | 6.96 | 6.96 | 6.96 |
| 10.45 | 10.45 | 10.45 | 10.45 | 10.45 | 10.45 | 10.45 | 10.45 | 10.45 | 10.45 |
| 18.05 | 18.05 | 18.05 | 18.05 | 18.05 | 18.05 | 18.05 | 18.05 | 18.05 | 18.05 |
| 60 | 60 | 60 | 60 | 60 | 59 | 60 | 60 | 60 | 60 |
| 32 | 32 | 32 | 32 | 32 | 32 | 32 | 32 | 32 | 32 |
| Two | Two | Two | Two | Two | Two | Two | Two | Two | Two |
| tow | tow | tow | tow | tow | tow | tow | tow | tow | tow |
| hooks | hooks | hooks | hooks | hooks | hooks | hooks | hooks | hooks | hooks |
| Pintle | Pintle | Pintle | Pintle | Pintle | Pintle | Pintle | Pintle | Pintle | Pintle |
| 60 | 60 | 60 | 60 | 60 | 60 | 60 | 60 | 60 | 60 |
| 3½ | 3½ | 3½ | 3½ | 3½ | 3½ | 3½ | 3½ | 3½ | 3½ |
| 200 | 200 | 200 | 200 | 200 | 200 | 200 | 200 | 200 | 200 |
| 7½ | 7½ | 7½ | 7½ | 7½ | 7½ | 7½ | 7½ | 7½ | 7½ |
| 9 | 9 | 9 | 9 | 9 | 9 | 9 | 9 | 9 | 9 |
| 3½ | 3½ | 3½ | 3½ | 3½ | 3½ | 3½ | 3½ | 3½ | 3½ |
| 9 | 9 | 9 | 9 | 9 | 9 | 9 | 9 | 9 | 9 |
| 60 | 60 | 60 | 60 | 60 | 60 | 60 | 60 | 60 | 60 |
| 6½ | 6½ | 6½ | 6½ | 6½ | 6½ | 6½ | 6½ | 6½ | 6½ |
| 12 | 12 | 12 | 12 | 12 | 12 | 12 | 12 | 12 | 12 |

TM 9-710
4

**BASIC HALF-TRACK VEHICLES (WHITE, AUTOCAR, and DIAMOND T)**

Figure 23—Multiple Gun Motor Carriage M16 (Left Rear)

Figure 24—81-mm Mortar Carrier M21 (Forward Firing)

Section III

## DRIVING CONTROLS AND OPERATION

|  | Paragraph |
|---|---|
| Controls | 5 |
| Operation of the vehicle | 6 |
| Towing the vehicle | 7 |

5. **CONTROLS** (fig. 25).

    *a.* **Windshield Wiper Control Buttons.** The two windshield wiper control buttons are part of the wiper units which are located at the bottom center panel of each windshield. Pull button out to start wiper, push button in to stop.

    *b.* **Panel Light Control Rheostat.** The instrument panel light control is located directly under the left-hand windshield wiper unit. Turn knob counterclockwise to illuminate instruments to desired intensity, turn clockwise to turn lights off. The service headlights must be in use before the panel lights will go on.

    *c.* **Electric Brake Load Control.** The electric brake load control is a radio-type dial rheostat located on the left side of the instrument cluster. The dial is marked "LIGHT," "MEDIUM," and "HEAVY," to cover varying trailer loads. Turn dial to right to increase braking on trailer brakes as trailer load increases.

    *d.* **Main Light Switch** (fig. 26). The main light switch, located directly above the electric brake control, is a four-position push-pull type switch. This switch controls the service and blackout headlights, and the service and blackout stop and taillights in the following manner.

    (1) OFF POSITION. Push switch button completely in to turn off all lights. NOTE: *Service stop lights cannot be used with button in this position.*

    (2) BLACKOUT POSITION. Pull switch button to first position to operate blackout headlights, and blackout stop, and taillights.

    (3) SERVICE LIGHTS POSITION. Depress lockout button and pull switch button to second position to operate service headlights, and service stop, and taillights.

    (4) SERVICE STOP LIGHT POSITION. Depress lockout button and pull switch button fully out to operate service stop light for daylight use.

    *e.* **Blackout Driving Light Switch** (fig. 25). The blackout driving light switch, located on the instrument panel to the right-hand center of the speedometer and marked "B. O. DRIVE", energizes the blackout driving light (if one is installed), which is a shielded type, used in addition to the standard blackout lights, when additional illumination is necessary during blackout conditions. Blackout driving switch will not operate unit until main light switch is in first or blackout position, as previously explained.

**TM 9-710**
**5**

**BASIC HALF-TRACK VEHICLES (WHITE, AUTOCAR, and DIAMOND T)**

Figure 25—Instruments and Controls

## DRIVING CONTROLS AND OPERATION

A—TACHOMETER
B—TROUBLE LIGHT RECEPTACLE
C—WINDSHIELD WIPER CONTROL—LEFT UNIT
D—PANEL LIGHT CONTROL RHEOSTAT
E—MAIN LIGHT SWITCH
F—INSTRUMENT CLUSTER
G—THROTTLE CONTROL
H—STARTER PUSH BUTTON
I—IGNITION SWITCH
J—SPEEDOMETER
K—COMPASS
L—FUEL TANK SELECTOR SWITCH
M—BLACKOUT DRIVING LIGHT SWITCH
N—DASH LIGHT
O—VOLTMETER
P—VOLTMETER PUSH BUTTON
Q—MAP COMPARTMENT DOOR
R—WINDSHIELD WIPER CONTROL—RIGHT UNIT
S—VEHICLE REGISTRATION PLATE
T—FIRE EXTINGUISHER
U—RADIATOR SHUTTER CONTROL LEVER
V—WINCH CAUTION PLATE
W—FRONT AXLE DRIVE SHIFT LEVER
X—VENTILATOR CONTROL—RIGHT HAND
Y—TRANSFER CASE SHIFT LEVER
Z—CHOKE CONTROL
AA—PARKING BRAKE LEVER
AB—ACCELERATOR PEDAL
AC—TRANSMISSION GEAR SHIFT LEVER
AD—P. T. O. SHIFT LEVER
AE—BRAKE PEDAL
AF—VENTILATOR CONTROL—LEFT HAND
AG—ELECTRIC BRAKE LOAD CONTROL
AH—CLUTCH PEDAL
AJ—GEAR SHIFT INSTRUMENT PLATE
AI—ENGINE CAUTION PLATE

RA PD 314003B

*Legend for Figure 25—Instruments and Controls*

## BASIC HALF-TRACK VEHICLES (WHITE, AUTOCAR, and DIAMOND T)

f. **Ignition Switch.** The ignition switch is marked "IGNITION," and is located between the instrument cluster and the speedometer. This switch, being the lever type, does not require a key. Turning the lever to the left turns the ignition on, returning it to the vertical position turns it off.

g. **Starter Push Button** (fig. 27). This button is on the dash just above the ignition switch between the instrument cluster and speedometer. To crank engine, turn ignition switch to the left and press starter push button. Release button the instant engine starts.

h. **Fuel Tank Selector Switch.** This is a toggle type switch, located just below the center strip of the windshield on the instrument panel. Push toggle to right for reading of right-hand tank supply. Push toggle to left for reading of left-hand tank supply. The ignition switch must be "ON" before a reading can be made.

i. **Dash Light.** The dash light is located just above the ammeter. The service headlights must be "ON" before it is operative. A knob, located at the lamp base, turns the dash light to the right to "ON" position; to the left turns it "OFF."

j. **Choke Control Button.** The control button marked "CHOKE" is located directly below the speedometer. This regulates the fuel and air mixture to aid starting when the engine is cold. Pull out just far enough to allow the engine to run smoothly during the warm-up period. Otherwise the button should remain at position while engine is in operation.

k. **Throttle Control Button.** The control button marked "THROTTLE" is located directly below the ignition switch and starter button. Pull this button out to regulate the speed of the engine during the warm-up period or during engine tests. Do not use the throttle control button to control the speed of the vehicle in motion.

l. **Ventilator Control Buttons.** Two ventilator control buttons of the push-pull type are located on the bottom edge of the dash marked "VENT." The right-hand ventilator control button is just to the right of the choke button, and the left-hand ventilator control button is just to the left of the throttle button. Pull buttons out to open ventilators.

m. **Horn Button.** The horn button is located at the center of the steering wheel. Press the horn button to operate the horn.

n. **Radiator Shutter Control Lever.** The radiator armor plate shutters are controlled by a lever located at the extreme right-hand side of the driver's compartment, just under the instrument panel. To open shutters, press button on top of lever handle releasing locking latch, then pull lever to extreme rear position and release button. To close shutters, press button and push lever to extreme forward position. There are three intermediate settings between fully open and fully closed positions.

o. **Front Axle Drive Shift Lever.** The front axle drive shift lever is the first lever starting at extreme right of the center floor plate. It has two positions. Push lever forward to engage the front axle

## DRIVING CONTROLS AND OPERATION

drive. Pull lever rearward to disengage front axle drive (fig. 28).

p. **Transfer Case Shift Lever.** The transfer case lever is the second lever from the right-hand side of the center floor plate. It has two positions. Push lever forward to put transfer case in low gear range. Pull lever rearward to put transfer case in high gear range (fig. 28).

q. **Transmission Gearshift Lever.** The transmission gearshift lever is the third lever from the right-hand side of the center floor plate. It is used in conjunction with the clutch pedal to select the various gear ratios or speeds provided in the transmission. The transmission has four speeds forward and one reverse (fig. 28).

r. **Clutch Pedal.** The clutch pedal is the pedal to the left of the steering column in the driver's compartment. Depressing the pedal

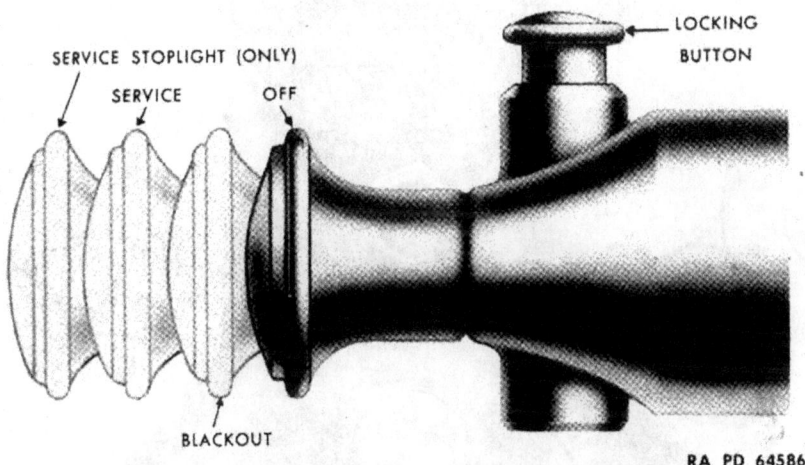

*Figure 26—Main Light Switch Operating Positions*

disengages the engine from the transmission so that transmission gears may be shifted. Releasing the pedal engages the clutch and connects the engine and transmission gears.

s. **Brake Pedal.** The brake pedal is the pedal to the right of the steering column in the driver's compartment. Press pedal down to apply the service brakes. Releasing pressure on the pedal releases the brakes as the pedal returns to normal position.

t. **Parking Brake Lever.** The parking brake lever is located to the right and rear of the transmission gearshift lever. To operate the parking brake, pull back on the lever and a spring-loaded catch will lock the lever in applied position. To release, depress button on top of lever releasing the latch, and push lever forward as far as possible. Only apply this brake after vehicle has come to a dead stop.

u. **Power Take-off Shift Lever.** The power take-off lever is the lever at the rear left-hand side of the center floor plate. It has three positions. When pushed forward, it operates the winch in reverse;

# TM 9-710
5-6

**BASIC HALF-TRACK VEHICLES (WHITE, AUTOCAR, and DIAMOND T)**

when pulled rearward, it operates the winch in forward speed; and setting the lever in the middle position places it in neutral. The clutch is depressed before shifting the power take-off lever into the desired position and releasing the clutch puts the winch in operation. Speed of operation is controlled by speed of the engine through the foot pedal accelerator.

v. **Accelerator Pedal.** The accelerator pedal is located in the driver's compartment on the toe plate to the right of the brake

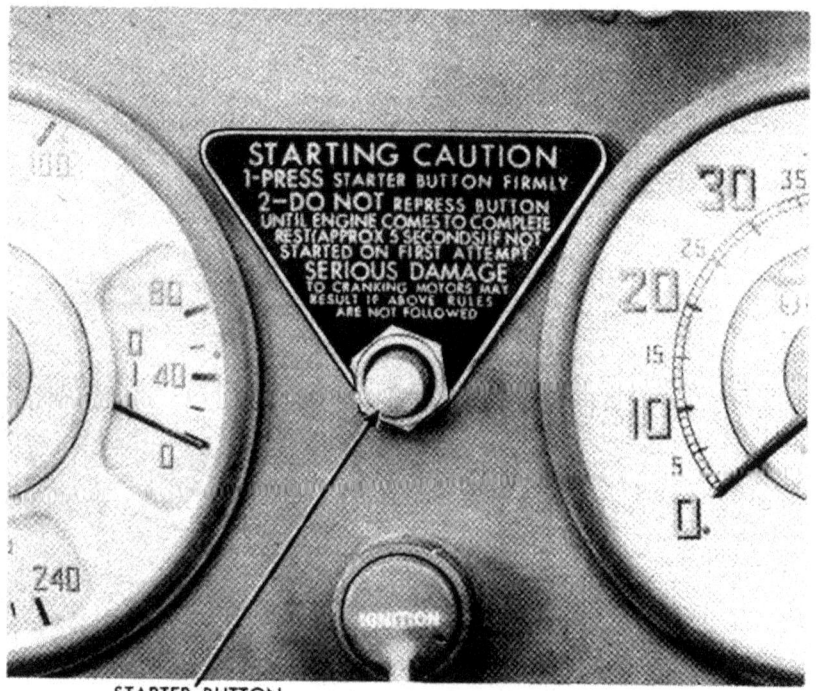

*Figure 27—Starter Button Caution Plate*

pedal. Engine and vehicle speed are controlled by this pedal, which is linked to the carburetor throttle.

## 6. OPERATION OF THE VEHICLE.

a. **Starting the Engine.**

(1) MAKE BEFORE-OPERATION INSPECTION. Refer to paragraph 18, Preventive Maintenance, Section VI.

(2) STARTING THE ENGINE. Apply the hand brake by pulling back on lever. Place the transmission shift lever in neutral position. Pull choke button out about half-way and pull hand throttle button out one-quarter inch. (If engine is warm these two steps will not be necessary). Move ignition switch lever to left to turn on ignition.

# DRIVING CONTROLS AND OPERATION

Depress clutch pedal disengaging the clutch. Press the starter button on instrument panel and crank the engine. Release pressure on starter button the instant the engine starts. Adjust throttle and choke until engine attains even idling speed. Release clutch pedal slowly.

(3) INSTRUMENT READINGS. Before operating the vehicle, check the instruments on the instrument panel for the following readings:

*(a) Tachometer.* The idling speed is approximately 400 revolutions per minute.

*(b) Electric Brake Control.* If towing a trailer, set this dial to the proper braking power indication.

*(c) Ammeter.* This should show a "positive" (+) reading.

*(d) Fuel Gage.* Take a reading of both tanks (using toggle switch) to assure a sufficient fuel supply.

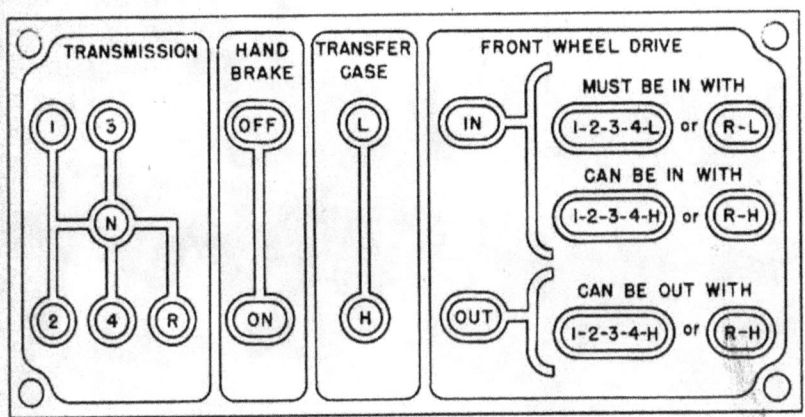

RA PD 24077

*Figure 28—Gearshift Diagram*

*(e) Engine Temperature Gage.* This should show a slow increase in temperature until the engine warms up, then it should show a maximum reading of 180°F.

*(f) Oil Pressure Gage.* This gage should show a reading of four to eight pounds, with engine idling, and a maximum pressure of 20 to 35 pounds with engine running at operating speed.

*(g) Voltmeter.* Press in switch button below the gage. The reading with engine stopped and no load on battery should be approximately 12 to 14 volts.

b. **Driving the Vehicle.**

(1) SHIFTING INTO LOW GEAR (fig. 28.) After engine has been started and checked for satisfactory performance, depress the clutch pedal and move the transmission lever from neutral position to the left and then forward, placing the transmission gears in (first gear) "LOW." If it is to be a level start under no great load, and solid underfoot, pull the transfer case shift lever to the rear, placing the

**BASIC HALF-TRACK VEHICLES (WHITE, AUTOCAR, and DIAMOND T)**

transfer case in "HIGH" range. NOTE: *If these conditions are reversed and the start is to be made under difficulties, push the transfer case lever forward into "LOW" and engage the front axle drive by pushing its lever forward to engaged position.*

(2) PUTTING VEHICLE IN MOTION. Release the parking brake by depressing the button on top of the handle, and push the lever forward as far as possible. Release the clutch pedal slowly, and at the same time, press the accelerator pedal the amount necessary to overcome the load and put the vehicle in motion.

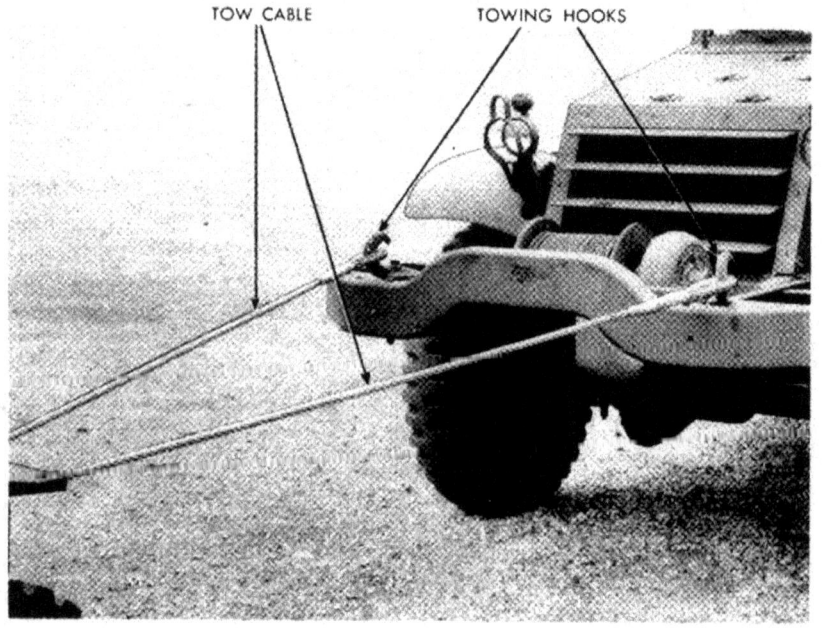

*Figure 29—Hook-up of Towing Cable on Front of Vehicle*

(3) SHIFTING TO HIGHER GEARS (fig. 28). As the vehicle gains speed, release the accelerator pedal, and push the clutch pedal down at the same time. Pull the transmission shift lever straight back to engage the "second" gear. Release the clutch and push down the accelerator as before, until the speed of the vehicle has increased enough for the next shift. Repeat the operation of releasing the accelerator and depressing the clutch, and shift the lever forward and into neutral; then shove it forward and to the right into "third" gear. Release the clutch and pick up more speed in "third", then repeat the operation of releasing the accelerator and depressing the clutch. Now pull the shift lever straight back and engage the "fourth" or "HIGH" gear; release the clutch pedal and control the speed of the vehicle with the accelerator.

**c. Double Clutching.** To shift the transmission gears smoothly, it is sometimes necessary to "double clutch." Push down the clutch

## DRIVING CONTROLS AND OPERATION

pedal disengaging the clutch, shift the transmission lever to neutral position and release the clutch pedal. Push down clutch pedal. Regulate engine speed with accelerator to equal new transmission speed. Shift transmission lever to gear selected. Release clutch slowly.

**d. Shifting the Transmission into Reverse** (fig. 28). Disengage the clutch and bring vehicle to a full stop. Move transmission shift lever into neutral, then to the right as far as possible, and rearward into "REVERSE" position. Release clutch pedal, and accelerate engine at the same time, and in the same manner, as when starting vehicle forward.

**e. Stopping the Vehicle.** Release the accelerator pedal and apply the brakes by slowly pushing in the brake pedal. When forward speed of the vehicle has decreased to about the idling speed of the engine, push in the clutch pedal. When the vehicle has been brought to a complete stop, shift the transmission into neutral, release the clutch pedal, and pull the hand brake as far rearward as possible.

**f. Stopping the Engine.** Turn the ignition switch to the right or "OFF" position, after completing instructions on stopping the vehicle.

## 7. TOWING THE VEHICLE.

**a. Towing to Start Vehicle** (fig. 29). To start the engine by towing, place the transfer case in high range and the transmission in fourth or high gear. Disengage the front axle. Disengage the clutch by holding foot pedal down. Adjust choke and throttle to suit climatic condition. After vehicle has gained speed, turn on the ignition switch and engage the clutch slowly. As soon as the engine is running smoothly, shift transmission into neutral and signal towing vehicle to stop.

**b. Towing Disabled Vehicle.** Towing of a disabled vehicle will depend upon the damage to the vehicle. If the wheels and tracks are not disabled, the vehicle can be towed by a connection made to one of the tow hooks on the front end of the vehicle, or to the rear pintle hook. In case either of the ends remains undamaged, the damaged end can be raised with a conventional towing hoist and the vehicle towed to a repair station. Place the towed vehicle in neutral with all drives disengaged. If the wheels or tracks cannot be used to support one end of the vehicle, special recovery equipment will have to be procured.

**TM 9-710**
**8-9**

**BASIC HALF-TRACK VEHICLES (WHITE, AUTOCAR, and DIAMOND T)**

Section IV

## AUXILIARY EQUIPMENT CONTROLS AND OPERATION

|  | Paragraph |
|---|---|
| Winch controls | 8 |
| Winch cable operation | 9 |

**8. WINCH CONTROLS.**

   a. **Drum Clutch Control.** A lever for engaging or disengaging the drum clutch by hand, is located on the clutch end of the winch (fig. 30). When this clutch is disengaged, the drum turns freely on drum shaft, being retarded only by the drag brake. CAUTION: *Do not disengage the drum clutch while winch is under load. Before using power on winch, determine that winch clutch is locked "IN" securely.*

*Figure 30—Winch Drum Clutch Control*

   b. **Power Take-off Control.** The lever for shifting the power take-off and operating the winch is the first one on the driver's right-hand side. The lever is held in neutral position by a hinged lock on the floor of the cab. Raise this lock before attempting to operate the lever. To unwind the winch cable, push the lever forward. To wind the cable, pull the lever to the rear of neutral position.

**9. WINCH CABLE OPERATION** (fig. 31).

   a. **To Hook On.** Disengage drum clutch and pull off required amount of cable. If winch is under load, reverse power take-off and run winch until load-pressure is released. NOTE: *The winch cable must*

32

## AUXILIARY EQUIPMENT CONTROLS AND OPERATION

*Figure 31—Caution Plate on Winch Operation*

not be wrapped around the load, with the hook around the cable, as this will damage cable.

　b. **To Pull.** Engage drum clutch securely, push down clutch pedal, shift power take-off into forward position, then slowly release truck clutch pedal. Control speed of winch by operation of engine accelerator pedal or hand throttle control.

　c. **To Stop Winch.** Push down clutch pedal and shift power take-off into neutral. Load will be held by the winch automatic worm brake.

　d. **To Release Load.** Push down clutch pedal, shift power take-off into reverse, and run out just enough cable to give a little slack. Push in clutch pedal and shift power take-off into neutral.

　e. **To Rewind Cable.** Reel cable on drum in the same manner as making a pull. Keep a slight tension on the cable, to assure tight wrapping. Make the first layer of cable winding trim and "close wrapped," tapping the strands in, tightly, with a wood block.

# TM 9-710

## BASIC HALF-TRACK VEHICLES (WHITE, AUTOCAR, and DIAMOND T)

Section V

## OPERATION UNDER UNUSUAL CONDITIONS

|  | Paragraph |
|---|---|
| Extreme heat | 10 |
| Extreme cold | 11 |
| Sandy terrain | 12 |
| Fording streams, or flood conditions | 13 |
| Muddy terrain or deep snow | 14 |
| Rough terrain | 15 |
| Gas contaminated areas | 16 |

### 10. EXTREME HEAT.

**a. Cooling System.**

(1) Make certain the system is clean and free flowing.

(2) Keep the water level as high as possible in the radiator tank.

(3) Adjust the fan belts to proper tension of 3/4-inch deflection.

(4) If the engine becomes overheated from lack of water, allow it to cool before adding water.

(5) Keep the radiator fins free of foreign materials, such as insects, leaves, and dirt.

(6) Use only clean, clear water to fill radiator. **NOTE:** *Do not use salt, or mineral water, solutions in the system.*

**b. Engine Care.**

(1) Use only the crankcase oil viscosities recommended in the Lubrication Guide for temperatures encountered.

(2) Inspect exhaust pipe and service if partially closed.

(3) Keep engine clean. Accumulations of dust and oil form an insulation against cooling air supplied by the fan.

(4) Keep all mountings, cylinder head nuts, and connections tight.

**c. Electrical System Care.**

(1) BATTERIES. Never allow batteries to become overheated. Guard against this in extreme heat conditions by opening the battery box while in operation allowing air to circulate around the batteries. Top connectors should not feel hot to the touch. If battery feels warm, turn on the lights to cut down charging rate to battery. This is particularly necessary on long runs.

(2) WIRING SYSTEM. Inspect carefully to detect any bare wire or other possibilities of short circuit.

(3) IGNITION.

*(a)* Check ignition timing occasionally, and adjust to avoid overheating due to incorrect timing.

*(b)* Examine distributor for proper operation of centrifugal advance, proper condition, and adjustment of distributor points.

*(c)* Check spark plugs and adjust to proper gap, 0.025 inch.

## OPERATION UNDER UNUSUAL CONDITIONS

(4) FUEL SYSTEM. Keep the air cleaner and its tube, connecting to the carburetor intake, as clean as possible.

**d. Clutch.** Keep the clutch in proper adjustment, to avoid clutch slippage, and racing of the engine without effective power to the driving axles.

**e. Transmission, Transfer Case, and Driving Axles.**

(1) Keep all vent holes clean and free.

(2) Examine housings for cracks and leaks.

(3) Make certain that proper lubricants, in proper quantities, are in the units (see Lubrication Guide).

## 11. EXTREME COLD.

**a. General.**

(1) Operation of automotive equipment at subzero temperatures presents problems that demand special precautions and careful servicing from both operation and maintenance personnel, if poor performance and total functional failure are to be avoided. The instructions given herein apply only at temperatures ranging between 0°F and —40°F. Automotive equipment can be operated efficiently at low temperatures if the instructions in this paragraph are observed.

(2) Extreme care must be exercised whenever a vehicle or part is moved from a warm place into subzero temperature, as moisture will immediately condense upon all surfaces, and freeze there.

(3) Lubrication of automotive equipment at temperatures above 0°F is covered by Lubrication Guides and applicable Ordnance Field Service Bulletins. The lubrication instructions contained in this paragraph will be followed only when temperatures below 0°F prevail. Subzero temperatures affect both metals and lubricants. Therefore, special attention must be given to lubrication and servicing of equipment when such temperatures are encountered.

**b. Gasoline for Low Temperatures.**

(1) Winter grade gasoline is designed to reduce cold weather starting difficulties; therefore the winter grade motor fuels procured under U. S. Army Specification 2-103, latest issue, will be used.

(2) Due to condensation of moisture in the air, water will accumulate in tanks and containers. At low temperatures, this water will form ice crystals that will clog fuel lines and carburetor jets unless the following precautions are taken:

(a) Strain the fuel through a chamois skin, or other type of strainer, that will prevent the passage of water. CAUTION: *Gasoline flowing over a surface generates static electricity that will result in a spark, unless some means is provided to ground the electricity. A metallic contact, between the container and the tank, must be provided to assure an effective ground.*

(b) Keep tank full, if possible. The more fuel there is in the tank, the smaller will be the volume of air from which moisture can be condensed.

TM 9-710
11

**BASIC HALF-TRACK VEHICLES (WHITE, AUTOCAR, and DIAMOND T)**

*(c)* Be sure that all containers are thoroughly clean and free from rust before storing fuel in them.

*(d)* If possible, after filling or moving a container, allow the fuel to settle before filling vehicle tank from it.

*(e)* Keep all closures of containers tightly covered to prevent snow, ice, dirt, and other foreign matter from entering.

c. **Lubrication of Engines Equipped with Winterization Kits.** Special winterization kits are prepared for all vehicles. When these kits are available, the following instructions for preparation and starting of engines will apply. NOTE: *If kits are not installed, see subparagraph d below for engine instructions. Instructions on all other parts of vehicle which follow apply whether kits are used or not.*

(1) VEHICLES WITH SHROUDS AND HEATERS. When shrouds and heaters are supplied, no engine oil dilution is necessary. For short shut-down periods, the vehicle should be parked in a sheltered spot, out of the wind if possible. If no shelter is available, park so that the vehicle does not face the wind. For long periods of shut-down, as in bivouac, park vehicle in as sheltered a place as possible. If built-in engine heater is supplied, drop bottom cover of heater. Make sure valve in gasoline supply line is open to heater. Open lighter hole in base of heater. Remove lighter tool from clip on side of heater, soak lighter tool with gasoline, ignite, and insert lighter tool in hole, lighting heater. Close lighter hole. If built-in heater is not supplied, connect standby heater to fuel supply. Hang heater from chassis under engine, or stand on ground under engine and level with leveling screws in legs, within 10 degrees of absolute level. Do not stand heater on snow. Light heater. Heater should burn with a blue flame in still air. Keep heater free of ice, and strainers clear. Change adjustment of heater only as last resort, and then, with extreme caution. Be sure all electrical equipment is turned off. Use windshield defrosters only when engine is running. Erect shroud over engine, and weight down at edges with stones or snow. Make shroud as tight as possible to keep out wind, but allow for air necessary for combustion of heater fuel. To start vehicles with built-in heaters, close bottom cover of heater. This will extinguish the heater. Leave gasoline supply valve open for other equipment. Forty-five minutes before it is intended to start, turn on battery heater. When start is to be made, turn off battery heater. Pull choke out ¾ to full. Do not manipulate choke until engine is running, and then with caution. Disengage clutch and operate cranking motor. After engine has started, it must be allowed to idle until cooling system temperature begins to rise. Check battery warming coil for leaks. Regulate engine temperature by use of shutters on radiators. Remove shroud, engine heater, and battery heater, and stow.

(2) VEHICLES WITHOUT SHROUDS AND HEATERS. In order to assure starting at subzero temperatures when no shrouds and heaters are provided, vehicles must be prepared for operation. Park vehicle in as sheltered a spot as possible and not facing the wind. Stop engine and check oil level in crankcase. If below "FULL," bring up to level with engine oil, crankcase grade. Start engine and, with engine idling, dilute crankcase oil. Lower dilution valve to fill diluting measure attached to

TM 9-710

## OPERATION UNDER UNUSUAL CONDITIONS

engine. Raise dilution valve to allow fuel to run into crankcase. Repeat once with full diluting measure, and once with half full measure. Note level of lubricant on dipstick after allowing engine to idle 10 to 15 minutes to mix diluent and lubricant. After each day's operation, check level of lubricant in crankcase. If below "FULL" mark, bring up to level with engine oil, crankcase grade, and then dilute. If above full mark, excess will indicate dilution remaining. Add dilution in required proportion to bring level to that encountered after initial dilution.

**d. Lubrication of Engines Not Equipped with Special Winterization Kits.** Several methods for keeping crankcase oil sufficiently fluid for proper lubrication are listed below. Preference should be given to the different methods in the order listed, according to the facilities available.

(1) Keep the vehicle in a heated inclosure when it is not being operated.

(2) When the engine has stopped, drain the crankcase oil while it is hot and store in a warm place until the vehicle is to be operated again. If warm storage is not available, heat the oil before reinstalling. Do not get the oil too hot; heat only to the point where the bare hand can be inserted without burning. Tag the vehicle in a conspicuous place in the cab to warn personnel that the crankcase is empty.

(3) If the vehicle is to be kept out-of-doors and if the crankcase cannot be drained, cover the engine with a tarpaulin. About 3 hours before the engine is to be started, place fire pots under the tarpaulin. A Van Prag, Primus-type, or other type blow-torch or ordinary kerosene lanterns may be used. With due consideration for the fire hazard involved, the flame may be applied directly to the oil pan.

(4) Dilute the crankcase oil with gasoline. The following dilutions will form mixtures for satisfactory starting at the temperature indicated:

| 0°F to —20°F | Below —20°F |
|---|---|
| ½ qt to each 4½ qt engine oil | 1 qt to each 5 qt engine oil |

(5) When crankcase oils are first diluted, run the engine 2 to 3 minutes at moderate speed to mix oil and diluent. If the vehicle is operated 4 hours or more at operating temperature, and if it is anticipated that the vehicle will be left standing unprotected for three hours or more, redilution will be necessary.

(6) The presence of a large percentage of light diluent will increase oil consumption, and for this reason, oil level should be checked frequently.

**e. Transmission, Differentials, and Transfer Case.**

(1) Universal gear lubricant, SAE 80, is suitable for use at temperatures as low as —20°F. For lower temperatures, universal gear lubricant, SAE 80, diluted with the fuel used by the engine in the proportion of one part fuel to six parts universal gear lubricant, must be used. When temperatures below —20°F are anticipated, drain transmission immediately after use, while lubricant is still warm. Refill to proper level with universal gear lubricant, SAE 80, diluted as noted above. After standing overnight at subzero temperatures, warm up transmission as follows:

(a) Warm up engine as provided in subparagraph c (1) above.

# TM 9-710

**BASIC HALF-TRACK VEHICLES (WHITE, AUTOCAR, and DIAMOND T)**

*(b)* Engage clutch and maintain engine speed at fast idle for five minutes or until gears can be engaged. Put transmission in low (1st) gear and drive vehicle for 100 yards, being careful not to stall engine.

**f. Chassis Lubricants.**

(1) TRACK SUSPENSION, REAR TRACK IDLER AND SUPPORT BEARINGS. Bogie wheels and track roller bearings must be removed, and washed in dry-cleaning solvent or Diesel fuel, and reassembled. Lubricate with engine oil, SAE 30. If removal of bearings and washing are impractical, bearings may be lubricated by forcing in engine oil, SAE 30, immediately after vehicle has been driven and when bearings are warm, forcing out the general purpose grease used above 0°F.

(2) DRIVING SPROCKET WHEEL BEARINGS, AND GREASE CUPS. Driving sprocket wheel bearings, and grease cups calling for general purpose grease, No. 2, must be lubricated with general purpose grease, No. 2, at all times. If repacking must be performed at such low temperatures that hand packing cannot be accomplished, grease, OD No. 00, may be used.

(3) UNIVERSAL JOINTS AND SLIP JOINTS. Universal joints and slip joints must be lubricated with grease, OD No. 00.

(4) CHASSIS POINTS. Chassis points must be lubricated with engine oil, SAE 30. CAUTION: *When temperatures below 0°F are no longer anticipated, the above bearings must be lubricated immediately with proper seasonal grade lubricant.*

(5) HYDROVAC CYLINDERS. Lubricate hydrovac cylinders with hydraulic oil.

**g. Protection of Cooling System.**

(1) Ethylene Glycol is prescribed for use as an antifreeze solution in vehicle radiators.

(2) The following table gives the approximate quantity of antifreeze necessary for various temperature conditions; however, check with an antifreeze solution hydrometer.

**Antifreeze Chart**

| Temperature F | +10 | 0 | —10 | —20 | —30 | —40 | —50 | —60 | —70 |
|---|---|---|---|---|---|---|---|---|---|
| Antifreeze Compound, (ethylene glycol type) (quarts) | 6½ | 8¼ | 9¾ | 11½ | 13 | 14¾ | 14¾ | 16¼ | 16¼ |

(3) Precautions to be taken before installing the antifreeze:

*(a)* Thoroughly flush the cooling system.

*(b)* Check the system for leaks; tighten the hose connections and replace if necessary; check the thermostat and water pump.

*(c)* Check the fan belts for adjustment or weakness. Do not use rubber fan belts at temperatures below —20°F. Use leather, fiber, or synthetic rubber fan belts.

**TM 9-710**
**11**

### OPERATION UNDER UNUSUAL CONDITIONS

**h. Protection of Electrical System.**

(1) GENERATOR AND CRANKING MOTOR. Check the brushes, commutators, and bearings. See that the commutators are clean. The large surges of current which occur when starting a cold motor require good contact between brushes and commutators.

(2) WIRING. Check and clean all connections, especially the battery terminals. Care should be taken that no short circuits are present.

(3) COIL. Check coil for proper functioning.

(4) DISTRIBUTOR. Clean thoroughly, and clean or replace points. Check the points frequently. In cold weather, slightly pitted points can prevent engine from starting.

(5) SPARK PLUGS. Clean, test, and replace, if necessary. If it is difficult to make the engine fire, reduce the gap 0.005 inch less than that recommended by the manufacturer. This will make ignition more effective at the reduced voltages likely to prevail.

(6) TIMING. Check timing carefully. Care should be taken that the spark is not unduly advanced or retarded.

(7) BATTERIES.

*(a)* The efficiency of batteries decreases sharply with decreasing temperatures, and becomes practically nil at —40°F. Do not try to start the engine with the battery when it has been chilled to temperatures below —30°F until battery has been heated. See that the battery is always fully charged, with the hydrometer reading between 1.275 and 1.300. A fully charged battery will not freeze at temperatures likely to be encountered even in arctic climates, but a fully discharged battery will freeze and rupture at 18°F.

*(b)* Maintain electrolyte level 3/8 inch above top of plates, using distilled water.

*(c)* Do not add water to batteries when they have been exposed to subzero temperatures, unless the battery is to be charged immediately afterward. If water is added and the battery not put on charge, the layer of water will stay at the top and freeze before it gets a chance to mix with the acid. Keep vent holes in filler plugs open. Keep terminals tight and clean. Apply a coating of PETROLATUM or GREASE, general purpose No. 0.

(8) LIGHTS. Inspect the lights carefully. Check for short circuits and presence of moisture around sockets.

(9) Before each start, see that the spark plugs, wiring, and other electrical equipment are free from ice.

**i. General Conditions.**

(1) Be sure that no heavy grease or dirt has been left on the cranking motor throw-out mechanism. Heavy grease or dirt may keep the gears from meshing or cause them to remain in mesh after the engine starts running. The latter will ruin the cranking motor and necessitate repairs.

(2) A full choke is necessary to secure the air-fuel ratio required for cold weather starting. Check the butterfly valve to see that it closes all the way and otherwise functions properly.

**BASIC HALF-TRACK VEHICLES (WHITE, AUTOCAR, and DIAMOND T)**

(3) Carburetors which give no appreciable trouble at normal temperatures may not operate satisfactorily at low temperatures. A fuel pump which will deliver enough gasoline at normal starting speeds of 500 revolutions per minute may have leaky valves or a diaphragm which will prevent delivering a sufficient quantity of fuel which, at the reduced temperature, will produce sufficient vapor to fire when turning at speeds of 30 to 60 revolutions per minute. Another source of trouble is the float needle valve which, although a close fit, must move freely. Different expansions of the metals used in the needle valve parts, may cause the needle valve to stick at extremely low temperatures.

(4) At temperatures below 0°F do not use oil in air cleaners. The oil will congeal and prevent the easy flow of air. At temperatures below 0°F, wash screens in dry-cleaning solvent, dry and replace. Ice and frost formations on the air cleaner screens may cause an abnormally high intake vacuum in the carburetor air horn hose, resulting in collapse.

(5) Full flow oil filters have a bypass valve. Below —30°F these filters must be bypassed, because the viscous oil will not flow freely through them. Other filters (bypass type) require no special attention.

(6) Remove and clean fuel system sediment bulb, strainers, etc., daily. Also drain fuel tank pump daily to remove water and dirt.

(7) Brake bands, particularly on new vehicles, have a tendency to bind when they are very cold. Always have a blow-torch handy to warm up these parts if they bind prior to moving, or attempting to move, the vehicle. Parking the vehicle with the brake released will eliminate most of the binding. Precaution must be taken, under these circumstances, to block the wheels or otherwise prevent movement of the vehicle.

(8) Inspect the vehicle frequently. Shock resistance of metals, or resistance against breaking, is greatly reduced at extremely low temperatures. Operation of vehicles on hard, frozen ground causes strain and jolting, which will result in screws breaking or nuts jarring loose.

(9) Disconnect oil-lubricated speedometer cables at the drive end when operating vehicles at temperatures of —30°F and below. These cables often fail to work properly at these temperatures, and sometimes break due to the excessive drag caused by the high viscosity of the oil with which they are lubricated.

*j.* **Lubricants.** For correct lubricants, refer to Product Guide, OFSB 6-2, latest issue.

*k.* **Cold Weather Accessories.** All necessary cold weather accessories are included in the cold weather starting kits being prepared for vehicles in cold climates (OFSB 6-11).

## 12. SANDY TERRAIN.

*a.* **Air Filters and Protective Measures.**

(1) In sand-storm operation, tie a single layer of medium fine knit cotton cloth, such as undershirt cloth, loosely over the oil breather holes to prevent grit from entering the crankcase.

**TM 9-710**

## OPERATION UNDER UNUSUAL CONDITIONS

(2) Using medium fine knit cotton cloth, form a loose bag over the entire air cleaner units for the engine and the hydrovac cylinder. Constant close supervision and daily inspection of the air filters are the only ways of insuring that sand will not get into the engine.

(3) Wipe all sand and dust off the caps of the crankcase and fuel tanks, and the spouts of the gasoline and oil containers, before using these units.

(4) Seal the instrument panel with masking tape to keep the dust from entering the instruments and causing their failure.

(5) Canvas boots for the distributor and front wheel joints help keep sand and grit from fouling these joints.

(6) Vehicles must be cleaned and lubricated more frequently when operating in sandy or desert terrain.

**b. Tires.**

(1) Operations in the desert will require movement over all types of terrain. Tires must be suitable for every type of surface which will be encountered. Most difficulty will be met in sand. Air pressure must be varied to suit the type of ground surface. Over sand or soft powdered clay, reduce the ground pressure per square inch by deflating the tires. The area of the tire in contact with the ground is thus increased, and the tire fits itself to the irregularities of the sand without breaking through the crust. The minimum pressure must be determined by test for each type of vehicle. NOTE: *Tires on flat base rims will spin on the rims if pressure is too low.*

## 13. FORDING STREAMS, OR FLOOD CONDITIONS.

**a. Flood Maintenance.** After fording shallow streams it is usually unnecessary to take any preventive maintenance steps. However, if the units have been submerged for several hours or more, because of fording deep streams or being in a flood area, it is necessary to remove all foreign matter that may have accumulated. This is done by dismantling the units submerged, washing each part in dry-cleaning solvent, and spreading a thin film of oil over the parts. In instances when emergency requirements make an immediate complete cleaning impossible, some damage may be prevented and the vehicle kept in service by the following procedure:

(1) BOGIE SUSPENSION. Remove bogie roller bearings, and clean and repack completely with recommended lubricant, and reassemble. Always replace grease retainers at roller hubs with new ones, since old, gritty retainers, if replaced, may damage or cut away the seat, and cause leakage.

(2) BRAKE SYSTEM. Remove the brake drums, and wipe the linings and anchor pins clean. Lubricate the pins. Drain the brake lines, flush the system with alcohol, and refill with new brake fluid.

(3) COOLING SYSTEM. If any grit or dirty water has seeped into the cooling system, drain out the liquid, then flush the system thoroughly, and refill with clean liquid. Clean the outside of the radiator case.

(4) ELECTRIC LIGHTING SYSTEM, BATTERY, AND ACCESSORIES. Wipe all wires and contact points clean and dry. Clean the battery ter-

**BASIC HALF-TRACK VEHICLES (WHITE, AUTOCAR, and DIAMOND T)**

minals and check the battery for signs of discharging because of short circuiting by the water or other foreign matter. Recharge battery, if necessary.

(5) FUEL SYSTEM. If any part of the fuel system has been submerged, drain and flush the system thoroughly, and refill with gasoline, using one-half pint of alcohol to each tankful of fuel to counteract the effect of the water. If any grit gets into the carburetor, it may be necessary to remove the carburetor and clean the jets and needle valve. NOTE: *In case the carburetor must be disassembled, refer to a higher echelon.*

(6) GENERAL. Lubricate the steering gear and all pedals, shafts, and linkages beneath the hood, and on the chassis. NOTE: *At the first opportune time, completely disassemble each unit and clean thoroughly.*

## 14. MUDDY TERRAIN OR DEEP SNOW.

a. Do not have the front wheels in a cramped position when starting to move the vehicle, and avoid making sharp turns.

b. When traction is impossible, utilize the winch and winch cable, if so equipped, to pull the vehicle to more solid ground. This operation may be accomplished as follows:

(1) Utilize any stationary, solid object as an anchor. This may be a large tree, another vehicle, or similar materials.

(2) Secure an anchor chain and pulley to this object, preferably thirty or forty feet behind the vehicle. Attach to this any standard pulley block of proper size.

(3) Unwind the winch cable from the drum, passing it through the pulley block and returning it to the front of the vehicle where the hook should be fastened through the tow hook.

(4) Operation of the winch from inside of cab can then be utilized to pull the mired vehicle to more solid ground.

c. When starting on slippery or icy roads, it is advisable to start the vehicle in second or third speeds with the engine running slowly until traction is secured. This operation in second or third speed gives a greater initial thrust at the contact point with the road surface, and offers less possibility of spinning.

## 15. ROUGH TERRAIN.

a. **Tires.** In rocky or boulder-strewn ground, tires must be as fully inflated as the age and condition of the tires permit. CAUTION: *At low pressure the innermost layer of canvas will be broken by the violent inward bending when a sharp rock is struck. The resulting chafing will wear out the inner tube even though no danger is apparent from the outside of the tire.*

b. **Electrical Difficulties.** The constant shock and vibration caused by the passage over rough ground frequently causes cable clips to shake loose, and cables are broken or shorted. Frequent inspection of cable clips should be made, and spring washers inserted under the nuts, if possible. Voltage control units may cause

## OPERATION UNDER UNUSUAL CONDITIONS

trouble because of breaking of wire in shunt-winding or sticking of regulator points. Drivers should watch the ammeter as carefully as any other instrument since overcharging, even when not sufficient to buckle the plates, always results in loss of battery water, most difficult to obtain in the desert. The high saline content of water issued for drinking and for radiators forbids its use in batteries.

c. **Loading.** The vehicle must be carefully loaded. Excessive breaking of springs has been a constant source of trouble in the vehicles used in the desert. The rough going is very hard on springs and they are quickly broken by overloading, improper distribution of load, or shifting of load while moving.

### 16. GAS CONTAMINATED AREAS.

a. For complete information on decontamination see Armored Force Field Manual, FM 17-59.

TM 9-710
17

**BASIC HALF-TRACK VEHICLES (WHITE, AUTOCAR, and DIAMOND T)**

Section VI

## INSPECTION AND PREVENTIVE MAINTENANCE SERVICES

|  | Paragraph |
|---|---|
| Purpose | 17 |
| Before-operation service | 18 |
| During-operation service | 19 |
| At-halt service | 20 |
| After-operation and weekly service | 21 |

**17. PURPOSE.**

a. To insure mechanical efficiency, it is necessary that the vehicle be systematically inspected at intervals each day it is operated and weekly, so defects may be discovered and corrected before they result in serious damage or failure. Certain scheduled maintenance services will be performed at these designated intervals. The services set forth in this section are those performed by driver or crew, before operation, during operation, at halt, and after operation and weekly.

b. Driver Preventive Maintenance Services are listed on the back of "Driver's Trip Ticket" and Preventive Maintenance Service Record W.D. Form No. 48 to cover vehicles of all types and models. Items peculiar to specific vehicles, but not listed on W.D. Form No. 48, are covered in manual procedures under the items to which they pertain. Certain items listed on the form that do not pertain to the vehicle involved are eliminated from the procedures as written into the manual. Every organization must thoroughly school each driver in performing the maintenance procedures set forth in manuals whether they are listed specifically on W.D. Form No. 48 or not.

c. The items listed on W.D. Form No. 48 that apply to this vehicle are expanded in this manual to provide specific procedures for accomplishment of the inspections and services. These services are arranged to facilitate inspection and conserve the time of the driver and are not necessarily in the same numerical order as shown on W.D. Form No. 48. The item numbers, however, are identical with those shown on that form.

d. The general inspection of each item applies also to any supporting member or connection, and generally includes a check to see whether or not the item is in good condition, correctly assembled, secure, or excessively worn.

e. The inspection for "good condition" is usually an external visual inspection to determine whether or not the unit is damaged beyond safe or serviceable limits. The term good condition is explained further by the following terms: not bent or twisted, not chafed or burned, not broken or cracked, not bare or frayed, not dented or collapsed, not torn or cut.

## INSPECTION AND PREVENTIVE MAINTENANCE SERVICES

f. The inspection of a unit to see that it is "correctly assembled" is usually an external visual inspection to see whether or not it is in its normal assembled position in the vehicle.

g. The inspection of a unit to determine if it is "secure" is usually an external visual examination, a hand feel, or a pry-bar check for looseness. Such an inspection should include any brackets, lock washers, lock nuts, locking wires, or cotter pins used in assembly.

h. "Excessively worn" will be understood to mean worn close-to, or beyond, serviceable limits, and likely to result in a failure if not replaced before the next scheduled inspection.

i. Any defects or unsatisfactory operating characteristics beyond the scope of first echelon to correct must be reported at the earliest opportunity to the designated individual in authority.

### 18. BEFORE-OPERATION SERVICE.

a. This inspection schedule is designed primarily as a check to see that the vehicle has not been tampered with, or sabotaged, since the "After-operation Service" was performed. Various combat conditions may have rendered the vehicle unsafe for operation and it is the duty of the driver to determine whether or not the vehicle is in condition to carry out any mission to which it may be assigned. This operation will not be entirely omitted, even in extreme tactical situations.

b. **Procedures.** Before-operation Service consists of inspecting items listed below according to the procedure described, and correcting or reporting any deficiencies. Upon completion of the service, results should be reported promptly to the designated individual in authority.

(1) ITEM 1, TAMPERING AND DAMAGE. Look for any injury to vehicle in general, its accessories or equipment which may have been caused by tampering or sabotage, collision, falling debris, or shell fire, since vehicle was parked. Look under hood for signs of tampering or sabotage, such as loosened or damaged accessories, lines, or linkage.

(2) ITEM 2, FIRE EXTINGUISHER. Inspect fire extinguisher for corrosion, full charge, clogged nozzle, and secure mounting.

(3) ITEM 3, FUEL, OIL, AND WATER. Check for leaks and tampering. Add fuel, oil, or water as needed. Report unusual losses. Have value of antifreeze checked if, during period when antifreeze is used, it becomes necessary to replenish a considerable amount of water.

(4) ITEM 4, ACCESSORIES AND DRIVES. Examine carburetor, generator, regulator, cranking motor, and water pump for loose connections or leaks, and security of mountings. Inspect fan belts for ¾-inch deflection.

(5) ITEM 6, LEAKS, GENERAL. Look on ground under vehicle for indications of fuel, oil, water, brake fluid, or gear oil leaks. Trace leaks to source, and correct, or report.

(6) ITEM 7, ENGINE WARM-UP. Start engine, observe cranking motor action, listen for unusual noise and adequate cranking speed.

TM 9-710
18

**BASIC HALF-TRACK VEHICLES (WHITE, AUTOCAR, and DIAMOND T)**

CAUTION: *Do not re-press starter button until engine comes to complete rest (approximately 5 seconds) if not started on first attempt.* Idle engine fast enough to run smoothly, (400 to 450 rpm). Proceed immediately with following services while vehicle is warming up.

(7) ITEM 8, CHOKE. As engine warms, push in choke as required for smooth operation.

(8) ITEM 9, INSTRUMENTS. Inspect instruments during warm-up for following indications:

(a) *Fuel Gage.* Fuel gage must show approximate amount of fuel in tanks according to position of toggle switch.

(b) *Oil Pressure Gage.* At normal vehicle operation speeds, pressure should be about 20 to 35 pounds. Pressure should not fall below 4 pounds at idle. If proper oil pressure is not indicated within 30 seconds, stop engine and report.

(c) *Temperature Indicator.* Temperature should rise slowly during warm-up. Normal operating temperature 155°F to 185°F. CAUTION: *Do not operate engine over 2,000 revolutions per minute until cooling system temperature has reached 160°F.*

(d) *Ammeter.* Ammeter should show a high charge for short period after starting, and a zero or positive (+) reading above 12 to 15 miles per hour with lights and accessories "off." A zero reading with lights and accessories "on" is normal.

(e) *Voltmeter.* Voltmeter, if vehicle is so equipped, should show a reading of not less than 12 volts, with engine stopped and no load on battery. An excessive drop (more than 2 or 3 volts under heavy load) will indicate battery or connection faults.

(f) *Tachometer.* Tachometer must indicate engine speed without excessive fluctuation or unusual noise.

(9) ITEM 10, HORN AND WINDSHIELD WIPERS. Sound horn, tactical situation permitting. Check both wipers for secure attachment, effective operation, and full blade contact through full stroke.

(10) ITEM 11, GLASS AND REAR VIEW MIRRORS. Clean glass and inspect for cracks, discoloration, or breakage.

(11) ITEM 12, LIGHTS. Try switches in each position and see if lamps respond. Inspect lights for good condition and secure mounting. Clean lenses.

(12) ITEM 13, WHEEL AND FLANGE NUTS. Observe for presence of wheel and flange nuts and tighten as needed.

(13) ITEM 14, TIRES AND TRACKS. Test tires with gage, if time permits. Normal pressure for combat tires is 55 pounds, tires cold. Make sure that valve caps are in place. Remove embedded objects from tire treads and rubber tracks. Inspect for cuts and bruises. Remove any stones or debris from track, or track suspension mechanism. Inspect tracks for proper tension; there should be ¾-inch sag midway between top roller and idler with 150-pound load.

(14) ITEM 15, SPRINGS AND SUSPENSION. Look for sagged or broken front springs, shifted leaves, loose or missing rebound clips, and loose U-bolts. Inspect volute and coil springs for breakage. Observe cap screws and nuts on bogie, idler, drive sprocket, drive sprocket hubs, track support rollers, and bogie wheels, for tightness.

## INSPECTION AND PREVENTIVE MAINTENANCE SERVICES

(15) ITEM 16, STEERING LINKAGE. Examine steering gear case, steering arm, drag link, tie rod, and Pitman arm, for secure mounting and good condition. Test adjustment by back-and-forth movement of steering wheel.

(16) ITEM 17, FENDERS, BUMPERS, OR ROLLER. Examine fenders, bumper, or roller, for secure mounting and serviceable condition. See that roller springs are in good condition, that front roller turns and is properly lubricated.

(17) ITEM 18, TOWING CONNECTIONS. Examine pintle and tow hooks for secure mounting and good condition.

(18) ITEM 19, BODY AND LOAD. Observe load for proper stowage; tarpaulins and curtains for adequate fastening and good condition. Check armament and ammunition for presence.

(19) ITEM 20, DECONTAMINATOR. Examine decontaminator for full charge and secure mounting.

(20) ITEM 21, TOOLS AND EQUIPMENT. Inspect tools and equipment for presence, serviceability, and proper stowage.

(21) ITEM 23, DRIVER'S PERMIT AND FORM NO. 26. Accident report form No. 26, vehicle manual, Lubrication Guide, and W.D. AGO form No. 478 must be present, legible, and safely stowed. Driver must have Driver's Permit on his person.

(22) ITEM 22, ENGINE OPERATION. Accelerate engine and observe for unusual noises, indicating compression or exhaust leaks, worn, damaged, loose, inadequately lubricated parts, or misfiring.

(23) ITEM 25, DURING-OPERATION SERVICE. Begin the "During-operation Service" immediately after the vehicle is in motion.

## 19. DURING-OPERATION SERVICE.

a. While vehicle is in motion, listen for any sounds such as rattles, knocks, squeals, or hums that may indicate trouble. Look for indications of trouble in cooling system and smoke from any part of the vehicle. Be on the alert to detect any odor of overheated components or units such as generator, brakes, or clutch, or fuel vapor from a leak in fuel system, exhaust gas, or other signs of trouble. Any time the brakes are used, gears shifted, or vehicle turned, consider this a test, and notice any unsatisfactory or unusual performance. Watch the instruments carefully. Notice promptly unusual instrument indication that may signify possible trouble in system to which the instrument pertains.

b. **Procedures.** During-operation Service consists of observing items listed below according to the procedures following each item, and investigating any indications of serious trouble. Notice minor deficiencies to be corrected or reported at earliest opportunity, usually next scheduled halt.

(1) ITEM 27, FOOT AND HAND BRAKES. Foot brakes must stop vehicle smoothly, without side pull, within reasonable distance, with at least one-third reserve pedal travel. Brake pedal should have ½-inch free travel. Hand brake must hold vehicle securely on reasonable incline with ¼-reserve ratchet travel.

## BASIC HALF-TRACK VEHICLES (WHITE, AUTOCAR, and DIAMOND T)

(2) ITEM 28, CLUTCH. Clutch must operate smoothly without chattering, grabbing, or slipping. Inspect for free pedal travel of 1 to 1½ inch.

(3) ITEM 29, TRANSMISSION AND POWER TAKE-OFF. Gearshift mechanism must operate smoothly, and gears must stay in mesh.

(4) ITEM 30, TRANSFER. Gearshift mechanism must operate smoothly. Gears must stay in mesh.

(5) ITEM 31, ENGINE AND CONTROLS. Observe whether or not engine responds readily to controls and has adequate pulling power without unusual noises, stalling, misfiring, overheating, or excessive exhaust smoke.

(6) ITEM 32, INSTRUMENTS. Observe readings of instruments frequently during operation, to see whether or not they are indicating properly and whether or not the systems to which they pertain are functioning properly.

(a) *Fuel Gage.* Fuel gage must show approximate amount of fuel in tank according to position of toggle switch.

(b) *Oil Pressure Gage.* At normal vehicle operating speeds, pressure should be about 20 to 35 pounds. Pressure should not fall below four pounds at idle.

(c) *Temperature Indicator.* Indicator hand should rise slowly during warm-up. Normal operating temperature is 155°F to 185°F. CAUTION: *Do not operate engine over 2,000 revolutions per minute until cooling system temperature has reached 160°F.*

(d) *Ammeter.* The ammeter should show a high charge for short period after starting and a zero or positive (+) reading above 12 to 15 miles per hour with lights and accessories off. A zero reading with lights and accessories on is normal.

(e) *Tachometer.* Tachometer must indicate engine speed without excessive fluctuation or unusual noise.

(f) *Speedometer.* Speedometer must show vehicle speed, accumulating trip mileage, and total mileage. Indicator hand should move steadily without unusual fluctuation.

(7) ITEM 33, STEERING GEAR. Observe steering mechanism for excessive pulling to either side, wandering, or shimmy.

(8) ITEM 34, RUNNING GEAR. Listen for unusual noises from wheels, axles, bogie, or track suspension mechanism.

(9) ITEM 35, BODY. Be alert for noise that could indicate shifting load, loose tarpaulin or curtains, loose or damaged panels, hardware, body attachments, or gun mounts. Observe towed vehicle for weaving, shifting of load, or loose tarpaulin.

## 20. AT-HALT SERVICE.

a. At-halt Service may be regarded as minimum maintenance procedures and should be performed under all tactical conditions even though more extensive maintenance services must be slighted or omitted altogether.

b. **Procedures.** At-halt Service consists of investigating any deficiencies noted during operation, inspecting items listed below accord-

## INSPECTION AND PREVENTIVE MAINTENANCE SERVICES

ing to the procedures following the items, and correcting any deficiencies found. Deficiencies not corrected should be reported promptly to the designated individual in authority.

(1) ITEM 38, FUEL, OIL, AND WATER. Examine fuel, oil, and water levels, and replenish as required. If during period when antifreeze is used, an abnormal amount of water is required to fill radiator, have coolant tested with a hydrometer and add antifreeze as necessary.

(2) ITEM 39, TEMPERATURES, (HUBS, BRAKE DRUMS, TRANSFER, TRANSMISSION, JACKSHAFT, AND FRONT AXLE). Feel brake drums, wheel hubs, transmission, transfer, front axle, and jackshaft, to see if they are abnormally hot. Examine all units for excessive oil leaks.

(3) ITEM 40, AXLE AND TRANSFER VENTS. Examine axle and transfer vents for presence. Must not be damaged or clogged.

(4) ITEM 41, PROPELLER SHAFT. Inspect propeller shaft and joints for looseness, damage, or oil leaks.

(5) ITEM 42, SPRINGS. Look for broken front spring leaves, loose clips, loose shackles, or loose U-bolts. Examine volute and coil springs for breakage.

(6) ITEM 43, STEERING LINKAGE. Examine steering control mechanism for damage or looseness. Investigate any irregularities noted during operation.

(7) ITEM 44, WHEEL AND FLANGE NUTS. Observe whether or not wheel, axle, and jackshaft flange nuts are present and tight. See that track suspension mechanism nuts are present and tight.

(8) ITEM 45, TIRES AND TRACKS. Inspect for flat tires, damage, cuts, or foreign matter embedded in treads. Remove stones or debris from track and track suspension. Inspect for $3/4$-inch sag, measured midway between top roller and idler, vehicle loaded normally, and with all slack in top of track. Track should be loaded with 150 pounds at point of measurement of sag.

(9) ITEM 46, LEAKS, GENERAL. Look around engine, and on ground beneath vehicle for excessive leaks. Trace the source; correct, or report the trouble.

(10) ITEM 47, ACCESSORIES AND BELTS. See that fan, water pump, and generator are secure, that fan belts are adjusted to deflection of $3/4$-inch and are not badly frayed.

(11) ITEM 48, AIR CLEANERS. If dusty or sandy conditions have been encountered, drop oil reservoir and examine for excessive dirt. Service, if required. Clean and reoil the oil filler breather each time air cleaner is serviced.

(12) ITEM 49, FENDERS, BUMPER, OR ROLLER. Inspect fenders, bumper, or roller for looseness or damage.

(13) ITEM 50, TOWING CONNECTIONS. Inspect pintle hook, trailer brake, and light socket attachment for serviceability.

(14) ITEM 51, BODY, LOAD, AND TARPAULINS. Inspect body for damage; vehicle and trailed vehicle loads for shifting. See that tarpaulins are properly secured and not damaged.

(15) ITEM 52, APPEARANCE AND GLASS. Clean glass and light lenses, and inspect vehicle for damage to body finish or markings.

**TM 9-710**
**21**

## BASIC HALF-TRACK VEHICLES (WHITE, AUTOCAR, and DIAMOND T)

**21. AFTER-OPERATION AND WEEKLY SERVICE.**

a. After-operation Service is particularly important because at this time the driver inspects his vehicle to detect any deficiencies that may have developed, and corrects those he is permitted to handle. He should report promptly, to the designated individual in authority, the results of his inspection. If this schedule is performed thoroughly, the vehicle should be ready to roll again on a moment's notice. The Before-operation Service with a few exceptions, is then necessary only to ascertain whether or not the vehicle is in the same condition in which it was left upon completion of the After-operation Service. The After-operation Service should never be entirely omitted even in extreme tactical situations, but may be reduced to the bare fundamental services outlined for the At-halt Service if necessary.

b. **Procedures.** When performing the After-operation Service, the driver must remember and consider any irregularities noticed during the day in the Before-operation, During-operation, and At-halt Services. The After-operation Service consists of inspecting and servicing the following items. Those items of the After-operation Service that are marked by an asterisk (*) require additional weekly services, the procedures for which are indicated in subparagraph *(b)* of each applicable item.

(1) ITEM 55, ENGINE OPERATION. Listen for missing, backfiring, noises, or vibration, that might indicate worn parts, loose mountings, faulty fuel mixture, or faulty ignition.

(2) ITEM 56, INSTRUMENTS. Inspect all instruments to see that they are securely connected and not damaged. Inspect compass for indication of true magnetic north; check with known direction or with compass of known accuracy in another vehicle.

(3) ITEM 57, HORN AND WINDSHIELD WIPERS. Inspect horn for good condition and secure mounting. Operate both windshield wipers, and see that blades contact glass effectively throughout full stroke.

(4) ITEM 54, FUEL, OIL, AND WATER. Check coolant and oil levels; add as needed. Fill fuel tank. Refill spare cans. During period when antifreeze is used, have hydrometer test made of coolant. If loss of coolant from boiling or other cause has been considerable, add antifreeze, with water, if required.

(5) ITEM 58, GLASS. Clean glass and examine for breakage.

(6) ITEM 59, LIGHTS. Observe whether or not lights "light" with switch at "ON" position, and go out when switch is "OFF." Observe stop light operation. Clean lenses.

(7) ITEM 60, FIRE EXTINGUISHER. Be sure fire extinguisher is full, securely mounted, and that the nozzle is clean.

(8) ITEM 61, DECONTAMINATOR. Examine decontaminator for good condition and secure mounting.

(9) ITEM 62, *BATTERY.

*(a)* See that battery is clean, securely mounted, and not leaking. See that electrolyte level reaches bottom of filler well when cap is removed from vent. (Electrolyte should stand ½ inch above plates). See that filler caps are in place with vents open. Clean terminals if dirty.

TM 9-710

## INSPECTION AND PREVENTIVE MAINTENANCE SERVICES

*(b) Weekly.* Clean top of battery, remove filler caps, and place cap on vents. Add clean water to top of filler well. Remove battery caps from vents (electrolyte level should fall to bottom of well). Replace battery caps on filler well. Clean corrosion from posts and terminals and apply light coating of grease. Tighten terminals as needed; tighten carrier clamp and hold-down bolts carefully to avoid damaging battery. Clean battery carrier, if corroded.

(10) ITEM 63, *ACCESSORIES AND BELTS.

*(a)* Test fan belts. Should have ¾-inch deflection. Examine belt for good condition.

*(b) Weekly.* Tighten all accessories such as carburetor, generator, regulator, cranking motor, fan, surge tank, water pump, and oil cooler.

(11) ITEM 64, *ELECTRICAL WIRING.

*(a)* See that ignition wiring and shielding is securely connected, clean, and undamaged.

*(b) Weekly.* Inspect ignition wiring and shielding for secure attachment and tight connections. Inspect exposed low tension wiring for secure attachment and tight connections. Insulators and conduits must not be cracked or chafed. Observe radio bonding and condensers for clean connections and secure attachment.

(12) ITEM 65, *AIR CLEANER AND BREATHER CAP.

*(a)* Examine oil in air cleaner to see that it is at proper level and not excessively dirty. Accumulation of dirt in cleaner cup must not exceed ½ inch. Clean and refill reservoir as required. Clean and reoil oil filler breather cap when so equipped.

*(b) Weekly.* Clean and service air cleaner and oil filler breather.

(13) ITEM 66, *FUEL FILTERS.

*(a)* Examine fuel filters for leaks.

*(b) Weekly.* Remove bowl from fuel pump fuel filter and clean out sediment and water. Be sure bowl is replaced tightly without leaks. Clean bowl from fuel filter at carburetor and tighten carefully to avoid leaks. Replace gaskets if necessary.

(14) ITEM 67, ENGINE CONTROLS. Examine engine controls for excessive wear or disconnected linkage.

(15) ITEM 68, *TIRES AND TRACKS.

*(a)* Inspect tires and tracks for cuts or abnormal tread wear. Remove foreign bodies from treads. Test tires for 55 pounds pressure (combat tires) when tires are cold. Inspect bogie wheel tires for cuts or separation from wheels. Remove oil or grease from tires or tracks. Remove sticks, stones, or other foreign material that may be lodged in track or suspension mechanism. Inspect for bent, loose, or broken track guides. Inspect track tension for ¾-inch sag between top roller and rear idler with load weighing about 150 pounds on track, near point of measurement. NOTE: *There should be ¾-inch sag with vehicle under normal load and on hard level surface, and load placed in such a manner that it does not twist the track.* CAUTION: *Do not park in mud or water during freezing weather, because of difficulty of loosening tracks.*

**TM 9-710**

**BASIC HALF-TRACK VEHICLES (WHITE, AUTOCAR, and DIAMOND T)**

*(b) Weekly.* Replace badly worn or otherwise unserviceable tires. Inspect tracks for excessive wear. Track should be removed when rubber on ground side has worn to extent that wear on steel cross plates and exposure of cables is imminent. Inspect for bent, loose, or broken track guides.

(16) ITEM 69, *SPRINGS.

*(a)* Examine front springs for sag, broken, or shifted leaves, loose or missing rebound clips, bolts, or shackles. Inspect volute and coil springs, for sag or breakage. Volute springs should be replaced if two or more coils are resting on seat.

*(b) Weekly.* Tighten spring bolts, nuts, shackles, and U-bolts as required.

(17) ITEM 70, STEERING LINKAGE. Inspect steering linkage for bent, loose, or inadequately lubricated parts.

(18) ITEM 71, PROPELLER SHAFT. Inspect propeller shaft and U-joints for loose connections, lubrication leaks, or damage.

(19) ITEM 72, *AXLE, TRANSFER, AND JACKSHAFT VENTS.

*(a)* Inspect axle, transfer and jackshaft vents for good condition, cleanliness, and secure attachment.

*(b) Weekly.* Remove, clean, and install vents. Make sure differential carrier mounting cap screws are tight.

(20) ITEM 73, LEAKS, GENERAL. Look under hood and beneath vehicle for indications of fuel, oil, water, or brake fluid leaks.

(21) ITEM 74, GEAR OIL LEVELS. After units have cooled, inspect differentials, transmission, and transfer lubricant levels. Look for leaks. Lubricant should be ½ inch below bottom of the filler hole (unit cool).

(22) ITEM 76, FENDERS, BUMPER, AND ROLLER. Inspect fenders, bumper, and roller for good condition and secure mounting.

(23) ITEM 77, TOWING CONNECTIONS. Inspect pintle and tow hooks and towed load connections for good condition and secure attachment.

(24) ITEM 78, BODY, LOAD, AND TARPAULINS. Inspect body, top, cab, and windshield for good condition; armament, ammunition, and load for proper mounting or stowage; tarpaulins for good condition and secure attachment. Inspect towed vehicle for proper stowage of load and good condition and fastening of tarpaulins.

(25) ITEM 79, ARMOR, FRONT ROLLER OR WINCH (ON VEHICLES SO EQUIPPED). Inspect body armor, cab, doors, hood, windshield covers and port hole covers for damage, broken welds, loose mounting bolts, screws, or rivets. Examine radiator shutters for good condition. Test operation of controls. Inspect front roller and front roller springs for good condition and secure mounting. Inspect winch for good condition and secure mounting. See that cable is properly wound and in good condition (not frayed) and that cable chain and hook are in good condition and securely attached. See that clutch moves freely and latches securely. Inspect winch propeller shaft for good condition.

(26) ITEM 81, GUN MOUNTS. Examine mounts of guns to see that they are secure and in good condition for immediate use. Test elevat-

## INSPECTION AND PREVENTIVE MAINTENANCE SERVICES

ing and traversing mechanism and firing controls for proper operation (on vehicles so equipped).

(27) ITEM 82, *TIGHTEN.

*(a)* Tighten any loose wheel drive flange, sprocket, idler, and support roller nuts. Tighten spring U-bolts, if loose.

*(b) Weekly.* Tighten all vehicle assembly or mounting bolts, nuts, or screws, that inspection indicates require tightening. Inspect for presence of cotter keys and locking wires.

(28) ITEM 83, *LUBRICATE AS NEEDED.

*(a)* Lubricate spring shackles and steering linkage, if lubrication is needed.

*(b) Weekly.* Lubricate points indicated on vehicle Lubrication Guide on a weekly or mileage basis. CAUTION: *Remove excess grease, which has been forced out of bogie wheel and top roller bearings, to avoid its contact with rubber tires and rubber tracks.*

(29) ITEM 84, *CLEAN ENGINE AND VEHICLE.

*(a)* Clean dirt and trash from inside of body. Remove excess dirt from exterior of engine.

*(b) Weekly.* Wash vehicle when possible; if not possible, wipe off thoroughly. Clean engine.

(30) ITEM 85, *TOOLS AND EQUIPMENT.

*(a)* See that all tools and equipment assigned to vehicle are present, serviceable, and securely stowed.

*(b) Weekly.* Check tools and equipment with vehicle stowage list.

**TM 9-710**
**22**

## BASIC HALF-TRACK VEHICLES (WHITE, AUTOCAR, and DIAMOND T)

Section VII

# LUBRICATION

|  | Paragraph |
|---|---|
| Lubrication Guide........................................ | 22 |
| Detailed lubrication instructions....................... | 23 |

**22. LUBRICATION GUIDE.**

*a.* War Department Lubrication Guide No. 21 (figs. 32 and 33) prescribes lubrication maintenance for Half-track Car M2A1. This guide is representative of the vehicles covered in this manual. For detailed lubrication instructions covering each vehicle, refer to War Department Lubrication Guides as listed below:

| Vehicle | Guide No. |
|---|---|
| Car, half-track, M2 and M2A1...................... | 21 |
| Carrier, personnel, M3 and M3A1................... | 22 |
| Carrier, mortar, 81-mm, half-track, M4 and M4A1...... | 23 |
| Carriage, motor, gun, 75-mm, M3 and M3A1.......... | 112 |
| Carriage, motor, 75-mm, howitzer, T30.............. | 111 |
| Carriage, motor, howitzer, 105-mm, T19............. | — |
| Carriage, motor, multiple gun, M13................. | 118 |
| Carriage, motor, multiple gun, M15 and M15A1....... | 131 |
| Carriage, motor, multiple gun, M16................. | 132 |
| Carrier, mortar, 81-mm, M21....................... | — |

*b.* A Lubrication Guide is placed on, or is issued with, each item of materiel, and must be carried with it at all times. In the event the materiel is received without a Guide, the using arms must immediately requisition a replacement from the Commanding Officer, Fort Wayne Ordnance Depot, Detroit 32, Michigan.

*c.* Lubrication instructions on the Guide are binding on all echelons of maintenance and there must be no deviations, except as indicated in subparagraph d below.

*d.* Service intervals specified on the Guide are for normal operating conditions. Reduce these intervals under extreme conditions such as excessively high or low temperatures, prolonged periods of high speed operation, continued operation in sand or dust, immersion in water, or exposure to moisture, any one of which may quickly destroy the protective qualities of the lubricant.

*e.* Lubricants are prescribed in the "Key" in accordance with three temperature ranges: above $+32°F$, $+32°F$ to $0°F$, and below $0°F$. Determine the time to change grades of lubricants by maintaining a close check on operation of the vehicle during the approach to change-over periods. Be particularly observant when starting the engine. Sluggish starting is an indication of lubricants thickening and the signal to change to grades prescribed for the next lower temperature range. Ordinarily it will be necessary to change grades of lubricants *only when air temperatures are consistently in the next higher or lower range,* unless malfunctioning occurs sooner due to lubricants being too thin or too heavy.

## LUBRICATION

**f. Localized Views.** Refer to series of illustrations (figs. 34 through 38) for localized views of various lubrication points. Caption under each view briefly describes the type of fitting, method of lubrication, and special information regarding the lubrication of that specific item. The illustrations or captions do not specify lubricant (except by symbols) or intervals at which points must be lubricated. Reference must be made to Lubrication Guides (figs. 32 and 33) for those items. Information on those items which require special lubrication operations will be found in respective sections of the manual.

### 23. DETAILED LUBRICATION INSTRUCTIONS.

**a. Lubrication Equipment.**

(1) Each piece of materiel is supplied with lubrication equipment adequate to maintain the materiel. This equipment must be cleaned both before and after use.

(2) Lubrication guns must be operated carefully and in such manner as to insure a proper distribution of the lubricant.

**b. Points of Application.**

(1) Lubrication fittings, grease cups, oilers, and oil holes are readily identifiable on the materiel by a red circle. Such lubricators and the surrounding surface must be wiped clean before lubricant is applied.

(2) Where relief valves are provided, apply new lubricant until the old lubricant is forced from the vent. Exceptions are specified in notes on the Lubrication Guide.

**c. Cleaning.** SOLVENT, dry-cleaning, or OIL, fuel, Diesel must be used to clean or wash all parts. Use of gasoline for this purpose is prohibited. After washing, parts must be thoroughly dried before applying lubricant.

**d. Lubrication Notes on Individual Units and Parts.** The following instructions supplement those notes on the Lubrication Guides (figs. 32 and 33) which pertain to lubrication and service of individual units and parts of the vehicle.

(1) AIR CLEANERS.

*(a) Oil Bath Type.* Daily, check level and refill engine air cleaner oil reservoir to bead level with used crankcase oil or OIL, engine, SAE 30 above +32°F, and SAE 10 from +32°F to 0°F. Below 0°F, remove oil and operate dry. Every 1,000 miles, daily under extreme dust conditions, remove air cleaner and wash all parts.

*(b) Element Type.* Every 1,000 miles, remove, wash curled hair in brake vacuum or hydrovac cylinder air cleaners and reoil with used crankcase oil or OIL, engine, SAE 30 above +32°F or SAE 10 from +32°F to 0°F. From 0°F to –40°F, use FLUID, shock-absorber, light. Below –40°F, wash and replace dry.

(2) BOGIE WHEELS. CAUTION: *Some modifications are sealed and have no relief valve, nor will lubricant come out bearing when full.* To prevent breaking seals, use low pressure gun and never force lubricant into these units.

# TM 9-710

## BASIC HALF-TRACK VEHICLES (WHITE, AUTOCAR, and DIAMOND T)

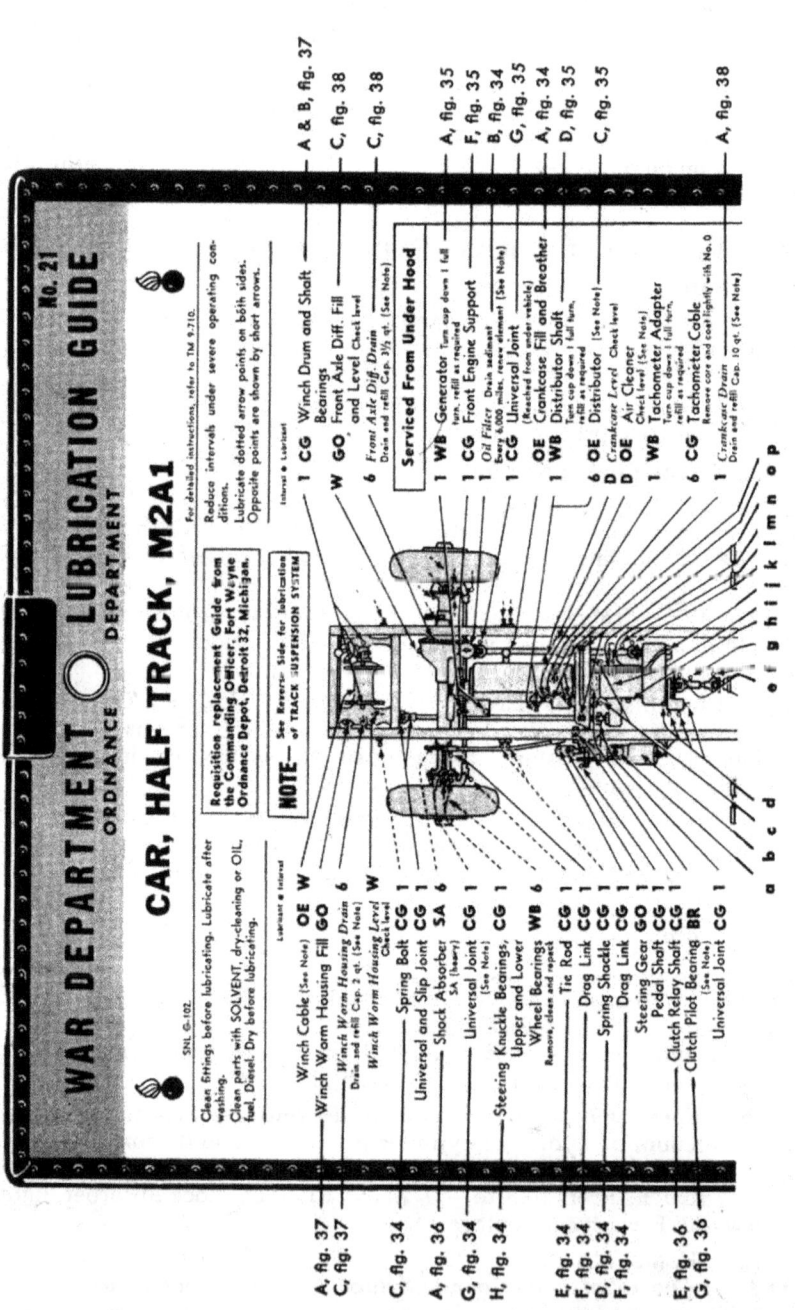

# LUBRICATION

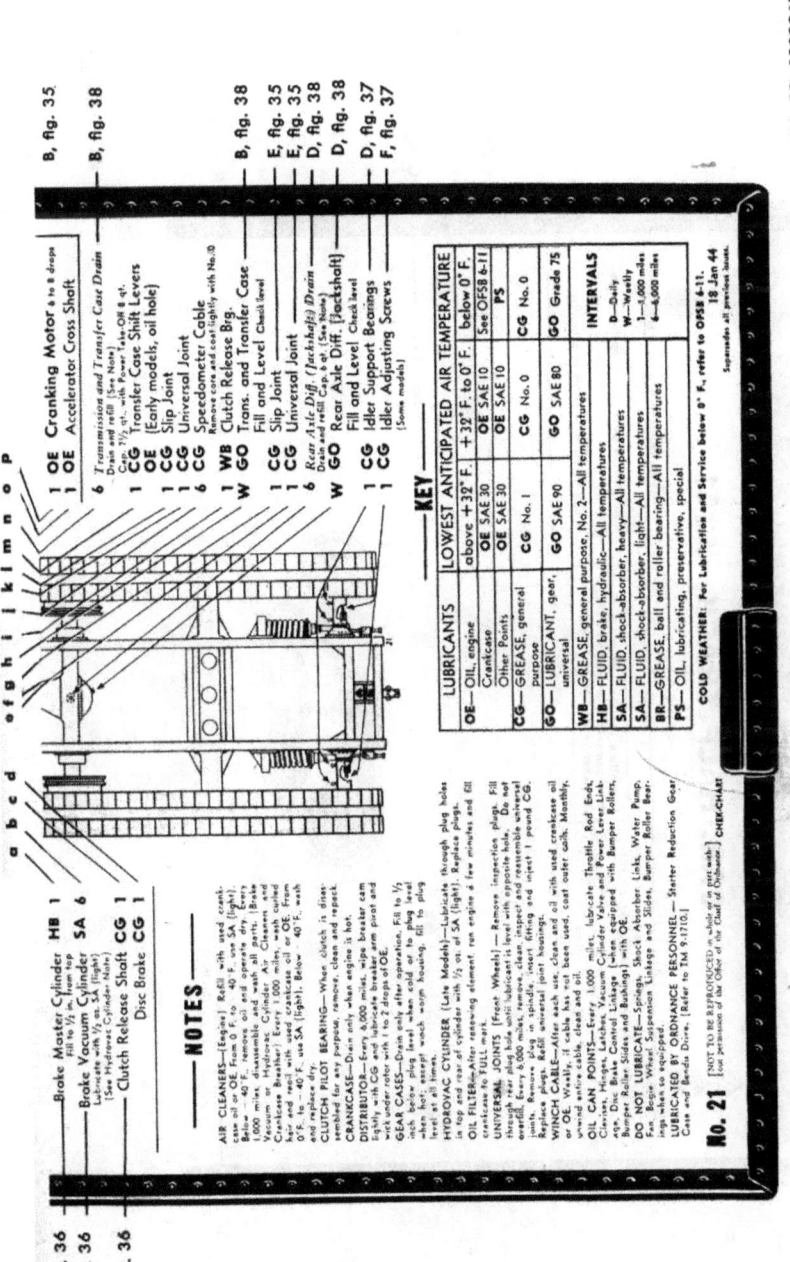

Figure 32—Lubrication Guide

# TM 9-710

## BASIC HALF-TRACK VEHICLES (WHITE, AUTOCAR, and DIAMOND T)

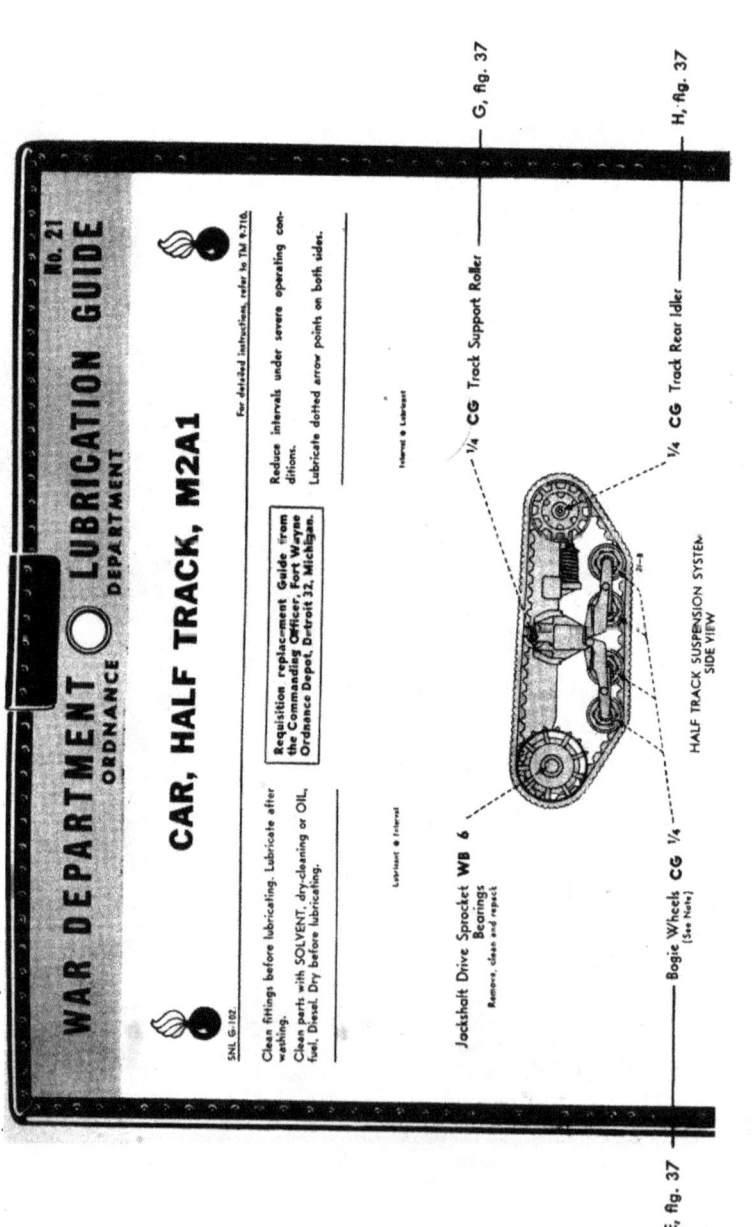

RA PD 330837

## LUBRICATION

TM 9-710
23

RA PD 330837B

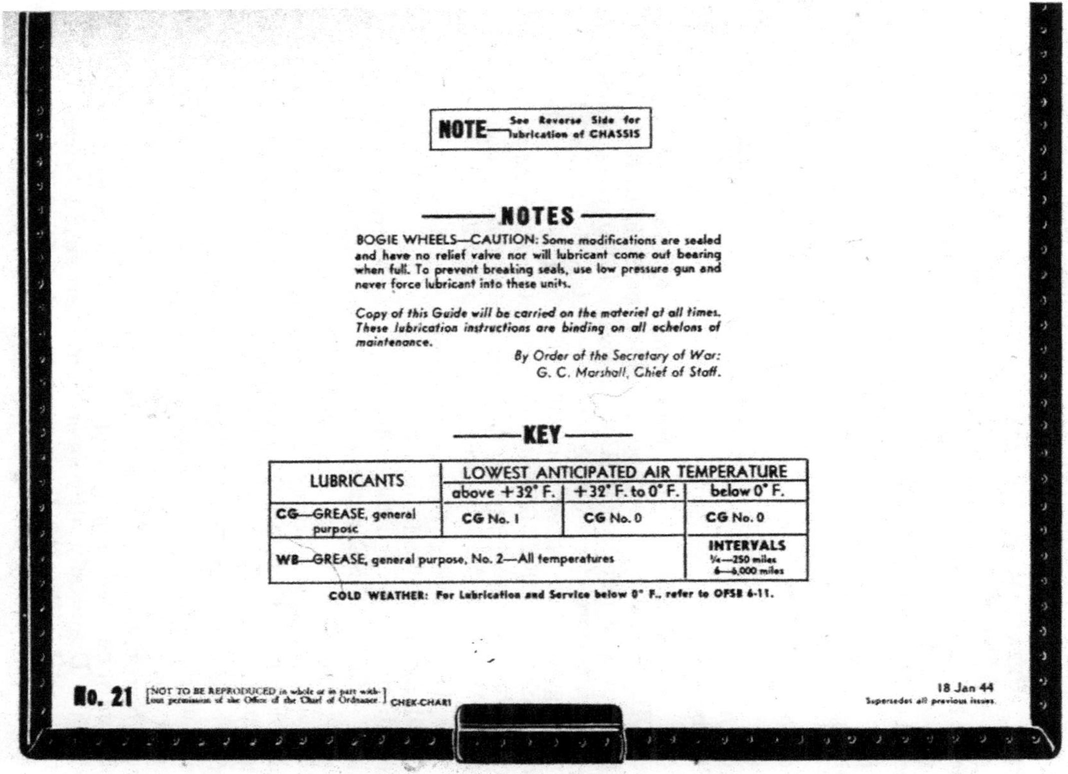

**NOTE** — See Reverse Side for Lubrication of CHASSIS

**— NOTES —**

BOGIE WHEELS—CAUTION: Some modifications are sealed and have no relief valve nor will lubricant come out bearing when full. To prevent breaking seals, use low pressure gun and never force lubricant into these units.

Copy of this Guide will be carried on the materiel at all times. These lubrication instructions are binding on all echelons of maintenance.

By Order of the Secretary of War:
G. C. Marshall, Chief of Staff.

**— KEY —**

| LUBRICANTS | LOWEST ANTICIPATED AIR TEMPERATURE | | |
|---|---|---|---|
| | above +32° F. | +32° F. to 0° F. | below 0° F. |
| CG—GREASE, general purpose. | CG No. 1 | CG No. 0 | CG No. 0 |
| WB—GREASE, general purpose, No. 2—All temperatures | | | INTERVALS ½—250 miles 6—6,000 miles |

COLD WEATHER: For Lubrication and Service below 0° F. refer to OFSB 6-11.

No. 21 [NOT TO BE REPRODUCED in whole or in part without permission of the Chief of Ordnance] CHEK-CHART

18 Jan 44
Supersedes all previous issues.

**Figure 33—Lubrication Guide**

59

## BASIC HALF-TRACK VEHICLES (WHITE, AUTOCAR, and DIAMOND T)

(3) BRAKE VACUUM CYLINDER AND HYDROVAC CYLINDER.

*(a) Brake Vacuum Cylinder, Early Models.* Every 6,000 miles, remove plug in front of cylinder and lubricate with one-half ounce of FLUID, shock-absorber, light. Disconnect piston and rotate to distribute oil on leather. Replace plugs.

*(b) Hydrovac Cylinder, Late Models.* Every 6,000 miles, lubricate through plug holes in top and rear of cylinder with one-half ounce of FLUID, shock-absorber, light.

(4) BREATHER AND VENTS.

*(a) Breather.* Every 1,000 miles, remove crankcase breather, wash curled hair and reoil with used crankcase oil or OIL, engine, SAE 30 above $+32°F$ or SAE 10 from $+32°F$ to $0°F$. From $0°F$ to $-40°F$, use FLUID, shock-absorber, light. Below $-40°F$, wash and replace dry.

*(b) Vents.* Flywheel housing, transmission, transfer case, differentials, and steering gear vents must be cleaned and kept open. Inspect each time lubricant level is checked, and each time vehicle is operated under extremely dirty or muddy conditions.

(5) CLUTCH PILOT BEARING. When clutch is disassembled for any other purpose, remove, clean and repack with GREASE, ball and roller bearing.

(6) CRANKCASE. Daily, check level and refill to "FULL" mark with OIL, engine, SAE 30 above $+32°F$ or SAE 10 from $+32°F$ to $0°F$. Below $0°F$ refer to OFSB 6-11. Every 1,000 miles, remove drain plug from bottom of crankcase and completely drain case. Drain only when engine is hot. After thoroughly draining, replace drain plug and refill crankcase to "FULL" mark on gage with correct lubricant to meet temperature requirements. Run engine a few minutes and recheck oil level. CAUTION: *Be sure pressure gage indicates oil is circulating.*

(7) DISTRIBUTOR. Every 1,000 miles, lubricate distributor shaft with GREASE, general purpose, No. 2, by turning grease cup down one full turn. Every 6,000 miles, wipe the distributor breaker cam lightly with GREASE, general purpose, No. 1 above $+32°F$ and No. 0 below $+32°F$. Also lubricate the breaker arm pivot and wick under rotor with one to two drops of OIL, engine, SAE 30 above $+32°F$, SAE 10 from $+32°F$ to $0°F$ or OIL, lubricating, preservative, special, below $0°F$.

(8) GEAR CASES. Differentials, transmission and transfer case, and winch worm housing only. Weekly, check level with truck on level ground and, if necessary, add lubricant to one-half inch below plug level when cold, or to plug level when hot; except winch worm housing which must be filled to plug level at all times. Every 6,000 miles, drain and refill. Drain only after operation when gear lubricant is warm. Refill with LUBRICANT, gear, universal, SAE 90 above $+32°F$, SAE 80 from $+32°F$ to $0°F$ or grade 75 below $0°F$.

(9) JACKSHAFT DRIVE SPROCKET BEARINGS. Every 6,000 miles, remove tracks, drive sprocket flanges, bearing hubs and bearings. Clean and repack bearings with GREASE, general purpose, No. 2.

(10) OIL FILTERS. Every 1,000 miles, remove drain plug from oil filter to drain sediment. Every 6,000 miles, or more often if filter be-

## LUBRICATION

comes clogged, remove filter element, clean inside of case, and install new element. After renewing element, run engine a few minutes, recheck crankcase oil level and fill to "FULL" mark with the correct grade of OIL, engine.

(11) UNIVERSAL JOINTS AND SLIP JOINTS. Use GREASE, general purpose, No. 1 for temperatures above +32°F or GREASE, general purpose, No. 0 below +32°F. Apply grease to universal joint until it overflows at the relief valve, and to the slip joint until lubricant is forced from the vent at the universal joint end of the spline.

(12) UNIVERSAL JOINTS (FRONT WHEELS). To fill, place vehicle on level ground. Remove the inspection plugs. Fill through rear plug hole until the lubricant is level with opposite hole. Replace the plugs. CAUTION: *Every 6,000 miles, remove, clean, inspect, and reassemble universal joints.* Remove plug in spindle, insert fitting and inject one pound GREASE, general purpose, No. 1 above +32°F or No. 0 below +32°F. Replace plugs. Refill universal joint housings.

(13) WHEEL BEARINGS. Remove bearing cone assemblies from hub. Wash bearings, cones, spindle, and inside of hub and dry thoroughly. Do not use compressed air. Inspect bearing races and replace if damaged. Wet the spindle, inside of hub, and hub cap with GREASE, general purpose, No. 2 to a maximum thickness of $\frac{1}{16}$ inch only to retard rust. Lubricate bearings with GREASE, general purpose, No. 2 with a packer, or by hand, kneading lubricant into all spaces in the bearing. Use extreme care to protect the bearings from dirt, and immediately reassemble and replace wheel. Do not fill hub or hub cap. The lubricant in the bearing is sufficient to provide lubrication until the next service period. Any excess might result in leakage into the drum. Adjust bearings (par. 137).

(14) WINCH CABLE. After each use, clean and oil with used crankcase oil or OIL, engine, SAE 30 above +32°F, SAE 10 from +32°F to 0°F, or OIL, lubricating, preservative, special, below 0°F. If cable has not been used, coat outer coils weekly. Unwind entire cable, clean and oil monthly.

(15) OILCAN POINTS. Every 1,000 miles, lubricate throttle rod ends, clevises, hinges, latches, vacuum cylinder valve and power lever linkage, disk brake control linkage (when equipped with bumper rollers, bumper roller slides and bushings) with OIL, engine, SAE 30 above +32°F, SAE 10 from +32°F to 0°F, OIL, lubricating, preservative, special, below 0°F.

(16) DO NOT LUBRICATE. Springs, shock absorber links, water pump, fan, bogie wheel suspension linkage and slides, bumper roller bearings (when so equipped).

e. **Points to be Lubricated by Ordnance Personnel Only.**

(1) CRANKING MOTOR REDUCTION GEAR CASE AND BENDIX DRIVE. Every 6,000 miles, remove and clean Bendix drive. Lubricate drive shaft outer bearing through oiler with OIL, engine, SAE 30 above +32°F, SAE 10 from +32°F to 0°F or OIL, lubricating, preservative, special, below 0°F. Every 6,000 miles, remove plug in top of reduction gear housing and refill with GREASE, general purpose, No. 1 above +32°F or No. 0 below +32°F. Yearly, disassemble, clean gears,

# TM 9-710
## 23
## BASIC HALF-TRACK VEHICLES (WHITE, AUTOCAR, and DIAMOND T)

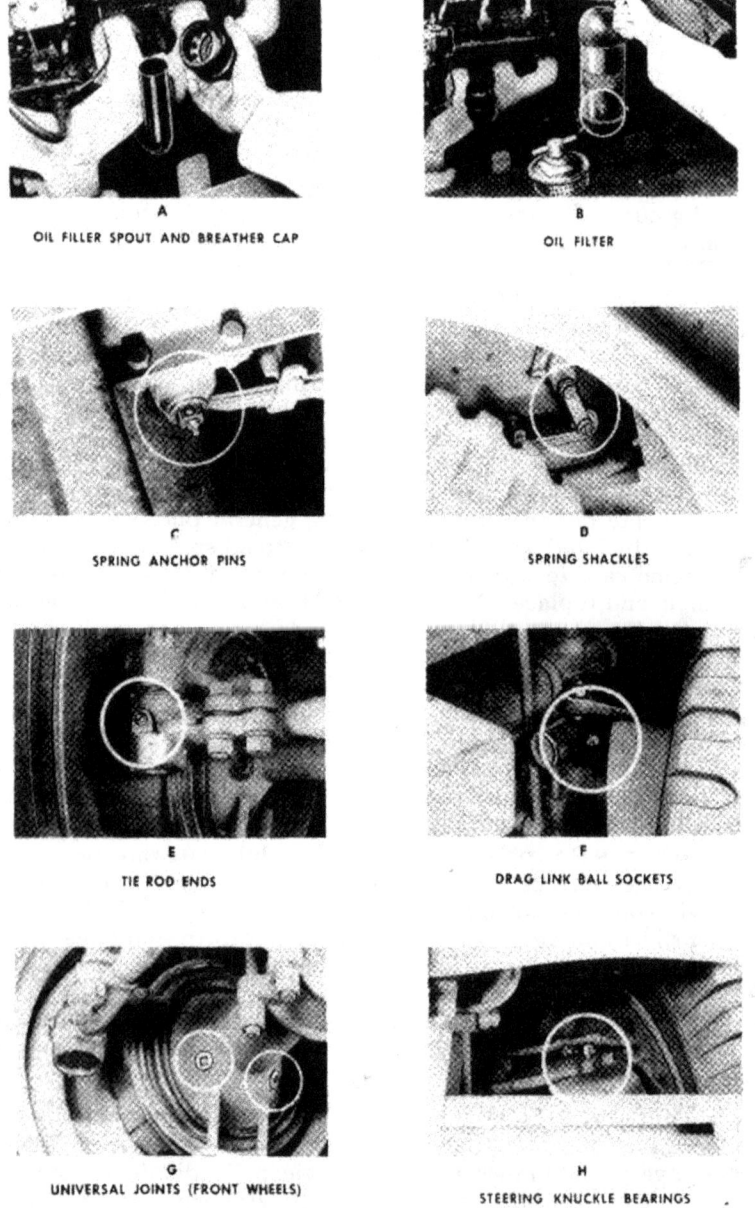

Figure 34—Localized Views

TM 9-710
23

## LUBRICATION

A
GENERATOR GREASE CUPS

B
CRANKING MOTOR OILERS

C
WICK UNDER DISTRIBUTOR ROTOR

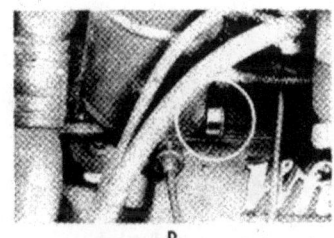

D
DISTRIBUTOR SHAFT GREASE CUP

E
REAR AXLE PROPELLER SHAFT AND SLIP JOINT FITTINGS

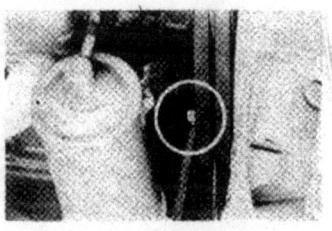

F
FRONT ENGINE SUPPORT

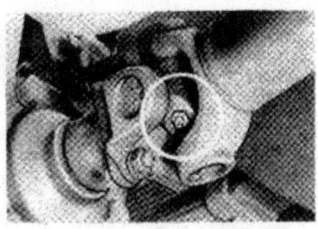

G
FRONT AXLE UNIVERSAL JOINT FITTING

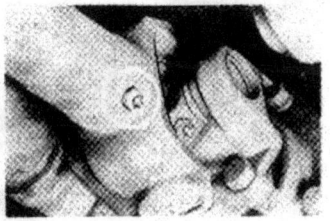

H
FRONT AXLE PROPELLER SHAFT SPLINE FITTING

RA PD 314009

*Figure 35—Localized Views*

**TM 9-710**
23

## BASIC HALF-TRACK VEHICLES (WHITE, AUTOCAR, and DIAMOND T)

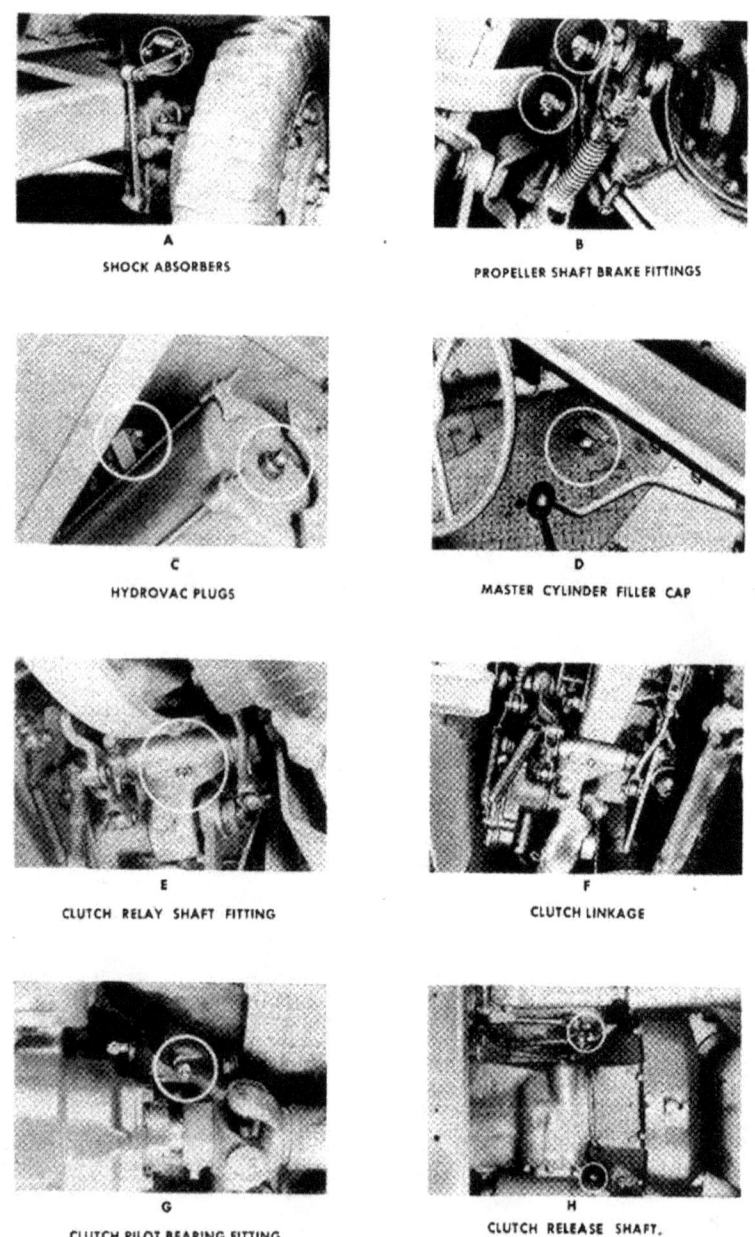

Figure 36—Localized Views

## LUBRICATION

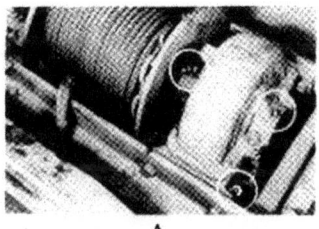

A
WINCH DRUM BEARING AND SHAFT FITTING
WORM HOUSING FILLER PLUG

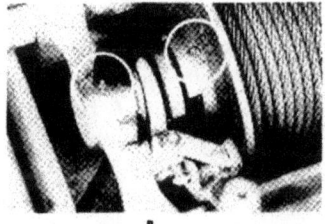

B
WINCH DRUM BEARING AND SHAFT FITTINGS

C
WINCH WORM HOUSING DRAIN PLUG.

D
IDLER SUPPORT BEARINGS

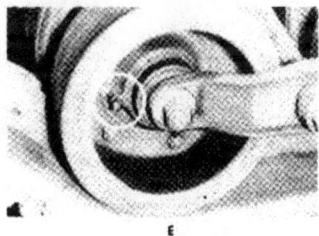

E
BOGIE WHEELS

F
IDLER ADJUSTING SCREWS

G
TRACK SUPPORT ROLLER

H
IDLER SPROCKET FITTING

RA PD 314011

*Figure 37—Localized Views*

**TM 9-710**
**23**

**BASIC HALF-TRACK VEHICLES (WHITE, AUTOCAR, and DIAMOND T)**

assemble, and refill housing with GREASE, general purpose, No. 1 above +32°F or No. 0 below +32°F.

**f. Reports and Records.**

(1) REPORTS. Report unsatisfactory performance of materiel to the Ordnance Officer responsible for maintenance.

(2) RECORDS. A record of lubrication may be maintained in the Duty Roster (W. D., A.G.O. Form No. 6).

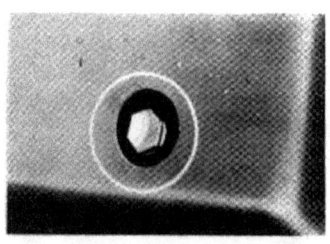
A
CRANKCASE DRAIN PLUG

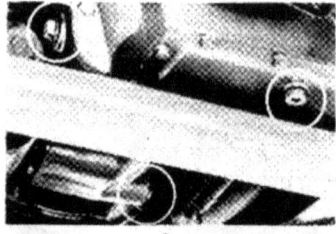
B
TRANSMISSION AND TRANSFER CASE PLUGS

C
FRONT AXLE DIFFERENTIAL PLUGS

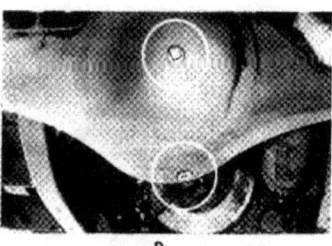
D
REAR AXLE DIFFERENTIAL PLUGS

RA PD 314012

*Figure 38—Localized Views*

TM 9-710
24-26

Section VIII

# TOOLS AND EQUIPMENT STOWAGE ON THE VEHICLE

| | Paragraph |
|---|---|
| Representative stowage lists. | 24 |
| Use of stowage lists. | 25 |
| Armament and ammunition, M3A1*. | 26 |
| Armament and ammunition, M16. | 27 |
| Gun tools and equipment, M3A1*. | 28 |
| Gun tools and equipment, M16. | 29 |
| Vehicle accessories, M3A1*. | 30 |
| Vehicle accessories, M16. | 31 |
| Vehicle tools and spare parts, M3A1*. | 32 |
| Vehicle tools and spare parts, M16. | 33 |

**24. REPRESENTATIVE STOWAGE LISTS.**

   a. This section of this manual combines two representative stowage lists, which apply to Personnel Carrier M3A1 and Multiple Gun Motor Carriage M16. These stowage lists do not include personal equipment which has no stowage on the vehicle, but is worn on the person, such as helmets, goggles, etc. These lists do not apply in full to all half-track vehicles covered by this manual, but merely are representative.

**25. USE OF STOWAGE LISTS.**

   a. Representative stowage lists given in this section of this manual are for information only. CAUTION: *These stowage lists are not intended as authority or basis for requisitioning.*

**26. ARMAMENT AND AMMUNITION, M3A1*.**

   a. Armament.

| Item | Number Carried | Where Carried |
|---|---|---|
| Gun, machine, cal. .30 model M1919A4 (flexible) | 1 | On carriage from mount M35 |
| Gun, machine, cal. .50 M2 H.B. (flexible) | 1 | On ring mount M49 |
| Gun, Thompson, submachine, cal. .45 M1928A1 or M1 | 1 | Above left gasoline tank, in brackets provided. |
| Rifle, M1 | 12 | In brackets provided behind left and right rear seats. |

   b. Ammunition.

| | | |
|---|---|---|
| Cal. .30 rounds (in ammunition boxes D44070 and belts C3951) | 7,750 | One 250 round box in front -floor well. Remainder of boxes and belts located where convenient. |

*Personnel Carrier M3A1.

TM 9-710
26-27

## BASIC HALF-TRACK VEHICLES (WHITE, AUTOCAR, and DIAMOND T)

| Item | Number Carried | Where Carried |
|---|---|---|
| Cal. .45 rounds | 540 | Under right rear seats. |
| Cal. .50 rounds (in boxes D73913) | 700 | One 100 round box on gun. Remainder of boxes located where convenient. |
| **c. Hand Grenades.** | | |
| Chemical A.T. (AW mixture) M1 | 2 | In box between front seats. |
| Fragmentation, MK II | 2 | In box between front seats. |
| Offensive, MK III (w/fuse, detonation hand grenades, M6) | 10 | In box between front seats. |
| Smoke M8 | 2 | In box between front seats. |
| Thermite, incendiary | 2 | In box between front seats. |
| CN-DM irritant M6 | 4 | In box between front seats. |
| **d. Mines.** | | |
| Mines, A.T. w/fuse M1 | 24 | Outside in rack left and right sides. |

## 27. ARMAMENT AND AMMUNITION, M16.

### a. Armament.

| Item | Number Carried | Where Carried |
|---|---|---|
| Adapter, grenade, cal. .30, M1903 rifle | 1 | In grenade chest. |
| Carbine, cal. .30 | 3 | 2 in right side fighting compartment; 1 in driver's compartment. |
| Gun, machine, cal. .50, M2 (without edgewater adapter) T.T. H.B. | 4 | Gun mount, M45. |
| Gun, Thompson, submachine, cal. .45, M1928A1 or M1 | 1 | Left side fighting compartment. |
| Rifle, cal. .30, M1903 | 1 | Driver's compartment. |

### b. Ammunition.

| Item | Number Carried | Where Carried |
|---|---|---|
| Cal. .45 rounds | 420 | Left side fighting compartment. |
| *Cal. .50 rounds, packed as follows: | 5,000 | In fighting compartment. |
| 200 round chests | **10 | |
| 200 round belts | 15 | |

### c. Hand Grenades.

| Item | Number Carried | Where Carried |
|---|---|---|
| Fragmentation, MK II | 12 | In box left side fighting compartment. |

*4,600 when radio set SCR 528 is used.
**Eight 200-round chests when radio set SCR 528 is used.

## TOOLS AND EQUIPMENT STOWAGE ON THE VEHICLE

| Item | Number Carried | Where Carried |
|---|---|---|
| Smoke, M8 | 12 | In box right side fighting compartment. |
| Thermite, incendiary | 2 | In floor well. |
| Grenades, rifle, M9A1 | 10 | Under radio shelf. |

### 28. GUN TOOLS AND EQUIPMENT, M3A1*

**a. Gun Accessories.**

(1) ACCESSORIES FOR CAL. .45 SUBMACHINE GUN.

| Item | Number Carried | Where Carried |
|---|---|---|
| Brush, chamber cleaning, M6 | 1 | Under left rear seats. |
| Brush, cleaning, cal. .45, M5 | 1 | Under left rear seats. |
| Case, accessories and spare parts M1918 w o contents | 1 | Under left rear seats. |
| Cover, assembly, Thompson submachine gun cal. .45 | 1 | On gun or under left rear seats. |
| Envelope, fabric, one button 3 x 3⅛-in. | 1 | Under left rear seats. |
| Magazine, 30 rounds (clip) | 18 | Under left rear seats. |
| Oiler, Thompson submachine gun | 1 | Under left rear seats. |
| Rod, cleaning | 1 | Under left rear seats. |
| Sling, gun M1923 (webbing) | 1 | On gun. |
| Thong | 1 | Under left rear seats. |

(2) ACCESSORIES FOR CAL. .30 MACHINE GUN.

| Item | Number Carried | Where Carried |
|---|---|---|
| Bag, empty, cartridge, cal. .30 or cal. .50 | 1 | On gun or under right rear seats. |
| Belt, ammunition, 250 rounds | 31 | In ammunition boxes provided. |
| Box, ammunition cal. .30, M1 | 31 | Located where convenient. |
| Brush, chamber cleaning, M6 | 1 | Under right rear seats. |
| Brush, cleaning cal. .30, M2 | 3 | Under right rear seats. |
| Can, tubular (w o contents) | 1 | Under right rear seats. |
| Case, cleaning rod, M1 | 1 | Under right rear seats. |
| Case, cover group | 1 | Under right rear seats. |
| Case, spare bolt, M2 (w o contents) | 3 | Under right rear seats. |
| Chest, steel, M5 (w o contents) | 1 | Under right rear seats. |
| Cover, cal. .30 machine gun | 1 | On gun or under right rear seats. |
| Cover, spare barrel | 1 | Under right rear seats. |
| Cover, tripod mount, M2 | 1 | On tripod. |
| Cover, tripod mount over-all | 1 | Outside rear door on brackets. |

*Personnel Carrier M3A1.

# TM 9-710

## BASIC HALF-TRACK VEHICLES (WHITE, AUTOCAR, and DIAMOND T)

| Item | Number Carried | Where Carried |
|---|---|---|
| Cradle, assembly (less ammunition tray, D36951) | 1 | On fixed pintle. |
| Envelope, spare parts, M1 (w/o contents) | 1 | Under right rear seats. |
| Extractor, ruptured cartridge, MK IV | 1 | Under right rear seats. |
| Mount, tripod, machine gun, cal. .30, M2 | 1 | On outside of rear door. |
| Oiler, rectangular 12-oz. | 1 | Under right rear seats. |
| Reflector, barrel cal. .30 | 1 | Under right rear seats. |
| Rod, cleaning jointed cal. .30, M1 | 1 | Under right rear seats. |
| Roll, spare parts, M13 w/o contents) | 1 | Under right rear seats. |
| Roll, tool, M12 (w/o contents) | 1 | Under right rear seats. |

(3) ACCESSORIES FOR CAL. .50 MACHINE GUN.

| Item | Number Carried | Where Carried |
|---|---|---|
| Bag, empty cartridge, cal. .30 or cal. .50 | 1 | On gun or under right rear seats. |
| Bag, metallic belt link | 1 | Under right rear seats. |
| Box, ammunition cal. .50, M2 | 7 | In light ammunition chest. |
| Brush, cleaning, cal. .50, M4 | 4 | Under right rear seats. |
| Carriage, assembly | 1 | On gun ring. |
| Case, cleaning rod, M15 | 1 | Under right rear seats. |
| Chute, metallic belt link, M1 | 1 | Under right rear seats. |
| Cover, cal. .50 A.A. machine gun | 1 | On gun or under right rear seats. |
| Cover, spare barrel, M13, 45-in. | 1 | Under right rear seats. |
| Cover, tripod mount, M1 | 1 | On tripod. |
| Cradle, assembly | 1 | On carriage. |
| Envelope, spare parts, M1 (w/o contents) | 2 | Under right rear seats. |
| Extractor, ruptured cartridge | 1 | Under right rear seats. |
| Mount, tripod, machine gun cal. .50, M3 | 1 | On side rear body in brackets provided. |
| Slide, belt feed, ass'y, B261110 | 1 | |
| Spring, belt feed pawl, A9351 | 1 | |
| Slide, sear | 1 | Under right rear seats. |
| Spring, belt feed lever plunger | 1 | Under right rear seats. |
| Spring, belt holding pawl | 1 | Under right rear seats. |
| Spring, cover extractor | 1 | Under right rear seats. |
| Spring, locking barrel | 1 | Under right rear seats. |

## TOOLS AND EQUIPMENT STOWAGE ON THE VEHICLE

| Item | Number Carried | Where Carried |
|---|---|---|
| Spring, sear | 1 | Under right rear seats. |
| Stud, bolt | 1 | Under right rear seats. |

b. Gun Spare Parts.

(1) SPARE PARTS FOR CAL. .45 SUBMACHINE GUN.

| | | |
|---|---|---|
| Disconnector, 6D | 1 | Under left rear seats. |
| Ejector, 4B (M1928A1 only) | 1 | Under left rear seats. |
| Ejector, assembly (M1 only) | 1 | Under left rear seats. |
| Extractor, 15A | 1 | Under left rear seats. |
| Pin, firing, 14A | 1 | Under left rear seats. |
| Rocker, 16D | 1 | Under left rear seats. |
| Spring, disconnector, 9A | 1 | Under left rear seats. |
| Spring, firing pin, 14C | 1 | Under left rear seats. |
| Spring, magazine catch, 9D | 1 | Under left rear seats. |
| Spring, recoil, 17C | 1 | Under left rear seats. |
| Spring, sear, 9B | 1 | Under left rear seats. |

(2) SPARE PARTS FOR CAL. .30 MACHINE GUN.

| | | |
|---|---|---|
| Band, lock, front barrel bearing. | 1 | Under right rear seats. |
| Band, lock, front barrel bearing plug | 1 | Under right rear seats. |
| Barrel | 1 | Under right rear seats. |
| Bolt, group, consisting of: | 1 | Under right rear seats. |

   1 Bolt, assembly, B147299
   1 Extractor, assembly, C121076
   1 Lever, cocking, B131317
   1 Pin, cocking lever, A20567
   1 Pin, firing, assembly, C9186
   1 Rod, driving spring, assembly, B147222
   1 Sear, C64137
   1 Spring, driving, B212654
   1 Spring, sear assembly, A131265

| | | |
|---|---|---|
| Cover group, consisting of: | 1 | Under right rear seats. |

   1 Cover assembly, C9801
   1 Lever, feed belt, B17503
   1 Pawl, feed belt, C8461
   1 Pin, belt feed pawl assembly, B131255

# TM 9-710
28

## BASIC HALF-TRACK VEHICLES (WHITE, AUTOCAR, and DIAMOND T)

| Item | Number Carried | Where Carried |
|---|---|---|
| 1 Pivot, belt feed lever, group assembly, B110529 | | |
| 1 Slide, feed belt, assembly, B131262 | | |
| 1 Spring, feed belt pawl, B147224 | | |
| 1 Spring, cover extractor, B17513 | | |
| Extension, barrel, group, consisting of: | 1 | Under right rear seats. |
|   1 Extension, barrel, assembly, C64139 | | |
|   1 Lock, breech, B147214 | | |
|   1 Pin, breech lock, assembly, B131253 | | |
|   1 Spring, locking barrel, B147230 | | |
| Frame, lock group, consisting of: | 1 | Under right rear seats. |
|   1 Accelerator, C64142 | | |
|   1 Frame, lock, assembly, C9182 | | |
|   1 Pin, accelerator, assembly, B131253 | | |
|   1 Pin, trigger, A20503 | | |
|   1 Plunger, barrel, assembly, B131251 | | |
|   1 Spring, barrel plunger, A135057 | | |
|   1 Spring, trigger pin, B147231 | | |
|   1 Trigger, C8476 | | |
| Lever, cocking | 1 | Under right rear seats. |
| Lever, feed belt | 1 | Under right reat seats. |
| Pawl, holding belt | 1 | Under right rear seats. |
| Pawl, feed belt | 1 | Under right rear seats. |
| Pin, accelerator, assembly | 1 | Under right rear seats. |
| Pin, belt holding pawl, split | 1 | Under right rear seats. |
| Pin, cocking lever | 1 | Under right rear seats. |
| Pin, firing, assembly | 1 | Under right rear seats. |
| Pin, trigger | 1 | Under right rear seats. |
| Plug, front barrel bearing | 1 | Under right rear seats. |
| Spring, belt holding pawl | 1 | Under right rear seats. |
| Spring, locking barrel | 1 | Under right reat seats. |
| Spring, sear, assembly | 1 | Under right rear seats. |
| Trigger | 1 | Under right rear seats. |

## TOOLS AND EQUIPMENT STOWAGE ON THE VEHICLE

| Item | Number Carried | Where Carried |
|---|---|---|
| (3) SPARE PARTS FOR CAL. .50 MACHINE GUN. | | |
| Barrel, assembly | 1 | Under right rear seats. |
| Disk, buffer | 1 | Under right rear seats. |
| Extension, firing pin assembly | 1 | Under right rear seats. |
| Extractor, assembly | 1 | Under right rear seats. |
| Lever, cocking | 1 | Under right rear seats. |
| Pin, cotter, belt feed lever pivot stud $3/32$ x $3/4$ in. | 1 | Under right rear seats. |
| Pin, cotter, cover pin $1/8$ x $3/8$ in. | 1 | Under right rear seats. |
| Pin, cotter, switch pivot $1/16$ x $3/4$ in. | 2 | Under right rear seats. |
| Pin firing | 1 | Under right rear seats. |
| Plunger, belt feed lever | 1 | Under right rear seats. |
| Rod, driving spring w/ spring assembly | 1 | Under right rear seats. |
| Slide, belt feed, group consisting of: | 1 | Under right rear seats. |
|   1 Arm, belt feed pawl, B8914 | | |
|   1 Pawl, feed belt, assy, B8961 | | |
|   1 Pin, belt feed pawl, assy, B8962 | | |

c. **Gun Tools.**

(1) TOOLS FOR CAL. .30 MACHINE GUN.

| Item | Number Carried | Where Carried |
|---|---|---|
| Oiler, filling, oil buffer | 1 | Under right rear seats. |
| Rod, jointed, cleaning, M7 | 1 | Under right rear seats. |
| Screwdriver, common, 3-in. blade | 1 | Under right rear seats. |
| Tray, ammunition | 1 | On cradle. |
| Wrench, combination, M6 | 1 | Under right rear seats. |
| Wrench, socket, front barrel bearing plug | 1 | Under right rear seats. |
| (2) TOOLS FOR CAL. .50 MACHINE GUN. | | |
| Wrench, combination, M2 | 1 | Under right rear seats. |

**29. GUN TOOLS AND EQUIPMENT, M16.**

a. **Gun Accessories.**

(1) ACCESSORIES FOR CAL. .45 SUBMACHINE GUN.

| Item | Number Carried | Where Carried |
|---|---|---|
| Brush, chamber cleaning, M6 | 1 | Center floor well. |
| Brush, cleaning, cal. .45, M5 | 1 | Center floor well. |

TM 9-710
29

**BASIC HALF-TRACK VEHICLES (WHITE, AUTOCAR, and DIAMOND T)**

| Item | Number Carried | Where Carried |
|---|---|---|
| Case, accessories and spare parts, M1918 (w o contents) | 1 | Center floor well. |
| Cover, assembly, Thompson, submachine gun cal. .45 | 1 | On gun. |
| Envelope, fabric, one button 3 x 3⅛ in. | 1 | Center floor well. |
| Magazine, 20 rounds (clip) | 21 | Container left side fighting compartment. |
| Oiler, Thompson submachine gun | 1 | Center floor well. |
| Rod, cleaning | 1 | Center floor well. |
| Sling, gun, M1923 (webbing) | 1 | Center floor well. |
| Thong | 1 | Center floor well. |

(2) ACCESSORIES FOR CAL. .50 MACHINE GUN.

| Item | Number Carried | Where Carried |
|---|---|---|
| Brush, cleaning, cal. .50, M4 | 24 | 6 in. each M5 chest. |
| Can, tubular, (w o contents) for spare parts | 4 | 1 in. each M5 chest. |
| Case, cleaning rod, M15 | 4 | 1 in. each M5 chest. |
| *Chest, ammunition, cal. .50, M2 | 10 | In fighting compartment. |
| Chest, steel, M5 (w o contents) | 4 | 2 in driver's compartment under seat; 2 in box in rear of vehicle. |
| Cover, (mult. cal. .50 machine gun mount) | 1 | On gun mount. |
| Crank, chest, ammunition, M2 | 3 | Center floor well. |

b. Gun Spare Parts.

(1) SPARE PARTS FOR CAL. .45 SUBMACHINE GUN.

| Item | Number Carried | Where Carried |
|---|---|---|
| Catalogue service parts (for vehicle) | 1 | Glove compartment. |
| Disconnector, 6D | 1 | Center floor well. |
| Ejector, 4B (M1928A1 only) | 1 | Center floor well. |
| Ejector, assembly (M1 only) | 1 | Center floor well. |
| Extractor, 15A | 1 | Center floor well. |
| Lamp, inspection 12-16 V. D.C. | 2 | Glove compartment. |
| Lamp, inspection | 1 | Glove compartment. |
| Link, self-closing (wheel chain repair) | 4 | Center floor well. |
| Lubrication Guide, War Dept. | 1 | In bracket, right door. |

*Eight when radio set SCR 528 is used.

74

## TOOLS AND EQUIPMENT STOWAGE ON THE VEHICLE

| Item | Number Carried | Where Carried |
|---|---|---|
| Manual, field for cal. .50, M2 H.B. | 1 | Glove compartment. |
| Manual, operating | 1 | Glove compartment. |
| Manual, technical for M.G. M.C., M16 | 1 | Glove compartment. |
| Manual, technical, mount M.G. mult. cal. .50, M45 | 1 | Glove compartment. |
| Mittens, asbestos, pairs | 2 | Center floor well. |
| Net, camouflage, 36- x 44-ft | 1 | Right front fender. |
| Nozzle, flexible, tube | 2 | Center floor well. |
| Oiler, (trigger type 1-pt) | 1 | Center floor well. |
| Pack, seat | 5 | On seat boxes. |
| Paulin, 12- x 12-ft. | 1 | Left front fender. |
| Pin, firing, 14A | 1 | Center floor well. |
| Pump, assembly, hand, air | 1 | Center floor well. |
| Rocker, 16D | 1 | Center floor well. |
| Roll, blanket | 5 | Box in rear of vehicle. |
| Snatch block | 1 | Center floor well. |
| Spring, disconnector, 9A | 1 | Center floor well. |
| Spring, firing pin, 14C | 1 | Center floor well. |
| Spring, magazine catch, 9D | 1 | Center floor well. |
| Spring, recoil, 17C | 1 | Center floor well. |
| Spring, sear, 9B | 1 | Center floor well. |
| Straps, fender, 36- x 1½-in. | 4 | 2 each front fender. |
| Tape, friction, ¾ in. wide, 30-ft. roll | 1 | Center floor well. |
| Wire, soft iron, 14 gage, 10 ft. long | 1 | Center floor well. |

(2) SPARE PARTS FOR CAL. .50 MACHINE GUN.

| Item | Number Carried | Where Carried |
|---|---|---|
| Accelerator | 4 | 1 in each M5 chest. |
| Arm, belt feed pawl | 4 | 1 in each M5 chest. |
| Bar, trigger | 4 | 1 in each M5 chest. |
| Barrel, assembly | 4 | In fighting compartment. |
| Collar, driving spring rod | 4 | 1 in each M5 chest. |
| Disk, buffer | 8 | 2 in each M5 chest. |
| Ejector | 4 | 1 in each M5 chest. |
| Envelope, spare parts, M1 (w/o contents) | 8 | 2 in each M5 chest. |
| Extension, firing pin, assembly | 8 | 2 in each M5 chest. |
| Extractor, assembly | 8 | 2 in each M5 chest. |
| Gage, head space and timing, cal. .50 B.M.G. | 4 | 1 in each M5 chest. |

# TM 9-710
29

## BASIC HALF-TRACK VEHICLES (WHITE, AUTOCAR, and DIAMOND T)

| Item | Number Carried | Where Carried |
|---|---|---|
| Lever, cocking | 4 | 1 in each M5 chest. |
| Lever, feed, belt | 4 | 1 in each M5 chest. |
| Lock, spring, oil buffer body | 4 | 1 in each M5 chest. |
| Nut, 3/8-16NC-2 | 4 | 1 in each M5 chest. |
| Oiler, rectangular, 12 oz. | 4 | 1 in each M5 chest. |
| Pawl, feed, belt, assembly | 4 | 1 in each M5 chest. |
| Pawl, holding, belt | 4 | 1 in each M5 chest. |
| Pin, accelerator, assembly | 4 | 1 in each M5 chest. |
| Pin, belt holding pawl, assembly | 8 | 2 in each M5 chest. |
| Pin, breech lock, assembly | 4 | 1 in each M5 chest. |
| Pin, cocking lever | 4 | 1 in each M5 chest. |
| Pin, cotter, split, S., 1/16- x 3/4-in. | 20 | 5 in each M5 chest. |
| Pin, cotter, split, S., 1/16- x 1-in. | 20 | 5 in each M5 chest. |
| Pin, cotter, split, S., 3/32- x 3/4-in. | 12 | 3 in each M5 chest. |
| Pin, cotter, split, S., 1/8- x 7/8-in. | 8 | 2 in each M5 chest. |
| Pin, firing | 8 | 2 in each M5 chest. |
| Pin, stop, driving spring rod collar | 4 | 1 in each M5 chest. |
| Pin, trigger bar, assembly | 4 | 1 in each M5 chest. |
| Plunger, belt feed lever | 8 | 2 in each M5 chest. |
| Reflector, barrel, cal. .50 | 4 | 1 in each M5 chest. |
| Rod, driving spring, w/ spring assembly | 8 | 2 in each M5 chest. |
| Rod, jointed, cleaning, M7 | 4 | 1 in each M5 chest. |
| Roll, spare parts, M14 (w/o contents) | 4 | 1 in each M5 chest. |
| Roll, tool, M10 (w/o contents) | 4 | 1 in each M5 chest. |
| Screw | 4 | 1 in each M5 chest. |
| Screw, cap, hex hd. | 4 | 1 in each M5 chest. |
| Screw, filler, oil buffer tube | 4 | 1 in each M5 chest. |
| Screw, retracting slide bracket, front | 8 | 2 in each M5 chest. |
| Screw, retracting slide bracket, rear | 16 | 4 in each M5 chest. |
| Sear | 4 | 1 in each M5 chest. |
| Slide, sear | 8 | 2 in each M5 chest. |
| Spring, belt feed lever plunger | 4 | 1 in each M5 chest. |

## TOOLS AND EQUIPMENT STOWAGE ON THE VEHICLE

| Item | Number Carried | Where Carried |
|---|---|---|
| Spring, belt feed pawl | 8 | 2 in each M5 chest. |
| Spring, belt holding pawl | 8 | 2 in each M5 chest. |
| Spring, cover, extractor | 8 | 2 in each M5 chest. |
| Spring, ejector | 4 | 1 in each M5 chest. |
| Spring, locking, barrel | 8 | 2 in each M5 chest. |
| Spring, oil buffer | 4 | 1 in each M5 chest. |
| Spring, retracting slide lever, R.H. | 4 | 1 in each M5 chest. |
| Spring, sear | 8 | 2 in each M5 chest. |
| Spring, side plate, trigger | 4 | 1 in each M5 chest. |
| Spring, side plate, trigger slide | 4 | 1 in each M5 chest. |
| Stop, sear, assembly | 4 | 1 in each M5 chest. |
| Stud, bolt | 8 | 2 in each M5 chest. |
| Washer, lock, toothed, reg., $\frac{1}{4}$-in. | 4 | 1 in each M5 chest. |
| Washer, lock, toothed, reg., $\frac{3}{8}$-in. | 4 | 1 in each M5 chest. |
| Washer, lock, $\frac{3}{8}$-in. | 4 | 1 in each M5 chest. |

c. Gun Tools.

(1) TOOLS FOR CAL. .50 MACHINE GUN.

| Item | Number Carried | Where Carried |
|---|---|---|
| Pliers, side-cut., parallel jaw, 6-in. | 4 | 1 in each M5 chest. |
| Punch, drive pin, 12-in. point | 4 | 1 in each M5 chest. |
| Punch, drive pin, 18-in. point | 4 | 1 in each M5 chest. |
| Screwdriver, common, 3-in. blade | 4 | 1 in each M5 chest. |
| Wrench, combination, M2 | 4 | 1 in each M5 chest. |
| Wrench, engrs., dble. hd., alloy-S., $\frac{7}{16}$- x $\frac{1}{2}$-in. | 4 | 1 in each M5 chest. |
| Wrench, engrs., dble. hd., alloy-S., $\frac{5}{8}$- x $\frac{3}{4}$-in. | 4 | 1 in each M5 chest. |
| Wrench, engrs., dble. hd., alloy-S., $\frac{7}{8}$- x 1-in. | 4 | 1 in each M5 chest. |

## 30. VEHICLE ACCESSORIES, M3A1.*

a. Sighting Equipment.

| Item | Number Carried | Where Carried |
|---|---|---|
| Binocular, M3, complete composed of:<br>1 Binocular M3<br>1 Case, carrying, M17 | 1 | On commander. |

*Personnel Carrier M3A1.

# TM 9-710
30

**BASIC HALF-TRACK VEHICLES (WHITE, AUTOCAR, and DIAMOND T)**

| Item | Number Carried | Where Carried |
|---|---|---|
| **b. Signaling Equipment.** | | |
| Antenna, complete w/cover | 1 | |
| Radio set SCR 193, 245, 506, 508, or 510 | 1 | In brackets provided. |
| **c. Rations.** | | |
| Type "C" two-day ration for 13 men, cans | 156 | Under left rear seat. |
| Type "D" one-day ration for 13 men, cans | 4 | Under left rear seat. |
| **d. Pioneer Tools** (fig. 41). | | |
| Ax, chopping, 5-lb. | 1 | Outside vehicle in brackets provided. |
| Cover, saw | 1 | Under right rear seat. |
| Crowbar, pinch point, 60-in. | 1 | Under left rear seats. |
| Mattock, pick, with handle M1 | 1 | Outside vehicle in brackets provided. |
| Saw, cross-cut (one-man, $4\frac{1}{2}$ ft long, w/handle) | 1 | Under right rear seat. |
| Shovel, short-handled | 1 | Outside vehicle in brackets provided. |
| **e. Accessories and Miscellaneous** (fig. 40). | | |
| Apparatus, decontaminating $1\frac{1}{2}$-qt., M2 (Spec. 197-54-113) | 1 | Right of right shutter handle, bracket fastened to plate. |
| Appliers, track chain | 2 | Rear floor well, in bag w/track chains. |
| Bag, field, canvas O.D. M1936 | 13 | Between individual's feet. |
| Bag, tool | 1 | Center floor well. |
| Bolt, connector, side chain (track chain repair) | 8 | Rear floor well. |
| Book, O.O. Form 7255 | 1 | In glove compartment. |
| Bow, top, (1 center, 1 rear) | 2 | Behind left rear seats. |
| Bucket, canvas, folding 18 qt | 1 | Rear floor well. |
| Cable, towing ($\frac{5}{8}$-in. x 15-ft) | 1 | On front bumper. |
| Canteen, M1910, with cup and cover, M1910 | 13 | On personnel. |
| Catalogue, service parts (for vehicle) | 1 | In glove compartment. |
| Chain, tire, front wheel (w/bag) (8.25 x 20) | 1 pr. | Rear floor well. |
| Chain, band track narrow | 1 pr. | Rear floor well. |
| Connector, side chain (track chain repair) | 8 | Rear floor well. |

## TOOLS AND EQUIPMENT STOWAGE ON THE VEHICLE

| Item | Number Carried | Where Carried |
|---|---|---|
| Container, water, 5-gal. Q.M.C. standard | 2 | In brackets on sides of cowl. |
| Curtain, canvas, R.H. w/flap | 1 | Behind left rear seats. |
| Curtain, canvas, L.H. w/flap | 1 | Behind left rear seats. |
| Envelope, waterproof | 1 | In driver's compartment. |
| Extinguisher, fire (2-lb $CO_2$) and bracket assembly | 1 | To right of right front seat. |
| Flashlight (specification 17-197) | 3 | In flashlight clips. |
| Gage, tire pressure | 1 | Center floor well. |
| Gun, lubricating, pressure (hand-operated) | 1 | Center floor well. |
| Key, map compartment | 2 | In map compartment lock. |
| Kit, first aid, 24-unit (Spec. 1553) | 1 | Under right rear seat. |
| Kit, tire repair, (hot patch w/clamp) | 1 | Center floor well. |
| Lamp, inspection 12-16V D.C. | 2 | In glove compartment. |
| Lamp, inspection | 1 | In glove compartment. |
| Link, self-closing (wheel chain repair) | 4 | Rear floor well. |
| Lubrication Guide, War Dept. | 1 | In bracket right door. |
| Manual, field, for A.T. mines | 1 | Under left rear seat. |
| Manual, field for cal. .30 M.G. M1919A4 | 1 | Under left rear seat. |
| Manual, field for cal. .50 M.G., M2 | 1 | Under left rear seat. |
| Manual, techincal for H.T.C., M3A1 | 1 | In glove compartment. |
| Mittens, asbestos | 2 pr. | Under left rear seats. |
| Net, camouflage 36- x 44-ft. | 1 | Under left rear seats. |
| Nozzle, flexible tube | 2 | Under left rear seat. |
| Oiler, (trigger type, 1-pt) | 1 | Center floor well. |
| Pack, seat | 13 | In crew compartment. |
| Pump, assembly, hand, air | 1 | Under left rear seat. |
| Rod, curtain, body | 2 | Behind left rear seats. |
| Rod, top bow support (front) | 1 | Behind left rear seats. |
| Rod, top bow support (center) | 2 | Behind left rear seats. |
| Rod, top bow support (rear) | 2 | Behind left rear seats. |
| Roll, blanket | 13 | Inside canvas seats. |
| Snatch block (when winch equipped) | 1 | Rear floor well. |
| Straps, fender, 36- x 1½-in. | 4 | On fenders. |

TM 9-710
30-31

## BASIC HALF-TRACK VEHICLES (WHITE, AUTOCAR, and DIAMOND T)

| Item | Number Carried | Where Carried |
|---|---|---|
| Strap, web | 1 | Behind left rear seats. |
| Strap, web (right front) | 1 | Behind left rear seats. |
| Strap, web (right rear) | 1 | Behind left rear seats. |
| Tape, friction, ¾ in. wide (30-ft roll) | 1 | Center floor well. |
| Top, canvas | 1 | On right front fender. |
| Bag, canvas | 1 | Behind left rear seats. |
| Bow, top, front | 1 | Behind left rear seats. |
| Wire, soft iron, 14 gage, 10 ft long | 1 | Center floor well. |

### 31. VEHICLE ACCESSORIES, M16.

**a. Sighting Equipment.**

| | | |
|---|---|---|
| Binocular, M3, complete, composed of: | 1 | On commander. |
| 1 Binocular, M3 | | |
| 1 Case, carrying M17 | | |

**b. Signaling Equipment.**

| | | |
|---|---|---|
| Antenna, complete w/cover | 1 | |
| Flag set, M238, composed of: | 1 | Right of commander's seat. |
| 1 Case, CS-90 | | |
| 1 Flag, MC-273 (red) | | |
| 1 Flag, MC-274 (orange) | | |
| 1 Flag, MC-275 (green) | | |
| 3 Flagstaff, MC-270 | | |
| Radio set SCR 510 or 528 or British No. 19 | 1 | |

**c. Rations.**

| | | |
|---|---|---|
| Type "C" 2-day rations for 5 men, cans | 60 | Under gun mount base. |
| Type "D" 1-day rations for 5 men, cans | 2 | Under gun mount base. |

**d. Pioneer Tools (fig. 41).**

| | | |
|---|---|---|
| Ax, (chopping, 5-lb) | 1 | Outside, below right door. |
| Crowbar, pinch point 60-in. | 1 | Rear fighting compartment. |
| Mattock, pick, with handle M1 | 1 | Outside, below left door. |
| Shovel, short-handled | 1 | Outside, below left door. |

**e. Accessories and Miscellaneous (fig. 40).**

| | | |
|---|---|---|
| Apparatus, decontaminating, 1½-qt, M2 (Spec. 197-54-113) | 1 | Left of driver's seat. |
| Applier, track chain | 2 | Center floor well. |

## TOOLS AND EQUIPMENT STOWAGE ON THE VEHICLE

| Item | Number Carried | Where Carried |
|---|---|---|
| Bag, tool | 1 | Center floor well. |
| Bag, field, canvas O.D. M1936 | 5 | Top of front gas tanks. |
| Bolt, connector, side chain (track chain repair) | 8 | Center floor well. |
| Bucket, canvas, folding 18-qt. | 1 | Behind driver's seat. |
| Bucket, water, galv. iron, 14-qt. | 1 | Left rear outside. |
| Cable, towing (¾-in. x 15-ft) | 1 | On front bumpers. |
| Canteen, M1910, with cup and cover M1910 | 5 | On troops. |
| Chain, tire, front wheel (w/bag) (8.25 x 20) | 1 pr. | Center floor well. |
| Chain, band track narrow, | 1 pr. | Center floor well. |
| Container, water, 5-gal (Q.M.C. Standard) | 2 | Outside, engine cowl. |
| Connector, side chain (track chain repair) | 8 | Center floor well. |
| Envelope, waterproof | 1 | In glove compartment. |
| Extinguisher, fire (2-lb $CO_2$) and bracket assembly | 1 | Right of driver's seat. |
| Flashlight (Specification 17-197) | 3 | In flashlight clips. |
| Gage, tire pressure | 1 | Center floor well. |
| Gun, lubricating, pressure (hand-operated) | 1 | Center floor well. |
| Key, map compartment | 2 | In map compartment lock. |
| Kit, first aid 24-unit (Spec. 1553) | 1 | Left side fighting compartment. |
| Kit, tire repair, (hot patch w/clamp) | 1 | Center floor well. |

## 32. VEHICLE TOOLS AND SPARE PARTS, M3A1.*

**a. Vehicle Spare Parts.**

| Item | Number Carried | Where Carried |
|---|---|---|
| Belt, fan, pair | 1 | Center floor well. |
| Body, elbow, fitting lubricating, 90°, ⅛-in. | 3 | Center floor well. |
| Caps, valve, tire | 5 | Center floor well. |
| Condenser, (distribution) and bracket (unassembled) | 1 | Center floor well. |
| Core, valve, tire | 5 | Center floor well. |
| Fitting, lubricating, straight, ⅛-in. | 6 | Center floor well. |

*Personnel Carrier M3A1.

# TM 9-710

## BASIC HALF-TRACK VEHICLES (WHITE, AUTOCAR, and DIAMOND T)

| Item | Number Carried | Where Carried |
|---|---|---|
| Guide, track | 4 | Center floor well. |
| Headlamp, service (spare) | 1 | Above left gas tank. |
| Nut | 4 | Center floor well. |
| Pin, winch drive (when winch equipped) | 6 | Center floor well. |
| Plug, pipe, 1/8-in. | 1 | Center floor well. |
| Plug, pipe, 1/4-in. | 1 | Center floor well. |
| Spark plug, assembly | 3 | Center floor well. |
| Washer, lock | 4 | Center floor well. |

b. Vehicle Tools (fig. 42).

| Item | Number Carried | Where Carried |
|---|---|---|
| Brush, scratch, wire, painter's handled | 1 | Center floor well. |
| Extension, (1/2-in. sq drive 10-in. long) | 1 | Center floor well. |
| Hammer, machinist, ball peen (32 oz) | 1 | Center floor well. |
| Handle, socket wrench (wheel bearing nut) | 1 | Center floor well. |
| Jack, assembly w handle (5-ton) | 1 | Center floor well. |
| Plier, combination, slip joint (8-in.) | 1 | Center floor well. |
| Ratchet, reversible, (1/2-in. sq drive 9-in.) | 1 | Center floor well. |
| Screwdriver, common, 6-in. blade | 1 | Center floor well. |
| Screwdriver, common, 8-in. blade | 1 | Center floor well. |
| Screwdriver, special purpose, 1 3/4-in. blade | 1 | Center floor well. |
| Wrench, adj. single end, 18-in. (modified to 2 3/16-in. opening) | 1 | Center floor well. |
| Wrench, eng. dble. hd. 7/16-in. and 1/2-in. | 1 | Center floor well. |
| Wrench, eng. dble. hd. 9/16-in. and 5/8-in. | 1 | Center floor well. |
| Wrench, eng. dble. hd. 3/4-in. and 15/16-in. | 1 | Center floor well. |
| Wrench, eng. dble. hd. 1 1/16-in. and 1 5/16-in. (special) | 1 | Center floor well. |
| Wrench, socket, (3/4-in. opening, 1/2-in. drive) | 1 | Center floor well. |
| Wrench, spark plug | 1 | Center floor well. |
| Wrench, wheel bearing nut | 1 | Center floor well. |
| Wrench, wheel nut | 1 | Center floor well. |

# TM 9-710

## TOOLS AND EQUIPMENT STOWAGE ON THE VEHICLE

### 33. VEHICLE TOOLS AND SPARE PARTS, M16.

**a. Vehicle Spare Parts.**

| Item | Number Carried | Where Carried |
|---|---|---|
| Belt, fan, pair | 1 | Center floor well. |
| Body, elbow, fitting, lubr. 90 deg., $\frac{1}{8}$-in. | 3 | Center floor well. |
| Cap, valve, tire | 5 | Center floor well. |
| Condenser, (distributor) and bracket (unassembled) | 1 | Center floor well. |
| Core, valve, tire | 5 | Center floor well. |
| Fitting, lubricating, straight $\frac{1}{8}$-in. | 6 | Center floor well. |
| Guide, track | 4 | Center floor well. |
| Headlamp, service (spare) | 1 | In spare lamp brackets. |
| Nut (for track guide) | 4 | Center floor well. |
| Pin, winch drive | 6 | Center floor well. |
| Plug, pipe, $\frac{1}{8}$-in. | 1 | Center floor well. |
| Plug, pipe, $\frac{1}{4}$-in. | 1 | Center floor well. |
| Plug, spark, assembly | 3 | Center floor well. |
| Washer, lock | 4 | Center floor well. |

**b. Vehicle Tools (fig. 42).**

| Item | Number Carried | Where Carried |
|---|---|---|
| Brush, scratch, wire, painter's handled | 1 | Center floor well. |
| Chisel, cold, $\frac{3}{4}$-in. | 1 | Center floor well. |
| Extension, $\frac{1}{2}$-in. sq drive 10-in. long | 1 | Center floor well. |
| File, hand, smooth, 8-in. | 1 | Center floor well. |
| File, 3-sq smooth, 6-in. | 1 | Center floor well. |
| Hammer, machinist, ball peen (32-oz) | 1 | Center floor well. |
| Handle, socket wrench (wheel bearing, nut) | 1 | Center floor well. |
| Jack, assembly w handle (5-ton) | 1 | Center floor well. |
| Plier, combination, slip joint (8-in.) | 1 | Center floor well. |
| Ratchet, reversible, $\frac{1}{2}$-in. sq drive, 9-in. | 1 | Center floor well. |
| Screwdriver, common, 6-in. blade | 1 | Center floor well. |
| Screwdriver, common, 8-in. blade | 1 | Center floor well. |
| Screwdriver, special purpose, $1\frac{3}{4}$-in. blade | 1 | Center floor well. |

# TM 9-710
## 33
## BASIC HALF-TRACK VEHICLES (WHITE, AUTOCAR, and DIAMOND T)

Figure 39 — Stowage Compartments, Open (Car M2)

**TM 9-710**

## TOOLS AND EQUIPMENT STOWAGE ON THE VEHICLE

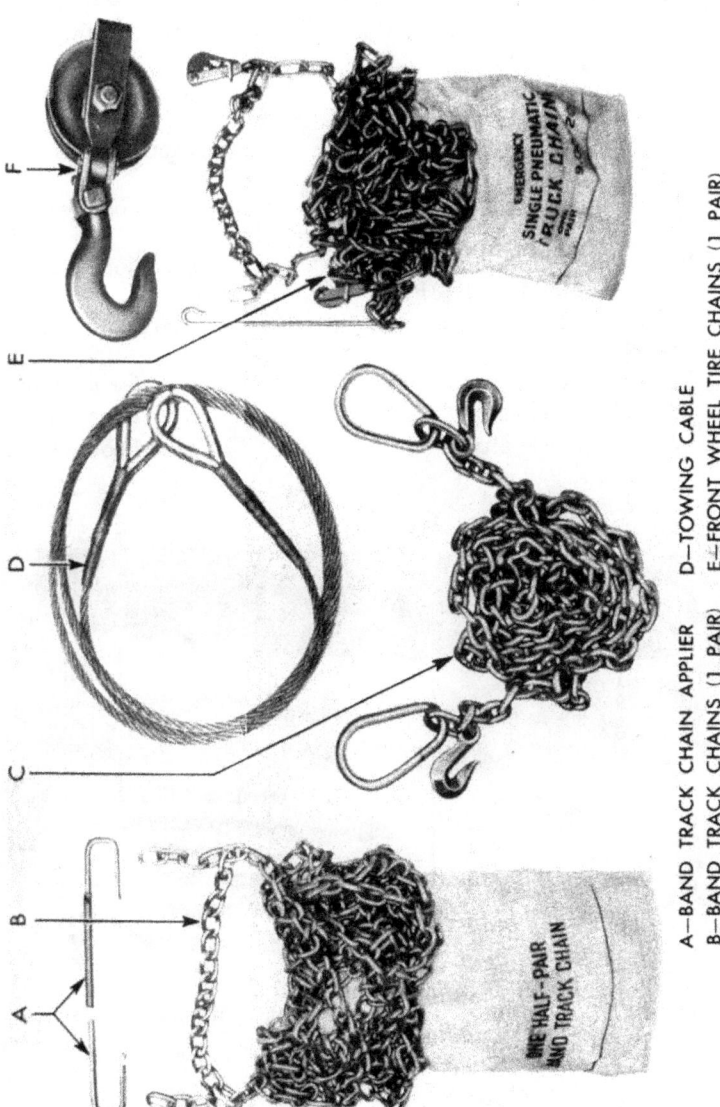

A—BAND TRACK CHAIN APPLIER   D—TOWING CABLE
B—BAND TRACK CHAINS (1 PAIR)  E—FRONT WHEEL TIRE CHAINS (1 PAIR)
C—TOWING CHAIN                F—SNATCH BLOCK

*Figure 40—Vehicle Accessories*

# TM 9-710
33

## BASIC HALF-TRACK VEHICLES (WHITE, AUTOCAR, and DIAMOND T)

| Item | Number Carried | Where Carried |
|---|---|---|
| Wrench, engr., dble. hd. $7/16$-in. and $1/2$-in. | 1 | Center floor well. |
| Wrench, engr. dble. hd. $9/16$-in. and $5/8$-in. | 1 | Center floor well. |
| Wrench, engr. dble. hd. $3/4$-in. and $15/16$-in. | 1 | Center floor well. |
| Wrench, engr. dble. hd. $1 1/16$-in. and $1 5/16$-in. (special) | 1 | Center floor well. |
| Wrench, adj. single end, 18-in. (modified to $2 3/16$-in.) | 1 | Center floor well. |
| Wrench, socket ($3/4$-in. opening, $1/2$-in. drive) | 1 | Center floor well. |
| Wrench, wheel bearing nut | 1 | Center floor well. |
| Wrench, wheel nut | 1 | Center floor well. |
| Wrench, spark plug | 1 | Center floor well. |

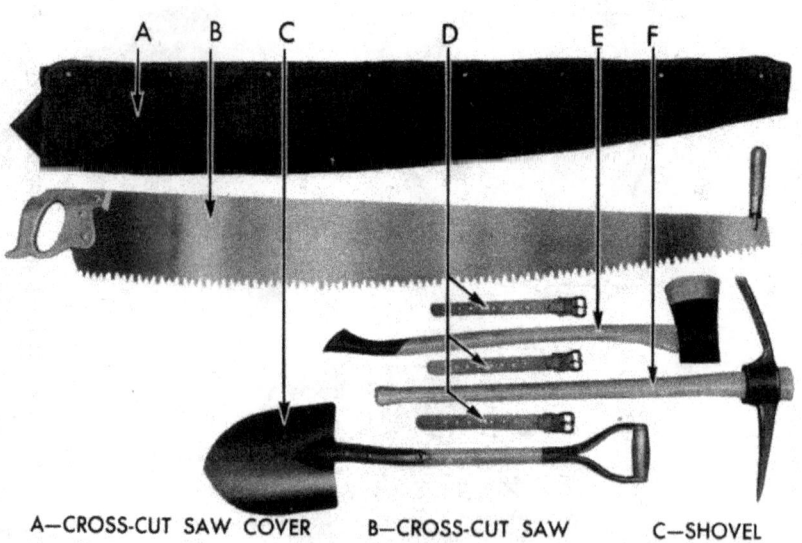

A—CROSS-CUT SAW COVER  B—CROSS-CUT SAW  C—SHOVEL
D—STRAPS  E—AXE  F—MATTOCK

RA PD 18348

*Figure 41—Pioneer Tools*

86

## TOOLS AND EQUIPMENT STOWAGE ON THE VEHICLE

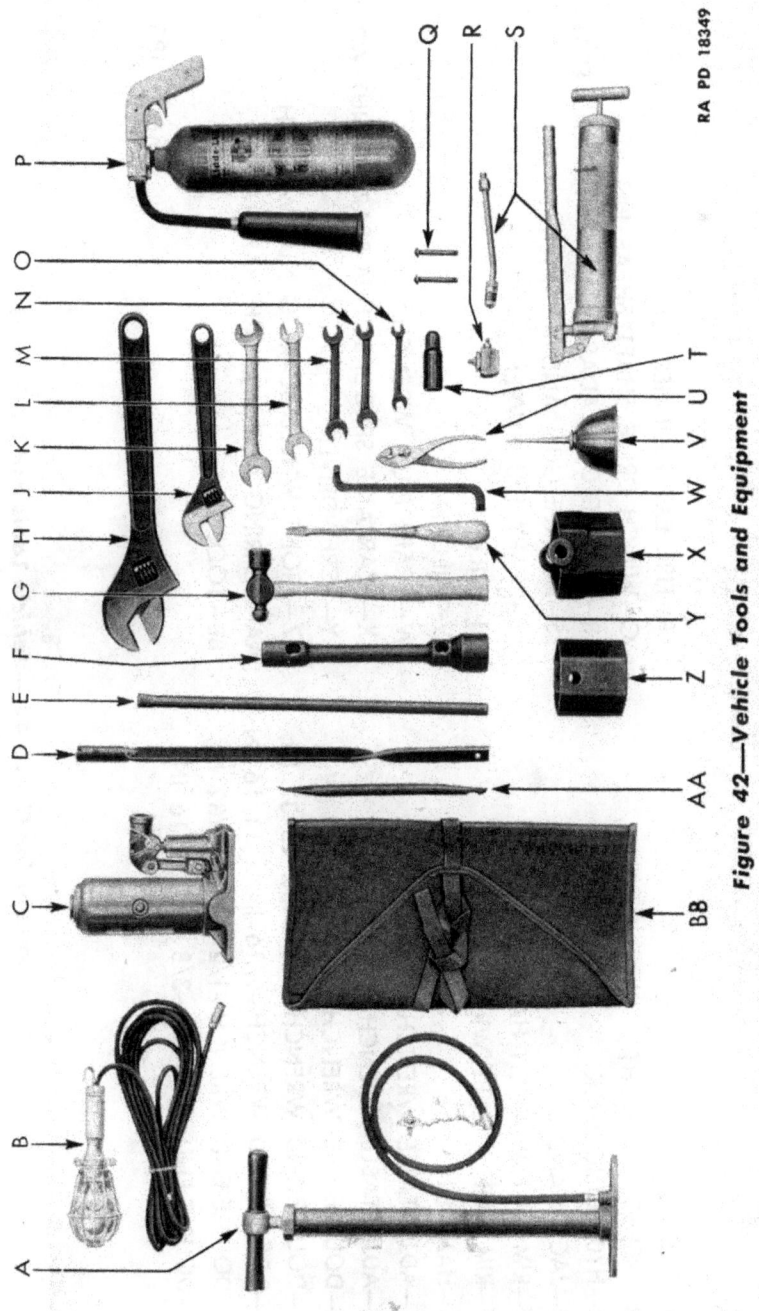

Figure 42—Vehicle Tools and Equipment

**TM 9-710**

**BASIC HALF-TRACK VEHICLES (WHITE, AUTOCAR, and DIAMOND T)**

A—TIRE PUMP
B—INSPECTION LIGHT
C—HYDRAULIC JACK
D—JACK HANDLE
E—RIM NUT WRENCH HANDLE
F—RIM NUT SOCKET WRENCH
G—HAMMER
H—ADJUSTABLE WRENCH—18 INCH
J—ADJUSTABLE WRENCH—12 INCH
K—DOUBLE-END WRENCH—3/4 IN. x 7/8 IN.
L—DOUBLE-END WRENCH—5/8 IN. x 25/32 IN.
M—DOUBLE-END WRENCH—9/16 IN. x 11/16 IN.
N—DOUBLE-END WRENCH—1/2 IN. x 19/32 IN.
O—DOUBLE-END WRENCH—3/8 IN. x 7/16 IN.
P—FIRE EXTINGUISHER ($CO_2$)
Q—WINCH DRIVE SHAFT SHEAR PIN
R—ALEMITE GUN ADAPTER (BUTTON HEAD FITTING)
S—ALEMITE GUN AND ADAPTER
T—SPARK PLUG WRENCH
U—PLIERS
V—OILCAN
W—DRAIN PLUG WRENCH
X—REAR AXLE SPROCKET HUB BEARING NUT WRENCH
Y—SCREWDRIVER
Z—FRONT WHEEL BEARING NUT WRENCH
AA—BEARING NUT WRENCH HANDLE
BB—TOOL BAG

RA PD 18349C

*Legend for Figure 42—Vehicle Tools and Equipment*

# TM 9-710

## TOOLS AND EQUIPMENT STOWAGE ON THE VEHICLE

Figure 43—Stowage Compartments, Open (Personnel Carrier M3)

*Figure 44—Stowage Compartments, Open (81-mm Mortar Carrier M4A1)*

**TM 9-710**
**33**

# TOOLS AND EQUIPMENT STOWAGE ON THE VEHICLE

*Figure 45—Stowage Compartments, Open (75-mm Gun Motor Carriage)*

# TM 9-710
## 33
### BASIC HALF-TRACK VEHICLES (WHITE, AUTOCAR, and DIAMOND T)

Figure 46—Stowage Compartments, Open (Multiple Gun Motor Carriage M15)

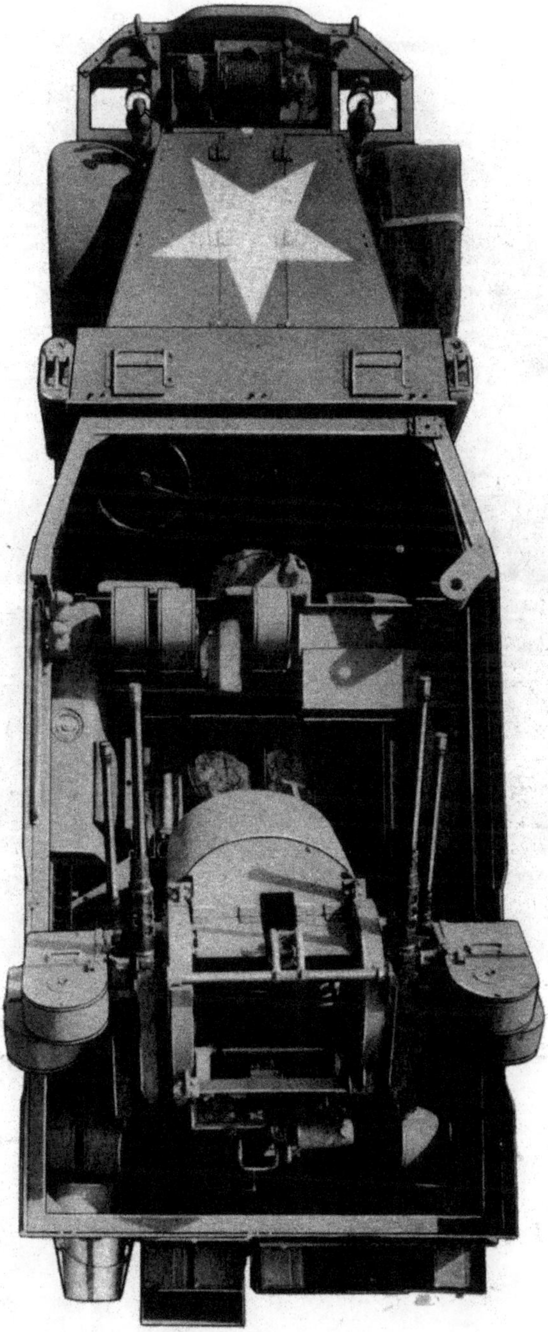

## TOOLS AND EQUIPMENT STOWAGE ON THE VEHICLE

Figure 47—Stowage Compartments, Open (Multiple Gun Motor Carriage M16)

RA PD 31401

*Figure 48—Stowage Compartments, Open (81-mm Mortar Carrier M21)*

TM 9-710
34-36

# PART TWO—VEHICLE MAINTENANCE INSTRUCTIONS

Section IX

# RECORD OF MODIFICATIONS AND NEW VEHICLE RUN-IN TESTS

|  | Paragraph |
|---|---|
| MWO and major unit assembly replacement record | 34 |
| Purpose of run-in test | 35 |
| Correction of deficiencies | 36 |
| Run-in procedures | 37 |

## 34. MWO AND MAJOR UNIT ASSEMBLY REPLACEMENT RECORD.

**a. Description.** Every vehicle is supplied with a copy of A.G.O. Form No. 478 which provides a means of keeping a record of each MWO (FSMWO) completed or major unit assembly replaced. This form includes spaces for the vehicle name and U.S.A. Registration Number, instructions for use, and information pertinent to the work to be accomplished. It is very important that the form be used as directed, and that it remain with the vehicle until the vehicle is removed from service.

**b. Instructions for Use.** Personnel performing modifications or major unit assembly replacements must record clearly on the form a description of the work completed, and must initial the form in the columns provided. When each modification is completed, record the date, hours and/or mileage, and MWO number. When major unit assemblies, such as engines, transmissions, transfer cases, are replaced, record the date, hours and/or mileage and nomenclature of the unit assembly. Minor repairs and minor parts and accessory replacements need not be recorded.

**c. Early Modifications.** Upon receipt by a third or fourth echelon repair facility of a vehicle for modification or repair, maintenance personnel will record the MWO numbers of modifications applied prior to the date of A.G.O. Form No. 478.

## 35. PURPOSE OF RUN-IN TEST.

**a.** When a new or reconditioned vehicle is first received at the using organization, it is necessary for second echelon personnel to determine whether or not the vehicle will operate satisfactorily when placed in service. For this purpose, inspect all accessories, subassemblies, assemblies, tools, and equipment to see that they are in place and correctly adjusted. In addition, they will perform a run-in test of at least 50 miles as directed in AR 850-15, paragraph 25, table III, according to procedures in paragraph 37 below.

## 36. CORRECTION OF DEFICIENCIES.

**a.** Deficiencies disclosed during the course of the run-in test will be treated as follows:

TM 9-710
36-37

### BASIC HALF-TRACK VEHICLES (WHITE, AUTOCAR, and DIAMOND T)

(1) Correct any deficiencies within the scope of the maintenance echelon of the using organization before the vehicle is placed in service.

(2) Refer deficiencies beyond the scope of the maintenance echelon of the using organization to a higher echelon for correction.

(3) Bring deficiencies of serious nature to the attention of the supplying organization.

### 37. RUN-IN TEST PROCEDURES.

**a. Preliminary Service.**

(1) FIRE EXTINGUISHER. See that portable extinguisher is present and in good condition. Test it momentarily for proper operation, and mount it securely.

(2) FUEL, OIL, AND WATER. Fill fuel tank. Check crankcase oil and coolant supply, and add as necessary to bring to correct levels. Allow room for expansion in fuel tank and radiator. During freezing weather, test value of antifreeze and add as necessary to protect cooling system against freezing. CAUTION: *If there is a tag attached to filler cap or steering wheel concerning engine oil in crankcase, follow instructions on tag before driving the vehicle.*

(3) FUEL FILTER. Inspect fuel filter for leaks, damage, secure mountings, and connections. Drain filter sediment bowl. If any appreciable amount of water or dirt is present, remove bowl, and clean bowl and element in dry-cleaning solvent. Also drain accumulated water or dirt from bottom of fuel tank. Drain only till fuel runs clean.

(4) BATTERY. Make hydrometer and voltage test of battery and level electrolyte to $3/8$ inch above plates with clean water if necessary.

(5) AIR CLEANER AND BREATHER CAP. Examine carburetor air cleaner and crank case breather cap to see if they are in good condition and secure. Remove oil cup, wash out in dry-cleaning solvent and refill reservoir to proper depth with fresh oil. On vehicles equipped with hydrovac brake booster, remove hair element, wash thoroughly in dry-cleaning solvent and saturate with engine oil. Replace hair in cleaner and reassemble.

(6) ACCESSORIES AND BELTS. See that accessories such as carburetor, generator, regulator, cranking motor, distributor, water pump, fan and oil filters are securely mounted, and that fan and generator drive belts are in good condition and adjusted to have $1/2$-inch deflection.

(7) ELECTRIC WIRING. Examine all accessible wiring and conduits to see if they are in good condition, securely connected, and properly supported.

(8) TIRES. Inspect for flat tires, damage, cuts or foreign matter embedded in tread. Proper pressure is 50 pounds. Remove stones or debris from tracks and track suspensions.

(9) WHEEL AND FLANGE NUTS. Observe whether or not wheel axle and jack shaft flange nuts are present and tight. See that track suspension mechanism nuts are present and tight.

(10) FENDERS AND BUMPERS. Inspect fenders and bumpers for looseness or damage.

**TM 9-710**
**37**

## RECORD OF MODIFICATIONS AND NEW VEHICLE RUN-IN TESTS

(11) TOWING CONNECTIONS. Inspect pintle hook, trailer brake, and light socket attachments for serviceability.

(12) BODY AND TARPAULIN. Inspect body for damage and tarpaulin for security.

(13) WINCH. When vehicle is so equipped inspect winch for damage, secure mountings and oil leaks. Test winch clutch mechanism for proper operation. Test drag brake to see if it holds drum from spinning and as cable is unwound; inspect it for wear, damage, and adequate lubrication. Test winch automatic brake by placing vehicle at top of steep incline, and attaching cable to another vehicle at bottom. While drawing towed vehicle up hill, release engine clutch; if towed vehicle backs down hill, brake needs adjustment. Start lowering vehicle down hill with winch; throw out engine clutch; if towed vehicle does not stop or drifts more than one or two inches, brake needs adjustment. See paragraph 37 b (3). After test, rewind cable evenly and tightly on drum and while winding, clean cable thoroughly and apply a film of engine oil.

(14) ARMOR AND FRONT ROLLER. Inspect all armor, armor shields, door and windshield, for good condition and secure mounting. Also see that front roller, when vehicle is so equipped, is securely mounted and can be revolved.

(15) LUBRICATE. Perform a complete lubrication of the vehicle, covering all intervals, according to the instructions in the Lubrication Guide, paragraph 23, except gear cases, wheel bearings, and other units covered in preceding procedures. Check all gear case oil levels, and add, as necessary, to bring to correct level; change only if condition of oil indicates the necessity, or if gear oil is not of proper grade for existing atmospheric temperature. NOTE: *Perform items (16) to (19) during lubrication.*

(16) SPRINGS AND SUSPENSIONS. Inspect front shock absorbers, front and rear springs, and rear bogie suspension volute spring seats, to see if all are in good condition, correctly assembled, and secure. Check for excessive leaks.

(17) STEERING LINKAGE. See that all steering arms, rods, and connections are in good condition and secure; and that gear case is securely mounted and not leaking excessively.

(18) PROPELLER SHAFTS, AND UNIVERSAL JOINTS. Inspect all shafts, and universal joints to see if they are in good condition, correctly assembled, alined, secure, and not leaking excessively at seals or vents. Be sure vent passages are not clogged.

(19) AXLE AND TRANSFER VENTS. See that axle housing and transfer case vents are present, in good condition, and not clogged.

(20) CHOKE. Examine choke to be sure it opens and closes fully in response to operation of choke button.

(21) ENGINE WARM-UP. Start engine, noting if cranking motor action is satisfactory, and any tendency toward difficult starting. Set hand throttle to run engine at fast idle during warm-up. Reset choke button so engine will run smoothly, and to prevent overchoking and oil dilution.

# TM 9-710

## BASIC HALF-TRACK VEHICLES (WHITE, AUTOCAR, and DIAMOND T)

(22) INSTRUMENTS.

*(a) Oil Gage.* Immediately after engine starts, observe if oil pressure is satisfactory. Normal operating pressure, hot is 30 to 35 pounds, and should not fall below 10 pounds at idle.

*(b) Ammeter.* Ammeter should show a high charge for short period after starting, and zero, or slight positive reading, above 12 to 15 miles per hour with lights and accessories off.

*(c) Temperature Gage.* Temperature should rise slowly during warm-up. Normal operating temperature 160°F to 185°F. CAUTION: *Do not operate engine over 2,000 revolutions per minute until cooling system temperature has reached 160°F.*

*(d) Fuel Gage.* Fuel gage must show approximate amount of fuel in tanks according to position of toggle switch.

*(e) Voltmeter.* Voltmeter should show a reading of not less than 12 volts with engine stopped and no load on battery. An excessive drop (more than 2 or 3 volts under heavy load) will indicate battery or connection faults.

*(f) Tachometer.* Tachometer must indicate engine speed without excessive fluctuation or unusual noise.

*(g) Compass.* Inspect compass for true indication of magnetic north by comparing with known direction or with a compass of known accuracy. See paragraph 165 h for instructions for compensating.

(23) ENGINE CONTROLS. Observe if engine responds properly to controls and if controls operate without excessive looseness or binding.

(24) HORN AND WINDSHIELD WIPERS. See that these items are in good condition and secure. If tactical situation permits, test horn for proper operation and tone. See if wiper arms will operate through their full range, and that blade contacts glass evenly and firmly.

(25) GLASS AND REAR VIEW MIRRORS. Clean all body glass and mirrors and inspect for looseness and damage. Adjust rear view mirrors for correct vision.

(26) LAMPS (LIGHTS) AND REFLECTORS. Clean lenses and inspect all units for looseness and damage. If tactical situation permits, open and close all light switches to see if lamps respond properly.

(27) LEAKS, GENERAL. Look under vehicle, and within engine compartment, for indications of fuel, oil, coolant, and brake fluid leaks. Trace any found to source and correct or report them.

(28) TOOLS AND EQUIPMENT. Check tools and On Vehicle Stowage Lists, paragraphs 24 to 33, to be sure all items are present, and see that they are serviceable and properly mounted or stowed.

**b. Run-in Test.**

(1) DASH INSTRUMENTS AND GAGES. Observe all instruments frequently, noting whether or not they operate within the prescribed limits, temperatures, and pressures.

(2) SPEEDOMETER. When vehicle is in motion, speedometer must show vehicle speed, accumulating trip mileage, and total mileage. Indicator hand should move steadily without unusual noise.

(3) BRAKES, FOOT AND HAND. Test service brakes to see if they stop vehicle effectively without side pull, chatter, or squealing. Pedal

## RECORD OF MODIFICATIONS AND NEW VEHICLE RUN-IN TESTS

should have ⅓ reserve travel. Parking brake must hold vehicle on a reasonable incline with ½-ratchet travel in reserve.

(4) CLUTCH. Make sure that clutch operates smoothly without chatter, grabbing, or slipping, and pedal has 1½-inch free travel.

(5) TRANSMISSION AND TRANSFER. Gearshift mechanism should operate without unusual noise, and not slip out of mesh. Test front axle declutching, and power take-off mechanism (on vehicles so equipped) for proper operation.

(6) STEERING. Observe steering action for binding or looseness, and note any excessive pull to one side, wander, shimmy, or wheel tramp. See that column bracket and wheel are secure. Pay particular attention to Pitman arm to see that it is secure.

(7) ENGINE. Be on alert for any abnormal engine operating characteristics or unusual noise such as lack of pulling power or acceleration; backfiring, misfiring, stalling, overheating, or excessive exhaust smoke.

(8) UNUSUAL NOISE. Be on the alert throughout road test for any unusual noise from body and attachments, running gear, suspensions or wheels, that might indicate looseness, damage, wear, inadequate lubrication, or underinflated tires.

(9) HALT VEHICLE AT 10-MILE INTERVALS FOR SERVICES (10) TO (13) BELOW.

(10) BRAKE BOOSTER OPERATION. With engine idling and vehicle stopped, depress brake slowly and note whether or not the booster can be felt assisting the movement of the pedal. On hydrovac, locate air cleaner and listen for air movement while pedal is being operated.

(11) TEMPERATURES. Cautiously hand-feel each brake drum and wheel hub for abnormal temperatures. Examine transmission, transfer case, and differential housings for indications of overheating and excessive lubricant leaks at seals, gaskets, or vents. NOTE: *Transfer case temperatures are normally higher than other gear cases.*

(12) LEAKS. With engine running, and fuel, engine oil, and cooling systems under pressure, look within engine compartment and under vehicle for indications of leaks.

(13) GUN ELEVATING AND TRAVERSING MECHANISM. Inspect skate mount, machine gun carriage, pintles and controls to see that they operate without any binding, excessive lash, or erratic action, and are securely mounted.

(14) TRACK TENSION. Inspect track tension for sag of ¾ inch midway between top roller and idler with 150-pound pressure on top of track.

c. **Vehicle Publications and Reports.**

(1) PUBLICATIONS. See that vehicle (Technical Manuals, Lubrication Guide, Standard Form No. 26—Driver's Report Accident, Motor Transportation and W.D., A.G.O. Form 478—MWO and Major Unit Assembly Replacement Record), are in the vehicle, legible, and properly stowed. NOTE: *U. S. A. registration number and vehicle nomenclature must be filled in, on Form No. 478 for new vehicles.*

(2) REPORTS. Upon completion of the Run-in Test, correct, or report, any deficiencies noted. Report general condition of the vehicle to designated individual in authority.

# TM 9-710
38-39

**BASIC HALF-TRACK VEHICLES (WHITE, AUTOCAR, and DIAMOND T)**

Section X

## ORGANIZATION TOOLS AND EQUIPMENT

|  | Paragraph |
|---|---|
| Organization standard tool sets | 38 |
| Special tools | 39 |

### 38. ORGANIZATION STANDARD TOOL SETS.

a. The organization standard tool sets are listed in SNL N-19. The availability of these sets to an organization can be found in the applicable Table of Equipment.

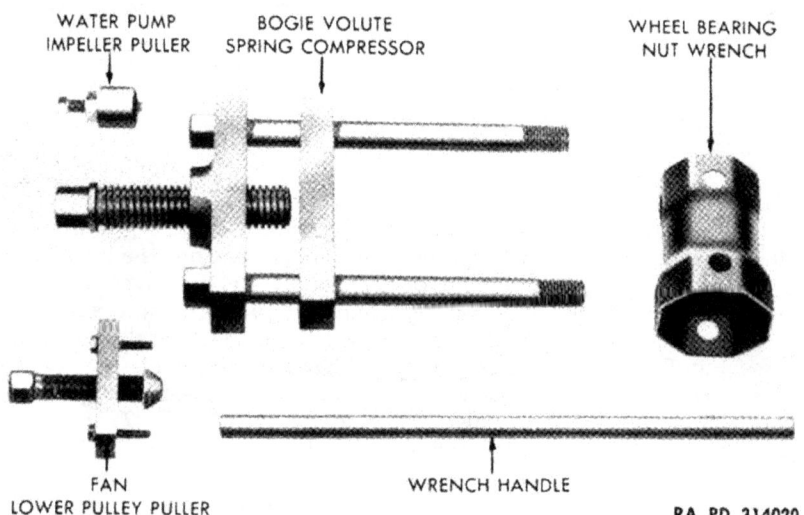

*Figure 49—Special Tools*

### 39. SPECIAL TOOLS.

a. Special tools are listed in the Organizational Spare Parts and Equipment Lists of the pertinent SNL's, as follows:

| Name | Mfrs. Tool No. | Federal Stock Number |
|---|---|---|
| Fan lower pulley puller | RSC 249 | 41P 2907-150 |
| Water pump impeller puller | RSB 364 | 41P 2958-60 |
| Wheel bearing nut socket wrench | ....... | 41W 2612-25 |
| Bogie volute spring compressor (2) | ....... | 41C 2559-50 |

TM 9-710
40

Section XI

# ORGANIZATIONAL PREVENTIVE MAINTENANCE SERVICES

|  | Paragraph |
|---|---|
| Second echelon preventive maintenance services | 40 |

**40. SECOND ECHELON PREVENTIVE MAINTENANCE SERVICES.**

a. Regular scheduled maintenance inspections and services are a preventive maintenance function of the using arms and are the responsibility of commanders of operating organizations.

(1) FREQUENCY. The frequencies of the preventive maintenance services outlined herein are considered a minimum requirement for normal operation of vehicles. Under unusual operating conditions such as extreme temperatures, dusty or sandy terrain, it may be necessary to perform certain maintenance services more frequently.

(2) FIRST ECHELON PARTICIPATION. The drivers should accompany their vehicles and assist the mechanics while periodic second echelon preventive maintenance services are performed. Ordinarily the driver should present the vehicle for a scheduled preventive maintenance service in a reasonably clean condition; that is, it should be dry and not caked with mud or grease to such an extent that inspection and servicing will be seriously hampered. However, the vehicle should not be washed or wiped thoroughly clean, since certain types of defects, such as cracks, leaks, and loose or shifted parts or assemblies, are more evident if the surfaces are slightly soiled or dusty.

(3) If instructions other than those contained in the general procedures in step (4) below, or the specific procedures in step (5) which follows, are required for the correct performance of a Preventive Maintenance Service, or for correction of a deficiency, other sections of the vehicle Operator's Manual pertaining to the item involved, or a designated individual in authority, should be consulted.

(4) GENERAL PROCEDURES. These general procedures are basic instructions which are to be followed when performing the services on the items listed in the specific procedures. NOTE: *The second echelon personnel must be thoroughly trained in these procedures so that they will apply them automatically.*

(a) When new, or overhauled, subassemblies are installed to correct deficiencies, care should be taken to see that they are clean, correctly installed, properly lubricated, and adjusted.

(b) When installing new lubricant retainer seals, a coating of the lubricant should be wiped over the sealing surface of the lip of the seal. When the new seal is a leather seal, it should be soaked in SAE No. 10 engine oil (warm if practicable) for at least 30 minutes. Then, the leather lip should be worked carefully by hand before installing the seal. The lip must not be scratched or marred.

(c) The general inspection of each item applies also to any supporting member or connection, and usually includes a check to see

## BASIC HALF-TRACK VEHICLES (WHITE, AUTOCAR, and DIAMOND T)

whether or not the item is in good condition, correctly assembled, secure, or excessively worn. The mechanics must be thoroughly trained in the following explanations of these terms.

1. The inspection for "good condition" is usually an external visual inspection to determine whether or not the unit is damaged beyond safe or serviceable limits and is explained further by the following: not bent or twisted, not chafed or burned, not broken or cracked, not bare or frayed, not dented or collapsed, not torn or cut.

2. The inspection of a unit to see that it is "correctly assembled" is usually an external visual inspection to see whether or not it is in its normal assembled position in the vehicle.

3. The inspection of a unit to determine if it is "secure" is usually an external visual examination, a hand-feel, or a pry-bar check for looseness. Such an inspection should include any brackets, lock washers, lock nuts, locking wires, or cotter pins used in assembly.

4. "Excessively worn" will be understood to mean worn close-to or beyond serviceable limits, and likely to result in a failure if not replaced before the next scheduled inspection.

*(d) Special Services.* These are indicated by repeating the item numbers in the columns which show the interval at which the services are to be performed, and show that the parts or assemblies are to receive certain mandatory services. For example, an item number in one or both columns opposite a "TIGHTEN" procedure, means that the actual tightening of the object must be performed. The special services include:

1. *Adjust.* Make all necessary adjustments in accordance with the pertinent section of the vehicle Operator's Manual, special bulletins, or other current directives.

2. *Clean.* Clean units of the vehicle with dry-cleaning solvent to remove excess lubricant, dirt, and other foreign material. After the parts are cleaned, rinse them in clean fluid and dry them thoroughly. Take care to keep the parts clean until reassembled, and be certain to keep cleaning fluid away from rubber or other material which it will damage. Clean the protective grease coating from new parts since this material is not a good lubricant.

3. *Special Lubrication.* This applies either to lubrication operations that do not appear on the vehicle lubrication chart and to items that do appear on such charts, but should be performed in connection with the maintenance operations if parts have to be disassembled for inspection or service.

4. *Serve.* This usually consists of performing special operations, such as replenishing battery water, draining and refilling units with oil, and changing the oil filter cartridge.

5. *Tighten.* All tightening operations should be performed with sufficient wrench torque (force on the wrench handle) to tighten the unit according to good mechanical practice. Use torque-indicating wrench where specified. Do not overtighten, as this may strip threads or cause distortion. Tightening will always be understood to include the correct installation of lock washers, lock nuts, and cotter pins provided to secure the tightening.

**TM 9-710**
**40**

## ORGANIZATIONAL PREVENTIVE MAINTENANCE SERVICES

(e) When conditions make it difficult to perform the complete Preventive Maintenance Procedures at one time, they can sometimes be handled in sections, planning to complete all operations within the week, if possible. All available time at halts, and in bivouac areas must be utilized to assure that maintenance operations are completed. When limited by the tactical situation, items with Special Services in the columns, should be given first consideration.

(f) The numbers of the preventive maintenance procedures that follow are identical with those outlined on W.D. AGO Form No. 461, which is the "Preventive Maintenance Service Work Sheet" for wheeled and half-track vehicles. Certain items on the work sheet that do not apply to this vehicle are not included in the procedures in this manual. In general, the numerical sequence of items on the work sheet is followed in the manual procedures, but in some instances, there is deviation for conservation of the mechanic's time and effort.

(5) SPECIFIC PROCEDURES. The procedures for performing each item in the 1,000-mile (monthly) and 6,000-mile (six-month) maintenance procedures are described in the following chart. Each page of the chart has two columns at its left side corresponding to the 6,000-mile and 1,000-mile maintenance respectively. Very often it will be found that a particular procedure does not apply to both scheduled maintenances. In order to determine which procedure to follow, look down the column corresponding to the maintenance due, and wherever an item number appears perform the operations indicated opposite the number.

### ROAD TEST

| MAINTENANCE | |  |
|---|---|---|
| 6000 Mile | 1000 Mile | |
|  |  | NOTE: *When tactical situations do not permit a full road test, perform those items which require little or no movement of the vehicle.* When a road test is possible, it should be 4, preferably 5, and not over 10 miles. |
| 1 | 1 | Before-operation Service. Perform the Before-operation Service as described in paragraph 18. |
| 3 | 3 | Instruments and Gages.<br>FUEL GAGE. Fuel gage must show approximate amount of fuel in tanks according to position of toggle switch.<br>OIL PRESSURE GAGE. If pressure fails to register within 30 seconds, stop engine, and correct or report. At normal vehicle operating speed, pressure should be about 20 to 35 pounds. Pressure should not fall below 4 pounds at idle.<br>ENGINE TEMPERATURE INDICATOR. Temperature should rise slowly during warm-up. Normal operating temperature 155°F to 185°F. CAUTION: *Do not operate engine over 2,000 revolutions per minute until cooling system temperature has reached 160°F.*<br>AMMETER. Ammeter should show a high charge for short period after starting, and zero or slight positive (+) reading above 12 to 15 miles per hour with lights |

# TM 9-710

## BASIC HALF-TRACK VEHICLES (WHITE, AUTOCAR, and DIAMOND T)

| MAINTENANCE | |
|---|---|
| 6000 Mile | 1000 Mile |
| | |
| | |
| | |
| | |
| 4 | 4 |
| | |
| 5 | 5 |
| | |
| | |
| | |
| | |
| | |
| | |
| | |
| 6 | 6 |
| | |
| | |
| | |
| 7 | 7 |
| | |
| | |
| | |
| 8 | 8 |
| | |
| 9 | 9 |

and accessories "OFF." A zero reading with lights and accessories "ON" is normal.

TACHOMETER. Tachometer must indicate engine speed without excessive fluctuation or unusual noise.

SPEEDOMETER. Speedometer must show vehicle speed, accumulating trip mileage, and total mileage. Indicator hand should move steadily without unusual fluctuation.

COMPASS. Inspect compass for true indication of magnetic north by comparing with known direction or with compass of known accuracy (par. 165).

Horns, and Windshield Wipers. When tactical situation permits, test horns. Operate windshield wipers. Inspect for complete contact throughout full arc of operation.

Brakes (Foot, Hand, and Trailer). Foot brakes must stop vehicle safely at fast rate, within reasonable distance. Brake pedal must have moderate, but not "hard" or "spongy" feel. Brakes must not pull vehicle to one side. Listen for unusual noise or chatter. Pedal should have one-third reserve travel. Hand brake, when set, must hold vehicle effectively on grade. One-quarter the ratchet travel should be reserve. Observe trailer brake operation when control switch is at light, medium, and heavy load settings, to determine whether or not operation is adequate, whether or not there is any unusual noise, side sway, or indication of unequalized brake action.

Clutch. Test for grab, drag, chatter, or noise that might indicate faulty adjustment, defective clutch parts, or dry release bearing. Pedal should have free travel of 1 to 1½ inch before meeting resistance. While running at low speed in high gear, depress accelerator fully, at same time applying brakes slightly, and observe if clutch appears to slip.

Transmission, Transfer, and Power Take-off. With vehicle in motion, shift through entire gear range. See that shifter mechanism operates freely without clashing, or jumping out of gear; that locking mechanism in transfer operates freely. Observe for unusual vibrations that might indicate loose mountings. Listen for unusual noises.

Steering. With the vehicle in motion, move steering wheel fully in both directions, observing for any looseness or binding. Test for wander, shimmy, or side pull, while vehicle is operated at normal speeds.

Engine. During road test, note any tendency of the engine to stall while decelerating to shift gears. Observe if engine has normal acceleration and pulling power in each speed when shifting through gear range from first to high. Make similar observation in high

# TM 9-710
## 40
**ORGANIZATIONAL PREVENTIVE MAINTENANCE SERVICES**

| MAINTENANCE | |
|---|---|
| 6000 Mile | 1000 Mile |
| 10 | 10 |
| 11 | 11 |
| 13 | 13 |
| 14 | 14 |
| 15 | 15 |
| 16 | 16 |
| 17 | 17 |

gear from low speed with wide-open throttle. During this operation, note any unusual engine noises, such as excessive "ping," which may indicate early timing, or too low octane fuel. Listen for other noises that might indicate damaged, excessively worn, or inadequately lubricated engine parts, accessories, or loose drive belts.

**Engine Noises.** Be alert for any unusual noise that may indicate looseness, damage, or excessive wear in body, wheels, tracks, suspension assembly, attachments and equipment.

**Brake Booster Operation, Hydrovac.** Test brakes to learn whether or not vacuum power unit assists in application. A quick test is to stop vehicle, with engine running, and listen for air movement in the Hydrovac air cleaner, while the brake pedal is being operated.

**Temperatures.** After completing road test run, feel brake drums and wheel hubs, cautiously, for abnormal temperatures. Cautiously feel front axle, jackshaft, transmission, and transfer for overheating. If excessive heat is found, cause should be investigated. Transfer normally operates at higher temperatures than other units.

**Leaks.** Look within engine compartment and under vehicle for engine oil, water, fuel, and brake fluid leaks. Determine source and correct.

**Track Tension.** Inspect track tension. There should be ¾- to 1-inch sag midway between top roller and idler with 150-pound pressure on top of track (par. 117). Vehicle should have normal load.

**Gear Oil Level and Leaks.** Examine front axle, jackshaft, transmission, transfer, and power take-off for lubricant level and leaks. NOTE: *The safe level range is from the lower edge of the filler hole, when hot, to one-half inch below, when cold.* When a change of oil in these units is due, drain and refill with specified lubricant.

## MAINTENANCE OPERATIONS
### Raise Vehicle and Block Safely.

**Unusual Noises.** With engine running, accelerate and decelerate engine momentarily, and listen for unusual noises that might indicate damaged, loose, or excessively worn engine parts, drive belts, or accessories. Locate and correct, or report, any unusual engine noises heard during road test. With transmission in third gear, operate transmission, transfer, propeller shafts, U-joints, front axle and jackshaft at constant moderate speed by use of hand throttle. Test for any unusual noise that might indicate damaged, loose, or

## TM 9-710

### BASIC HALF-TRACK VEHICLES (WHITE, AUTOCAR, and DIAMOND T)

| MAINTENANCE | | |
|---|---|---|
| 6000 Mile | 1000 Mile | |
| | | excessively worn parts. Observe for vibrations which may indicate looseness or lack of balance. Locate, correct, or report any faults indicated by noise during road test. |
| 18 | 18 | Cylinder Head and Gasket. Examine for cracks or indications of oil, water, or compression leaks around cap screws and gaskets. CAUTION: *Cylinder heads should not ordinarily be tightened unless there is definite indication of looseness or leaks.* |
| | 20 | Spark Plugs. Wipe off and examine insulators without removing plugs. Wipe shields and reinstall. |
| 20 | | CLEAN AND ADJUST. Remove plugs, clean in an abrasive cleaner, inspect for cracked insulators and burned electrodes. Adjust gap to 0.025 inch. NOTE: *Test compression before installing plugs.* |
| 21 | | Compression Test. Normal compression is 120 pounds at normal cranking speed; should not vary more than 10 pounds between cylinders. Pressure on any cylinder should not drop below 90 pounds. |
| 22 | 22 | Battery. Examine case for leaks. Clean and dry cables and terminals. Grease terminals and posts lightly, and tighten terminals. Tighten hold-down and clamping bolts, if loose. CAUTION: *Tighten bolts carefully to avoid breaking battery case.* Test specific gravity reading. Record readings on W.D., A.G.O. Form No. 461. Reading of less than 1.225 indicates need for recharge. Bring electrolyte level to ½ inch above plates. NOTE: *Fill to top of filler well with cap mounted on vent hole.* |
| 22 | | HIGH RATE DISCHARGE TEST. Make a high rate discharge test of battery. Report if difference in reading between cells is more than 30 percent. |
| 23 | 23 | Crankcase. Inspect crankcase, valve covers, timing gear cover, and clutch housing for oil leaks, and check oil level. NOTE: *When an oil change is due, drain crankcase and refill with specified oil.* Do not start engine again until item No. 24 is completed. |
| 24 | 24 | Oil Filter. Inspect oil filter for leakage or loose mountings. |
| 24 | | RENEW FILTER ELEMENT. Remove filter element. Clean oil filter case and install new filter cartridge. Be sure to check for oil leaks after starting engine. CAUTION: *In refilling crankcase, when installing new oil filter, allow sufficient additional oil to wet new filter cartridge completely.* |
| 25 | 25 | Radiator. Observe cooling system, including radiator, hose, and surge tank, for good condition, secure mounting, or leakage. Examine coolant for contamination. If |

## ORGANIZATIONAL PREVENTIVE MAINTENANCE SERVICES

| MAINTENANCE | |
|---|---|
| 6000 Mile | 1000 Mile |
| 25 | |
| 26 | 26 |
| 27 | 27 |
| 27 | |
| 29 | 29 |
| 31 | 31 |
| 31 | |
| 32 | 32 |

antifreeze is used, make hydrometer test for temperature encountered. Clean dirt, insects, and trash from exterior of core.

TIGHTEN. Tighten radiator and surge tank mountings and hose.

Water Pump, Fan, and Shroud. Observe water pump for leaks. Test shaft for end play and loose bearings. Inspect fan and shroud for good condition and secure mounting.

Generator, Cranking Motor, and Switch. Examine generator and cranking motor for good condition and secure mounting, and wiring connections for secure attachment.

COMMUTATORS. Remove inspection covers of generators and cranking motor, see that commutators and brushes are in good condition and not excessively worn; that brushes are free in holders, and brush connecting wires are secure and not chafing. Dirty commutators must be cleaned with flint paper No. 2/0. Blow out dust with compressed air. Tighten cranking motor mounting nuts securely.

Drive Belts and Pulleys. Check fan and generator drive belts for good condition, and drive pulleys and hubs for good condition and security. Adjust drive belts to ¾-inch deflection.

Distributor. Remove shielding from distributor, clean and examine for good condition, correct assembly, secure mounting, and serviceability. Inspect for cracks in cap and rotor arm, corrosion of terminals and connections, and burning of the outer end of conductor strap. Breaker points must be in good condition, alined, and adjusted to 0.017 to 0.018-inch gap. Replace points if burned, pitted, or excessively worn. Inspect distributor shaft for looseness by trying to move with fingers. Test centrifugal advance by finger rotation for normal range of movement, and for return, when released, without binding or sticking. CAUTION: *Make sure all shielding joints are clean and tight as unit is reassembled.*

SERVE. If breaker plate assembly is excessively worn or dirty, remove distributor, clean in dry-cleaning solvent, and dry with compressed air. Inspect for good condition; lubricate as specified in Lubrication Guide; and reinstall in position for timing. Adjust breaker point gap to 0.017 to 0.018 inch.

Coil and Wiring. Inspect coil for good condition, cleanliness, and secure mounting. Inspect high tension wiring for secure fastening at all support mountings and terminals. See that insulation and connections are

# TM 9-710

## BASIC HALF-TRACK VEHICLES (WHITE, AUTOCAR, and DIAMOND T)

| MAINTENANCE | | |
|---|---|---|
| 6000 Mile | 1000 Mile | |
| 33 | 33 | clean. Inspect all low voltage wiring in engine compartment for good condition, cleanliness, and secure attachment.<br>**Manifolds.** Inspect intake and exhaust manifolds for good condition and secure attachment. Look for leaks in manifold gaskets. |
| 30 | 30 | **Tachometer Drive and Adapter.** Examine tachometer drive and adapter to see that they are in good condition, correctly assembled, and securely mounted. Inspect flexible drive shaft for indications of oil leaks. |
| 34 | 34 | **Air Cleaner.** Inspect carburetor air cleaner for good condition, secure mounting, and oil leaks. Remove air cleaner and wash all parts in dry-cleaning solvent. Replace, and refill to proper level with engine oil, crankcase grade. |
| 35 | 35 | **Breather Caps.** Inspect oil filler breather cap and ventilator to see that they are in good condition, correctly assembled, and that ventilator tube is open. Clean breather cap in dry-cleaning solvent and reoil. |
| 36 | 36 | **Carburetor (Choke, Throttle, and Linkage).** Inspect choke, throttle, and linkage to see that they are in good condition, correctly assembled, and securely attached. |
| 37 | 37 | **Fuel Filter and Lines.** Inspect fuel filter at carburetor, sediment bowl on fuel pump, fuel lines and connections to see that they are in good condition and securely mounted, and do not leak. Remove fuel filter cup; clean cup and element, being careful not to damage element. Clean sediment bowl and screen from fuel pump. Use new gaskets if required. After assembling, recheck for leaks. |
| 38 | 38 | **Fuel Pump.** Inspect fuel and vacuum pump for good condition, security, and leaks. Attach test gage, and with engine idling, note whether or not pressure and vacuum are satisfactory. Normal pressure is $2\frac{1}{2}$ to 4 pounds. Normal vacuum is 8 to 10 inches. |
| 39 | 39 | **Cranking Motor.** Start engine, observing whether or not drive engages and disengages without excessive noise, and whether or not motor has adequate cranking speed. |
| 40 | 40 | **Leaks.** Look in engine compartment and under vehicle for engine oil, fuel, brake fluid, and water leaks. |
| 41 | 41 | **Ignition Timing.** With engine running, check ignition timing with neon timing light. Observe whether or not centrifugal control advances spark, as engine is accelerated slowly. Adjust timing as required. |
| 42 | 42 | **Engine Idle and Vacuum Test.** Connect vacuum gage to intake manifold, adjust engine to normal idle speed by means of throttle stop screw, then adjust idle |

# TM 9-710
## 40

## ORGANIZATIONAL PREVENTIVE MAINTENANCE SERVICES

| MAINTENANCE | |
|---|---|
| 6000 Mile | 1000 Mile |
| 43 | 43 |
| 47 | 47 |
| 106 | 106 |
| 106 | |
| 107 | 107 |
| 107 | |
| 108 | |
| 109 | |

mixture until vacuum gage indicates maximum reading. If latter adjustment changes idle speed appreciably, reset idle speed and mixture until both are satisfactory.

Regulator Unit. Observe regulator unit for good condition, secure connections, and mounting. Connect low voltage circuit tester, and test voltage regulator, current regulator, and cut-out for proper generator output control. Follow instructions which accompany test instrument.

### CHASSIS, BODY, AND ATTACHMENTS

Tires and Rims. Inspect tires for good condition. Observe for excessive wear, cuts, tears, and breaks. Remove any foreign objects from treads. See that all valve caps are present and secure. If directional tread tires are used, they should be mounted with closed end of chevron meeting ground first.

Tracks, Guides, and Tread Wear. Examine tracks for good condition and proper position on sprockets and rollers. See that guides are all present, not excessively worn, and securely attached. Inspect tracks for excessive wear, cuts, tears, breaks between tread, lugs, stones embedded in tracks. Remove stones or debris lodged between tracks and rollers, or which may be lodged in the suspension system.

SERVE. Remove tracks, using "C" clamps to block bogie suspension system properly. Tighten all track guide nuts with torque indicating wrench (100 foot-pounds).

Sprockets, Flanges, Bearings, and Seals. Examine sprockets and flanges for good condition, secure attachment, and any indications of oil leaks from seals.

CLEAN. Disassemble and clean sprocket hubs, bearings, and oil seals. Examine rollers, races, and cages, to see that they are in good condition. It is not necessary to remove them from hubs. CAUTION: *Be sure to perform items 108 and 109 before and during reassembly.* Lubricate and adjust bearings, using new oil seals. Tighten all hub flange, sprocket flange, and jackshaft flange nuts securely.

Brake Drums, Supports, and Cylinders. Clean all dirt and grease from brake drums, shoes, and backing plate parts thoroughly, keeping dry-cleaning solvent away from brake linings and wheel cylinder boots. Examine drums and brake backing plates for good condition and secure mounting. Inspect drums for excessive wear or scoring. Inspect brake cylinders for good condition and secure mounting. Look for leaks.

Brake Shoes (Linings, Guides, and Anchors). Inspect linings for wear, to determine whether or not

# TM 9-710
40

## BASIC HALF-TRACK VEHICLES (WHITE, AUTOCAR, and DIAMOND T)

| MAINTENANCE | |
|---|---|
| 6000 Mile | 1000 Mile |
| | | rivets may score drums within the next 1,000 miles of operation. Install new linings if inspection determines necessity. |
| 109 | 109 | ADJUST. Adjust brakes by minor adjustment method. If new linings have been installed, use major adjustment method. Clearances are: Heel 0.005 inch, toe 0.010 inch. |
| 110 | 110 | Idlers (Flanges and Bearings). Examine idler wheels and flanges for good condition, secure mounting, and any indication of oil leaks from seals. |
| 110 | | CLEAN. Disassemble and clean idler hubs, bearings, and oil seals. Examine bearings and races for good condition. Pack idler bearings, and after bearings are installed and adjusted, and cap is reinstalled, apply additional lubricant through grease fitting until full. Tighten all hub and flange nuts securely. |
| 111 | 111 | Idler (Posts, Shackles, Shafts, Adjusting Rods, and Brackets). Examine idler posts, shackles, shafts, adjusting rods, and brackets for good condition correct assembly, and secure mounting. Make sure that idler spring adjusting screws and idler stop screws are waterproofed and taped. |
| 112 | 112 | Frame Brackets and Cross Tube. Examine for good condition and secure mounting. |
| 112 | | TIGHTEN. Tighten frame bracket and cross tube mounting bolts securely. |
| 113 | 113 | Bogie (Crab Assemblies, Springs, Slides, Plates, Arms, and Bolts). Examine bogie crab assemblies, springs, slides, plates, arms, and bolts for good condition and secure mounting. See that the slides are not excessively worn. Examine springs for good condition, proper seating in the spring blocks, and that they have not taken a permanent set. (Two or more coils resting on seat indicates permanent set, and need for spring replacement). |
| 114 | 114 | Bogie Rollers (Lower and Upper) (Tires, Bearings, Seals, and Bolts). Examine upper rollers and brackets, and lower rollers and tires for good condition, proper alinement with track, and secure mounting. Observe whether or not tires are secure on lower rollers and not excessively worn, paying particular attention to cuts or gouged spots in tires. See that lubricant is not leaking excessively from seals. |
| 114 | | CLEAN. Remove and clean bogie lower rollers, bearings, and seals. Examine bolts, links, and bearings for good condition. As bearings are reinstalled, pack with specified lubricant. After reassembling, apply additional grease through grease fitting until entire hub is filled. |
| 115 | 115 | Track Tension (Vehicle on Ground). Adjust track tension for ¾-inch sag midway between track support |

## ORGANIZATIONAL PREVENTIVE MAINTENANCE SERVICES

| MAINTENANCE | |
|---|---|
| 6000 Mile | 1000 Mile |
| 115 | |
| 55 | 55 |
| 55 | |
| 56 | 56 |
| 57 | 57 |
| 57 | |
| 58 | 58 |
| 58 | |
| 60 | |

roller and idler, with track loaded to equivalent of 150 pounds.

TRACK ADJUSTMENT. Track adjustment should be made when performing 6,000-mile maintenance service after vehicle has been lowered to ground.

Steering Knuckles (Joints, Bearings, Seals, and Boots). Examine steering knuckle housings and steering arm for good condition. Observe whether or not outside seals and dust boots are in good condition and secure. Obtain sample of lubricant from each knuckle; inspect for contamination.

CLEAN. Remove constant velocity U-joint assembly without disassembling U-joint. Clean steering knuckles and axle U-joint assembly parts. Observe parts for good condition. As knuckle pivot bearings and drive joints are installed, lubricate by packing lubricant into pivot bearings and constant velocity U-joint until it fills all space between balls, cages, and races. Be sure to install shims and spacers in the original position from which they were removed at disassembly to insure correct pivot bearing and axle end play adjustment, and also any required new lubricant retainer seals and gaskets.

Front Springs. Examine front springs, spring clips, spring leaves, U-bolts, hangers, and shackles for good condition, correct assembly, and secure mounting. Observe whether or not springs have excessive sag. Tighten U-bolts securely.

Steering (Tie Rod, Drag Link, Steering Arm, Pitman Arm, Seals, Gear, Column, and Wheel). Examine to see that steering wheel, column, gear, and linkage are in good condition, securely and correctly assembled and mounted. Inspect steering gear case lubricant for proper level. See that case is not leaking. Test steering gear for satisfactory adjustment.

TIGHTEN. Tighten Pitman arm shaft nut and steering gear case assembly and mounting nuts and cap screws securely. CAUTION: *Loosen steering column bracket when tightening steering gear case mounting nuts so as not to distort column.*

Front Shock Absorbers and Links. Examine shock absorber bodies and links for good condition and secure mounting. Look for fluid leaks.

SERVE. Fill shock absorber bodies with specified fluid. Disconnect link and check for normal action. Work arm several times and add fluid. Repeat operation until air is expelled and reservoir is full.

Front Wheels. Inspect wheels for good condition. Revolve and observe if they have excessive run-out. Listen

# TM 9-710
40

**BASIC HALF-TRACK VEHICLES (WHITE, AUTOCAR, and DIAMOND T)**

| MAINTENANCE | |
|---|---|
| 6000 Mile | 1000 Mile |
| | |
| | |
| | |
| | |
| | |
| | |
| | |
| | |
| | |
| 60 | |
| | |
| 61 | 61 |
| | |
| | |
| | |
| | |
| 62 | 62 |
| | |
| | |
| | |
| | |
| | |
| 62 | |
| | |
| 63 | 63 |
| | |
| | |
| | |
| 64 | 64 |
| | |
| | |
| | |
| | |
| | |
| 65 | 65 |

for indications of dry or damaged wheel bearings. Without removing wheels, examine for evidence of looseness in wheel bearing or adjustment. Inspect drive flanges and drums for lubricant or brake fluid leaks. Examine drive flanges and nuts to see that they are in good condition and secure. NOTE: *If vehicle has been operated recently in deep water, remove one wheel to see whether or not lubricant appears contaminated.* Clean and lubricate bearings of removed wheel before reinstalling. At such time also inspect brake linings for wear or damage from grease. If inspection indicates contamination of bearing lubricant, serve other wheel in same manner. Clean and inspect brake linings, shoes, brake cylinders and backing plates for good condition and secure mounting. Inspect brake lining for excessive wear. Look for grease and brake fluid leaks.

SERVE. Remove front wheels. Clean and inspect wheel bearings, lubricate, and reassemble. Adjust bearings.

Front Axle. If front axle appears to be out of line, measure distance from front spring eyebolt to center of axle spring pad on each side. This distance should be about the same on each side. Inspect axle housing for good condition. Examine housing and pinion shaft seal for leaks. Test pinion shaft for excessive end play. Clean axle housing vent thoroughly.

Front Propeller Shaft (Joints and Alinement, Seals and Flanges). Inspect front propeller shaft for good condition, correct and secure assembly and mounting. Inspect U-joints for proper alinement and excessive wear. Slip joints should be free, not excessively worn, and well lubricated; seals of U-joints and slip joints should not leak excessively.

TIGHTEN. Tighten U-joint assembly and companion flange bolts securely.

Engine Mountings. Inspect engine mountings for good condition and secure bolting. If mounting bolts are loose, tighten properly. Remove oil or grease from rubber mountings. Apply brake fluid if rubber is hard or cracked.

Hand Brake (Ratchet and Pawl, Linkage, Disk, and Lining). Examine hand brake ratchet and pawl and linkage for good condition and secure mounting. See that brake disk is not scored or oily, and that brake lining is not oil-soaked or worn thin. Adjust clearance between brake disk and lining to $\frac{1}{32}$ inch at brake shoe center.

Clutch Pedal (Free Travel, Linkage, and Return Spring.) Examine to see that pedal free travel is 1 to

112

## ORGANIZATIONAL PREVENTIVE MAINTENANCE SERVICES

| MAINTENANCE ||
|---|---|
| 6000 Mile | 1000 Mile |

| 6000 Mile | 1000 Mile | |
|---|---|---|
| | | 1½ inch, that the pedal is securely mounted, clutch operating linkage in good condition, secure, and not excessively worn. See that return spring is intact and has sufficient tension. |
| 65 | | ADJUST. Adjust clutch pedal free travel to 1 to 1½ inch. |
| 66 | 66 | Brake Pedal. Brake pedal should have ⅓-reserve travel. Inspect brake linkage for good condition and secure mounting. See that return spring is intact and has sufficient tension. |
| 67 | 67 | Brake Master Cylinder (Vent, Fluid Level, Leaks, and Switch). Examine brake master cylinder for good condition and secure mounting; see that boot is properly installed, and observe for indication of fluid leaks. Fill master cylinder reservoir to correct level, allow approximately one-quarter inch for expansion. Clean vent. |
| 68 | 68 | Brake Booster, Hydrovac (Linkage, Air Cleaner Hose, and Slave Cylinder). Inspect hydrovac units and connections for good condition, correct assembly, and secure mounting. See that operating and control linkage does not bind. Observe whether or not brake fluid is leaking from slave cylinder. Clean and oil air cleaner element. |
| 71 | 71 | Transmission (Mounting, Seals, Power Take-off, and Linkage). Inspect transmission case for good condition, seals and gaskets for leaks, and control linkage for good condition, proper connections, and secure mounting. Clean vent. |
| 71 | | TIGHTEN. Tighten all transmission and power take-off mounting and external assembly bolts and cap screws securely. |
| 72 | 72 | Transfer (Mountings, Linkage, and Seals.) Inspect transfer case for good condition, security of mounting, and observe seals for leaks. Tighten mountings and external assembly nuts and cap screws securely. |
| 73 | 73 | Rear Propeller Shaft (Joints and Alinement, Seals and Flanges). Inspect for good condition, correct assembly, and secure mounting. Inspect U-joints for good condition and proper alinement. Slip joints should be free, not excessively worn, and well lubricated. Seals of U-joints and slip joints should not leak excessively. |
| 73 | | TIGHTEN. Tighten U-joint assembly and companion flange bolts securely. |
| 75 | 75 | Jackshaft (Pinion End Play, Seals and Vents). Inspect to see that jackshaft housing is in good con- |

## BASIC HALF-TRACK VEHICLES (WHITE, AUTOCAR, and DIAMOND T)

| MAINTENANCE | |
|---|---|
| 6000 Mile | 1000 Mile |
| 79 | 79 |

dition and not leaking. Examine pinion shaft for excessive end play, and seals for leaks. Clean jackshaft housing vent thoroughly. Tighten U-bolts securely.

**Body Mountings.** Inspect body mountings for security; tighten loose bolts.

| 80 | 80 |
|---|---|

**Frame (Rails and Cross Members).** Inspect frame brackets, side rails, and cross members to see that they are in good condition, secure, and correctly alined.

| 81 | 81 |
|---|---|

**Wiring, Conduits, and Grommets.** Examine these items to see that they are in good condition, properly supported, and securely connected.

| 82 | 82 |
|---|---|

**Fuel Tanks, Fittings, and Lines.** Examine for good condition and secure mounting. Inspect caps for defective gaskets or plugged vents. See that lines and fittings are in good condition, securely supported, and not leaking.

| 82 | |
|---|---|

DRAIN. Drain accumulated water and sediment from bottom of tank by removing fuel tank drain plugs. Drain briefly until fuel runs clear.

| 83 | 83 |
|---|---|

**Brake Lines (Fittings and Hose).** Examine brake lines, fittings, and hose beneath vehicle and on jackshaft housing, to see that they are in good condition and secure. Observe for fluid leakage.

| 84 | 84 |
|---|---|

**Exhaust Pipes and Muffler.** Examine exhaust pipes and muffler for secure mounting and good condition. Observe for evidence of leaks. Examine tail pipe to see that it is securely clamped at both inner and outer ends.

| 85 | 85 |
|---|---|

**Vehicle Lubrication.** If due, lubricate in accordance with Lubrication Guide, Section VII, and current lubrication directives, using only clean lubricant and omitting items that have had special lubrication during this service. Replace damaged or missing fittings, vents, flexible lines, or plugs.

### LOWER VEHICLE TO GROUND

| 86 | 86 |
|---|---|

**Toe-in and Turning Stops.** With front wheels on the ground in straight-ahead position, and using a proper toe-in gage, see that front wheel toe-in is within specified limits ($\frac{1}{8}$ inch plus or minus $\frac{1}{16}$ inch). Check wheel turning stops for presence and secure mounting. Turn wheels both directions to see that they engage the stops, and to see that tires clear all parts of vehicle in extreme positions. If there is any indication that tires scuff against vehicle, or abnormal front drive U-joint wear because of excessive turning angle, report for a check of turning angle by higher echelon.

| 87 | 87 |
|---|---|

**Winch (Clutch, Brake, Drive, Shearpin, Cable, and Guide).** Inspect for good condition, correct assembly, and secure mounting. See that clutch moves

## ORGANIZATIONAL PREVENTIVE MAINTENANCE SERVICES

| MAINTENANCE ||
|---|---|
| 6000 Mile | 1000 Mile |
| 87 | |
| 89 | 89 |
| 91 | 91 |
| 93 | 93 |
| 94 | 94 |
| 95 | 95 |
| 96 | 96 |
| 97 | 97 |
| 98 | 98 |
| 101 | 101 |

freely and latches securely, that the drag-brake lining is in good condition, secure, and correctly adjusted. Inspect automatic brake to see that lining is securely mounted, and not excessively worn. Examine propeller shaft for proper assembly, loose or worn U-joints. See that proper shearpin is installed and in good condition. Oil level in worm gear case should be at drain plug level. Lubricate winch clutch, shaft, and operating arm with engine oil. Move the clutch back and forth several times during application of lubricant to be sure it is free. Unwind cable and inspect it for broken or frayed strands and for flat or rusty spots.

CLEAN AND SERVE. Clean entire length of cable with cloth saturated with fuel oil or dry-cleaning solvent. Wipe off excess fluid and rewind cable on drum, coating it as rewound, with engine oil. Used engine oil is satisfactory. Drain worm gear case and refill to correct level.

Tractor-to-trailer Wiring and Connections. Examine to see that tractor-to-trailer wiring and connections are in good condition and securely fastened, so they will not chafe or interfere with working parts. Examine connection fittings for good condition and secure attachment.

Lights (Head, Tail, Stop, and Blackout). Test switches and lamps to see that they operate properly. Be sure to include stop light and blackout light. Inspect all lights for good condition, secure attachment, clean lenses, and inspect for broken lenses.

Front Bumper or Roller, Tow Hooks, and Brush Guards. Inspect to see that bumper or roller, tow hooks, and brush guards are in good condition and properly mounted.

Hood (Hinges and Fasteners). See that hood, hinges, fasteners, and props are in good condition and securely mounted. Lubricate hinges lightly.

Front Fenders and Running Boards. Inspect front fenders and running boards for good condition and secure mounting.

Body. Inspect doors, hardware, glass, top, and frame, curtains and fasteners, seats, safety straps, grab rails, and ventilators for good condition and secure mounting.

Heater and Fan (if Provided). See that heater is securely mounted, in good condition, and not leaking. Turn on switches, see that fan operates properly and listen for excessive noise.

Circuit Breaker. Examine circuit breakers to see that they are clean, in good condition, and that electrical connections are tight.

Rear Bumpers and Pintle Hook. Examine rear body plates which serve as bumpers, and pintle hook for

## TM 9-710

**BASIC HALF-TRACK VEHICLES (WHITE, AUTOCAR, and DIAMOND T)**

| MAINTENANCE | |
|---|---|
| 6000 Mile | 1000 Mile |
| | |
| | |
| 102 | 102 |
| | |
| | |
| | |
| | |
| 103 | 103 |
| | |
| | |
| | |
| | |
| | |
| 104 | 104 |
| | |
| | |
| | |
| 105 | 105 |
| | |
| | |
| | |
| 129 | 129 |
| | |
| | |
| | |
| 131 | 131 |
| | |
| | |
| | |
| | |
| 132 | 132 |
| | |
| 133 | 133 |
| 134 | 134 |
| | |
| 135 | 135 |
| | |
| | |

good condition and secure mounting. Check pintle and latch to see that they operate properly, are adequately lubricated, and whether or not the lock pin is attached with chain. Inspect spring for breakage and drawbar for excessive wear.

**Armor Plate.** Examine armor plate for good condition and secure attachment. Examine body, cowl, windshield armor plate and port covers for good condition and secure mounting. Note whether or not hinges and fasteners are adequately lubricated. CAUTION: *Do not overlubricate so as to affect paint.*

**Paint and Markings.** Examine paint of entire vehicle to see that it is in good condition, paying particular attention to any bright spots in finish that might cause glare or reflection. Inspect vehicle markings and identification for legibility. Inspect identification plates, and their mountings, if furnished, for good condition and secure attachment.

**Radio Bondings (Suppressors, Filters, Condensers, and Shielding).** Examine radio bonding, suppressors, filters, condensers, and shielding to see that their bonding connections are in good condition, clean, and securely mounted.

**Armament.** Inspect guns, mounts, rails, spare parts and covers for good condition, cleanliness, and secure mountings. Refer all mounted guns, spare gun parts, and covers to armorer or gun commander for inspections and service.

**Electric Brake.** Inspect application controller and linkage for good condition, secure mounting, and good electrical connections. Make sure spring tension adjusting nut on controller arm is present and properly adjusted.

**Tools (Vehicle and Pioneer).** Check tools against stowage lists for presence. Inspect for good condition, cleanliness, and proper stowage or secure mounting. Any tools mounted on outside of vehicle, which have bright or polished surfaces should be painted or otherwise treated to avoid glare or reflection.

**Fire Extinguisher.** Inspect fire extinguisher for full charge, good condition, secure mounting, and clean nozzle.

**Decontaminator.** Inspect decontaminator for good condition, secure mounting, and full charge.

**First Aid Kit.** Inspect first aid kit for good condition and presence of all items. Report deficiencies immediately.

**Publications and Form No. 26A.** The vehicle manuals and parts lists, Lubrication Guide, and Standard Accident Form No. 26A should be present, legible, and properly stowed.

# TM 9-710
## 40

## ORGANIZATIONAL PREVENTIVE MAINTENANCE SERVICES

| MAINTENANCE | | |
|---|---|---|
| 6000 Mile | 1000 Mile | |
| 136 | 136 | **Traction Devices (Chains).** Check to see that chains are in good condition, clean, not excessively worn, protected against rust, and properly stowed. |
| 137 | 137 | **Tow Chains.** See that any provided towing devices are in good condition, clean, and properly stowed. |
| 138 | 138 | **Spare Shearpins and Bulbs.** See that proper number and sizes of spare shearpins and light bulbs are present, in good condition, and properly stowed. |
| 139 | 139 | **Water Cans and Brackets.** See that cans and brackets are in good condition and securely mounted. Make sure that caps fit cans tightly, and are secured to can with chain. Examine cans for leaks. |
| 140 | 140 | **Bucket.** Check to see that bucket is present, in good condition, clean, and properly stowed. |
| 141 | | **Modification (Modification Work Orders Completed).** Inspect the vehicle to determine whether all Modification Work Orders have been completed and entered on W.D., A.G.O. Form 478. Enter any replacement of Major Unit Assembly made at time of this service. |
| 142 | 142 | **Final Road Test.** Make final road test, rechecking items 2 to 15 inclusive. Be sure to recheck transmission and transfer case, jackshaft and front axle, to see that lubricant is at correct level and not leaking. Confine road test to minimum distance necessary to make satisfactory observations. Correct or report all deficiencies found during final road test. |

TM 9-710
41-42

**BASIC HALF-TRACK VEHICLES (WHITE, AUTOCAR, and DIAMOND T)**

Section XII

# TROUBLE SHOOTING

|  | Paragraph |
|---|---|
| General | 41 |
| Engine | 42 |
| Fuel system | 43 |
| Cooling system | 44 |
| Ignition system | 45 |
| Cranking motor and generating system | 46 |
| Clutch | 47 |
| Transmission | 48 |
| Transfer case and power take-off | 49 |
| Front axle | 50 |
| Rear axle—jackshaft | 51 |
| Brake system | 52 |
| Wheels | 53 |
| Springs | 54 |
| Steering | 55 |
| Windshield wipers (body and frame) | 56 |
| Lighting and switches | 57 |

**41. GENERAL.**

a. This section contains trouble shooting information and tests which can be made to determine causes of trouble that may develop in vehicles under average climatic conditions (above 32°F). Each trouble symptom given under the unit or system involved, is followed by a list of possible causes of the trouble. The tests to determine the exact trouble are explained after each possible cause.

**42. ENGINE.**

a. **Engine Will Not Turn.**

(1) PISTON LOCK OR SEIZURE. Remove the spark plugs from the engine, put vehicle transmission into high gear and pull vehicle. This should revolve the crankshaft and relieve the seizure. If the engine turns, stop towing, install spark plugs, and attempt starting with the cranking motor. If the engine does not turn over, it indicates internal damage. Report to higher authority.

(2) CRANKING MOTOR INOPERATIVE. See paragraph 46.

(3) INCORRECT CRANKCASE OIL VISCOSITY. Drain crankcase and refill with proper grade of oil (par. 23).

b. **Engine Turns but Will Not Start.**

(1) EMPTY FUEL TANKS. Fill tanks with proper grade of fuel.

(2) IMPROPER GRADE OF FUEL. Fill tanks with proper grade of fuel.

## TROUBLE SHOOTING

(3) INOPERATIVE IGNITION SYSTEM. Remove a cable from a spark plug. Turn ignition switch on and crank the engine with the cranking motor, while holding the spark plug cable terminal one-fourth inch from the cylinder head. If a spark does not jump this gap to the cylinder head, the ignition is faulty. See paragraph 45.

(4) INOPERATIVE FUEL SYSTEM. Unscrew coupling nut at carburetor fuel line fitting and crank engine with cranking motor, ignition switch off. If a weak or no flow is apparent, it indicates that no fuel is reaching the carburetor due to a defective fuel pump or clogged lines. See paragraph 43.

(5) CRANKING SPEED TOO SLOW. See paragraph 46.

c. **Engine Does Not Develop Full Power.**

(1) FAULTY IGNITION. See paragraph 45.

(2) IMPROPER GRADE OF FUEL. Check, drain, and fill tanks with proper grade (par. 23).

(3) PREIGNITION. If the proper grade of fuel and proper spark plugs are being used, check ignition timing (par. 95). If this does not locate the trouble, it indicates faulty internal operation in the engine. Report to higher authority.

(4) FAULTY OPERATION OF FUEL SYSTEM. See paragraph 43.

(5) LOW ENGINE COMPRESSION. Test engine cylinder compression (par. 59). If found to be below recommended limits, report to higher authority.

(6) IMPROPER VALVE TIMING. With satisfactory performance of fuel and ignition systems, proper compression, and sufficient oil in lubricating system, if engine does not operate smoothly, improper valve timing is indicated. Report to higher authority.

d. **Engine Misfires.**

(1) FAULTY IGNITION SYSTEM. See paragraph 45.

(2) LOW ENGINE COMPRESSION. See step (5) above.

(3) IMPROPER CARBURETOR ADJUSTMENT. Adjust carburetor (par. 77).

(4) CLOGGED FUEL TANK CAP VENTS OR FUEL LINES. See paragraph 43.

(5) FOREIGN SUBSTANCE IN FUEL. Remove filter bowls of fuel pump and carburetor and examine for water, oil, dirt, etc.

e. **Engine "Knocks" or "Pings."**

(1) IMPROPER DISTRIBUTOR SETTING. A sharp "knock," heard upon quick acceleration indicates improper setting of the distributor for the fuel being used. Check distributor spark setting (par. 95). If the distributor is properly set, the knock indicates excess carbon in the combustion chamber.

(2) WORN OR FAULTY INTERNAL PARTS. A sharp, hollow, slapping sound, when pulling on level ground, or when starting a cold engine, indicates a worn piston or piston pin. Refer to proper authority. A dull, regular knock in time with crankshaft speed indicates loose or burned connecting rod or main bearings. Report to higher authority.

## BASIC HALF-TRACK VEHICLES (WHITE, AUTOCAR, and DIAMOND T)

f. **Engine Overheats.**

(1) LACK OF COOLANT IN SYSTEM. Fill cooling system (par. 83).

(2) FROZEN OR CLOGGED COOLING SYSTEM. See paragraph 44.

(3) IMPROPER CARBURETOR ADJUSTMENT. A too lean mixture of fuel in the carburetor will cause slow overheating of the engine. Check and adjust the fuel mixture (par. 77).

g. **Engine "Pops" and "Spits" When Running.**

(1) WEAK OR BROKEN VALVE SPRINGS. Remove valve cover plates and observe action of valve springs (engine running). Report faulty parts to proper authority.

(2) EARLY VALVE TIMING. If valve spring operation is satisfactory, and the engine continues to "pop" and "spit," it indicates early valve timing. Report to proper authority.

h. **Excessive Oil Consumption.**

(1) IMPROPER OIL VISCOSITY. Check, drain, and refill with proper grade.

(2) EXTERNAL OIL LEAKS. Inspect for leaks. Replace faulty gaskets.

i. **Engine Will Not Stop.**

(1) OVERHEATED COMBUSTION CHAMBERS. When the engine continues to run after the ignition switch is turned off, it indicates excessive heat in the combustion chambers, caused by improper fuel adjustment or carbon deposits. Clean carbon (par. 61), and adjust fuel mixture (par. 77).

(2) FAULTY OPERATION OF IGNITION SWITCH. After engine is stopped, turn ignition switch "ON" and "OFF" while observing ammeter and fuel gages. A defective switch will not deflect these pointers. If this condition exists, replace switch.

## 43. FUEL SYSTEM.

a. **No Fuel Flow at Carburetor.**

(1) LEAKAGE IN SYSTEM. Check entire system from fitting at bottom of fuel tank, along the lines to the fuel filter, fuel pump, and carburetor, for evidence of fuel leaks. Tighten loose fittings and replace defective parts.

(2) CLOGGED FUEL SYSTEM. Check the entire system for obstructions in the units, starting at the fuel tank end of the system.

(3) FAULTY FUEL PUMP. Check the effectiveness of the fuel pump by cranking the engine, with ignition switch off, after disconnecting the pump-to-carburetor fuel line at the front of the fuel pump. If the pump produces good pressure, it indicates faulty carburetor operation.

b. **Faulty Engine Performance with Full Fuel Flow at Carburetor.**

(1) IMPURITIES IN SYSTEM. Impurities, such as water and oil, can be detected in the sediment bowls of the fuel pump and fuel filter. Remove these units, being careful not to empty them in so doing. By slowly pouring out the contents, any impure solutions can be seen at once,

**TM 9-710**
43-45

## TROUBLE SHOOTING

as they will not mix with the fuel. Condensation of air, caused by rapid temperature changes, often produces a considerable amount of water in the fuel tanks. If the check shows water deposits in the sediment bowls, clean them, then drain the tanks of a gallon of fuel each. This should remove the water from the system.

(2) CLOGGED AIR CLEANER SYSTEM. Check air cleaner screens for clogged condition. Wash screens in dry-cleaning solvent and replace filter oil.

(3) FAULTY CARBURETOR ACTION. With engine running, adjust carburetor mixture at spring screw at top of carburetor. If this fails to improve engine performance, report to higher authority.

(4) FAULTY CARBURETOR CONTROLS. Check the setting and operation of the choke butterfly valve in the carburetor intake. Make sure that its normal position (wide open) is maintained. If its operation is faulty, report to proper authority.

### 44. COOLING SYSTEM.

**a. Engine Cooling System Overheats.**

(1) LACK OF COOLANT. Refill system.

(2) FAULTY THERMOSTAT OPERATION. Test thermostat and replace if faulty (par. 89).

(3) FAULTY WATER PUMP OPERATION. Test flow; replace pump if faulty (par. 84).

(4) CLOGGED SYSTEM. Flush and clean system (par. 87).

(5) HOSE LEAKING. Tighten clamps or replace faulty hose.

(6) FROZEN RADIATOR OR LINES. When the engine overheats very quickly, it indicates a complete clogging of the cooling system, either from ice, slush, or some foreign obstruction. If evidence of freezing is found, cover the radiator with a heavy cloth or tarpaulin and run the engine slowly, shutting it off each time the engine temperature gage passes 200°F. Repeat this operation until the coolant thaws. If the obstruction is not snow or ice, reverse-flush the cooling system (par. 87).

(7) LOOSE OR OPEN DRAIN COCKS AND PLUGS. Inspect and tighten.

(8) DAMAGED RADIATOR CORE. Seal or replace radiator.

### 45. IGNITION SYSTEM.

**a. No Spark at Spark Plugs.**

(1) FAULTY CABLES OR TERMINALS. Inspect all cables and terminals for cleanness and condition. Replace defective parts.

(2) FAULTY IGNITION COIL. Pull the coil-distributor cable from the terminal at the center of the distributor head and hold it about 3/8 inch from any convenient metal ground. "Make" and "break" the primary circuit by operating the starting motor (with the ignition switch "on"). A weak spark or no spark indicates a faulty coil. Replace coil. If a "hot" spark is obtained, install the cable in the distributor terminal and proceed.

(3) FAULTY DISTRIBUTOR OPERATION. Check inside and outside of distributor cover for cracks and moisture. Turn on ignition switch,

**BASIC HALF-TRACK VEHICLES (WHITE, AUTOCAR, and DIAMOND T)**

crank the engine, and with the distributor head removed, check for excessive arcing at the breaker points. This will indicate a defective distributor condenser. Replace condenser (par. 93). Pull coil-distributor cable from terminal at center of distributor. Remove cover and hold the cable terminal 3/8 inch from the rotor. Create secondary voltage by "making" and "breaking" primary circuit (step (2) above). If a spark occurs it indicates a grounded rotor. Replace rotor (par. 93).

    b. **Full Spark at Plugs, with Faulty Engine Performance.**

  (1) IGNITION OUT OF TIME. Time ignition (par. 95).

### 46. CRANKING MOTOR AND GENERATING SYSTEM.

    a. **No Cranking Motor Action When Switch is Closed.**

(1) FAULTY CRANKING MOTOR SWITCH. Test lights and horn for battery power. Push starter button and observe ammeter on instrument panel. No deflection of this gage (with ignition switch on) indicates a faulty cranking motor switch. Replace faulty unit.

(2) FAULTY OPERATION OF SOLENOID. If no sound or action is obtained at cranking motor when switch is depressed, it indicates an open circuit to the cranking motor. Check for broken cables or loose terminals. If these are found satisfactory, and the ammeter deflects when the starter button is pushed, it indicates faulty operation of the solenoid switch. Replace solenoid switch.

(3) CRANKING MOTOR INOPERATIVE. A clicking sound when the starter button is depressed indicates operation of the solenoid. If this is obtained it indicates a grounded or inoperative cranking motor. Replace cranking motor (par. 98).

    b. **Cranking Motor Hums When Switch Is Closed.**

(1) CRANKING MOTOR DRIVE DEFECTIVE. Clean cranking motor drive. If still inoperative, replace cranking motor (par. 98).

(2) CRANKING MOTOR MOUNTING BOLTS LOOSE, CAUSING MIS-ALINEMENT. Tighten mounting bolts.

    c. **Cranking Motor Not Strong Enough to Start Engine.**

(1) BATTERY WEAK OR COMPLETELY DISCHARGED. Replace or recharge battery.

(2) LOOSE OR CORRODED CONNECTIONS. Tighten and clean connections. Coat with petrolatum.

(3) CRANKING MOTOR COMMUTATOR BURNED OR DIRTY. Inspect, clean, or replace (par. 98).

(4) CRANKING MOTOR ARMATURE BURNED. Replace cranking motor (par. 98).

    d. **Cranking Motor Turns Over Engine, But Will Not Start.**

(1) WEAK BATTERY. Replace or recharge battery (par. 153).

(2) BATTERY TERMINALS CORRODED OR LOOSE CONNECTIONS. Tighten and clean connections. Coat with petrolatum.

    e. **Running Engine Misses.**

(1) BATTERY TERMINALS CORRODED OR LOOSE CONNECTIONS. Tighten and clean connections. Coat battery posts with petrolatum.

## TROUBLE SHOOTING

**f. Battery Not Receiving Charge from Generator.**

(1) CIRCUIT BREAKER FAULTY. If the ammeter on the instrument panel shows a heavy discharge when the generator is not running and all switches are off except the battery master switch, disconnect the battery lead marked "B" in the regulator terminal box. If the condition is corrected, the regulator circuit breaker contact points are stuck. If the ammeter on the instrument panel does not show charge until generator is running at high speed, the regulator circuit breaker is adjusted to operate at too high a voltage. In either of these cases, replace the regulator (par. 100).

(2) REGULATOR INOPERATIVE. Start the engine and observe ammeter on the instrument panel. If no charging rate is indicated, connect the battery and armature terminals marked "B" and "A" together in the regulator terminal box using a short piece of insulated wire. Hold jumper wire across the two terminals and watch the ammeter. If reading is obtained, the regulator is not connecting the generator to the battery. If this test does not reveal the trouble, connect the battery and field terminals together with the jumper wire. If a reading is obtained, the regulator is not allowing current to reach the generator field coils, preventing charge. If excessive charge is experienced and the batteries and circuits test properly, the trouble is caused by improper regulator adjustment. In either case, the regulator is inoperative.

(3) GENERATOR INOPERATIVE. If regulator tests have been made and no charge is obtained, connect a test voltmeter between armature terminal marked "A" in regulator terminal box and ground (hull). This test will show if generator is charging. If no voltage reading is shown, leave the voltmeter connected and connect the battery and field terminals marked "B" and "F" together with the jumper wire. A flash will be seen and the test voltmeter will show a reading when the jumper wire is connected, if the circuit is complete. Check the ammeter on the instrument panel. If a charge is shown, the trouble has been corrected by flashing the fields which has increased the magnetism or properly polarized the field coil shoes. If no reading is obtained on the voltmeter, inspect the terminals at the generator for loose or broken connections. If no trouble is observed in the connections or leads, the generator is inoperative.

**g. Ammeter Does Not Show Charge.**

(1) GENERATOR CIRCUIT BREAKER OPEN. Reset generator circuit breaker.

(2) AMMETER INOPERATIVE. If the ammeter fails to register a charge, turn on all lights and see if a discharge is shown. If no discharge is observed, connect a new ammeter temporarily to the leads in the instrument panel. If a reading is obtained, the ammeter is faulty. If no reading is obtained, test wiring from ammeter to shunt for open circuit.

(3) REGULATOR INOPERATIVE. See f (2) above.

(4) GENERATOR INOPERATIVE. See f (3) above.

(5) LOOSE OR CORRODED CONNECTIONS. Clean and tighten connections.

# TM 9-710

## BASIC HALF-TRACK VEHICLES (WHITE, AUTOCAR, and DIAMOND T)

(6) GENERATOR GROUND STRAP LOOSE OR BROKEN. Inspect ground strap. Tighten or replace.

**h. Ammeter Shows Excessive Charge.**

(1) CURRENT REGULATOR IMPROPERLY ADJUSTED. See f (1) above.

(2) BATTERIES RUN DOWN. Test batteries (par. 153). Recharge or replace.

(3) BATTERIES SHORTED INTERNALLY. Test batteries and replace if faulty (par. 153).

**i. Ammeter Shows Discharge with Engine Running.**

(1) GENERATOR NOT OPERATING. See f (3) above.

(2) REGULATOR CIRCUIT BREAKER CUT-IN VOLTAGE TOO HIGH. See f (3) above.

(3) GENERATOR DRIVE BELTS LOOSE OR BROKEN. Tighten or replace belts (par. 86).

**j. Ammeter Shows Heavy Discharge with Engine Stopped.**

(1) SHORTED CIRCUITS. Check system for current leaks.

(2) REGULATOR CIRCUIT BREAKER POINTS STUCK. See f (1) above.

(3) AMMETER HAND STICKING OR AMMETER BURNED OUT. Tap ammeter with heel of hand, and if not corrected, replace instrument cluster (par. 161).

**k. Ammeter Hand Fluctuates Rapidly.**

(1) GENERATOR DRIVE BELTS LOOSE. Tighten or replace belts (par. 86).

(2) GENERATOR GROUND STRAP LOOSE OR BROKEN. Tighten or replace ground strap.

(3) REGULATOR CIRCUIT BREAKER CUT-IN VOLTAGE TOO LOW OR CONTRACTS BURNED. See (5) below.

(4) REGULATOR LOOSE, NOT PROPERLY GROUNDED, OR VIBRATING AGAINST OTHER EQUIPMENT. Tighten regulator on mountings, inspect ground straps, and relieve interference.

(5) GENERATOR OR REGULATOR FAULTY. If ammeter needle fluctuates rapidly, while generator is running, test all regulator and generator mountings to see if they are tight, and inspect for broken ground straps. If ground straps and mountings are satisfactory, the condition is caused by incorrect setting of regulator circuit breaker, worn generator brushes, faulty generator drive belts, or regulator bumping against other equipment. If inspection reveals that the generator drive belts are properly adjusted (par. 86) and there is no interference with the regulator, connect a jumper wire between battery terminal marked "B" and armature terminal marked "A" in the regulator terminal box. If the fluctuation stops with the jumper wire connected, indicating that

## TROUBLE SHOOTING

the regulator circuit breaker points have been vibrating, replace the regulator (par. 100). If fluctuation continues, indicating that the generator is at fault, replace the generator (par. 99).

### 47. CLUTCH.
  a. **Slipping.**
  (1) IMPROPER ADJUSTMENT. Adjust clutch (par. 70).
  (2) OILY PRESSURE FACINGS. Clean and correct cause. Inspect rear crankshaft oil seal. Inspect overlubrication of pilot bearing. Replace pressure plate assembly if proper condition cannot be restored (par. 71).
  (3) WEAK CLUTCH SPRINGS. Report to higher authority.
  (4) WORN CLUTCH FACINGS. Report to higher authority.
  (5) STICKING CLUTCH SLEEVE. Inspect pull-back springs.
  b. **Rattling.**
  (1) LOOSE RELEASE YOKE. Report to higher authority.
  (2) WEAK OR BROKEN PULL-BACK SPRINGS. Report to higher authority.
  (3) IMPROPER PEDAL ADJUSTMENT. Adjust pedal (par. 70).
  c. **Chattering.**
  (1) BROKEN PULL-BACK SPRING. Report to higher authority.
  (2) OILY OR BURNED FACINGS. Clean driven member assembly, or report to higher authority.
  (3) STICKING CLUTCH SLEEVE. Report to higher authority.

### 48. TRANSMISSION.
  a. **Stiffness in Gearshifting.**
  (1) INSUFFICIENT LUBRICATION. Fill to level plug with proper lubricant.
  (2) IMPROPER LUBRICANT. Fill with proper grade.
  b. **Impossible to Shift Gears.**
  (1) SHIFTING YOKES BROKEN OR BENT. Report to higher authority, or replace complete assembly.
  (2) BROKEN GEAR TEETH. Report to higher authority or replace complete assembly (par. 102).
  (3) HOUSING AND ASSEMBLY OUT OF ALINEMENT. Inspect and relocate or replace complete assembly if the unit is damaged (par. 102).
  c. **Excess Noise in Operation.**
  (1) ASSEMBLY OUT OF ALINEMENT. Relocate and tighten (par. 103).
  (2) FAULTY GEARS. Report to higher authority or replace transmission (par. 102).
  (3) WORN BEARINGS. Report to higher authority or replace transmission (par. 102).

## BASIC HALF-TRACK VEHICLES (WHITE, AUTOCAR, and DIAMOND T)

(4) WORN GEAR TEETH. Report to higher authority or replace transmission (par. 102).

(5) WORN SHAFT SPLINES. Report to higher authority or replace transmission (par. 102).

(6) IMPROPER LUBRICANT. Drain and refill with proper grade.

(7) INSUFFICIENT LUBRICANT. Fill to level plug with proper lubricant.

**d. Excess Heat in Operation.**

(1) LACK OF LUBRICANT. Fill to level plug with proper lubricant.

(2) IMPROPER LUBRICANT. Drain and refill with proper lubricant.

(3) ASSEMBLY OUT OF ALINEMENT. Relocate and tighten (par. 102).

### 49. TRANSFER CASE AND POWER TAKE-OFF.

**a. Excess Noise in Operation.**

(1) INSUFFICIENT LUBRICANT. Fill to level plug with proper lubricant.

(2) IMPROPER LUBRICANT. Drain and fill with proper lubricant.

(3) DEFECTIVE GEARS. Report to higher authority or replace complete assembly (par. 102).

(4) EXCESS GEAR LASH. Report to higher authority or replace complete assembly.

(5) WORN BEARINGS. Report to higher authority or replace complete assembly.

(6) LOOSE GEARS. Report to higher authority or replace complete assembly.

(7) INSTALLATION OUT OF LINE. Relocate unit and tighten supports.

**b. Overheating.**

(1) INSUFFICIENT LUBRICANT. Fill to level plug with proper lubricant.

(2) IMPROPER LUBRICANT. Drain and fill with proper grade.

**c. Loss of Lubricant.**

(1) IMPROPER GRADE LUBRICANT. Drain and fill with proper grade.

(2) DEFECTIVE GASKETS OR SEALS. Report to higher authority.

(3) CRACKED OR BROKEN HOUSING. Report to higher authority.

### 50. FRONT AXLE.

**a. Hard Steering.**

(1) FRONT AXLE SHIFTED. Relocate and tighten spring clip nuts (par. 111).

(2) BENT FRAME. Report to higher authority.

(3) EXCESSIVE CASTER. Report to higher authority.

(4) TIRES UNDERINFLATED. Inspect and inflate to proper pressure (70 pounds).

## TROUBLE SHOOTING

(5) TIGHTNESS IN TIE ROD OR DRAG LINK JOINTS. Inspect and correct joints for wear, adjustment, and lubrication (pars. 109 and 142).

(6) TIGHTNESS IN STEERING GEAR ASSEMBLY. Inspect and correct adjustment of steering gear, alinement of steering column, and lubrication of steering gear (par. 141).

(7) IMPROPER TOE-IN. Adjust the tie rod yoke (par. 109).

b. **Low Speed Shimmy.**

(1) TOO MUCH OR TOO LITTLE CASTER. Report to higher authority.

(2) LOOSE FRONT WHEEL BEARINGS. Adjust, replace if adjustment does not correct (par. 137).

(3) LOOSE OR WORN STEERING MECHANISM. Inspect and adjust, tighten or replace—ball joints, bracket, steering gear to frame, Pitman arm, spring shackles, and spring U-bolts (pars. 109, 139, 141, and 142).

(4) ECCENTRIC WHEELS. Replace wheel or tire.

(5) TIE ROD LOOSE. Tighten or replace worn parts.

c. **High Speed Shimmy.**

(1) FRONT WHEELS WOBBLE. Report to higher authority or replace.

(2) RUPTURED OR WEAK TIRE CARCASS. Replace tire.

(3) DRAGGING FRONT WHEEL BRAKES. Adjust brakes.

d. **Wandering.**

(1) BENT AXLE PARTS. Report to higher authority.

(2) LOOSE FRONT WHEEL BEARINGS. Adjust bearings (par. 137).

(3) FRONT BRAKE DRUMS OUT-OF-ROUND. Report to higher authority.

(4) TIRES UNDERINFLATED. Correct inflation.

(5) ZERO OR REVERSE CASTER. Report to higher authority.

(6) EXCESSIVE ERROR IN TOE-IN. Correct toe-in (par. 108).

(7) AXLES SHIFTED. Relocate axles (par. 111).

(8) TIGHT STEERING ASSEMBLY OR GEAR. Adjust defective part.

(9) LOOSE WHEELS. Inspect and tighten wheel nuts.

## 51. REAR AXLE—JACKSHAFT.

a. **Axle Noises.**

(1) CONTINUOUS HUM. Adjust sprocket wheel bearings. Fill axle centers to level plug with proper lubricants.

(2) COASTING HUM. Inspect sprocket wheel bearings. If source of trouble is not located, report to proper authority.

(3) PULLING HUM. Report to higher authority.

b. **Backlash.**

(1) LOOSE AXLE SHAFT FLANGE. Tighten axle flange nuts.

(2) EXCESSIVE CLEARANCE AT AXLE SHAFT SPLINES. Report to higher authority.

## BASIC HALF-TRACK VEHICLES (WHITE, AUTOCAR, and DIAMOND T)

c. Grease Leakage.

(1) GREASE APPEARING ON BRAKES. Inspect seals and replace if faulty.

d. Dull Thud in Time with Speed of Truck.

(1) BROKEN GEAR TOOTH IN AXLE. Report to higher authority.

## 52. BRAKE SYSTEM.

a. No Resistance to Pressure on Foot Pedal.

(1) INSUFFICIENT BRAKE FLUID. Refill master cylinder.

(2) LINING WEAR. Adjust brakes for lining wear (par. 132).

(3) INCORRECT BRAKE SHOE ADJUSTMENT. Adjust brake shoes (par. 132).

(4) LEAKAGE IN SYSTEM. Inspect the brake wheel cylinders, brake fluid lines, the master cylinder, and Hydrovac unit for evidence of leaks. If caused by loose fittings, tighten the fittings. If caused by faulty or broken parts, replace the faulty unit.

(5) IMPROPER MASTER CYLINDER ROD ADJUSTMENT. Inspect the master cylinder rod for full travel adjustment. The piston in the master cylinder should (in released brake position) be completely toward the front end of the master cylinder. If this position is not maintained it will allow too great travel of the foot pedal. Adjust the rod with the adjusting nut and lock nut.

b. Brake Pedal Has "Spongy" Action.

(1) AIR IN SYSTEM. Bleed system (par. 122).

(2) INSUFFICIENT BRAKE FLUID. Refill master cylinder (par. 129).

c. No Brake Action with Hard Pedal Pressure.

(1) IMPROPERLY ADJUSTED BRAKE SHOES. Adjust brake shoes (par. 122).

(2) FAULTY OPERATION OF HYDROVAC UNIT. Replace unit or report to higher authority.

(3) WORN BRAKE LININGS. Replace linings (par. 132).

d. All Brakes Drag (with Pedal Released).

(1) INSUFFICIENT BRAKE SHOE CLEARANCE. Inspect and adjust clearance if insufficient (par. 122).

(2) IMPROPER MASTER CYLINDER ROD ADJUSTMENT. Adjust rod (par. 123).

(3) WEAK OR BROKEN PEDAL RETURN SPRING. Replace faulty spring.

e. One Brake Drags.

(1) WEAK OR BROKEN BRAKE SHOE RETURN SPRING. Replace faulty unit (par. 132).

(2) BRAKE SHOE BINDING ON ANCHOR PIN. Remove shoe, clean, and lubricate anchor pin.

(3) INSUFFICIENT BRAKE SHOE CLEARANCE. Inspect and adjust clearance if insufficient.

## TROUBLE SHOOTING

f. **Brakes "Grab" When Pedal Is Depressed.**
(1) BRAKE SHOE CLEARANCE TOO GREAT. Adjust clearance (par. 122).
(2) GREASE OR OIL ON LININGS. Clean linings.

g. **Noisy Brakes.**
(1) BENT OR BROKEN BACKING PLATE. Replace backing plate.
(2) DAMAGED BRAKE SHOES. Replace shoes (par. 132).
(3) BRAKE DRUMS OUT-OF-ROUND. Replace drums or report to higher authority.
(4) DIRT IN LININGS. Clean brake linings.

h. **Propeller Shaft Brake Does Not Hold When Applied.**
(1) LININGS WORN OUT. Replace linings.
(2) LININGS AND BRAKE SHOES IMPROPERLY ADJUSTED. Adjust brake (par. 132).

## 53. WHEELS.

a. **Hard Steering.**
(1) TIRES UNDERINFLATED. Inflate to proper pressure (55 pounds).
(2) DEFECTIVE WHEEL BEARING. Replace defective units (par. 137).
(3) UNEQUAL CAMBER. Report to higher authority.
(4) BENT OR DAMAGED WHEEL. Report to proper authority or replace wheel (par. 135).
(5) LOOSE WHEEL. Tighten wheel nuts.

b. **Noisy Operation.**
(1) LOOSE WHEEL NUTS. Tighten nuts.
(2) LOOSE TIRE RIM. Tighten rim nuts.
(3) DAMAGED WHEEL. Replace wheel (par. 135).

c. **Air Leakage.**
(1) VALVE CAP MISSING OR BROKEN. Replace with new cap.
(2) DEFECTIVE VALVE CORE. Replace with new core.
(3) PUNCTURE OR TORN TUBE. Repair if possible, or replace.

d. **Excess Track Noise in Operation.**
(1) BROKEN OR BENT GUIDE PLATES. Inspect and if plates are faulty, replace track (par. 117).
(2) IMPROPER TRACK TENSION. Adjust track tension (par. 117).
(3) DAMAGED IDLER WHEEL. Replace unit (par. 117).
(4) DAMAGED DRIVE SPROCKET WHEEL. Replace unit (par. 136).

## 54. SPRINGS.

a. **Hard Riding.**
(1) DRY SPRING SHACKLES OR BOLTS. Lubricate units (par. 23).
(2) BROKEN SHACKLE PINS. Replace defective parts (par. 139).

**BASIC HALF-TRACK VEHICLES (WHITE, AUTOCAR, and DIAMOND T)**

b. **Excessive Spring Action.**

(1) BROKEN LEAVES. Replace spring (par. 139).

(2) BROKEN SPRING CLIPS. Replace clip.

c. **Hard Steering.**

(1) SPRING SHIFTED. Relocate spring and tighten clips (par. 139).

(2) BROKEN LEAVES. Replace spring (par. 139).

d. **Noisy Operation.**

(1) DRY SHACKLES OR BOLTS. Lubricate units (par. 23).

(2) BROKEN BRACKETS OR SHACKLES. Replace defective unit (par. 139).

## 55. STEERING.

a. **Hard Steering.**

(1) TIRES UNDERINFLATED. Inspect and inflate to proper pressure (55 pounds).

(2) EXCESSIVE FRICTION IN TIE ROD OR DRAG LINK JOINTS. Inspect and adjust or lubricate as required.

(3) EXCESSIVE FRICTION IN STEERING GEAR ASSEMBLY. Inspect lubrication, and if not corrected, report to higher authority.

b. **Low Speed Shimmy.**

(1) TIRES UNDERINFLATED. Inspect and inflate to proper pressure (55 pounds).

(2) TOO MUCH OR TOO LITTLE CASTER. Report to higher authority.

(3) LOOSE FRONT WHEEL BEARINGS. Adjust bearings (par. 137).

(4) LOOSE OR WORN STEERING MECHANISM. Inspect and adjust or replace ball joints, steering gear mounting (housing-to-frame), Pitman arm, spring shackles, and U-bolts.

(5) ECCENTRIC WHEELS. Replace wheel or tire.

(6) FRONT SPRING HANGERS LOOSE ON FRAME. Tighten hangers.

(7) UNEQUAL FRONT WHEEL CAMBER. Report to higher authority.

(8) WEAK OR SAGGED FRONT SPRINGS. Inspect for broken leaves and replace. Check for overlubrication and wash off excess oil.

(9) DRAG LINK OUT OF LINE. Inspect and correct alinement.

(10) FRONT BRAKE DRUMS OUT-OF-ROUND (SHIMMY ONLY WHEN BRAKES ARE APPLIED). Report to higher authority.

c. **High Speed Shimmy.**

(1) TIRES UNDERINFLATED. Inspect and inflate to proper pressure (55 pounds).

(2) TOO MUCH OR TOO LITTLE CASTER. Report to higher authority.

(3) LOOSE FRONT WHEEL BEARINGS. Adjust bearings (par. 137).

(4) LOOSE OR WORN STEERING MECHANISM. Inspect and adjust or replace ball joints, steering gear mounting (housing-to-frame), Pitman arm, spring shackles and U-bolts.

(5) ECCENTRIC WHEELS. Replace wheel or tire.

## TROUBLE SHOOTING

(6) FRONT SPRING HANGERS LOOSE ON FRAME. Tighten hangers.

(7) UNEQUAL FRONT WHEEL CAMBER. Report to higher authority.

(8) WEAK OR SAGGED FRONT SPRINGS. Inspect for broken leaves and replace. Check for overlubrication and wash off excess oil.

(9) DRAG LINK OUT OF LINE. Inspect and correct alinement.

(10) FRONT BRAKE DRUMS OUT-OF-ROUND (SHIMMY ONLY WHEN BRAKES ARE APPLIED). Report to higher authority.

(11) DAMAGED WHEEL DISKS. Report to higher authority or replace wheel.

(12) FRONT WHEELS OUT OF BALANCE. Report to higher authority or replace wheels.

(13) RUPTURED OR WEAK SPOT IN TIRE. Replace tire (par. 138).

(14) DRAGGING FRONT WHEEL BRAKES. Adjust brakes (par. 132).

d. **Steering Wander.**

(1) TIRES UNDERINFLATED. Inflate to proper pressure (55 pounds).

(2) ZERO OR REVERSE CASTER. Report to higher authority.

(3) EXCESS ERROR IN TOE-IN. Correct toe-in (par. 108).

(4) AXLE SHIFTED IN SPRINGS. Relocate and tighten (par. 111).

(5) TIGHT STEERING ASSEMBLY. Adjust (par. 141).

(6) LOOSE WHEELS. Tighten.

## 56. WINDSHIELD WIPERS (BODY AND FRAME).

a. **Wiper Moves Too Slowly.**

(1) INSUFFICIENT PRESSURE. Inspect lines and connections for leaks, and replace if necessary.

(2) CLOGGED PORTS. Replace wiper assembly.

(3) LACK OF LUBRICANT. Replace wiper assembly.

b. **Wiper Will Not Oscillate.**

(1) ONE SET OF PORTS CLOGGED. Replace wiper assembly.

(2) LACK OF LUBRICANT. Replace wiper assembly.

c. **Wiper Will Not Move.**

(1) LINE SPLIT OR CONNECTION BROKEN. Inspect and replace damaged part.

(2) CLOGGED PORTS. Replace wiper assembly.

(3) WIPER BLADE STUCK. Free blade and check operation.

d. **Wiper Blade Streaking Windshield.**

(1) DIRT ON WINDSHIELD. Clean windshield.

(2) WORN OR DAMAGED BLADE. Replace blade assembly.

## 57. LIGHTING AND SWITCHES.

a. **Engine Will Not Start.**

(1) IGNITION SWITCH OFF. Close switch.

**BASIC HALF-TRACK VEHICLES (WHITE, AUTOCAR, and DIAMOND T)**

b. Lights of Vehicle Stay Bright When Starting Switch Is Closed.

(1) OPEN CIRCUIT IN CRANKING MOTOR. Refer to paragraph 46.

(2) CRANKING MOTOR SWITCH OPEN. Inspect switch.

c. Lights of Vehicle Go Very Dim or Out When Cranking Motor Switch Is Closed.

(1) DISCHARGED BATTERY. Replace or recharge battery.

(2) POOR CONNECTION AT BATTERY TERMINALS OR ELSEWHERE IN CIRCUIT. Tighten connections.

# TM 9-710
## 58

### Section XIII

## ENGINE DATA, MAINTENANCE, AND ADJUSTMENT IN VEHICLE

|  | Paragraph |
|---|---|
| Description and tabulated data | 58 |
| Tune-up | 59 |
| Cylinder head and gasket removal | 60 |
| Carbon removal | 61 |
| Cylinder head and gasket installation | 62 |
| Oil pan and guard | 63 |
| Oil temperature regulator | 64 |
| Oil filter | 65 |
| Crankcase ventilator | 66 |

### 58. DESCRIPTION AND TABULATED DATA.

**a. Description.** The engine is a six-cylinder, gasoline, four-stroke cycle, L-head type (figs. 50 and 51). The serial number is stamped on a pad on the left side of the crankcase. The cylinders and crankcase are cast in a block. The cylinder head is cast in one piece. The intake and exhaust manifolds, carburetor, oil filler pipe, oil filter, and oil bayonet gage are on the right-hand side. The generator, cranking motor, fuel and vacuum pump, distributor, and oil temperature regulator are on the left-hand side. The water pump is mounted on the front of the engine at the rear of the fan hub. The generator, fan and water pump are driven directly from the crankshaft pulley by dual V-type belts. The four water drain locations are: the radiator outlet pipe drain cock; the water pump drain cock on bottom rear of water pump; the cylinder block drain cock; and the drain cock at the right rear side of the engine block. The engine is equipped with a vibration damper on the front end of the crankshaft.

**b. Tabulated Data.**

| | |
|---|---|
| Make | White |
| Model | 160 AX |
| Cylinders | 6 |
| Bore | 4 in. |
| Stroke | 5⅛ in. |
| Displacement (cubic inches) | 386 cu in. |
| Compression ratio | 6.44 to 1 |
| Firing order | 1-5-3-6-2-4 |
| Brake horsepower (developed at 3,000 rpm) | 147 |
| Torque at 1,200 rpm | 325 ft-lb |
| Crankcase capacity (dry) | 12 qt |
| Oil drain location | Bottom of crankcase |
| Cooling system capacity (less heater) | 24 qt |

# TM 9-710
59

**BASIC HALF-TRACK VEHICLES (WHITE, AUTOCAR, and DIAMOND T)**

## 59. TUNE-UP.

a. **Compression Test** (fig. 52). Before starting with engine tune-up procedure, a test of engine compression should be made since an engine without fairly even compression in all cylinders cannot be successfully tuned. Make test in the following manner:

(1) Shut off ignition, pull throttle all the way out and remove spark plugs.

(2) Insert compression gage in a spark plug hole and crank engine several revolutions with cranking motor. Note highest compression

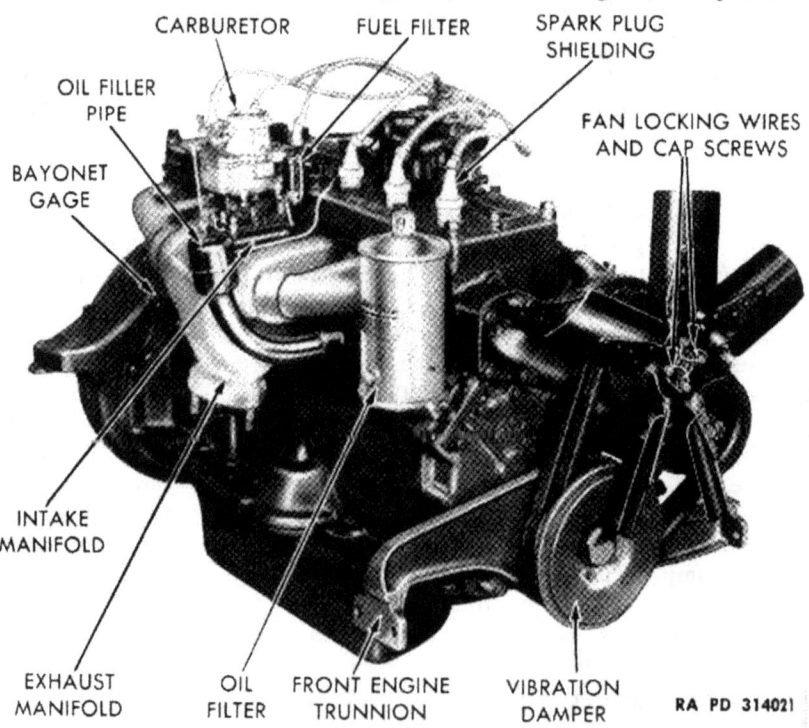

*Figure 50—Engine and Accessories*

reading on gage and record this reading. Repeat this operation at each cylinder.

(3) Compression reading of approximately 120 pounds per cylinder is desirable. A variation within approximately ten pounds limit is normal. If the compression is too low, the cause (either piston rings, valves, or cylinder head gasket) should be checked and corrected. To detect loss of compression through the piston rings, pour a liberal quantity of oil through a spark plug hole onto top of piston, allow enough time for the oil to spread around the piston, and then proceed with a second compression test reading. If the compression increases materially in cylinder so treated, it indicates a defective piston seal. An extremely low reading in any two adjacent cylinders might indicate a

**TM 9-710**
**59**

## ENGINE DATA, MAINTENANCE, AND ADJUSTMENT IN VEHICLE

leaky cylinder head gasket. If readings indicate need of engine overhaul, notify higher authority.

   b. **Ignition System.**

   (1) SPARK PLUGS (fig. 53). Inspect plugs for cracked, blistered, or fouled porcelains and worn electrodes. Test and clean the plugs. Use a round feeler gage and adjust spark gap to 0.025 by bending the side electrode (fig. 53). NOTE: *Do not bend the center electrode.*

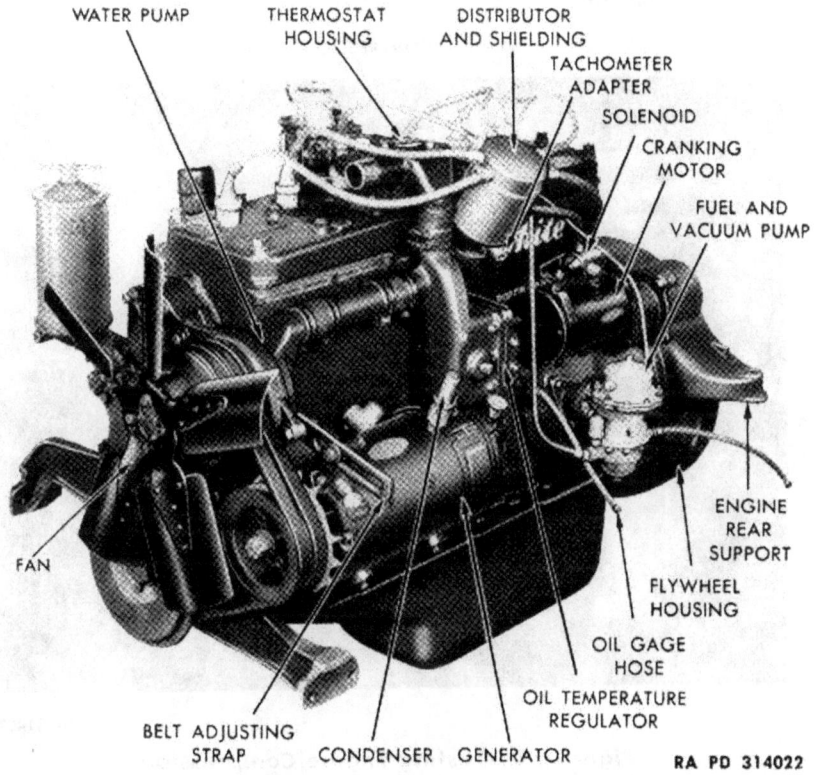

*Figure 51—Engine and Accessories*

   (2) DISTRIBUTOR. Remove cap and examine it for condition (cracks) and cleanliness. Inspect to see if posts are in good condition. Remove rotor and clean the spring contact point. Inspect the breaker points and if they are slightly pitted or burned, clean with a distributor point file, otherwise replace (par. 93). See that the automatic advance weights operate freely.

   (3) COIL. Examine terminals for tight connections and clean the outside of the coil. Test with coil tester and replace if coil is weak.

   (4) BATTERY AND IGNITION CABLES. Clean and tighten terminals and cables on battery. Test battery power using hydrometer, etc., for reading 0.1200 to 0.1275. Fill battery to ½ inch above the plates with

## BASIC HALF-TRACK VEHICLES (WHITE, AUTOCAR, and DIAMOND T)

distilled water. Inspect and correct ignition cables which have frayed or oil soaked insulation, broken wiring or loose terminals.

(5) IGNITION TIMING. Test ignition timing to see that it is adjusted to fire with marking on flywheel (fig. 98). Attach one end of a neon timing light to No. 1 spark plug and ground the other end. Run the engine at a slow idle. The flashes of the neon light should synchronize perfectly with the marking on the flywheel. Rotate the distributor body (fig. 54) to retard or advance the spark until the flash and the flywheel markings coincide.

*Figure 52—Testing Engine Compression*

c. **Fuel System.**

(1) AIR CLEANER. Remove the lower bowl and clean out dirty oil and sludge accumulation. Replace with fresh oil (to oil level bead) of same grade as used in crankcase. Wash the foreign material from air cleaner filtering screen and assembly by flushing the unit in dry-cleaning solvent (par. 78). Inspect both ends of the air tube outlet hose for signs of leaks or disintegration. Replace hose if deteriorated.

(2) CARBURETOR. Set throttle idle stop screw with engine warmed up, so tachometer registers approximately 400 revolutions per minute. Adjust idling screws until engine runs evenly and steadily. Examine gasket between carburetor flange and manifold for possible leak; also the gasket between intake manifold and engine block if engine will not idle evenly.

## ENGINE DATA, MAINTENANCE, AND ADJUSTMENT IN VEHICLE

(3) MANIFOLD HEAT CONTROL. Observe the action of the heater valve assembly. The heater valve shaft must work freely and respond to the action of the thermostatic spring control.

(4) FUEL PUMP. Remove bottom sediment bowl by unscrewing the cap screw at bottom of the unit. Clean the bowl and screen in dry-cleaning solvent. Dry thoroughly and install bowl, screen, and gasket. Examine for leakage after installation. Replace gasket if damaged.

(5) FUEL FILTER. Remove the sediment bowl and clean bowl and filtering screen in dry-cleaning solvent and dry thoroughly. Install the bowl, screen, and gasket and examine for leaks.

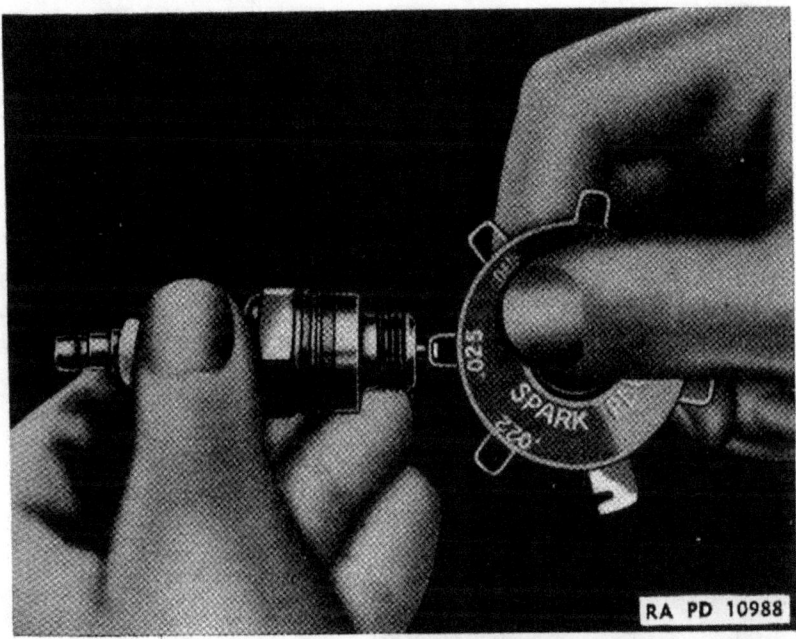

*Figure 53—Measuring Spark Plug Gap*

d. **Generator.** Observe charging rate at ammeter. Ammeter should show "plus" charge when engine is running. With engine off and electrical accessories on, the ammeter should show "minus" charge. Engine speed will vary the ammeter reading.

## 60. CYLINDER HEAD AND GASKET REMOVAL.

a. **Drain Coolant.** Drain coolant in system to a point below the level of coolant in the cylinder head by opening the drain cock in the radiator outlet pipe at lower left-hand side of radiator.

b. **Remove Hood.** Unhook the two latches at each side of hood and raise the sides high enough to rest them on the radiator shield corner. Unscrew and remove three bolts and safety nuts at each end of the center panel. Lift entire hood assembly from vehicle (fig. 65).

## TM 9-710
### BASIC HALF-TRACK VEHICLES (WHITE, AUTOCAR, and DIAMOND T)

c. **Remove Spark Plugs.** Unscrew the knurled coupling nuts on the six spark plug shields and lift off the upper shield assembly. Unscrew and remove the spark plugs, gaskets, and lower shields.

d. **Remove Breather Pipe Vent Tube and Engine Temperature Gage Bulb.** Unscrew coupling nut on crankcase vent tube at cylinder head, loosen hose clamp on vent tube at air cleaner end and pull line from connecting hose. Unscrew fitting on engine temperature gage bulb in cylinder head and lift unit from head.

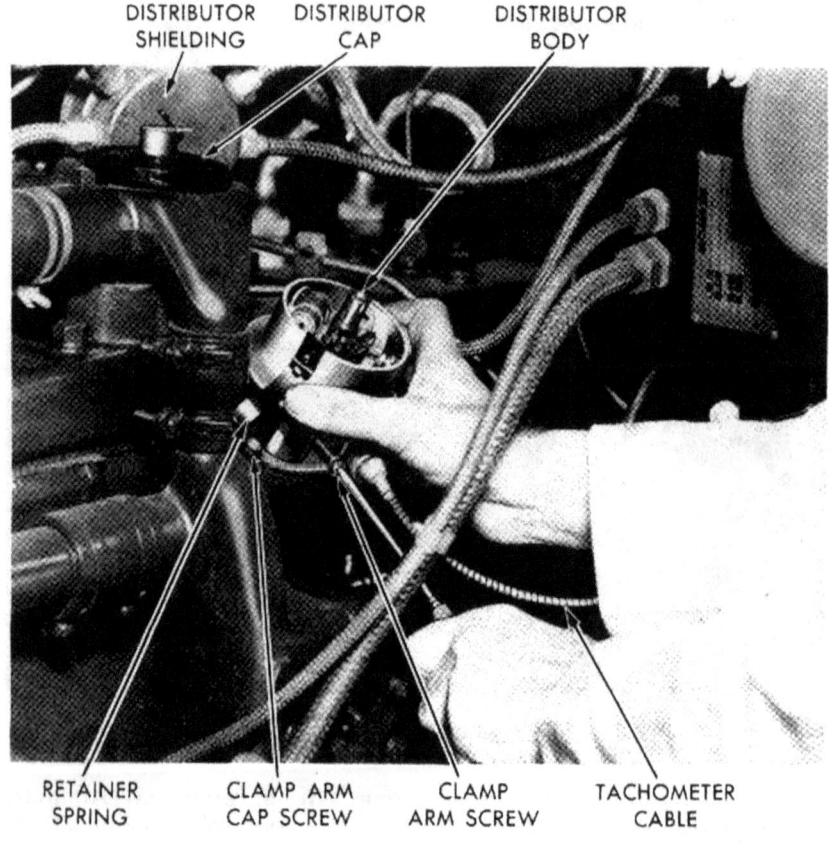

*Figure 54—Rotating Distributor Body to Advance Spark*

e. **Remove Fuel and Vacuum Lines.** Unscrew fuel line coupling nuts at fittings on lower front of vacuum-fuel pump (on left-hand side of engine) and upper front of carburetor fuel filter. Unscrew vacuum line coupling nuts at fitting on intake manifold and top rear of vacuum-fuel pump. Unscrew and remove cap screw from the clip which holds the fuel and vacuum lines to the head. Lift lines and clip from head.

f. **Remove Thermostat and Housing.** Refer to paragraph 89.

g. **Remove Head and Gasket.** Unscrew and remove 22 cylinder

## ENGINE DATA, MAINTENANCE, AND ADJUSTMENT IN VEHICLE

head cap screws and plain washers. Use a pinch bar on lugs at right-hand side of head to loosen, then lift head and gasket from engine.

### 61. CARBON REMOVAL.

a. **Plug Water Openings.** Plug all water openings and bolt holes in the top of the cylinder block with pieces of rags.

b. **Clean Carbon.** (fig. 55). At the time of removing cylinder head, clean the carbon deposits from the inside of the head, the top of the block, and the valves. Use a drill equipped with a carbon scraping wire brush if available. If drill is not available use a putty knife or file. Clean

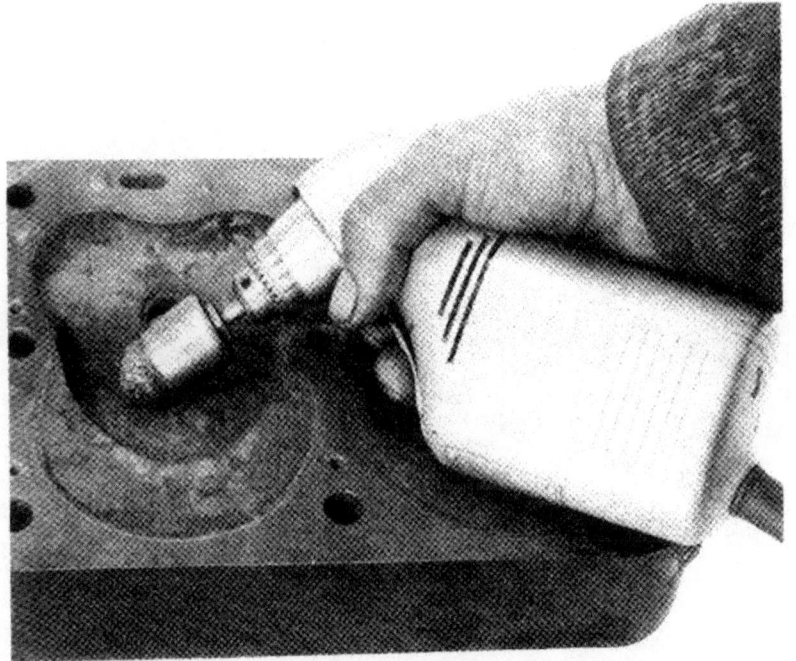

RA PD 3461

*Figure 55—Removing Carbon from Cylinder Head*

all surfaces and remove loosened carbon by blowing with air hose or wiping with cloth.

### 62. CYLINDER HEAD AND GASKET INSTALLATION.

a. **Replace Gasket.** Clean the surfaces of both cylinder head and block and place a new gasket in position.

b. **Install Cylinder Head.** Place the cylinder head in position on the block and gasket. Install cylinder head cap screws and plain washers, and partially tighten the 22 cap screws. Use a tension wrench to tighten the cap screws to a reading of 195 to 200 foot-pounds. Follow the tightening sequence shown in figure 56. Make a final check of the cap screw tension after engine has been thoroughly warmed up.

## TM 9-710

### BASIC HALF-TRACK VEHICLES (WHITE, AUTOCAR, and DIAMOND T)

c. **Install Fuel and Vacuum Lines.** Install fuel line at fitting on lower front of the vacuum-fuel pump and upper front of carburetor fuel filter and tighten the coupling nuts. Install vacuum line at fitting on intake manifold and top rear of vacuum-fuel pump and tighten coupling nuts. Install clip with cap screw holding the fuel line and vacuum line to cylinder head at the rear of the thermostat housing.

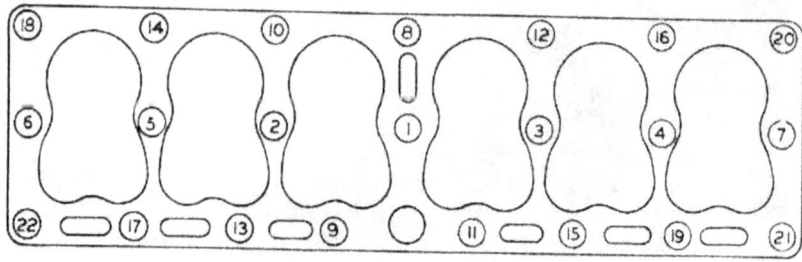

RA PD 3438

*Figure 56—Tightening Sequence, Cylinder Head Cap Screws*

d. **Install Breather Pipe Vent Tube and Engine Temperature Gage Bulb.** Insert crankcase vent tube in hose connection on air cleaner and tighten hose clamp; install coupling nut on cylinder head and tighten. Insert engine temperature gage bulb into the cylinder head and tighten nut on fitting.

e. **Install Thermostat Housing.** Refer to paragraph 89.

f. **Install Radiator Inlet Pipe and Hose.** Slip hose over connections at thermostat housing and radiator inlet and tighten the hose clamps.

**TM 9-710**
**62-63**

## ENGINE DATA, MAINTENANCE, AND ADJUSTMENT IN VEHICLE

g. **Install Spark Plugs.** Insert and tighten the six spark plugs with shields and gaskets. Install the upper shield assembly and tighten the round knurled coupling nuts by hand pressure only.

h. **Install Hood** (fig. 65). Place the hood in position with the three holes in each end of the center panel section lined up with corresponding holes in the dash and radiator shield. Install and tighten three bolts and safety nuts at each end of center panel. Lower the side panels and secure by fastening the two hand latches on each side of hood.

i. **Refill Cooling System.** Pour required amount of coolant in the radiator filler cap neck and inspect hose and head gasket for signs of any leakage.

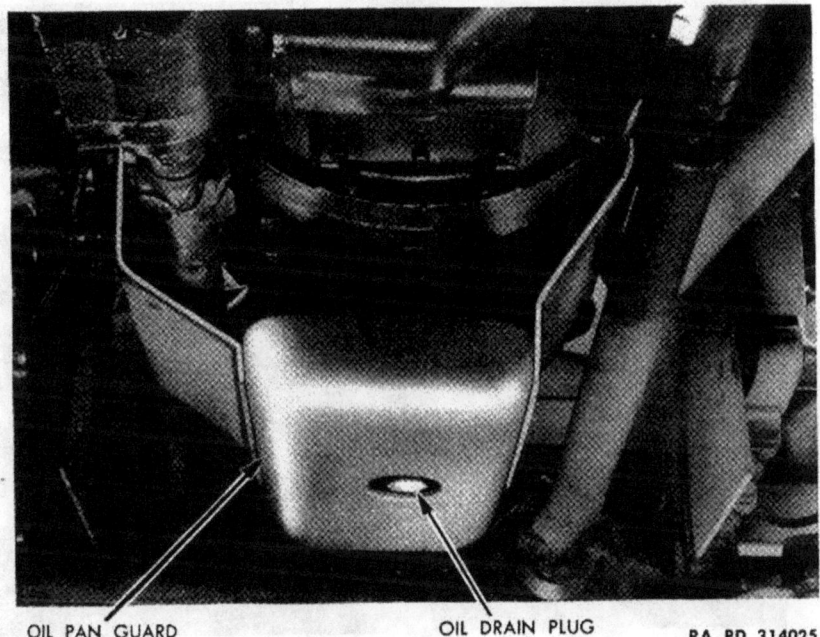

*Figure 57—Oil Pan Guard Installed*

### 63. OIL PAN AND GUARD.

a. **Removal.**

(1) DRAIN OIL. Unscrew and remove oil drain plug and gasket from bottom center of oil pan. Drain oil pan thoroughly. Clean the magnetic plug and screw plug and gasket into place.

(2) REMOVE GUARD (fig. 57). Remove six nuts, lock washers, and bolts from left-hand side of guard; five nuts, lock washers, and bolts from right-hand side of guard and remove the guard.

(3) REMOVE OIL PAN (fig. 58). Remove 26 cap screws and lock washers securing oil pan to crankcase. Lower oil pan to floor.

b. **Cleaning.** Wash pan out with dry-cleaning solvent and wipe dry. Scrape off any gasket pieces which may be sticking to the flange

# TM 9-710
63-64

## BASIC HALF-TRACK VEHICLES (WHITE, AUTOCAR, and DIAMOND T)

of the oil pan. Clean the magnetic drain plug of all articles adhering to it. Use a new drain plug gasket and screw drain plug into pan.

c. **Installation.**

(1) REPLACE GASKET. Clean the flange on bottom of crankcase of all foreign materials. Apply shellac to flange and place a new gasket in position.

(2) INSTALL OIL PAN. Lift oil pan to its proper position; install and partially tighten the 26 cap screws and lock washers. NOTE: *The three front cap screws use copper washers, as steel washers will not*

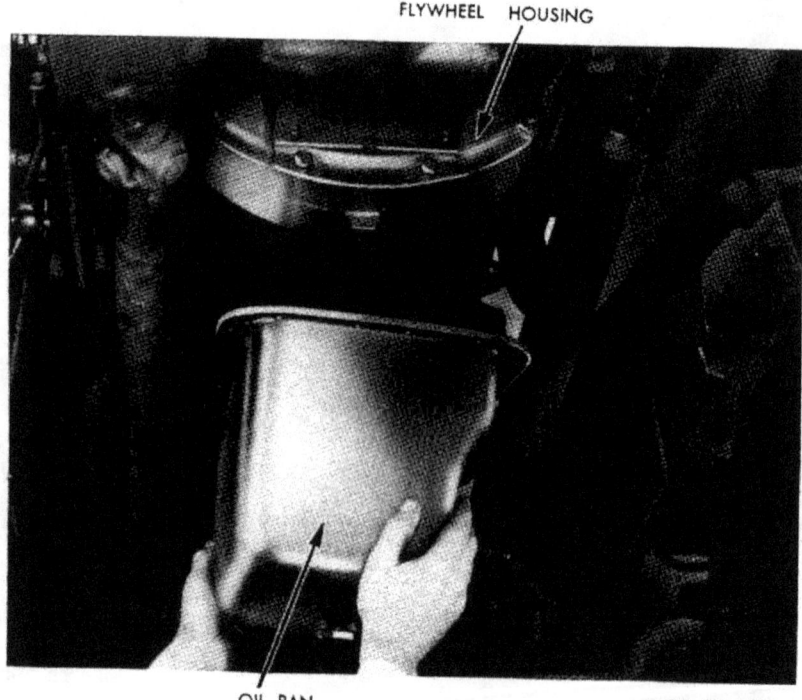

*Figure 58—Removing Oil Pan*

*retain the oil at this point.* Tighten all the cap screws a few turns at a time until all are secured with the same pressure.

(3) REFILL CRANKCASE. Pour 10 quarts of the specified grade of oil into the crankcase through the oil filler pipe. Check the oil level with the dipstick. Inspect the oil pan flange for leaks.

(4) INSTALL GUARD. Install guard in proper position and secure with six bolts, lock washers, and nuts on the left-hand side, five bolts, lock washers and nuts on the right-hand side.

## 64. OIL TEMPERATURE REGULATOR.

a. **Description and Tabulated Data.**

(1) DESCRIPTION AND OPERATION (fig. 60). The oil temperature regulator is bolted to the left-hand side of the crankcase directly below

# TM 9-710

## ENGINE DATA, MAINTENANCE, AND ADJUSTMENT IN VEHICLE

the distributor. The purpose of this unit is to maintain the engine oil at an even temperature. Oil is forced under pressure through a bellows type cooler inside a jacket which is surrounded by water from the cooling system of the vehicle. This tends to raise the temperature of the oil sooner when the engine is first started, and also keeps the oil at a normal operating temperature after warming up.

(2) TABULATED DATA.
Make............Harrison Radiator Corporation
Model..............................HE 30-6
Type..................................8 plate
Manufacturer's No...................8501562

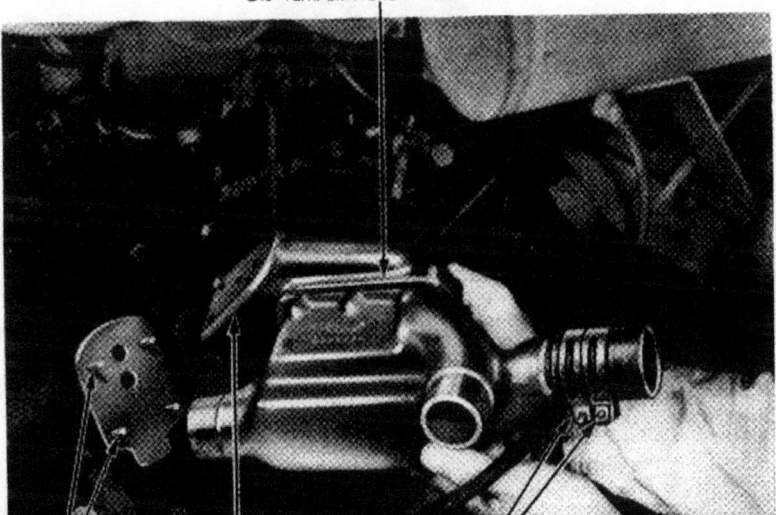

*Figure 59—Removing Oil Temperature Regulator*

b. **Removal.**

(1) DRAIN COOLING SYSTEM. Open drain cocks in radiator outlet pipe at bottom left-hand side of radiator, and at left-hand center of cylinder block, and drain cooling system.

(2) DISCONNECT HOSE CONNECTIONS. Loosen hose clamps on hose connection between lower radiator inlet pipe and bottom of oil temperature regulator. Loosen hose clamps on hose connection at front end of oil temperature regulator to water pump pipe. Loosen hose clamps at top hose connection of oil temperature regulator-to-thermostat housing.

(3) REMOVE OIL TEMPERATURE REGULATOR (fig. 59). Remove four nuts and lock washers securing oil temperature regulator and gasket to crankcase. Pull assembly and gasket from hose and studs.

## TM 9-710
## BASIC HALF-TRACK VEHICLES (WHITE, AUTOCAR, and DIAMOND T)

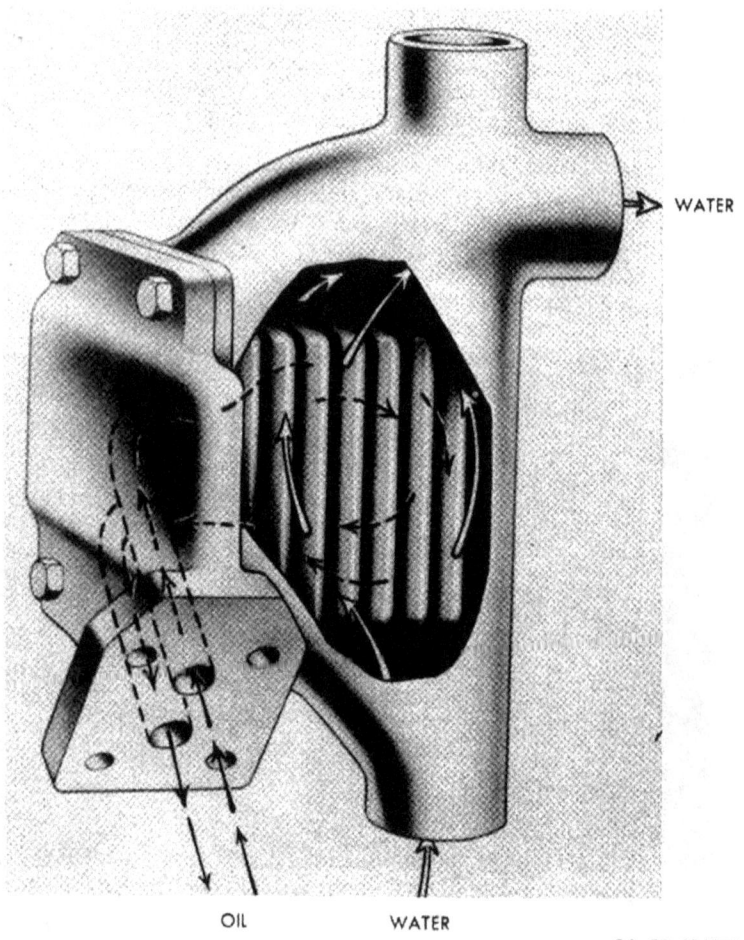

*Figure 60—Sectional View of Passage of Water and Oil through Oil Temperature Regulator*

c. Installation.

(1) INSTALL OIL TEMPERATURE REGULATOR. Replace gasket between oil temperature regulator and engine block and position assembly on the studs and gasket. Install and tighten four lock washers and nuts to attaching studs.

(2) CONNECT HOSE CONNECTIONS. Slip hose connection from oil temperature regulator to thermostat, into place; also the hose connection from oil temperature regulator to radiator outlet pipe connection, and from oil temperature regulator to water pump pipe. Tighten hose clamps on all three hose.

**TM 9-710**
**64-65**

## ENGINE DATA, MAINTENANCE, AND ADJUSTMENT IN VEHICLE

(3) REFILL COOLING SYSTEM. Pour required amount of coolant into radiator filler cap neck after closing the drain cock on radiator outlet pipe.

(4) BYPASSING (fig. 61). If no replacement unit is available for a damaged or faulty oil temperature regulator, the unit may be bypassed by drilling or chiseling away the web (metal between oil passages) of the oil cooler bracket, to a depth equal to the diameter of the oil passage. This metal is taken from the web at the flange face which fastens to the engine block. Replace faulty cooling element as quickly as possible. When replacing element, install a new bracket.

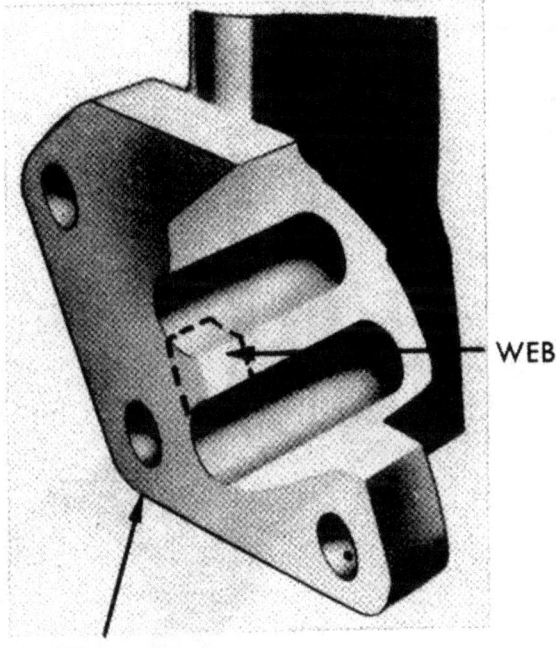

*Figure 61—Sectional View Showing Part of Regulator to be Removed to Bypass Oil Temperature Regulator*

65. **OIL FILTER** (fig. 62).

   a. **Description and Tabulated Data.**

   (1) DESCRIPTION. The oil filter is the partial flow cartridge type with no outside connecting oil lines. It is mounted on the front right-hand corner of the engine block with the oil lines enclosed in the base of the mounting bracket.

   (2) TABULATED DATA.
   Make............De Luxe Products Corporation
   Model ............................CS-602W
   Type ...............................cartridge

145

TM 9-710
65-66

**BASIC HALF-TRACK VEHICLES (WHITE, AUTOCAR, and DIAMOND T)**

  b. **Maintenance.** Examine the oil on the bayonet gage and when sludge accumulation is apparent or when the oil becomes a dark opaque color, replace the cartridge as follows:

  (1) REMOVE ELEMENT. Unscrew T-handle at top of filter and lift off cover, gasket, and handle. Lift out oil filtering element and discard.

  (2) DRAIN SUMP. Unscrew and remove drain plug at bottom of filter. Flush and clean the sump with dry-cleaning solvent and wipe dry. Install and tighten the drain plug.

  (3) INSTALL ELEMENT. Insert new filtering element. Install gasket and cover. Secure by installing and tightening T-handle by hand. NOTE: *It will be necessary to add oil after changing element to bring oil in crankcase up to full mark.*

RA PD 314030

*Figure 62—Oil Filter (Sectional View)*

  c. **Removal.** Remove four cap screws and lock washers securing oil filter and base to engine block. Lift off oil filter assembly and base gasket.

  d. **Installation.** Place oil filter assembly and base gasket in proper position on right front corner of engine and secure with four lock washers and cap screws.

**66. CRANKCASE VENTILATOR.**

  a. **Description.** Ventilation of the crankcase is accomplished by a vent tube running from inside the crankcase to the bottom of the air cleaner. The suction of the intake system through the air cleaner and crankcase vent tube withdraws fumes from the crankcase. The air thus withdrawn is replaced by air passing through openings inside the oil

## ENGINE DATA, MAINTENANCE, AND ADJUSTMENT IN VEHICLE

filler cap. The cap has a filter built into it which cleans the air drawn into the crankcase.

**b. Maintenance.** Keep vent tube connections tight and inspect the hose connection between copper vent tube and air cleaner and replace if hose is disintegrated. Clean the oil filler cap in dry-cleaning solvent and blow dry with compressed air.

**c. Removal.** Loosen hose clamps on the breather tube hose at bottom of air cleaner. Unscrew fitting on breather tube connection to the cylinder head and lift off breather tube assembly.

**d. Installation.** Install the breather tube hose to connection at bottom of air cleaner with two hose clamps on hose. Insert plain end of breather tube in hose and tighten hose clamps. Install other end of breather tube to cylinder head opening and tighten coupling nut on fitting.

TM 9-710
67

**BASIC HALF-TRACK VEHICLES (WHITE, AUTOCAR, and DIAMOND T)**

Section XIV

# ENGINE REMOVAL AND INSTALLATION

|  | Paragraph |
|---|---|
| Engine removal | 67 |
| Engine installation | 68 |

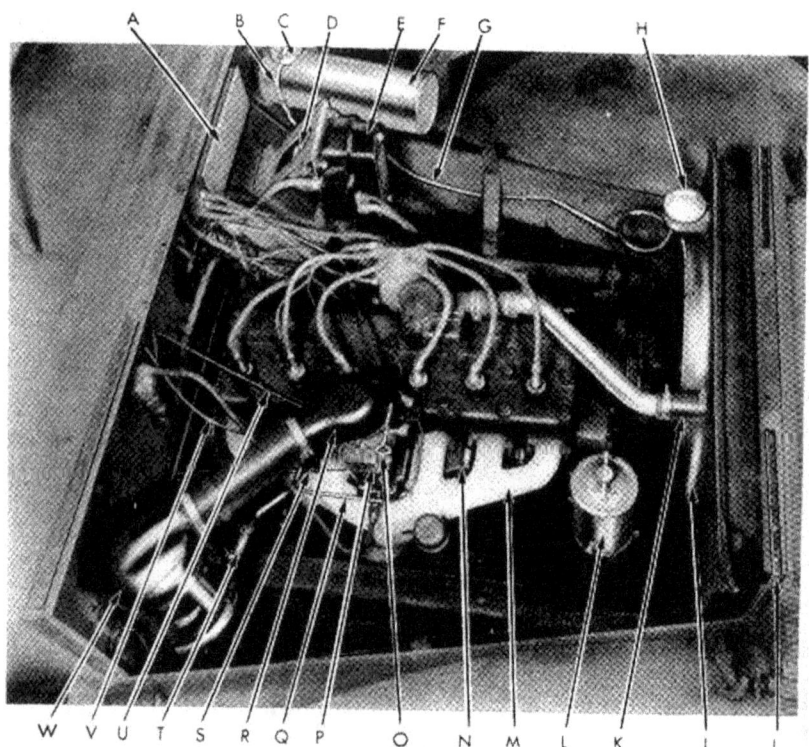

A—IGNITION COIL BOX
B—OVERFLOW
C—PRESSURE CAP
D—HYDROVAC AIR CLEANER
E—VOLTAGE REGULATOR
F—SURGE TANK
G—SURGE TANK LINE
H—RADIATOR FILLER CAP
I—ANTI-SQUEAK
J—SHROUD
K—RADIATOR INLET PIPE
L—OIL FILTER
M—EXHAUST MANIFOLD
N—INTAKE MANIFOLD
O—THUMB SCREW
P—CARBURETOR
Q—THROTTLE ROD
R—AIR CLEANER HORN
S—THROTTLE ROD RETURN SPRING
T—CRANKCASE BREATHER TUBE HOSE
U—HAND THROTTLE CABLE
V—CHOKE CABLE
W—AIR CLEANER

RA PD 314031

*Figure 63—Engine Installed*

TM 9-710
67

## ENGINE REMOVAL AND INSTALLATION

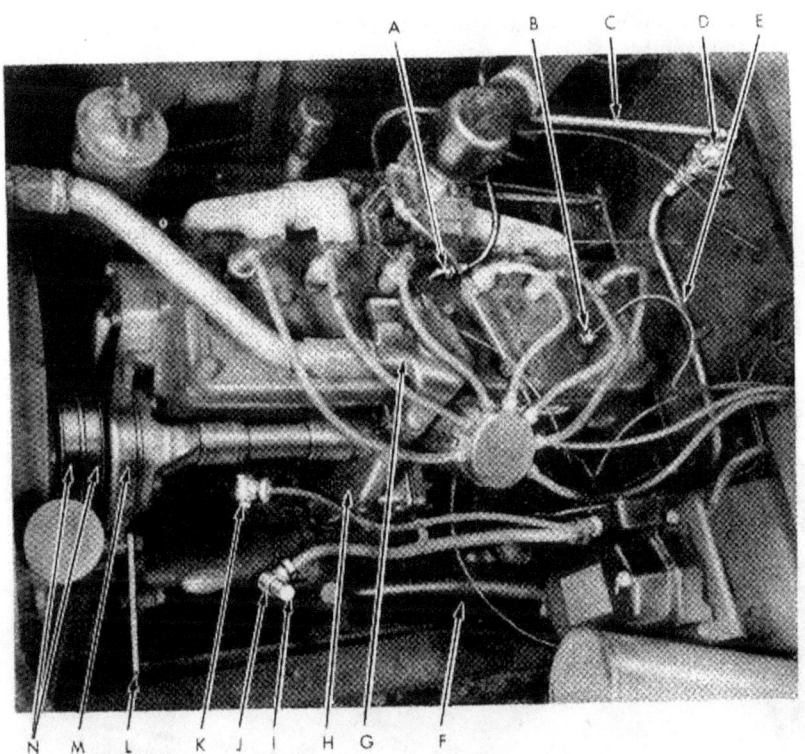

A—CRANKCASE BREATHER TUBE COUPLING
B—WATER TEMPERATURE GAGE BULB
C—INTAKE TO CHECK VALVE VACUUM LINE
D—CHECK VALVE
E—CHECK VALVE TO HYDROVAC VACUUM LINE
F—CAB VENTILATOR AIR FUNNEL
G—THERMOSTAT HOUSING
H—OIL TEMPERATURE REGULATOR
I—CONDENSER
J—ARMATURE TERMINAL
K—FIELD TERMINAL SHIELD
L—ADJUSTING STRAP
M—WATER PUMP
N—FAN BELTS

RA PD 314032

*Figure 64—Engine Installed*

**67. ENGINE REMOVAL** (figs. 63 and 64).

a. **Disconnect Battery Terminals.** Remove two cap screws and lock washers from front end of battery box cover located on right front of running board and slide cover aside. Disconnect and tape the negative terminal cable of battery and slide cover back in place.

b. **Remove Hood.** Drop the latches at each side of hood and raise sides of hood, resting them on the edge of the cowl. Remove three bolts and safety nuts from each end of the hood center panel. Remove hood assembly using rope sling and hoist (fig. 65). Remove two bolts and safety nuts holding the top cross member of the radiator louver assembly to the upright brackets. Punch out bottom rivet holding radiator anti-

149

# TM 9-710

## BASIC HALF-TRACK VEHICLES (WHITE, AUTOCAR, and DIAMOND T)

squeak to each side of radiator. Lift off top cross member of radiator shutter assembly.

c. **Remove Cab Ventilator Air Funnel.** Remove nut, lock washer, and bolt holding air funnel clamp to engine side shield. Loosen screw clamp holding ventilator tube to box on toeboard and remove flexible tube and funnel.

d. **Remove Oil Pan Guard.** Remove six nuts, lock washers, and bolts, holding oil pan guard to frame on the left side, and five nuts, lock washers, and bolts on the right side and lower guard to floor.

e. **Remove Winch Propeller Shaft.** Unscrew jam nut on the set screw holding the propeller shaft universal joint to the power take-off

*Figure 65—Removing Hood*

shaft and back off set screw. Push propeller shaft forward (the slip joint at winch end will allow the rear universal joint to clear the power take-off shaft) then pull propeller shaft free of front universal slip joint and remove propeller shaft.

f. **Drain Coolant and Disconnect Radiator Hose, Pipes, and Lines.** Open drain cock in radiator outlet pipe at bottom left corner of radiator, and the drain cock in engine block just below the oil temperature regulator, and drain coolant. Loosen hose clamps on radiator inlet pipe at radiator and thermostat housing and remove hose and pipe. Loosen hose clamps on radiator outlet pipe at radiator and bottom of oil temperature regulator; remove nut, bolt, and lock washer holding pipe bracket to generator bracket and remove pipe. Unscrew coupling nut on both ends of surge tank line, remove nut, lock washer, and bolt holding clip to side panel and lift off surge tank line.

## ENGINE REMOVAL AND INSTALLATION

g. **Remove Oil Filter.** Remove four cap screws and lock washers securing oil filter and base to engine block. Lift off oil filter assembly and base gasket.

h. **Remove Water Pump and Fan Assembly** (fig. 83). Remove nut, lock washer, and bolt holding belt adjusting strap to water pump housing. Loosen hose clamps on pipe from water pump to oil temperature regulator. Remove six cap screws and lock washers attaching water pump housing to block. Remove V-belts from drive shaft pulley and generator pulley and lift off fan and water pump assembly with spacer gasket and belts.

i. **Remove Radiator and Shroud** (fig. 87). Remove cotter pin, nut, washers, and coil spring from each of the two bottom radiator studs at the underside of the frame cross member. Remove nuts and lock washers from the two side radiator stabilizer rods and pull rods off studs. Lift radiator and shroud out of the shutter front. Lift off the two anti-squeak pads at the bottom studs of the radiator.

j. **Disconnect Tachometer Cable.** Unscrew coupling nut on tachometer cable at adapter just below distributor and place cable to one side.

k. **Disconnect Lines.** Unscrew coupling nut and pull engine temperature gage bulb from the cylinder head and tie in a safe position on cowl. Unscrew coupling nut on oil line at left side of engine below front end of cranking motor and pull line to one side. Shut off the fuel line at the transfer valve behind the driver's seat and unscrew coupling nut on fuel line at rear side of fuel pump. Unscrew coupling nut on vacuum line to windshield wipers at top front of vacuum-fuel pump and pull line to one side. Unscrew coupling nuts on vacuum line running from center of intake manifold to brake check valve and remove line.

l. **Remove Air Cleaner Tube and Crankcase Breather Tube.** Loosen thumb screw on air cleaner horn clamp at top of carburetor; loosen hose clamp at air cleaner and pull hose and horn from assembly. Loosen hose clamp on crankcase breather tube at air cleaner end and unscrew coupling nut holding tube to top of cylinder head and remove tube.

m. **Disconnect Carburetor Controls.** Unscrew nut and lock washer on ball socket joint of accelerator throttle rod at carburetor and lower this end. Unhook return spring from clip on stud at carburetor. Loosen set screw on choke and hand throttle wires, at carburetor. Unscrew clamps holding the choke and throttle cables in position, and remove cables to position on cowl. Pull accelerator pedal free of rod inside driver's compartment. Remove nut, lockwasher, and bolt from throttle bell crank under left toeboard and place rod assembly to one side.

n. **Disconnect Exhaust Pipe at Manifold.** Unscrew three high hex nuts from exhaust manifold studs at connection to exhaust pipe.

o. **Disconnect Cranking Motor Terminals.** Unscrew nut, washers, and lock washer holding battery cable to solenoid switch and remove cable. Unscrew nut and washer holding starter button cable to switch (red wire on top of solenoid switch) and remove wire. Remove cap screw and clamp holding cable conduit to cranking motor housing.

TM 9-710

## BASIC HALF-TRACK VEHICLES (WHITE, AUTOCAR, and DIAMOND T)

p. **Disconnect Distributor and Generator Cables.** Remove ignition coil box cover on cowl. Unscrew nut on low tension cable (small wire at top of coil) and remove wire from coil. Unscrew clamp screw holding high tension cable to center post of coil and pull out cable. Unscrew coupling nuts holding cable shielding to coil box and remove cables and shielding from coil box. Unscrew cap from field terminal shield, on side of generator next to engine, and remove nut, and lock washer, from terminal therein. Unscrew nut on shielding and remove cable and shielding from terminal post. Remove condenser from armature terminal shield of generator and remove nut and lock washer from terminal post therein. Unscrew nut on shielding, holding shielding and cable to terminal shield, and remove cable assembly. Tie the generator cables in safe position on cowl.

FRONT TRUNNION BRACKET　　　ENGINE REAR SUPPORT
RA PD 314034

*Figure 66—Engine Supports*

q. **Remove Floor Plates and Disconnect Clutch Release Lever.** Remove nuts, bolts, and lock washers holding small floor plate around transfer case levers. Lift off small plate after unscrewing knob on transfer case lever. Remove nuts, lock washers, and bolts holding tunnel floor plate over transmission and remove plate. Remove nuts, lock washers, and bolts holding left floor plate, and remove plate. Remove nut, lock washer, bolt, and clamp holding brake vacuum line to lower right corner of left toeboard. Disconnect clutch release lever rod, loosen clamp bolt, and remove lever from shaft.

r. **Remove Engine Support Bolts** (fig. 66). Remove cotter pin, castle nut, bolt, and washer from the rear engine support at each side of flywheel housing. Remove two nuts, lock washers, and bolts from each side of front engine trunnion.

s. **Block-up Transmission.** Place a jack under forward end of transmission housing to hold it in normal running position and remove 12 cap screws and lock washers holding transmission bell housing to flywheel housing. Remove bottom inspection plate from bell housing and disconnect flexible grease tube at the bottom of throwout bearing.

# ENGINE REMOVAL AND INSTALLATION

1. **Remove Engine from Chassis** (fig. 67). Place a figure eight sling of ¾-inch rope around the engine. Run rope through front of engine manifold, around and under front of engine, cross over at the hook on hoist, through rear of manifold down around flywheel housing, and return to hook. Draw up slack in rope with hoist. Raise engine one inch, disconnect exhaust pipe from manifold, then pull forward, disengaging clutch from transmission splined shaft and proceed to lift engine from chassis.

## 68. ENGINE INSTALLATION.

a. **Install Engine on Chassis.** Insert the small end of a clutch alining tool or mandrel through the clutch plate hub and aline clutch

*Figure 67—Method of Attaching Rope Sling to Engine*

plate hub and clutch throwout bearing. Remove inspection plate from bottom of transmission and jack up transmission until transmission splined shaft is centered between the rear engine mounts. Sling engine with three-quarter inch manila rope as shown in figure 67. Attach sling to a hoist of one-ton capacity and hoist engine to position. Lower engine carefully and engage the transmission splined shaft with the pilot bearing and clutch spline after carefully alining both units. Attach lubricator tube to the throwout bearing, and tilt clutch release lever fork toward rear of vehicle. Aline front and rear engine mounts, exhaust pipe flange, and lower engine to frame. NOTE: *If clutch and transmission splined shaft are not correctly alined the engine will be held in a forward position. Also the engine may push the transmission toward the rear approximately an inch in installation, because the transmission and its spring support mounting can slip rearward because of the slip joint connection of the rear propeller shaft.* Install two rear engine support bolts, washers, castle nuts, and cotter pins. Install four front trunnion bolts, lock washers, and nuts. Secure exhaust pipe and gasket to manifold studs with three high hex nuts.

TM 9-710
68

## BASIC HALF-TRACK VEHICLES (WHITE, AUTOCAR, and DIAMOND T)

b. **Secure Transmission.** If transmission has slipped rearward, use a bar to pry it forward. Install the battery cable clips and 12 cap screws and lock washers through transmission bellhousing to flywheel housing. Tighten screws evenly to prevent transmission splined shaft from binding in flywheel pilot bearing.

c. **Install Clutch Release Lever.** Inspect clutch release lever fork through inspection plate hole at bottom of transmission, to see if it has free movement between clutch throwout bearing and clutch spring plate hub. Install clutch release lever in proper position on release shaft and tighten clamp bolt. Connect clutch release lever to end yoke. Install bottom inspection plate cover. Install clamp to vacuum brake line on lower right corner of left toeboard. Remove jack supporting transmission and rope sling from engine.

d. **Install Radiator and Shroud.** Hoist radiator and shroud in rope sling (fig. 87) and lower into position making certain the two antisqueak pads are in place over the studs on the bottom of the radiator. Secure radiator side stabilizer rods to studs with lock washers and nuts. Install coil spring, washer, and castellated nut on the two bottom studs. Tighten nuts, leaving a small space between each coil of the spring, and secure nuts with cotter pins.

e. **Install Water Pump and Fan Assembly** (fig. 83). Install water pump and fan assembly with belts and spacer gasket to engine block and connecting water pipe. Secure assembly to block with six lock washers and cap screws. Slip belts over pulleys of crankshaft and generator and install belt adjusting strap to water pump housing, securing strap with bolt, lock washer, and nut. Adjust belts to proper tension (par. 86) and secure setting.

f. **Install Oil Filter.** Place oil filter assembly and base gasket in proper position on right front corner of engine and secure with four lock washers and cap screws.

g. **Connect Carburetor Controls.** Push accelerator pedal onto rod inside of driver's compartment. Connect throttle bell crank to assembly and secure with bolt, lock washer, and nut. Install throttle rod and return spring to carburetor. Install choke and throttle wire assembly to carburetor, and secure clamps and set screws.

h. **Install Air Cleaner Tube and Crankcase Breather Tube.** Install air cleaner hose and horn assembly to carburetor and air cleaner; secure horn to top of carburetor with thumb screw clamp, and the hose connection to air cleaner with hose clamp. Install crankcase breather tube to hose at bottom of air cleaner and tighten the hose clamp; secure opposite end to cylinder head with coupling nut.

i. **Install Lines.** Install brake vacuum line to bottom of check valve and intake manifold. Insert engine temperature gage bulb in cylinder head opening and secure with coupling nut. Install oil pressure line to fitting on left side of engine. Install the fuel line from the fuel tank to the rear of fuel pump and turn on fuel at transfer valve. Install vacuum line to top of vacuum fuel pump.

j. **Install Tachometer Cable.** Install tachometer cable to adapter at bottom of distributor and secure with coupling nut.

## ENGINE REMOVAL AND INSTALLATION

k. **Install Cranking Motor Terminals.** Install battery cable to terminal on side of the solenoid switch and secure with washer, lock washer, and nut. Install starter button cable to top of solenoid switch and secure with washer and nut. Install clamp with cap screw securing cable conduit to cranking motor housing.

l. **Install Distributor and Generator Cables.** Install low tension cable and shielding to coil and secure with nut (fig. 92). Install high tension cable and shielding to coil and secure with clamp screw. Secure shielding and nuts to connections at coil box and install box cover. Install cables and shielding to terminal posts on generator (fig. 101). Install condenser into top of armature terminal shield of generator and cap on the field terminal shield.

m. **Install Cab Ventilator Air Funnel.** Place ventilator tube in box on toeboard and secure with screw clamp. Install air funnel and clamp to engine side shield and secure with bolt, lock washer, and nut.

n. **Install Radiator Hose, Pipes, and Lines.** Install and tighten the inlet and outlet hose and pipes on radiator. Secure radiator outlet pipe bracket to generator bracket with bolt, lock washer, and nut. Install radiator surge tank line to surge tank and radiator filler spout and secure coupling nuts; secure surge tank line clip to side panel with bolt, lock washer, and nut. Close drain cocks and refill system.

o. **Install Winch Propeller Shaft.** Install winch propeller shaft to winch worm drive shaft universal joint by inserting propeller shaft spline end through opening in bottom corner of radiator and armor shield. Pull rear end of winch propeller shaft onto the power take-off shaft and Woodruff key and secure connection with screw and jam nut.

p. **Install Oil Pan Guard.** Install oil pan guard in proper position and secure left-hand side to frame with six bolts, lock washers, and nuts, and the right-hand side with five bolts, lock washers, and nuts.

q. **Install Hood.** Install the top cross member of the radiator shutter assembly and secure with two bolts and safety nuts. Secure the antisqueak pads to the radiator with two rivets. Sling the hood with a rope sling and hoist it into position to install (fig. 65). Secure the rear center panel of hood to cowl with three bolts and safety nuts; secure the front end of center panel to radiator shutter assembly with three bolts and safety nuts. Remove rope sling, lower side panels of hood, and fasten hood latches.

r. **Install Battery Terminals.** Slide battery box cover aside and remove tape from negative terminal cable. Install cable to negative terminal of battery and secure battery box cover with lock washers and cap screws.

s. **Install Floor Plates.** Install center floor plate over transmission tunnel and secure with bolts, lock washers, and nuts. Slip small section of center floor plate over transfer case levers and secure. Screw round knob onto transfer case shift lever. Install left-hand floor plate and secure with bolts, lock washers, and nuts.

**TM 9-710**
**69**

**BASIC HALF-TRACK VEHICLES (WHITE, AUTOCAR, and DIAMOND T)**

A - RELEASE BEARING OIL TUBE. W/LUBRICATOR
B - BEARING RETAINING RING
C - RELEASE BEARING
D - SLEEVE
E - CLUTCH RELEASE BEARING COVER
F - SHIFTER YOKE BUTTON
G - SLEEVE BUSHING
H - CLUTCH TO FLYWHEEL SCREW  W/LOCK WASHER
J - ADJUSTING RING
K - ADJUSTING RING LOCK
L - LOCKSCREW. W/LOCKWASHER

RA PD 314036

*Figure 68—Clutch Installed*

TM 9-710
69-70

Section XV

# CLUTCH

|   | Paragraph |
|---|---|
| Description and tabulated data | 69 |
| Adjustments | 70 |
| Removal | 71 |
| Installation | 72 |

## 69. DESCRIPTION AND TABULATED DATA.

**a. Description.** The clutch is a single-plate, dry-disk type and is secured to the engine flywheel (fig. 68). It provides a flexible connection between the engine and transmission, cushioning the stress of power applied to the driving train, and assists in the selection of transmission speeds.

**b. Tabulated Data.**
  Make ........................................ Spicer
  Model No. ................................... 001863
  Type ................................. Dry, single-plate

## 70. ADJUSTMENTS.

**a. Free Pedal Adjustment.**

(1) GENERAL. Maintain the free pedal travel at one inch to 1½ inches. Natural wear on the clutch facing will cause this measurement to decrease. Less than one-half inch free movement will require ad-

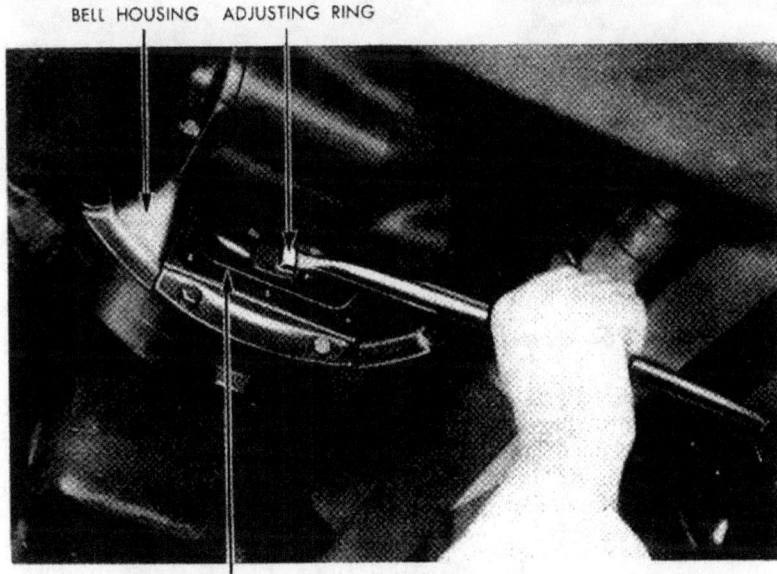

*Figure 69—Turning Adjusting Ring*

# TM 9-710

## BASIC HALF-TRACK VEHICLES (WHITE, AUTOCAR, and DIAMOND T)

justment. The adjustment is made on the clutch adjusting ring located inside the clutch housing, after removing inspection plate at bottom of housing (fig. 69). NOTE: *When properly adjusted, the space between the clutch release bearing and the clutch spring plate hub will be not more than one-half inch, nor less than three-eighths of an inch.*

(2) REMOVE ADJUSTING RING LOCK. Unscrew and remove the cap screw, lock washer, and adjusting ring lock.

*Figure 70—Clutch Springs Blocked for Clutch Removal*

(3) ADJUST PEDAL TRAVEL. Partially depress clutch pedal. Rotate clutch adjusting ring clockwise by tapping lugs on rim of ring with hammer and a brass drift (fig. 69). Test pedal "lash" and move adjusting ring until "lash" is correct. If proper adjustment cannot be obtained by adjusting ring, new clutch facings are required. Refer to proper authority.

(4) INSTALL ADJUSTING RING LOCK PLATE. Line up lugs on locking ring rim so lock can be installed between them. Secure lock plate with lock washer and cap screw, and install inspection plate cover.

## CLUTCH

**71. REMOVAL.**

a. **Block Clutch Springs.** Remove the clutch bottom inspection plate, depress clutch pedal, and insert two pieces of wood three-quarter inch square by three inches long between the release bearing housing and the spring plate hub. Release clutch pedal and proceed to remove transmission and transfer case.

b. **Remove Transmission and Transfer Case Assembly.** See paragraph 102.

c. **Remove Clutch.** Install a spare clutch shaft (or mandrel) of the correct size, to support the clutch. Loosen twelve cap screws and lock washers one turn at a time to prevent distortion, until the diaphragm spring pressure is completely released. Remove cap screws and lock washers, and lift out clutch assembly.

**72. INSTALLATION.**

a. **Block Clutch Springs** (fig. 70). Place clutch assembly in an arbor press with the clutch release bearing housing on the top side. Compress ring assembly and install two wood blocks three-quarter inch square by three inches long between the release bearing housing and the spring plate hub.

b. **Install Clutch Driven Disk.** Test disk with straightedge to make sure it is true. Set disk in place in the flywheel housing with the splined hub facing out.

c. **Install Clutch Assembly.** Push the clutch alining shaft through the disk hub and into the pilot bearing opening. Place clutch assembly with release bearing housing facing out, on the alining shaft and line up holes in clutch outer rim with holes in the flywheel. Install and secure the twelve lock washers and cap screws, tightening cap screws a few turns at a time until all are evenly secured. Remove the clutch alining shaft but leave the wood blocks in place until the transmission is installed.

d. **Install Transmission.** Refer to paragraph 103.

TM 9-710
73

**BASIC HALF-TRACK VEHICLES (WHITE, AUTOCAR, and DIAMOND T)**

Section XVI

## FUEL SYSTEM

|  | Paragraph |
|---|---|
| Description and tabulated data for system | 73 |
| Fuel tanks | 74 |
| Fuel and vacuum pump | 75 |
| Fuel filter | 76 |
| Carburetor | 77 |
| Air cleaner | 78 |

### 73. DESCRIPTION AND TABULATED DATA FOR SYSTEM.

**a. Description.** The air-fuel system consists of two fuel tanks, a transfer and shut-off valve (fig. 72), combination fuel and vacuum pump, fuel filter, carburetor, air cleaner, throttle and choke controls, and engine manifolds (fig. 71). Flexible fuel lines and connections are inserted at points between the tanks, the anchored lines, and the fuel pump, to eliminate breakage from vibration.

**b. Operation.** Fuel is drawn from the tanks by vacuum created within the fuel pump through transfer and shut-off valve into the pump, and is then forced in the required amounts by the fuel pump to the filter and carburetor. The fuel is broken into particles and mixed with air in the carburetor, and is then drawn into the intake manifold and cylinders.

**c. Tabulated Data.**

(1) FUEL AND VACUUM PUMP.
  Make .................................................. A. C.
  Model No. ......................................... 1537524
  Type ................... combination fuel and vacuum
  Location ........................... left rear of engine

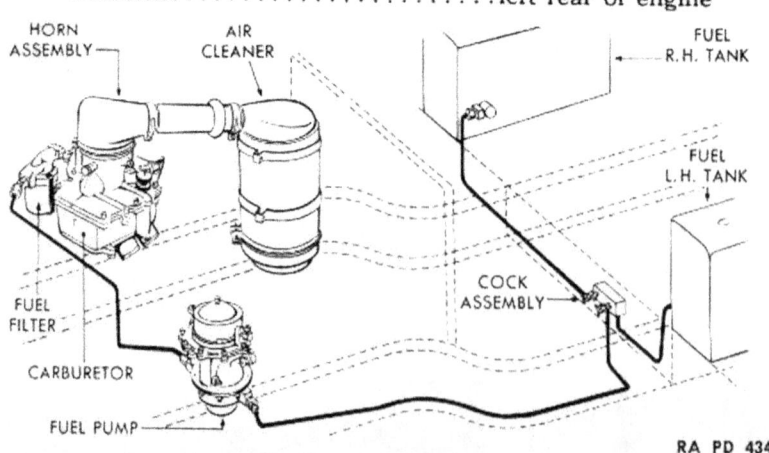

Figure 71—Fuel System

TM 9-710
73-74

## FUEL SYSTEM

(2) FUEL FILTER.
Make ................................. Zenith
Model No........................... F349X3
Type ........................ metallic element
Location .............. attached to carburetor

(3) CARBURETOR.
Make ............................. Stromberg
Model No. ........................... 380053
Type .................. duplex downdraft aero
Location .................... above manifolds

(4) AIR CLEANER.
Make ............................ Donaldson
Model No. ............................. E787
Type............................... oil bath
Location ............... cowl right-hand side

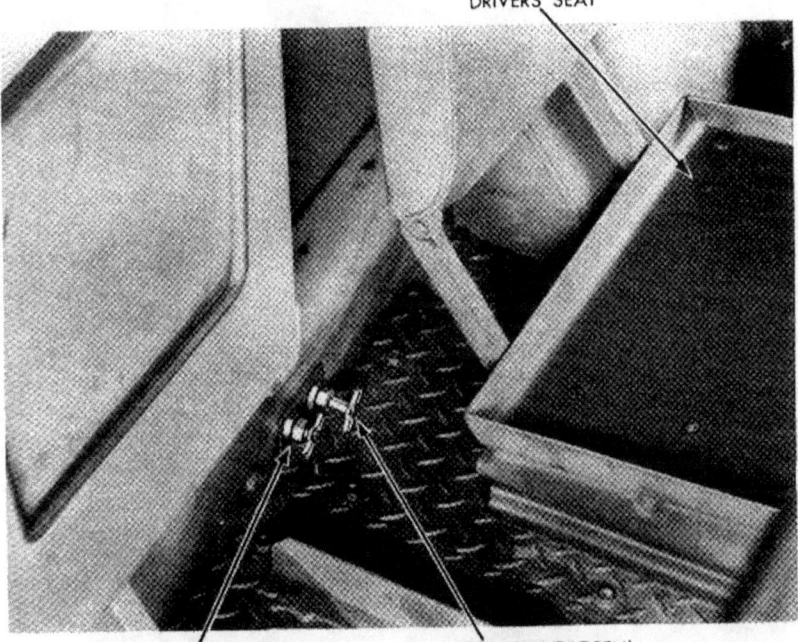

TRANSFER VALVE (CLOSED)   TRANSFER VALVE (OPEN)
(RIGHT HAND TANK)          (LEFT HAND TANK)     RA PD 314039

*Figure 72—Fuel Tank Transfer Valve*

74. **FUEL TANKS.**

a. **Description.** Two tanks of 30 gallons capacity each are provided on each vehicle (fig. 73). Locations differ, but all are within the body. A self-sealing composition covers each tank. The filler cap has a small breather valve which allows air to replace the fuel withdrawn by the fuel pump, and to allow the escape of expanded gases. A special screen is provided at the opening of the filler cap which acts as a flame arrester in case of a spark occurring when filling the tanks. A drain

**TM 9-710**
74

**BASIC HALF-TRACK VEHICLES (WHITE, AUTOCAR, and DIAMOND T)**

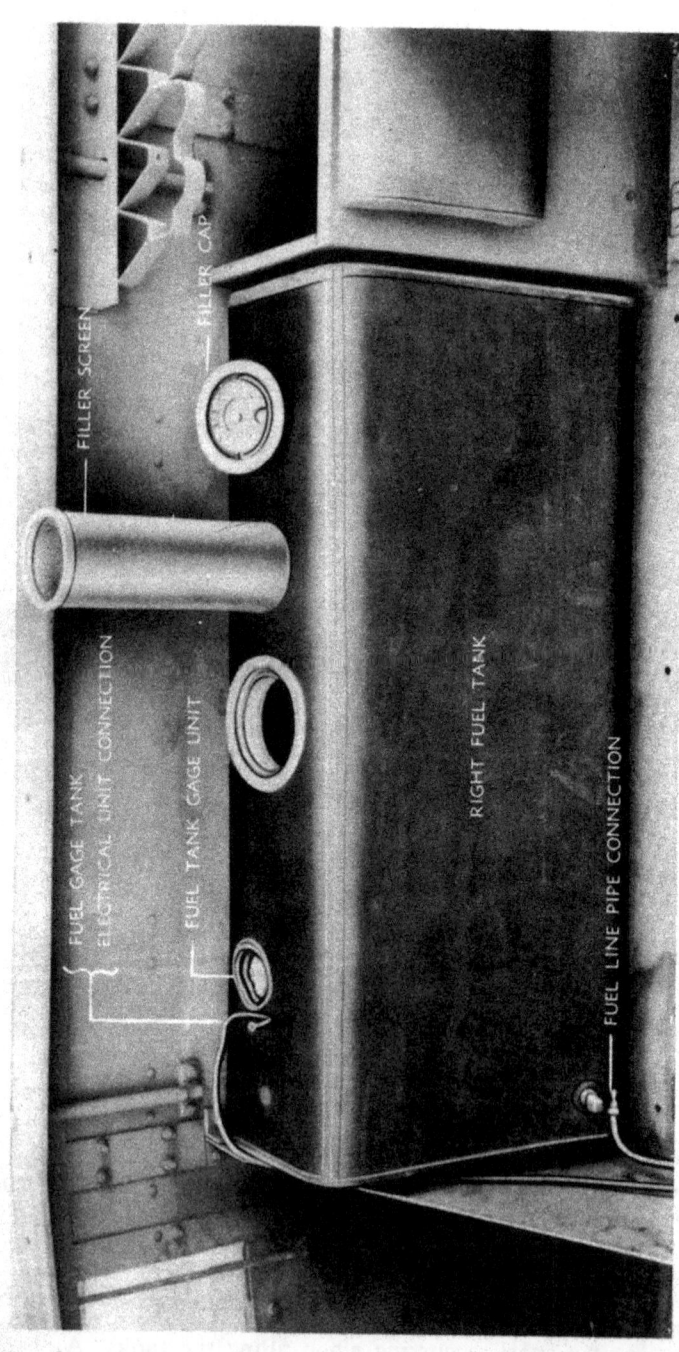

Figure 73—Fuel Tank Details

## FUEL SYSTEM

plug is recessed into the bottom of each tank. Each tank has a gage connected electrically to the dash toggle switch for a reading of the amount of fuel in either tank. The ignition switch must be turned on before a reading can be made.

b. **Maintenance.** Examine the breather valve in the filler cap to see that it is clean and free to open and close. Remove the flame arrester from the filler cap opening. Clean the flame arrester screen with compressed air and reinstall. Inspect the tanks and lines at regular intervals for leaks and loose connections. Drain the tanks seasonally or oftener, if dirty, to clean out sediment and condensation.

c. **Removal.**

(1) DRAIN TANKS. Unscrew the drain plug recessed in the bottom of the tank. This plug is removed from outside of body just above top of tracks. Install drain plug after tank is drained.

(2) REMOVE TANK COVER PLATE. Disconnect fuel line connection at front inside corner of tank by unscrewing coupling nut. Unscrew and remove six bolts and self-locking nuts from the top flange of tank cover plate where it is attached to the side of the body. Unscrew and remove three self-locking nuts from bolts attaching bottom flange of tank cover plate to the floor of the vehicle. Remove tank cover plate and padding.

(3) DISCONNECT ELECTRICAL CONNECTION. Disconnect electrical connection from gage terminals at top of fuel tank.

(4) REMOVE TANK. Slide tank out from under brackets and remove tank from vehicle.

d. **Installation.**

(1) INSTALL TANK. Place tank in position with the fuel line connection at the front end of tank and facing the inside of vehicle. Connect the electrical connection to top of tank fuel gage terminals and tighten securely.

(2) INSTALL TANK COVER PLATE. Place tank padding in position and install tank cover plate, securing with six bolts and self-locking nuts along the top flange to side of body. Secure bottom flange to floor of vehicle with three bolts and self-locking nuts. Position padding and tank plate so fuel line elbow is exposed.

(3) CONNECT FUEL LINE. Install fuel line to tank elbow connection and secure with fuel line coupling nut.

(4) REFILL FUEL TANK. Remove filler cap and pour fuel into tank through filler tank opening. Inspect drain plug and fuel line connection for leaks.

## 75. FUEL AND VACUUM PUMP.

a. **Description and Operation.** The combination fuel and vacuum pump (fig. 74) is located at the left rear of the engine and is attached to the crankcase. It is operated by the rotation of an eccentric on the engine camshaft against a rocker arm on the pump. The rocker arm operates a diaphragm against spring pressure creating suction and pumping forces. Two chambers, independent of each other, are built

**TM 9-710**
75

**BASIC HALF-TRACK VEHICLES (WHITE, AUTOCAR, and DIAMOND T)**

A—VACUUM LINE TO WINDSHIELD WIPERS
B—VACUUM LINE TO INTAKE MANIFOLD
C—VACUUM PUMP
D—MOUNTING CAP SCREW AND LOCK WASHER
E—FUEL OUTLET LINE
F—AIR DOME
G—FUEL BOWL

RA PD 314040

*Figure 74—Fuel and Vacuum Pump*

## FUEL SYSTEM

into this pump. The upper one acts as a vacuum booster for the windshield wiper and the lower one supplies fuel to the carburetor. An air dome on the lower chamber fuel outlet eliminates "surging" of fuel as it is forced to the carburetor.

b. **Removal.**

(1) D'SCONNECT VACUUM AND FUEL LINES. Unscrew coupling nuts and disconnect fittings on the vacuum lines at top part of pump. Shut off fuel line at transfer valve back of driver's seat. Unscrew coupling nuts and disconnect fittings on the fuel lines at bottom of pump.

(2) REMOVE PUMP. Remove two cap screws with lock washers and pull pump and gasket from adapter.

c. **Installation.**

(1) INSTALL PUMP. Use a new gasket and position the pump to block. Insert the two cap screws and lock washers and tighten.

(2) CONNECT FUEL AND VACUUM LINES. Install coupling nuts and tighten fuel line connections. Turn on fuel at transfer valve back of driver's seat. Install coupling nuts and tighten vacuum line connections.

### 76. FUEL FILTER.

a. **Description.** The fuel filter consists of a metal element located in a bowl which is secured to the inlet and outlet cover fitting with a bail wire and thumb screw. The filter is connected to the carburetor between the fuel line from the fuel pump and the fuel bowl on the carburetor. This filters impurities from the fuel which settle in the bowl provided. Later models have a metal bowl (replacing the former glass sediment bowl).

b. **Maintenance.** Unscrew thumb screw on bottom of filter bowl and swing thumb screw and bail wire from bowl. Remove bowl and gasket, and filtering element. Clean bowl and element with dry-cleaning solvent and dry thoroughly. Inspect gasket for good condition, and replace with a new one if there is any doubt of its serviceability. Install gasket, filter bowl, and screening element carefully. Swing bail wire and thumb screw into position and tighten by hand. Examine fuel lines and bowl gasket for leaks after starting engine.

c. **Removal.** Disconnect fuel inlet line at fuel filter by unscrewing fuel line coupling nut. Remove filter from front end of carburetor by unscrewing square fitting, connecting filter to carburetor. Unscrew and remove square fitting from filter.

d. **Installation.** Screw the square fitting into the fuel filter. Install filter with square fitting to front of carburetor. Connect fuel inlet line to fuel filter inlet and secure with coupling nut.

### 77. CARBURETOR.

a. **Description.** The carburetor (fig. 75) is the duplex-downdraft-aero type with dual throttles. It is secured to four studs on the top of the intake manifold on the right-hand side of the engine. The choke is manually controlled. Metering jets are fixed with the exception of the idling jets, which are adjustable.

# TM 9-710

## BASIC HALF-TRACK VEHICLES (WHITE, AUTOCAR, and DIAMOND T)

- A—AIR CLEANER
- B—AIR CLEANER AIR TUBE
- C—HAND THROTTLE CABLE
- D—AIR CLEANER HORN
- E—CHOKE WIRE
- F—THUMB SCREW
- G—CARBURETOR
- H—FUEL INLET LINE
- I—FUEL FILTER
- J—AIR CLEANER MOUNTING BRACKET
- K—AIR CLEANER CLAMP RING
- L—OIL BOWL
- M—THUMB SCREW
- N—BREATHER TUBE HOSE
- O—THROTTLE RETURN SPRING
- P—VACUUM LINE TO CHECK VALVE
- Q—THROTTLE ROD
- R—VACUUM LINE TO VACUUM PUMP

RA PD 314041

*Figure 75—Carburetor and Air Cleaner Assembly*

b. Adjustment.

(1) IDLING. With the engine warmed up, set the throttle stop screw so the tachometer will register approximately 400 revolutions per minute. Adjust the two idling screws, one at a time, until the engine idles smoothly (fig. 76). Turn the idling adjusting screws clockwise for a lean mixture; counterclockwise for a rich mixture.

(2) CHOKE. Loosen thumb screw on air cleaner at top of carburetor; lift horn and observe action of choke butterfly when manually operated. Adjust choke control wire so butterfly valve is fully open (vertical) when push button is against instrument panel, and fully closed with button pulled out.

TM 9-710
77

**FUEL SYSTEM**

c. **Carburetor Removal.**

(1) REMOVE AIR INTAKE TUBE. Loosen air cleaner horn connection by unscrewing thumb screw at top of carburetor. Unscrew hose clamp at air cleaner end and lift tube and horn from assembly.

(2) REMOVE THROTTLE ROD AND RETURN SPRING. Unscrew nut and lock washer on ball socket joint of throttle rod at carburetor connection and lower this end. Unhook return spring from clip on stud at carburetor.

(3) DISCONNECT CONTROL WIRES. Loosen set screws on choke wire and hand throttle wire at carburetor and pull wire from connections.

IDLER SCREWS

RA PD 314042

*Figure 76—Adjusting Carburetor Idler Screws*

(4) REMOVE FILTER. Unscrew coupling nut on fuel line at fuel filter and disconnect line at filter. Unscrew filter square fitting from carburetor.

(5) REMOVE CARBURETOR. Unscrew and remove four nuts and lock washers at base flange of carburetor. Lift and remove bracket clip which supports hand throttle cable. Lift and remove return spring clip. Lift carburetor and gasket from engine.

d. **Carburetor Installation.**

(1) INSTALL CARBURETOR. Use a new gasket and clean contact surfaces. Place carburetor in proper position on the four studs (filter hole toward front of engine). Install bracket clip support for throttle

## TM 9-710
## 77-78

### BASIC HALF-TRACK VEHICLES (WHITE, AUTOCAR, and DIAMOND T)

wire on rear left stud. Install throttle return spring clip on rear right stud. Install and tighten four lock washers and nuts.

(2) INSTALL FUEL FILTER AND CONNECT LINE. Screw filter and square fitting into front of carburetor. Install fuel line at fitting on filter and tighten coupling nut.

(3) INSTALL CONTROL WIRES. Insert choke wire and throttle wire in proper fittings and tighten set screws.

(4) INSTALL THROTTLE ROD AND RETURN SPRING. Install throttle rod ball socket joint to throttle lever (right side of carburetor) and tighten lock washer and nut.

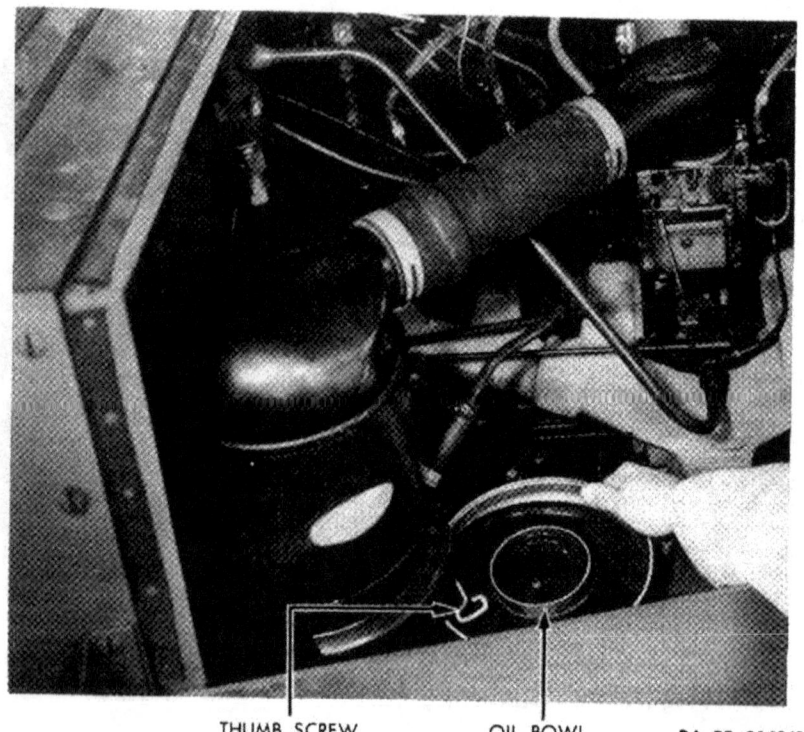

THUMB SCREW        OIL BOWL        RA PD 314043

*Figure 77—Removal of Air Cleaner Oil Bowl*

(5) INSTALL AIR INTAKE TUBE. Shove air intake tube on air cleaner elbow and air cleaner horn on top of carburetor. Tighten thumb screw at carburetor end and hose clamp at air cleaner end.

### 78. AIR CLEANER (fig. 75).

a. **Description.** The air cleaner is an oil bath type; mounted on the right-hand side of the cowl. It is equipped with a breather pipe which draws fumes out of the crankcase and feeds them to the carburetor. It filters all air entering the carburetor.

## FUEL SYSTEM

**b. Maintenance.**

(1) CLEAN OIL BOWL. Unscrew thumb screw and release clamp ring holding oil bowl at bottom of unit (fig. 77). Remove bowl from assembly and flush thoroughly. Fill bowl to oil bead with clean engine oil.

(2) CLEAN FILTERING SCREENS. The filtering screens must be kept open and clear of dust and foreign material. Remove assembly from dash and wash in kerosene. Blow screens out thoroughly with compressed air, if available.

**c. Removal.**

(1) REMOVE AIR TUBE. Loosen thumb screw on air cleaner horn clamp at top of carburetor; loosen hose clamp at air cleaner and pull hose and horn from assembly.

(2) DISCONNECT BREATHER TUBE. Loosen hose clamps at air cleaner end and push hose up on breather tube.

(3) REMOVE AIR CLEANER FROM DASH. Unscrew and remove four nuts and lock washers from bolts holding air cleaner brackets to dash.

**d. Installation.**

(1) INSTALL AIR CLEANER. Place air cleaner in proper position on dash. Insert four bolts through brackets and dash, install and tighten four lock washers and nuts.

(2) CONNECT BREATHER TUBE. Shove hose down breather tube to connection on air cleaner bowl and tighten hose clamps.

(3) INSTALL AIR TUBE. Place tube in proper position and tighten thumb screw clamp on horn (at carburetor) and hose clamp (at air cleaner).

TM 9-710
79

**BASIC HALF-TRACK VEHICLES (WHITE, AUTOCAR, and DIAMOND T)**

Section XVII

## INTAKE AND EXHAUST SYSTEM

|  | Paragraph |
|---|---|
| Description of system | 79 |
| Maintenance | 80 |
| Intake and exhaust manifolds and gasket | 81 |
| Exhaust pipe, muffler, and tail pipe | 82 |

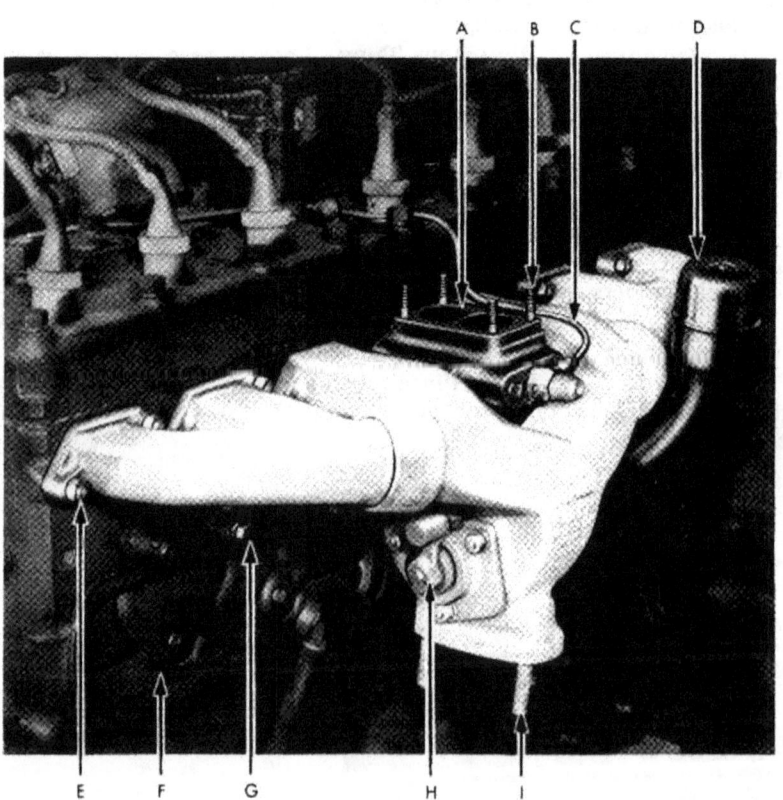

A—INTAKE MANIFOLD
B—CARBURETOR STUD
C—VACUUM PUMP LINE
D—OIL FILLER PIPE
E—EXHAUST MANIFOLD STUD, LOCK WASHER, AND NUT
F—VALVE COVER
G—INTAKE MANIFOLD CAP SCREW AND LOCK WASHER
H—HEATER VALVE ASSEMBLY
I—EXHAUST PIPE STUD

RA PD 314044

*Figure 78—Intake and Exhaust Manifolds*

170

## INTAKE AND EXHAUST SYSTEM

### 79. DESCRIPTION OF SYSTEM.

a. **Intake.** The intake manifold is of one-piece cast iron construction and is attached to the cylinder block with cap screws and lock washers (fig. 78). Three plugs for accessory connections are located near the center of the manifold. The center plug has been removed and a fitting inserted connecting two air suction lines which operate the windshield wipers and the vacuum booster on the service brakes.

b. **Exhaust.** The exhaust manifold is made up of three-piece cast iron construction and attached to the block with studs and nuts. A heater valve assembly is incorporated in the lower part of the exhaust manifold to direct heat to the intake manifold, preheating the fuel and air mixture. The outlet of the exhaust connects to the exhaust pipe and muffler, which carry away the exhaust fumes. NOTE: *The ex-*

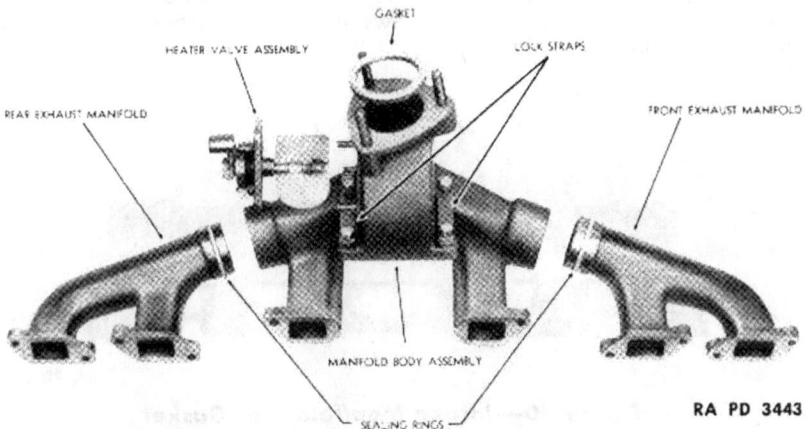

*Figure 79—Exhaust Manifold Details*

*haust and intake manifold gasket is a one-piece gasket, making it mandatory to remove both units and replace this gasket if either manifold is disturbed.*

### 80. MAINTENANCE.

a. **Intake.** Examine the intake manifold for any flaws or cracks that would let air enter the system, except through the regular channels. Inspect the gaskets between carburetor and manifold and the manifold and block for air leaks and replace if faulty. Tighten the manifold nuts and cap screws at regular maintenance intervals.

b. **Exhaust.** Keep the end of the tail pipe open. Back pressure caused by partially closed or clogged tail pipe or muffler will cause faulty engine performance. Inspect muffler and exhaust pipes for damage, corrosion and tightness. Test gaskets for seal. Replace units whenever leaks develop.

## BASIC HALF-TRACK VEHICLES (WHITE, AUTOCAR, and DIAMOND T)

### 81. INTAKE AND EXHAUST MANIFOLDS AND GASKET
(figs. 79 and 80).

**a. Removal.**

(1) REMOVE CARBURETOR. Refer to paragraph 77.

(2) REMOVE VACUUM LINES. Unscrew the flared tube nuts on each end of the vacuum line connecting intake manifold and the check valve on the dash. Unscrew coupling nut on the vacuum pump line connection to intake manifold and disconnect line.

(3) REMOVE OIL FILLER PIPE. Remove three cap screws and lock washers which attach oil filler pipe to the front valve cover and lift off the oil filler pipe.

(4) REMOVE INTAKE AND EXHAUST MANIFOLD ASSEMBLY. Remove 10 nuts and lock washers from exhaust manifold studs. Disconnect exhaust pipe and gasket from bottom of exhaust manifold by removing 3 high hex nuts from studs in exhaust manifold. Remove 12 intake manifold holding cap screws and lock washers and lift off manifolds and gasket.

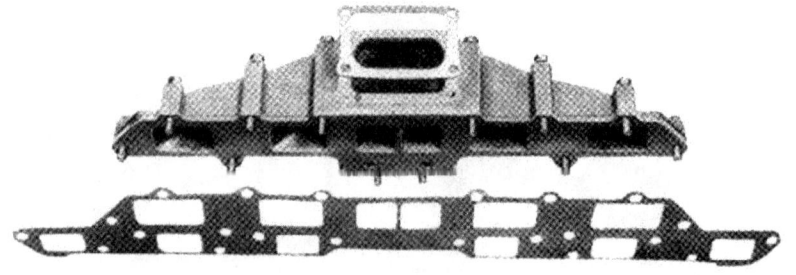

RA PD 3442

*Figure 80—Intake Manifold and Gasket*

**b. Installation.**

(1) INSTALL INTAKE AND EXHAUST MANIFOLD ASSEMBLY. Clean thoroughly the areas where manifold gasket is to be installed. Place a new manifold gasket in position on studs in engine block. Install manifolds on gasket and studs and secure with 12 cap screws and lock washers installed in the intake manifold and 10 nuts and lock washers on the studs of the exhaust manifold. Install a new gasket between exhaust manifold and exhaust pipe and secure the assembly with three high hex nuts installed on the studs at bottom of the exhaust manifold.

(2) INSTALL OIL FILLER PIPE. Place the oil filler pipe in position on front valve cover and secure with three cap screws and lock washers.

(3) INSTALL VACUUM LINES. Install vacuum pump line to the intake manifold fitting and secure with coupling nut. Install vacuum line connecting check valve and intake manifold and secure with the flared tube nut on each end of line.

(4) INSTALL CARBURETOR. Refer to paragraph 77.

## INTAKE AND EXHAUST SYSTEM

### 82. EXHAUST PIPE, MUFFLER, AND TAIL PIPE.

   a. **Removal of Exhaust Pipe.** Remove three exhaust manifold flange nuts; loosen pipe-to-muffler band clamp and remove exhaust pipe, flange, and gasket from assembly.

   b. **Installation of Exhaust Pipe.** Insert exhaust pipe into muffler band clamp and inlet pipe. Push exhaust pipe up into exhaust manifold and pull up ring gasket and flange, securing flange to exhaust manifold studs with three high hex nuts. Tighten muffler band clamp.

   c. **Removal of Muffler.** Loosen band clamp at connection of exhaust pipe to muffler. Remove U-bolt clamp securing front end of muffler to frame bracket. Remove the band clamp connecting rear of muffler and front end of tail pipe to frame bracket. Loosen U-bolt clamp at tail pipe outer end and pull tail pipe from rear of muffler. Remove muffler and insulation around inlet pipe of muffler.

   d. **Installation of Muffler.** Install muffler inlet pipe and insulation to connection with exhaust pipe and tighten band clamp. Install tail pipe to outlet end of muffler and secure with band clamp to frame bracket. Tighten the U-bolt clamp on the outer end of the tail pipe. Install the U-bolt clamp to the front end of the muffler to frame bracket.

   e. **Removal of Tail Pipe.** Loosen clamp bolt nut at rear of muffler. Remove U-bolt clamp at outer end of tail pipe and pull off tail pipe.

   f. **Installation of Tail Pipe.** Install tail pipe to rear of muffler and tighten clamp bolt. Install U-bolt clamp at outer end of tail pipe and tighten nuts.

# TM 9-710

## BASIC HALF-TRACK VEHICLES (WHITE, AUTOCAR, and DIAMOND T)

Section XVIII

## COOLING SYSTEM

|  | Paragraph |
|---|---|
| Description of system and tabulated data | 83 |
| Water pump | 84 |
| Fan | 85 |
| Belts | 86 |
| Radiator and shroud | 87 |
| Surge tank | 88 |
| Thermostat | 89 |

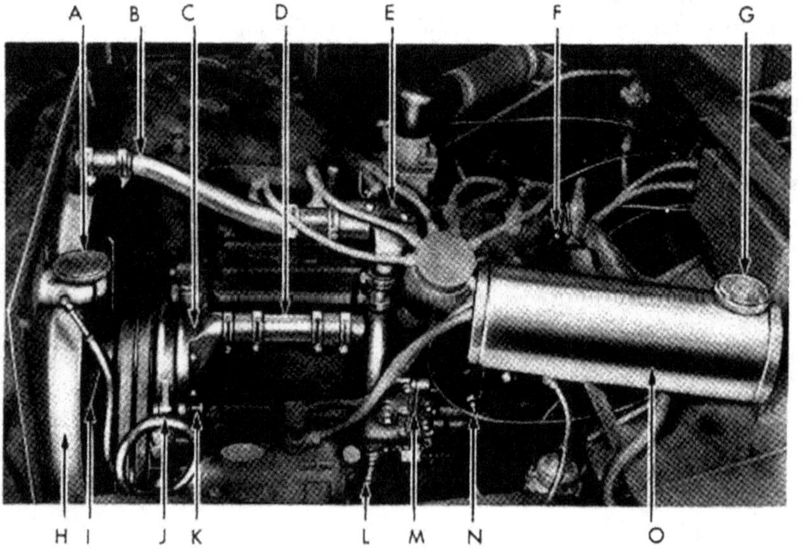

A—RADIATOR FILLER CAP
B—RADIATOR INLET PIPE
C—WATER PUMP
D—OIL TEMPERATURE REGULATOR TO WATER PUMP PIPE
E—THERMOSTAT HOUSING
F—ENGINE TEMPERATURE INDICATOR BULB
G—SURGE TANK PRESSURE CAP
H—FAN SHROUD
I—FAN
J—SURGE TANK LINE
K—WATER PUMP DRAIN COCK
L—RADIATOR OUTLET TO OIL TEMPERATURE REGULATOR PIPE
M—OIL TEMPERATURE REGULATOR
N—CYLINDER BLOCK DRAIN COCK
O—SURGE TANK

RA PD 314045

*Figure 81—Cooling System*

## 83. DESCRIPTION OF SYSTEM AND TABULATED DATA.

**a. Description.** The cooling system consists of a radiator, shroud, fan, water pump, thermostat, surge tank, connecting lines and hose

## COOLING SYSTEM

(fig. 81). This is a pressure cooling system, increasing the temperature at which the coolant will reach the boiling point. This results in less evaporation of the coolant in hot climates. The cooling system holds 24 quarts (less heater). The four drain locations are: drain cock at bottom of the water pump housing; drain cock at the left center side of cylinder block in front of cranking motor; drain cock in radiator outlet pipe at bottom left side of radiator; and drain plug in the right-hand side of the block at the rear of the manifolds. The filler cap is located at top of radiator on left-hand side under the hood.

b. **Tabulated Data.**

(1) WATER PUMP.
  Make .......................... White Motor
  Model No. ......................... 372671
  Type ........................... centrifugal
  Drive ......................... dual V-belts

(2) FAN BLADE.
  Make ...................... Hayes Industries
  Model No. ....................... W-12A-32
  Type ............................. 5-blade

(3) FAN BELTS.
  Width and length ............. 7/8 in. x 49 in.
  Model No. ............... White No. 372659
  (matched set)
  Type ............................. V-belt

(4) RADIATOR.
  Make ............................. Modine
  Model No. .......................... 8D-3833
  Type ......................... tubular core

(5) THERMOSTAT.
  Make ........................ Fulton Sylphon
  Model No. ................. (White) 372759
  Type ............................. bellows

## 84. WATER PUMP.

a. **Description.** The water pump is a centrifugal, packless type and requires no external lubrication or adjustment (fig. 82). It is mounted at the front end of the cylinder block and is driven by V-belts from the fan pulley. The water pump shaft rotates in two ball bearings. The fan hub is pressed on the front end of the shaft and the impeller on the rear end.

b. **Removal** (fig. 83).

(1) DRAIN SYSTEM. Open drain cock in radiator outlet pipe at bottom left-hand side of radiator and drain cooling system to a point below the level of water pump.

(2) DISCONNECT HOSE. Unscrew hose clamps on hose connection pipe running to oil temperature regulator and release hose at water pump elbow.

(3) REMOVE THE BELT ADJUSTING STRAP. Remove two bolts,

## TM 9-710

## BASIC HALF-TRACK VEHICLES (WHITE, AUTOCAR, and DIAMOND T)

Figure 82—Water Pump and Fan

## COOLING SYSTEM

RA PD 3613

*Figure 83—Removal of Water Pump and Fan Assembly*

nuts, and lock washers from the belt tension adjusting strap, and remove the strap (fig. 82).

(4) REMOVE BELTS FROM GENERATOR PULLEY. Loosen the two generator mounting bolts at the bottom of the generator (fig. 67), and lift the generator upward, releasing tension on the belts. Slip the belts off the generator and crankshaft pulleys.

(5) REMOVE PUMP. Remove six cap screws and lock washers attaching water pump assembly to front end of block. Lift off fan and pump assembly (with belts) and the spacer gasket between the pump and cylinder block.

c. Installation.

(1) INSTALL PUMP. Insert a new spacer gasket between the pump and the cylinder block. NOTE: *Neglecting to install this spacer will cause the belts to run out of line with the pulleys.* Place the fan and pump assembly (with the belts on the fan pulleys) in proper position,

# TM 9-710
## BASIC HALF-TRACK VEHICLES (WHITE, AUTOCAR, and DIAMOND T)

RA PD 3552

*Figure 84—Fan Belt Installed*

pushing the pump elbow into the connecting hose. Install and tighten six lock washers and cap screws. Tighten the hose clamps at the hose connection between the water pump elbow and the water pipe to the oil temperature regulator.

(2) INSTALL BELTS. Lift the generator upward, and install belts on pulleys of the generator and crankshaft.

(3) INSTALL BELT ADJUSTING STRAP. Install and secure the adjusting strap with two bolts, lock washers, and nuts. NOTE: *The slotted hole in the strap must be used with the bolt installed in the generator to provide adjustment for the belts.*

(4) SECURE GENERATOR AND ADJUST BELTS. Tighten the four generator mounting bracket nuts and bolts and adjust the belts to the recommended tension (par. 86). Tighten the nut and lock washer on the bolt through the adjusting strap slot to maintain the adjustment.

## COOLING SYSTEM

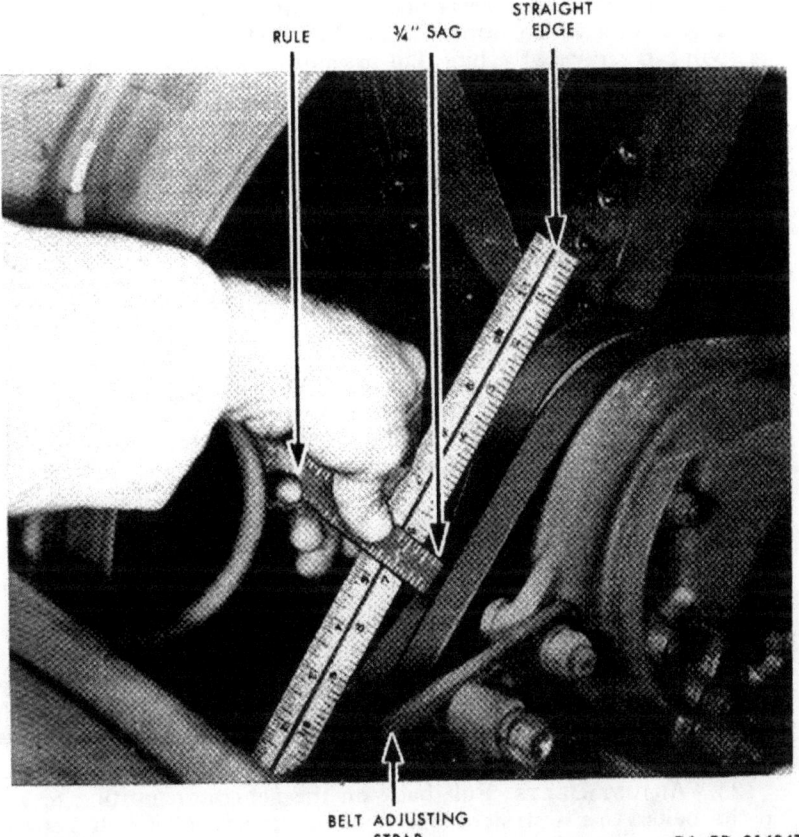

Figure 85—Adjusting Fan Belt

(5) REFILL COOLING SYSTEM. Pour required amount of coolant into radiator filler cap neck after closing the drain cock at radiator outlet pipe.

85. FAN.

a. **Description.** The flow of air through the radiator core and over the engine is maintained by the movement of the vehicle and a five-bladed fan revolving within the radiator shroud. The fan is secured to the pulley of the water pump. Two V-belts connect the pulleys of the fan and water pump assembly with the pulleys on the generator and the engine crankshaft. The pulley on the engine crankshaft furnishes the driving power for these units.

b. **Maintenance.** Examine the fan blade assembly for bent blades and restore them to original setting. Replace the entire assembly when blades cannot be brought back to proper shape or are otherwise damaged.

## BASIC HALF-TRACK VEHICLES (WHITE, AUTOCAR, and DIAMOND T)

c. **Removal.** Cut and remove the two locking wires from the four cap screws which attach fan assembly to the pulley. Remove the four cap screws attaching fan assembly to pump pulley and lift off fan assembly.

d. **Installation.** Place the fan assembly in position, lining up the cap screw holes with holes in the pulley. Install and tighten the four cap screws. Pull two new locking wires through the heads of the cap screws and twist the ends of the wire in a twist lock (fig. 50).

## 86. BELTS.

a. **Description.** Two matched V-type belts drive the fan, water pump, and generator (fig. 84). Driving power for the belts is obtained from the pulley located on the front of the engine crankshaft.

b. **Maintenance.** Examine the fan belts for cracks and defects. A belt that is fouled with grease or oil will soon deteriorate, and if cleaning shows it to be worn or not running true, replace belt. Belts must be replaced in matched sets only.

c. **Removal.** Loosen nut on the generator adjusting arm bolt. Loosen, but do not remove, the two generator mounting bracket bolts. Lift the generator, releasing tension on the belts. Slip belts off crankshaft pulley and generator pulley, and lift belts over fan blades and out.

d. **Installation.**

(1) INSTALL BELTS. Work the belts over the blades of fan to fan pulley. Push the generator toward the engine as far as possible. Slip the belts over the pulleys of the crankshaft and generator. Tighten the generator mounting bracket bolts.

(2) ADJUST BELTS. Pull back on the generator, putting tension on the belts. Use a straightedge on longest section of belt between upper and lower pulleys, press down on center of belt with a rule (fig. 85), and adjust belt to ¾-inch sag. Tighten locking nut on slotted adjusting arm and check setting.

## 87. RADIATOR AND SHROUD.

a. **Description.** The radiator is a tubular type with brass tanks. The core is supported by a cross strap and tie rods to the frame side members, and rests on two "anti-squeak" pads. A shroud is attached to the assembly to assist in the deflection of air to the fan blades. The radiator drain cock is located in the bottom left-hand corner of the outlet pipe. The overflow pipe, connected to a surge tank, provides a pressure cooling system. The filler cap is located under the hood on the left-hand side at the top of radiator. CAUTION: *Under no conditions should either radiator cap or surge tank cap be removed when the heat indicator reading is higher than 185°F.* If this is done, the operator may be seriously scalded by the steam which would immediately be formed.

b. **Maintenance.**

(1) SERVICING. Clean, flush, and tighten the cooling system every

## COOLING SYSTEM

6,000 miles. Replace all worn or deteriorated hose. Clean radiator fins of all foreign material.

(2) CLEANING. Drain one gallon of water from cooling system, then add the cleaning solution (one-half pound of soda ash, or sal soda, to a gallon of clean water). Run the engine until coolant heats thoroughly. Drain the system by disconnecting the lower hose connection.

(3) FLUSHING. Leave radiator and surge tank caps in place. Remove the thermostat from thermostat housing, then install housing (par. 89). Disconnect the lower hose connections on the radiator. Connect the flushing hose to lower radiator pipe so the system will

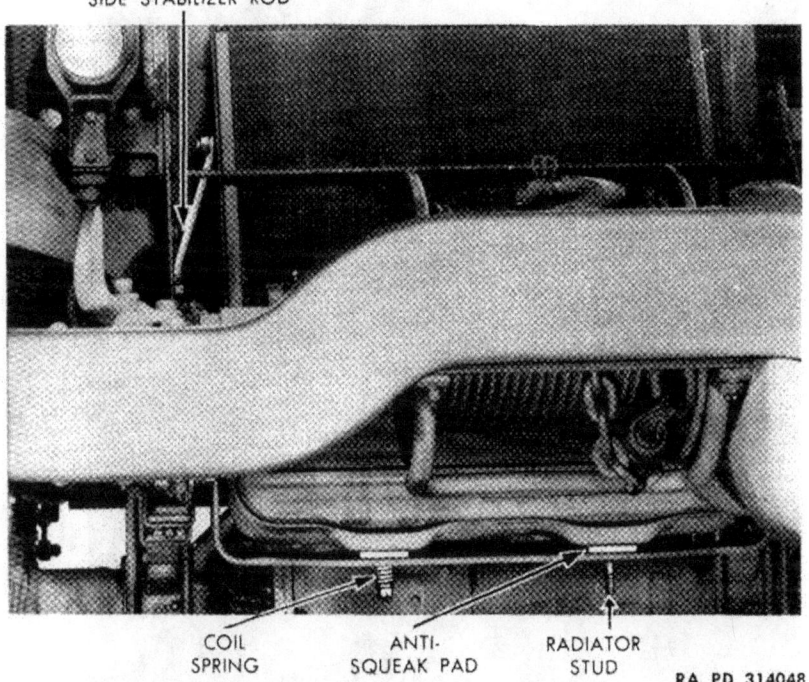

*Figure 86—Radiator Connections to Frame*

be flushed in the opposite direction to normal flow. Force water through system until the water (coming out of engine inlet pipe) is clean. Connect and tighten the hose connections, and install the thermostat (par. 89). Refill the cooling system.

c. **Removal.**

(1) DRAIN SYSTEM. Open drain cock in radiator outlet pipe at bottom left-hand corner of the radiator.

(2) REMOVE HOOD. Refer to paragraph 67 b.

(3) REMOVE RADIATOR HOSE AND PIPES. Loosen hose clamps on the hose and pipe connecting thermostat housing to radiator inlet pipe, and remove pipe and hose. Loosen hose clamps on hose and pipe con-

**TM 9-710**
**87**

**BASIC HALF-TRACK VEHICLES (WHITE, AUTOCAR, and DIAMOND T)**

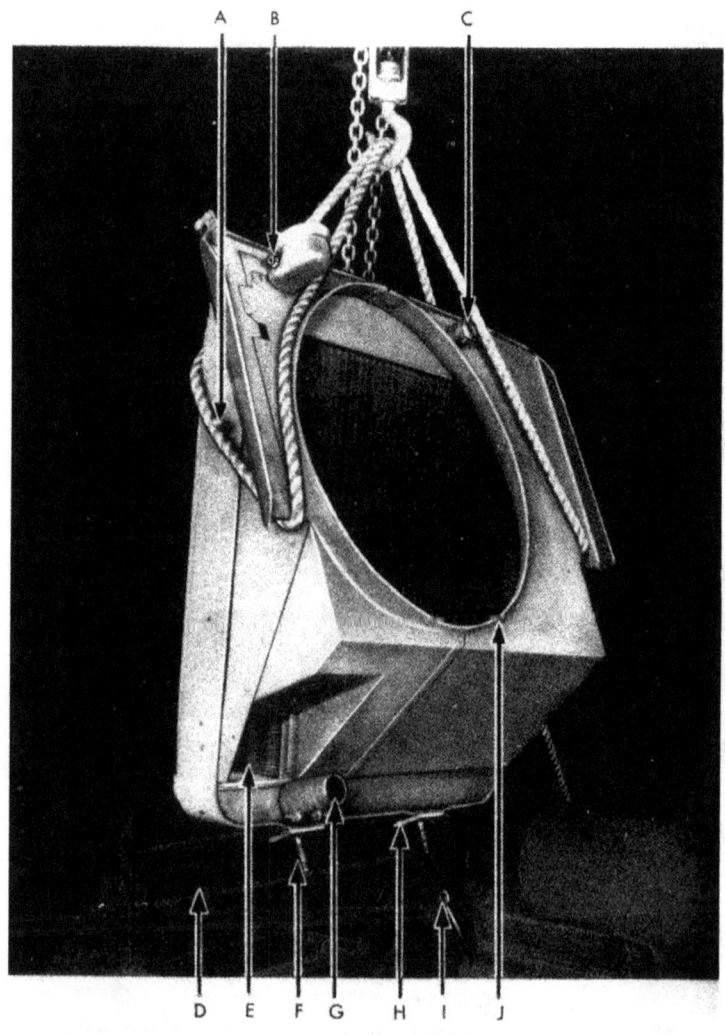

A—STABILIZER ROD STUD
B—SURGE TANK LINE CONNECTION
C—RADIATOR INLET
D—SHUTTER ASSEMBLY
E—OPENING FOR WINCH PROPELLER SHAFT
F—BOTTOM STUD
G—RADIATOR OUTLET
H—ANTI-SQUEAK PAD
I—STABILIZER ROD
J—SHROUD

RA PD 314049

*Figure 87—Removing Radiator and Shroud*

TM 9-710
87-88

## COOLING SYSTEM

necting radiator outlet pipe to bottom of the oil temperature regulator, and remove pipe and hose. Unscrew coupling nut on surge tank line at radiator filler spout and disconnect surge tank line.

(4) REMOVE OIL FILTER. Unscrew four cap screws and lock washers holding oil filter and base to engine block. Remove assembly and base gasket.

(5) REMOVE BELTS, FAN, AND WATER PUMP. Refer to paragraphs 84 through 86.

(6) REMOVE RADIATOR (figs. 86 and 87). Remove a cotter pin, nut, washer, and coil spring from each of the two bottom radiator studs at the underside of the frame cross member. Remove nuts and lock washers from the two side radiator stabilizer rods and pull rods off studs. Lift radiator and shroud out of the shutter front. Lift off the two anti-squeak pads at the bottom studs of the radiator.

d. **Installation.**

(1) INSTALL RADIATOR AND SHROUD. Place the two anti-squeak pads in position on the frame cross member so the bottom radiator studs enter the holes in the pads and frame. Install coil spring, washer, and nut on the bottom studs. Tighten nut, leaving a small space between each coil of the spring, and secure castellated nut with cotter pin. Install the two side radiator stabilizer rods, and secure by installing and tightening lock washers and nuts.

(2) INSTALL WATER PUMP, FAN, AND BELTS. Refer to paragraphs 84 through 86.

(3) CONNECT RADIATOR HOSE AND PIPES. Install the water pipe and two hose connecting radiator to thermostat housing, and tighten hose clamps. Install the water pipe and hose to lower connection of radiator and oil temperature regulator, and tighten hose clamps. Install surge tank line to radiator filler spout and secure with coupling nut.

(4) INSTALL OIL FILTER. Place oil filter and base gasket in proper position on engine block and secure with four lock washers and cap screws.

(5) INSTALL HOOD. Refer to paragraph 68.

(6) REFILL COOLING SYSTEM. Close the drain cock on radiator outlet pipe and fill radiator at filler cap neck. Screw filler cap on securely.

**88. SURGE TANK** (fig. 88).

a. **Description and Operation.**

(1) DESCRIPTION. The surge tank assembly consists of a cylindrical tank of 5-quart capacity fitted with a sealing cap containing a set of pressure and vacuum release valves. It is mounted with bolts, washers, and nuts on the sloping portion of the dash, under the left side of hood. It is connected to the radiator filler neck by a line.

(2) OPERATION. As the temperature of the coolant reaches the point where it evaporates, the steam is conducted through the connecting tube from the radiator filler neck to the surge tank. The tank cap will retain it up to a safe predetermined point and condensation of

## TM 9-710

**BASIC HALF-TRACK VEHICLES (WHITE, AUTOCAR, and DIAMOND T)**

the steam takes place. If the pressure exceeds 8 or 9 pounds, a valve in the pressure cap on the surge tank will open and release a sufficient amount of steam to relieve the pressure to a safe point. When the temperature of the coolant decreases, the water thus formed siphons back into the main cooling system. The pressure cap is also equipped to admit atmosphere to the system when the pressure in the surge tank falls one pound, or more, below outside atmospheric pressure. This occurs when the system is in the cooling stage after extreme heating of the coolant. NOTE: *As the coolant is under pressure after a certain temperature is reached, there will be a resulting increase in tem-*

Figure 88—Surge Tank, Pressure Cap, and Line

*perature of the coolant shown on the heat indicator on instrument panel.* The operator should not become alarmed when this occurs, as these higher temperatures will be proper under certain conditions. The heat indicator may sometimes reach 220°F under extremely severe climatic conditions. CAUTION: *When necessary to add coolant, it should be added through the radiator filler neck opening only and not through the surge tank.* Removal of pressure cap on the surge tank should not be necessary unless replacement of cap, or cleaning of tank, is required.

**b. Removal.** Disconnect line running from surge tank to radiator filler neck by unscrewing coupling nut at end of line at the radiator filler neck. Remove two bolts, nuts, lock washers, and reinforcing plate from each mounting bracket, and lift out tank with mounting brackets attached.

## COOLING SYSTEM

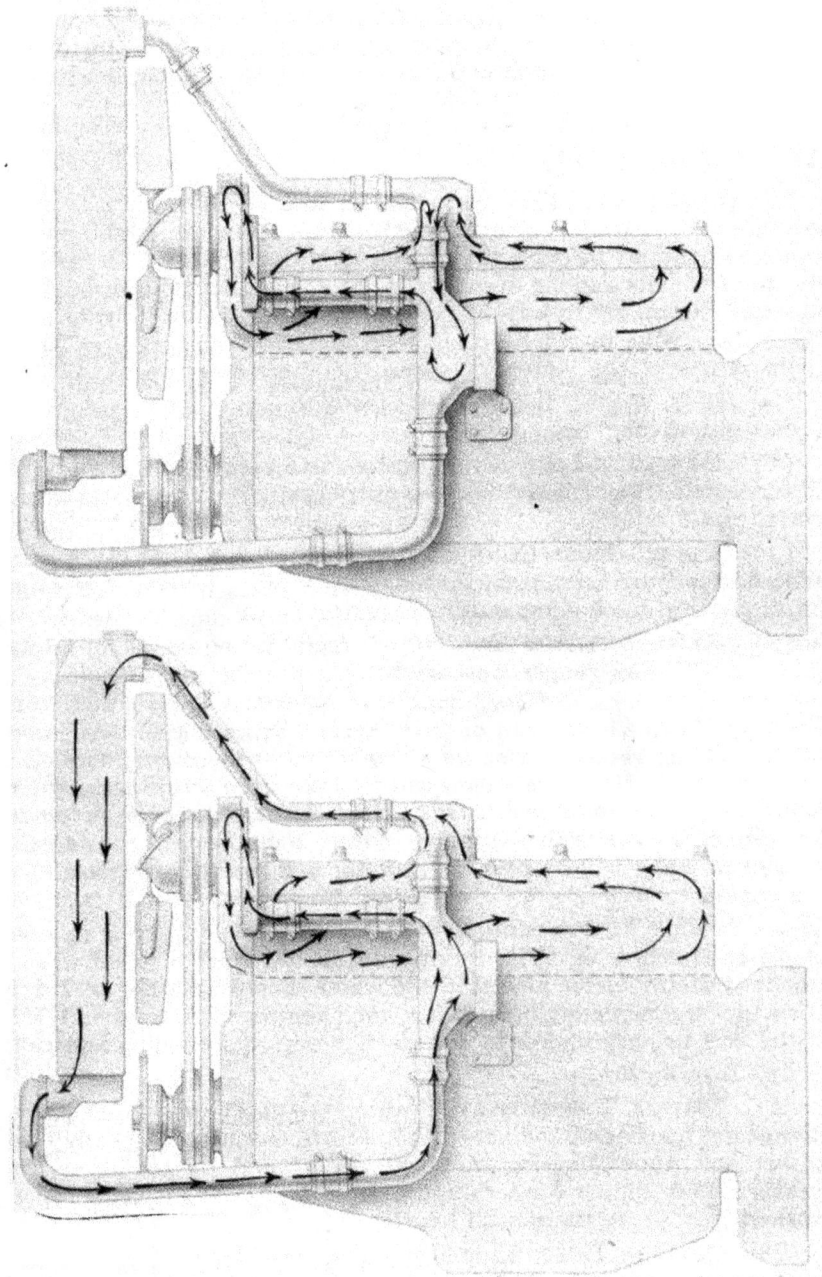

Figure 89—Water Flow Through Cooling System

## BASIC HALF-TRACK VEHICLES (WHITE, AUTOCAR, and DIAMOND T)

c. **Installation.** Install tank and attached mounting bracket so the holes in the mounting brackets line up with holes in the cowl. Insert two bolts through each of the mounting brackets and cowl and secure with reinforcing plate, two lock washers, and nuts. Install line from surge tank to radiator filler neck and secure coupling nut at radiator end.

## 89. THERMOSTAT.

a. **Description.** The thermostat is located at the water outlet passage in the cylinder head. It controls the temperature and path of water circulation through the cooling system (fig. 89). "Bypassing" the water in the cooling system so that it does not flow through the radiator during the warm-up period, shortens the length of time it takes the engine to reach an efficient operating temperature. As the temperature of the water increases, the thermostat opens, allowing flow of water through the radiator (fig. 89).

b. **Removal.**

(1) DRAIN COOLANT. Drain system to a point below the level of the coolant in the cylinder head by opening drain cock in the radiator outlet pipe.

(2) LOOSEN HOSE CONNECTIONS. Loosen two hose clamps and slide hose off the thermostat housing outlet pipe. Loosen hose clamp on thermostat-to-oil temperature regulator housing.

(3) REMOVE THERMOSTAT. Unscrew and remove three cap screws, lock washers, and copper washers holding the thermostat housing to the engine block. Lift off and remove in succession: upper thermostat housing, gasket, thermostat assembly, lower thermostat housing, gasket. CAUTION: *If the engine must be operated without the thermostat, plug the by-pass pipe which extends vertically from the oil temperature regulator housing on the left side of the engine to the elbow on the left side of the thermostat housing. If this is not done, a considerable volume of water will by-pass the radiator and result in overheating of the engine.*

c. **Testing Thermostat.** Test the thermostat by placing in a pan of water and heating. The thermostat should start to open when a standard thermometer placed in the water shows a reading of 155°F. It should be completely open when water temperature reaches 175°F. If the unit being tested does not meet these requirements, replace it.

d. **Installation.**

(1) INSTALL THERMOSTAT. Position the gasket and lower part of thermostat housing on cylinder head. Insert thermostat assembly. Set gasket and upper housing in place. Insert and tighten three lock washers, three copper washers, and three cap screws. Place the copper washers next to the thermostat housing.

(2) CONNECT HOSE. Slide hose on top radiator pipe on front end of thermostat housing, and the hose connection between thermostat and oil temperature regulator into position. Tighten hose clamps.

(3) REFILL COOLING SYSTEM. Pour required amount of coolant into radiator through filler spout, and inspect system for leaks.

## Section XIX

## IGNITION SYSTEM

| | Paragraph |
|---|---|
| Description of system and tabulated data | 90 |
| Ignition switch | 91 |
| Ignition coil | 92 |
| Distributor | 93 |
| Spark plugs | 94 |
| Engine timing | 95 |
| Ignition wiring and shielding | 96 |

### 90. DESCRIPTION OF SYSTEM AND TABULATED DATA.

**a. Description.** The ignition system consists of a battery, ignition coil, distributor, condenser, low and high tension wiring, and spark plugs (figs. 90 and 91). These are two distinct circuits in the system. The primary (low tension) circuit includes the battery, the distributor contact points and circuit breaking mechanism, the primary of the ignition coil, and the condenser. The secondary (high tension) circuit includes the secondary of the ignition coil, rotor and distributor cap, high tension wiring and spark plugs.

**b. Operation.** With the ignition switch turned on and the distributor contact points closed, current flows through the primary winding of the ignition coil and builds up a strong magnetic field in the coil. This magnetic field collapses and induces a high voltage in the secondary winding of the coil every time the distributor contact points open. This induced high voltage is distributed to the spark plugs at correct "firing" intervals by the distributor cap and rotor and the high tension wires between distributor cap and spark plugs.

**c. Tabulated Data.**

    (1) IGNITION COIL.
        Make ............................ Delco-Remy
        Model ............................... 1883956
        Type ................................ shielded
    (2) DISTRIBUTOR.
        Make ............................ Delco-Remy
        Model ............................... 1110174
        Type .......................... full automatic
    (3) SPARK PLUGS.
        Make ............................... Champion
        Model .................................. J-10
        Size ................................. 14-mm

### 91. IGNITION SWITCH.

**a. Description.** The switch is the keyless, lever type. Throw the lever to the left to close ignition circuit. The "OFF" position of the lever is vertical.

**TM 9-710**

**BASIC HALF-TRACK VEHICLES (WHITE, AUTOCAR, and DIAMOND T)**

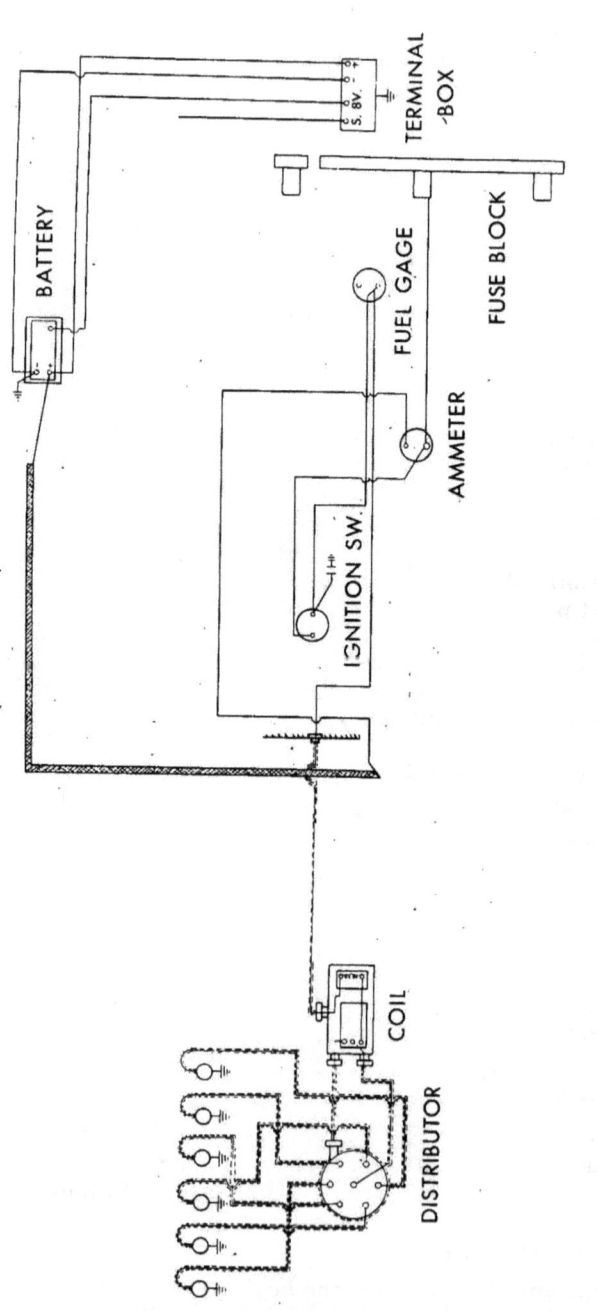

*Figure 90—Ignition System Wiring Diagram*

## IGNITION SYSTEM

*Figure 91—Ignition System Installed*

# TM 9-710
91-92

## BASIC HALF-TRACK VEHICLES (WHITE, AUTOCAR, and DIAMOND T)

*b.* **Removal.** Unscrew two thumb screws and pull off bottom cover of box on back of instrument panel. Disconnect wiring leads to switch at terminals. Insert a small, stiff drift in the hole in the face of the switch lever and press in release catch. Pull out lever. Insert a small drift in countersunk hole in locking nut on front of panel and tap lightly. Unscrew and remove nut. Lift switch from panel.

*c.* **Installation.** Place switch in position in panel. Install locking nut on front of panel and tighten by tapping with a small drift. Snap lever into place on switch. Install and tighten wiring at terminals on back of switch. Place bottom cover on box and install, and tighten, two thumb screws.

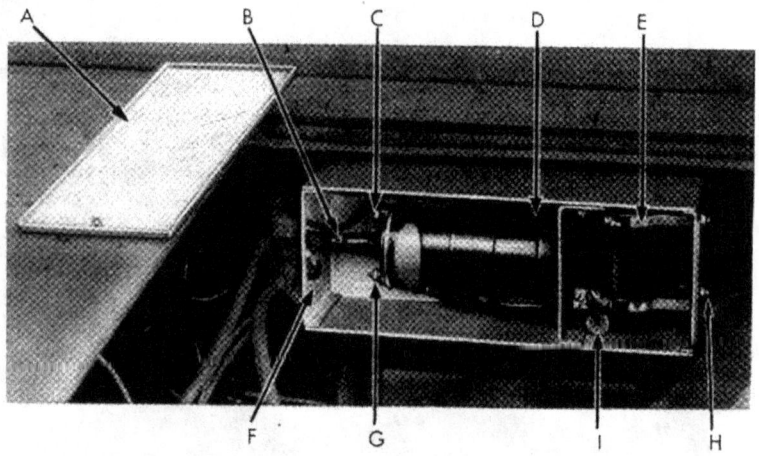

A—SHIELD BOX COVER
B—HIGH TENSION CABLE
C—LOW TENSION WIRE (NEGATIVE)
D—IGNITION COIL
E—FILTER COIL
F—SHIELD BOX
G—LOW TENSION WIRE (POSITIVE)
H—MOUNTING SCREW
I—CONDENSER

RA PD 314054

*Figure 92—Ignition Coil Assembly Installed*

## 92. IGNITION COIL (fig. 92).

*a.* **Description.** The ignition coil is mounted in a shield box on the left side of the engine cowl. A filter coil and condenser (for radio shielding) are connected in the circuit, and are mounted in the shielding box with the ignition coil. The heavy cable at the right center of the coil leads to the distributor cap. The negative low tension wire (upper terminal at right end) leads to the distributor points. The positive low tension wire leads to the filter coil and filter condenser.

*b.* **Removal of Component Units.**

(1) REMOVE IGNITION COIL. Unscrew lock and lift off shielding box cover. Unscrew and pull off locking cap at right end of distributor (fig. 93), and pull coil-to-distributor cable from coil. Unscrew nuts on

## IGNITION SYSTEM

top and bottom terminals (at right end of coil) and disconnect wires. Unscrew two nuts and lock washers and pull coil and bracket from box.

(2) REMOVE FILTER COIL. Remove shielding box cover. Disconnect terminals at top and bottom of coil. Unscrew and remove two nuts, toothed lock washers, and bolts from coil bracket (left side). Lift coil from box.

(3) REMOVE FILTER COIL CONDENSER. Remove filter coil. Disconnect terminal wire at condenser. Unscrew and remove two screws in condenser bracket and lift out condenser.

c. Installation of Component Units.

(1) INSTALL IGNITION COIL. Place coil and bracket in position in shielding box, with tapered end of coil to the right. Install and tighten two lock washers and nuts on bracket bolts. Install low tension wiring on top and bottom terminals at right end of coil. Insert high tension cable in connection at right end center of coil and install and tighten locking cap. Place shielding box cover in position and screw fastener shut.

(2) INSTALL FILTER COIL. Place coil in position. Insert and tighten two bolts, lock washers, and nuts through box and coil bracket. Install wiring at upper and lower coil terminals.

(3) INSTALL FILTER COIL CONDENSER. Place condenser and bracket in position in coil box, and insert and tighten two screws. Install condenser wire at terminal.

93. DISTRIBUTOR.

a. Description. The distributor is a six-cylinder, fully automatic, sealed type, having a built-in centrifugal-advance mechanism (fig. 93). The unit is equipped with complete shielding for radio suppression. The distributor drive shaft, which rotates clockwise, when viewed from the top of the unit, is driven by the camshaft through an extension of the oil pump shaft. The tachometer driver adapter is built into the body of the distributor.

b. Maintenance and Adjustment.

(1) BREAKER POINT REMOVAL. Unscrew and remove nut holding contact arm spring and pull spring from stud. Unscrew two contact support screws and lift off contact arm and contact support.

(2) BREAKER POINT DRESSING. Resurface the contacts on a moderately coarse oilstone, rounding their faces slightly so that the point of contact will be near the center and not at the edge. A contact file used to dress points should not be used on other metals. NOTE: *Never use emery cloth for points.*

(3) BREAKER POINT INSTALLATION. Place contact support in position and insert and partially tighten two screws. Install contact arm spring on stud and install and tighten nut. Set breaker arm tension to, from 17 to 21 ounces, on a spring scale. (Tension is changed by shifting the spring in the slot.)

**TM 9-710**
93

## BASIC HALF-TRACK VEHICLES (WHITE, AUTOCAR, and DIAMOND T)

A—BODY SHIELD
B—HIGH TENSION CAP SHIELD ASSEMBLY
C—DISTRIBUTOR CAP
D—RETAINER SPRING
E—LOW TENSION LEAD WITH SHIELDING
F—DISTRIBUTOR ASSEMBLY
G—CLAMP ARM CAP SCREW AND LOCK WASHER
H—TACHOMETER ADAPTER
I—CLAMP ARM SCREW
J—DISTRIBUTOR GREASE CUP

RA PD 314055

*Figure 93—Distributor Installed*

(4) BREAKER POINT ADJUSTMENT (fig. 94).

(a) Turn engine over until breaker contacts are fully separated. (The fiber rubbing block on the breaker arm will be on the highest point of the cam.)

(b) Loosen the lock nut on the contact screw, and adjust to obtain maximum gap of 0.017 to 0.018 inch, with points fully separated (fig. 94). Point opening for new points may be checked with a feeler gage, but the roughness of used points makes point setting with a feeler gage unsatisfactory. A dial indicator or contact angle meter should be used to check the point opening of used points. When setting contact point opening with a feeler gage, check opening for every cam lobe. The dif-

## IGNITION SYSTEM

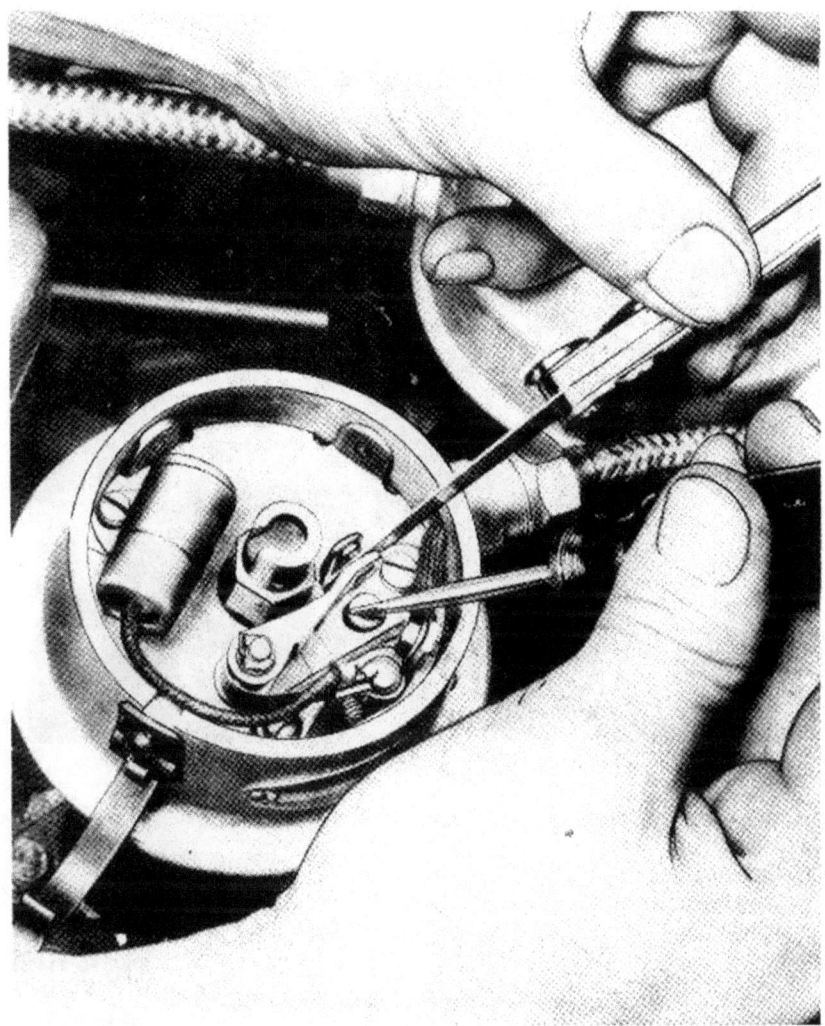

RA PD 3567

*Figure 94—Adjusting Distributor Breaker Point*

ference should not exceed 0.001 inch. If the difference is 0.002 inch or the cams are eccentric (center of cam not at center of rotation), replace distributor.

(c) Tighten nut on contact screw and recheck gap. Insert narrow strip of soft paper between the contacts, and turn the engine until the contacts close. Draw the paper back and forth to remove any oil or grease remaining on the point surfaces.

(d) Install the rotor, and check the cam setting by rocking back and forth as far as the slack in the distributor gear will permit. If the setting is correct, the points should open and close.

# TM 9-710
93

## BASIC HALF-TRACK VEHICLES (WHITE, AUTOCAR, and DIAMOND T)

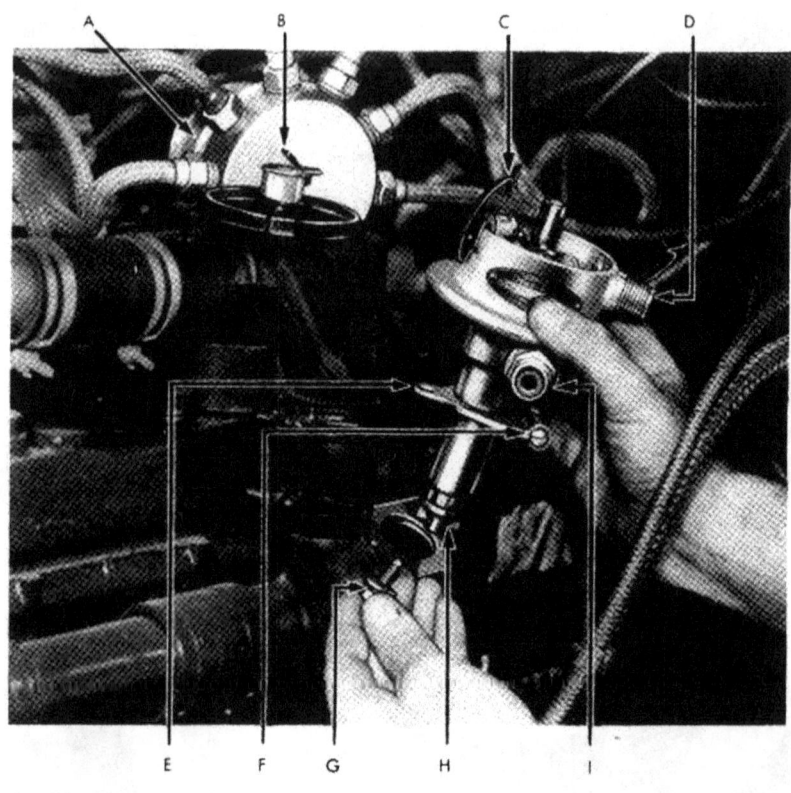

A—HIGH TENSION CAP SHIELD ASSEMBLY
B—ROTOR
C—RETAINER SPRING
D—LOW TENSION LEAD SHIELDING SCREW
E—CLAMP ARM
F—CLAMP ARM SCREW
G—CLAMP ARM TO BLOCK CAP SCREW
H—DISTRIBUTOR COUPLING
I—TACHOMETER DRIVE ADAPTER SCREW

RA PD 314056

*Figure 95—Removal of Distributor*

(e) Try out the engine at various speeds after replacing distributor cap. If the engine does not run smoothly and develop its full power, check spark plugs and ignition wiring before retiming.

(5) CONDENSER REMOVAL. Disconnect condenser wire at terminal in distributor. Unscrew clamp screw and slide condenser from clamp.

(6) CONDENSER INSTALLATION. Place unit in clamp and tighten clamp screw. Install condenser wire at terminal and install and tighten nut.

(7) DISTRIBUTOR CAP CLEANING. Unlatch and remove distributor body shield. Lift up distributor cap shielding and pull spark plug cables from cap. Remove cap from distributor and clean outside and

# TM 9-710

## IGNITION SYSTEM

inside with a soft, clean cloth. Install wiring to cap and cap to distributor.

c. **Distributor Removal** (fig. 95).

(1) REMOVE SHIELDING AND TACHOMETER CABLE. Unfasten the catch of the body shield. Unfold the two semicylindrical halves around the hinge pin and remove shield. Unscrew coupling nut at tachometer adapter and pull tachometer cable from adapter.

(2) REMOVE CAP. Turn down the retainer springs at the sides of the distributor, and lift off the high-tension insulator cap. NOTE: *The shielded spark plug cables attached at the cap shield, and the leads connected to the insulator cap need not be uncoupled.*

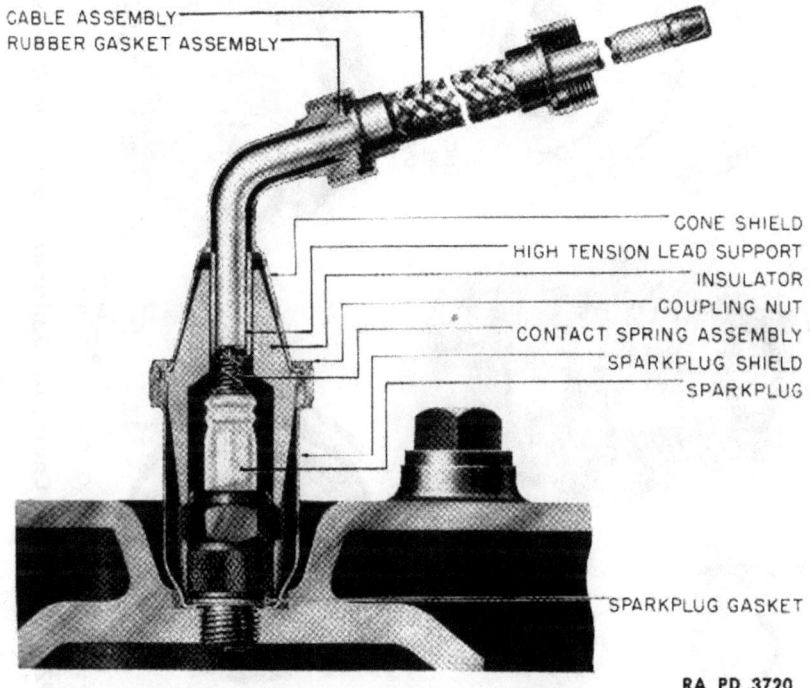

*Figure 96—Spark Plug and Shielding (Sectional View)*

(3) REMOVE WIRING. Detach the shielded low-tension lead from the body of the distributor, and loosen the screw inside, which connects this lead with the breaker points.

(4) REMOVE DISTRIBUTOR. Remove the cap screw and lock washer holding the clamp arm to engine block. Mark position of rotor on distributor and lift out distributor.

d. **Distributor Installation.**

(1) PLACE DISTRIBUTOR IN ASSEMBLY. Place unit in shaft housing, using marks to line up and seat coupling in oil pump shaft fitting. Install and tighten clamp arm cap screw and lock washer.

# TM 9-710

**BASIC HALF-TRACK VEHICLES (WHITE, AUTOCAR; and DIAMOND T)**

Figure 97—Illustrated Causes for Deficient Spark Plug Operation

## IGNITION SYSTEM

(2) INSTALL WIRING. Install low tension lead to breaker point terminal and install shielding cap at distributor body.

(3) INSTALL CAP, SHIELDING, AND TACHOMETER CABLE. Place cap in proper position on body and snap up spring latches to secure. Place distributor body shield in position to hold cap shield, and turn catch to secure. Install tachometer cable to adapter at bottom of distributor and secure with coupling nut.

### 94. SPARK PLUGS.

a. **Description.** The plugs used are standard 14-mm. They are completely shielded for radio suppression (fig. 96).

b. **Removal.** Unscrew round coupling nut on spark plug shielding and lift off upper shielding assembly and cable. Unscrew plug with spark plug wrench and lift out plug and lower shielding.

c. **Maintenance.**

(1) CLEANING. Clean excess carbon and other deposits from the electrodes of the plugs each time the plugs are removed (fig. 97).

(2) REGAPPING. Check spark plug gaps with a feeler gage each 1,000 miles. Test plugs with a spark plug tester each 4,000 miles. Set gap to 0.025 inch.

d. **Installation.** Place new spark plug gasket inside lower plug shielding. Place lower shielding in position over spark plug hole. Install plug and tighten with spark-plug wrench. Install upper shielding assembly and cable and tighten coupling nut on plug shield.

### 95. ENGINE TIMING.

a. **Inspect Breaker Points.** Inspect the breaker points in the distributor carefully to make sure that they are in good condition and have the correct gap of 0.017 to 0.018 inch maximum, when fully separated (fig. 94).

b. **Position No. 1 Piston on Top Dead Center.** Remove No. 1 spark plug. Turn the engine over in the direction of normal running (counterclockwise looking at fan from driver's seat) until the No. 1 piston reaches top dead center on the compression stroke, as indicated by holding thumb over spark plug opening until pressure is felt. Center the pointer on flywheel housing on the flywheel "X" mark (ball between words TOP and DC) at the inspection hole (fig. 98).

c. **Adjust Distributor.** Following the spark plug wire, trace the lead from the No. 1 plug to the distributor; the rotor contact should have a position opposite the No. 1 terminal in the cap. If this is not the case, loosen the advance arm clamp screw, and rotate the body of the distributor around its shaft, until the No. 1 terminal is opposite the rotor contact with the points just beginning to break open. The opening can be checked by a feeler of a very thin, strong paper, or by the ammeter, when the ignition switch is turned on. Be sure to tighten the advance arm clamp screw after making the adjustment. On this position, the No. 1 cylinder will fire at idling speed with fully retarded spark at top dead center. The firing order is 1-5-3-6-2-4.

# TM 9-710

## BASIC HALF-TRACK VEHICLES (WHITE, AUTOCAR, and DIAMOND T)

d. **Test Timing** (fig. 98). If a neon timing light is available, a final check should be made. Make a white chalk mark 1/16-inch wide, on the top dead center ball on the flywheel. Remove the cable from the No. 1 spark plug, and connect one lead of the light to the No. 1 spark plug, and the other to the No. 1 cable. Start the engine and let it run at idling speed, directing the light flash in the opening in the flywheel housing. Check the position of the chalk line in relation to pointer in the inspection hole; the chalk mark should line up exactly with the pointer. If it fails to do so, loosen the distributor advance arm

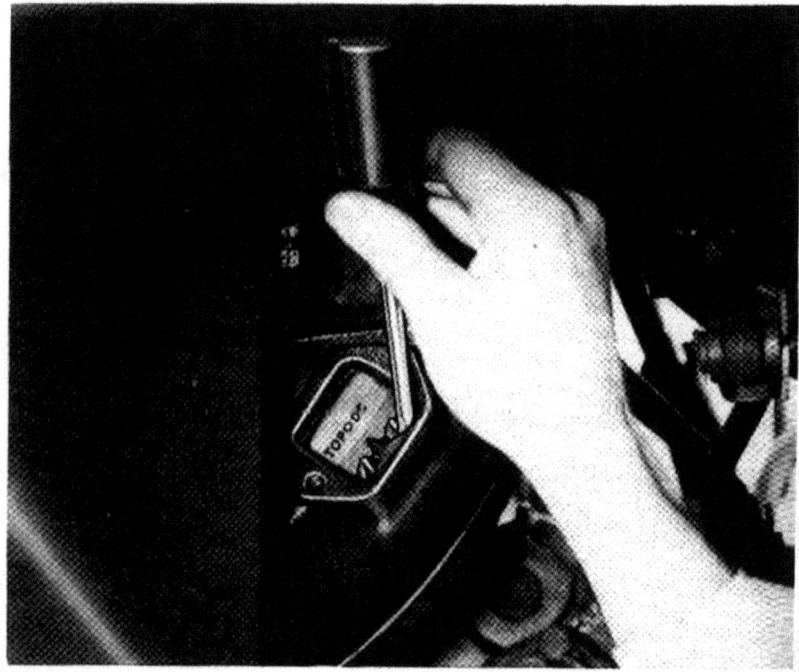

RA PD 314057

*Figure 98—Timing Engine Flywheel*

clamp screw, and rotate the distributor clockwise to advance, or counterclockwise to retard, ignition, as required. NOTE: *If the chalk mark blurs or widens out during test timing, it is an indication of a worn distributor shaft, sticking governor weights, weak governor weight springs, improper breaker contact adjustment, or excessive wear in the distributor drive gears. The difficulty should be investigated and corrected, or reported to higher authority.*

## 96. IGNITION WIRING AND SHIELDING.

a. **Description.** All electrical interference producing radio static, is suppressed in this vehicle by the use of shielding. The shielding covers all low and high tension wiring, the spark plugs, distributor, and

## IGNITION SYSTEM

ignition coil. The entire system grounds all radiating electrical waves within itself.

b. **Maintenance.** Inspect all wiring and shielding at regular intervals. Keep clean and dry. Keep all fittings clean and tight.

c. **Removal.**

(1) REMOVE DISTRIBUTOR BODY SHIELD. Unfasten shield catch, swing halves apart, and pull from assembly.

(2) REMOVE DISTRIBUTOR CAP SHIELD. Remove body shield. Unscrew all plug-to-distributor shielding nuts at cap couplings. Pull cables from distributor cap and through cap shielding, and remove cap shielding.

(3) REMOVE DISTRIBUTOR TO SPARK PLUG WIRE AND SHIELDING. Unscrew coupling nut at distributor cap shield. Unscrew coupling nut at distributor. Pull wire from distributor cap and remove wire and shield from engine. NOTE: *If wire is to be replaced, tie a strong cord to the distributor end, pull wire out from the spark plug end.* This line may then be used to pull the new cable through the shield.

(4) REMOVE DISTRIBUTOR TO COIL WIRE AND SHIELDING. Disconnect wiring at distributor and coil ends. Unscrew shielding coupling nuts on shielding at distributor body and coil box, and lift shielding and wiring from vehicle.

d. **Installation.**

(1) INSTALL DISTRIBUTOR TO SPARK PLUG WIRE AND SHIELDING. Place wire and shield in proper position. Install wire at spark plug. Run wire through hole in cap shield and install in distributor cap. Install and tighten shielding coupling nut at cap shield.

(2) INSTALL DISTRIBUTOR TO COIL WIRE AND SHIELDING. Place wiring and shields in position. Connect wiring at terminals in distributor and coil box. Install and tighten shield coupling nuts at distributor and coil box.

(3) INSTALL DISTRIBUTOR CAP SHIELD. Place shield in position. Push cables through proper holes and insert in proper cap fittings. Install and tighten coupling nuts at cap shield.

(4) INSTALL DISTRIBUTOR BODY SHIELD. Place shield in position, close halves, and fasten latch.

# TM 9-710

**BASIC HALF-TRACK VEHICLES (WHITE, AUTOCAR, and DIAMOND T)**

Section XX

## STARTING AND GENERATING SYSTEM

|  | Paragraph |
|---|---|
| Description of system and tabulated data | 97 |
| Cranking motor | 98 |
| Generator | 99 |
| Voltage regulator | 100 |

## 97. DESCRIPTION OF SYSTEM AND TABULATED DATA.

**a. Description.** The starting and generating system include the cranking motor, generator, voltage regulator, and their attaching parts (fig. 99). Complete description of the units in this system are given below.

**b. Tabulated Data.**

(1) CRANKING MOTOR.
   Make .................... Delco-Remy
   Model ................... 1108533
   Type .................... gear reduction

(2) GENERATOR.
   Make .................... Delco-Remy
   Model ................... 1117308
   Type .................... shunt wound

(3) VOLTAGE REGULATOR.
   Make .................... Delco-Remy
   Model ................... 1118488
   Type .................... 12-volt

## 98. CRANKING MOTOR.

**a. Description.** The cranking motor is a gear-reduction type, and is secured to the flywheel housing on the left side of the engine (fig. 100). Power is transmitted to the engine flywheel ring gear through a right-hand Bendix drive. A removable cover band around the field frame permits inspection of the commutator and brush connections.

**b. Removal.** Disconnect battery cable at terminal on top of motor and tape the end. Disconnect cranking motor switch wire from solenoid terminal. Remove three cap screws and lock washers which secure motor to flywheel housing, and lift carefully from engine.

**c. Installation.** Place cranking motor in position on engine, insert and tighten three lock washers and cap screws. Connect switch wire on solenoid terminal and install and tighten terminal lock washer and nut. Remove tape and clean battery cable terminal. Install cable on cranking motor terminal and install and tighten lock washer and nut.

## STARTING AND GENERATING SYSTEM

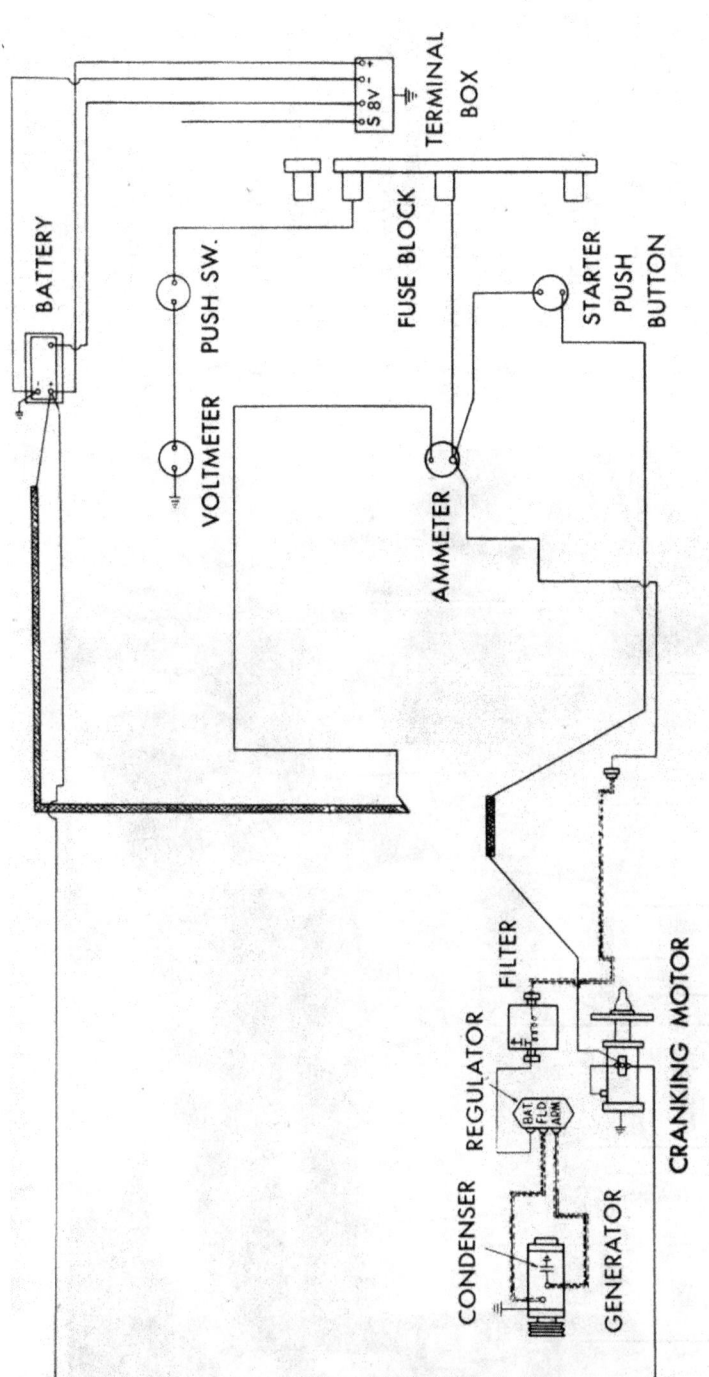

*Figure 99—Starting and Generating System Wiring Diagram*

## BASIC HALF-TRACK VEHICLES (WHITE, AUTOCAR, and DIAMOND T)

A — OILER
B — COMMUTER COVER BAND
C — SWITCH CONNECTOR STRAP
D — TERMINAL STUD, W/NUT (2) WASHER AND LOCK WASHER (2)
E — SWITCH TO BATTERY TERMINAL, W/NUT, WASHER AND LOCK WASHER
F — SWITCH TO BUTTON TERMINAL, W/NUT AND LOCK WASHER
G — SWITCH TO SCREW (2), W/LOCK WASHER
H — MAGNETIC SWITCH
J — PLUG
K — DRIVE HOUSING
L — CRANKING MOTOR TO HOUSING SCREW (3), W/LOCK WASHER (3)

RA PD 314059

Figure 100—Cranking Motor Installed

## STARTING AND GENERATING SYSTEM

**99. GENERATOR.**

**a. Description.** The generator (fig. 101) is a shunt wound unit having counterclockwise rotation as viewed from the commutator end. The unit is secured to the left side of the crankcase by a bracket and is belt-driven through a dual sheave pulley. Belt tension is maintained by adjusting the slotted supporting strap. The terminals are shielded to reduce radio interference. Cold output under control of the regulator is 55 amperes at 900 revolutions per minute. A removable cover band around the field frame permits the inspection of the commutator and brush connections.

**b. Removal.**

(1) DISCONNECT FIELD AND ARMATURE WIRES. Unscrew armature condenser from armature terminal shield housing (fig. 101). Unscrew coupling nut of cable shielding. Remove terminal nut and remove wire and cable. Remove cap from field terminal shield. Remove terminal nut. Unscrew shielding coupling nut and remove wire and shielding conduit.

(2) REMOVE GENERATOR DRIVE BELTS. Remove adjusting nut, lock washer, and bolt from generator adjusting strap. Loosen adjusting strap at water pump and push aside. Loosen, but do not remove bolts on generator bracket and lift generator. Pry belts off generator pulley.

(3) REMOVE GENERATOR. Remove two nuts, lock washers, and bolts from generator bracket (fig. 67). Lift out generator and bracket assembly.

**c. Installation.**

(1) INSTALL GENERATOR ON BRACKET. Place generator in position on bracket. Install two bolts, lock washers, and nuts holding generator to bracket and tighten nuts fingertight.

(2) INSTALL AND ADJUST DRIVE BELTS. Lift generator and slide drive belts over generator pulley. Swing adjusting strap into position and insert adjusting bolt, lock washer, and nut. Adjust drive belt tension (par. 86), and tighten all nuts.

(3) CONNECT GENERATOR FIELD AND ARMATURE WIRES. Connect field cable at terminal and tighten terminal nut. Install shielding cap and shielding coupling nut at terminal shielding and tighten. Connect armature cable at terminal and tighten terminal nut. Install and tighten coupling nut at terminal shield housing. Install condenser and housing to top of terminal housing.

(4) POLARIZE GENERATOR. Reverse polarity will cause vibrating points to vibrate and burn. To make certain that generator has correct polarity after regulator is reconnected, momentarily connect battery terminal of regulator to the field terminal before starting the engine. Momentary surge of battery current will correctly polarize generator.

**100. VOLTAGE REGULATOR.**

**a. Description and Operation.** The generator output to the electrical system is controlled automatically by a voltage regulator (fig. 102), which is mounted to the left on the engine side of the dash. The regulator consists of three separate and distinct elements, described

**BASIC HALF-TRACK VEHICLES (WHITE, AUTOCAR, and DIAMOND T)**

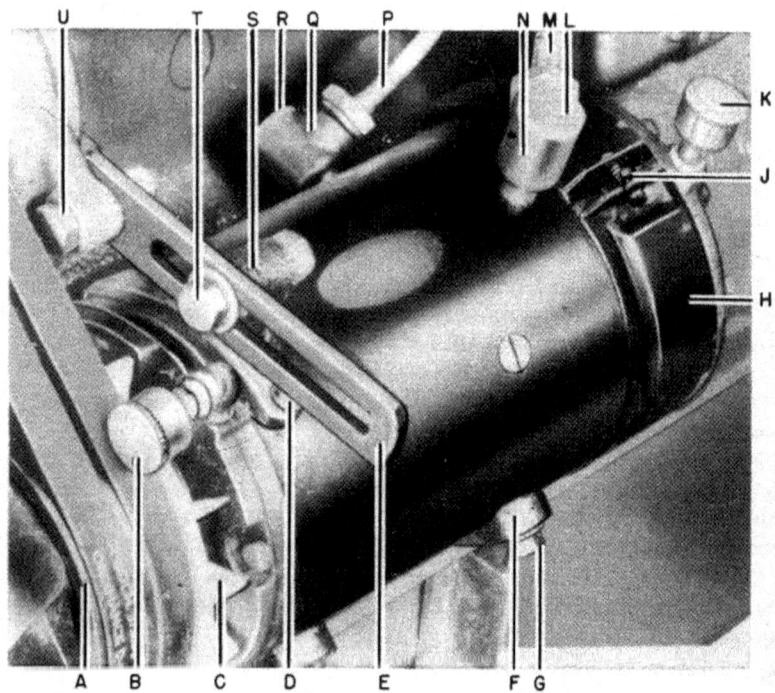

A - GENERATOR PULLEY, W/SHAFT NUT, WASHER, AND COTTER PIN
B - GREASE CUP W/ELBOW, FOR DRIVE END BALL BEARING
C - GENERATOR FAN
D - BRACKET TO GENERATOR SCREW (2), W/LOCK WASHER (2)
E - ADJUSTMENT SLOTTED STRAP
F - GENERATOR SUPPORT BRACKET
G - BRACKET TO GENERATOR SCREW (4), W/LOCK WASHER (4)
H - COMMUTATOR COVER BAND
J - COVER BAND SCREW, W/NUT
K - GREASE CUP FOR COMUTATOR END BALL BEARING
L - ARMATURE TERMINAL SHIELD CAP
M - GENERATOR ARMATURE (PLUS) TO REGULATOR, W/SHIELDING
N - ARMATURE TERMINAL SHIELD, W/TERMINAL STUD BUSHING (2)
P - GENERATOR FIELD TO REGULATOR SHIELDING W/CABLE
Q - FIELD TERMINAL SHIELD, W/TERMINAL STUD BUSHING (2)
R - FIELD TERMINAL SHIELD CAP
S - FAN BELT ADJUSTING BRACKET
T - STRAP TO GENERATOR BRACKET BOLT, W/NUT AND WASHERS
U - STRAP TO PUMP BOLT, W/NUT AND LOCK WASHER

RA PD 3556

*Figure 101—Generator Installed*

## STARTING AND GENERATING SYSTEM

as a cut-out or reverse current relay, the voltage-regulator relay, and a current limiting relay, all of which are mounted on the same base under a common cover and shielded.

(1) CUT-OUT RELAY. The function of this automatic switch is to close the circuit between the generator armature and the battery when the circuit is operating at a speed sufficient to develop voltage (approximately 13.5 volts) in excess of the system to which it is connected, and

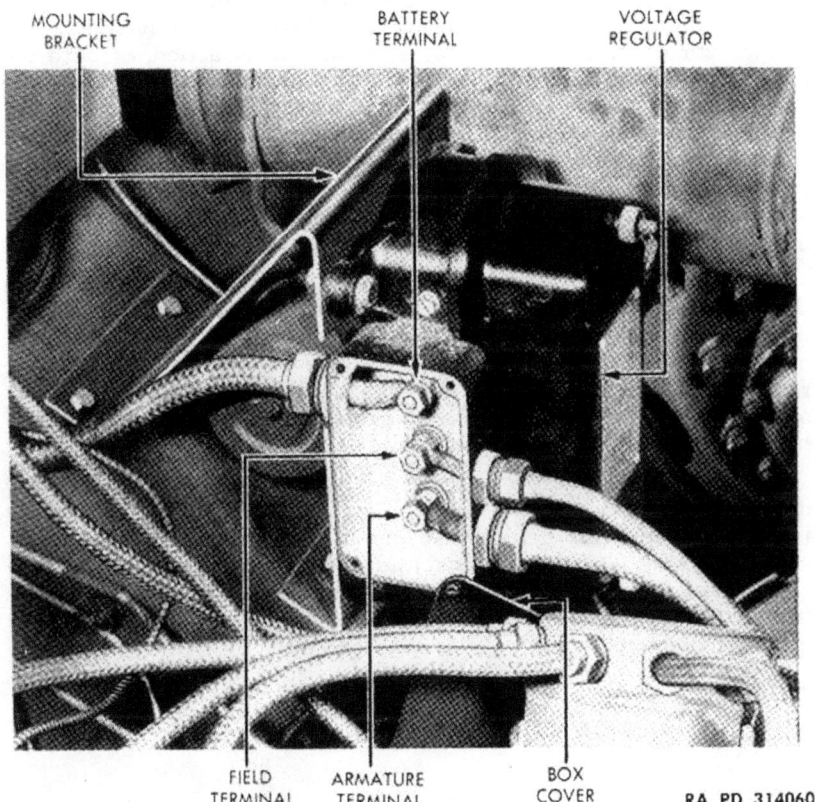

*Figure 102—Voltage Regulator Installed*

to open the circuit when the generator is at a standstill or low speed and thus prevent discharge of the battery through the generator.

(2) VOLTAGE REGULATOR RELAY. The function of this vibrating type unit is to control the generator field and prevent the generated voltage from exceeding a predetermined value (approximately 15.0 volts on open circuit). A constant voltage is maintained and at the same time limited to protect the system equipment from excessive voltage surges. The regulator cannot increase the generator output beyond the designed maximum.

## BASIC HALF-TRACK VEHICLES (WHITE, AUTOCAR, and DIAMOND T)

(3) CURRENT REGULATOR RELAY. This unit is similar in construction to the voltage regulator relay, but its action depends on the load requirement rather than the generated voltage. It functions to protect the generator from an excessive current output by opening the circuit at a predetermined circuit value (55 amperes). The normal current output varies in proportion to the state of battery charge and the requirements of the vehicle electrical accessories.

b. **Failure in Operation.** In the event of an emergency involving the voltage regulator, it would be practical to disconnect the field terminal lead at the generator to prevent the latter from developing any voltage while operating with the regulator out of action, or until the particular trouble can be identified and corrected. In case contacts of the regulator relays tend to seal, the generator has no protection electrically other than to have its field and armature terminals disconnected, since it cannot readily be removed if the engine is to continue running and retain the belt drive for the fan. The best procedure, if materiel is available, is to replace a voltage regulator when there is any indication of trouble that cannot be simply determined and corrected.

c. **Removal.** Unscrew shielding coupling nuts on armature cable shield (large shield) and field cable shield (small shield) at front of box which is secured to right side of regulator. Unscrew shielding coupling nut of battery cable shield at rear of this box. Remove four screws and cover from this box. Remove the three nuts and lock washers and disconnect the terminals. Remove four nuts, lock washers, and bolts holding regulator to bracket and remove regulator.

d. **Installation.** Place regulator in position on bracket and secure it with four bolts, lock washers, and nuts. Install battery cable (top terminal); generator field cable (middle terminal); and generator armature cable (bottom terminal), and secure with lock washers and nuts. Install shielding coupling nuts on outside of terminal box. Install box cover and secure with four screws. **NOTE:** *After regulator is installed, polarize generator* (par. 99 c (4)).

TM 9-710
101-102

Section XXI

# TRANSMISSION, TRANSFER CASE, AND POWER TAKE-OFF

|  | Paragraph |
|---|---|
| Description and tabulated data | 101 |
| Removal | 102 |
| Installation | 103 |

## 101. DESCRIPTION AND TABULATED DATA.

**a. Transmission** (fig. 103). The transmission and transfer case are bolted together to form an integral unit. The front of the transmission is attached to the clutch bell housing. The transmission shift lever is mounted on the top of the transmission; the hand brake lever and power take-off on the left-hand side; the transfer case and front axle shift levers on the right-hand side. The transmission is equipped with four speeds forward and one speed reverse.

**b. Transfer Case** (fig. 103). The transfer case is bolted to the rear of the transmission. This end of the assembly is suspended by a spring pressure plate and arched spring strap, the ends of which ride on pads on top of the frame side rails (fig. 103). This unit is part of the power train by which the rear axle (jackshaft) and the front axle are driven. High and low speed gears contained in this unit are used in conjunction with the gear speeds in the transmission to adapt the available power of the vehicle to best suit road and load conditions. The speedometer drive gears are fully enclosed in a small housing at the rear end of the front axle drive shaft and engage with a gear on this shaft. These gears are lubricated by the oil contained in the transfer case.

**c. Power Take-off** (fig. 103). The power take-off is mounted on the left side of the transmission and is the unit through which the winch receives its driving power. A propeller shaft connects the power take-off with the winch worm shaft and is controlled by the clutch and power take-off lever in the driver's compartment. The speed of the winch is controlled by the engine speed. This unit is lubricated by oil from the transmission case.

**d. Tabulated Data.**

(1) TRANSMISSION-TRANSFER CASE ASSEMBLY.
  Make .................................................. Spicer
  Model No. .............................................. 3641
  Type .......... 4-speed (with front axle declutching)
  Oil capacity (transmission-transfer case) ....... 7½ qt

(2) POWER TAKE-OFF.
  Make .............................................. Brown-Lipe
  Model No. ............................................ 001904
  Oil capacity (transmission-transfer case
    with power take-off) ............................. 9 qt

## 102. REMOVAL.

**a. Drain Lubricant.** Unscrew and remove the drain plug at bottom right-hand side of transmission, and drain lubricant from trans-

**TM 9-710**
**102**

**BASIC HALF-TRACK VEHICLES (WHITE, AUTOCAR, and DIAMOND T)**

A—CLUTCH RELEASE LEVER
B—BELL HOUSING
C—POWER TAKE-OFF SHIFT LEVER
D—TRANSMISSION SHIFT LEVER
E—HAND BRAKE LEVER
F—SHIFT LEVER CONNECTING LINK
G—TRANSFER CASE SHIFT LEVER
H—FRONT AXLE SHIFT LEVER
I—SPEEDOMETER CABLE COUPLING
J—TRANSMISSION SUPPORT SPRING
K—POWER TAKE-OFF ASSEMBLY
L—TRANSMISSION CASE PROTECTOR
M—PROPELLER SHAFT BRAKE ASSEMBLY
N—SPRING PRESSURE PLATE
O—BRAKE DISK
P—PROPELLER SHAFT

RA PD 314061

*Figure 103—Transmission, Transfer Case, and Power Take-off Installed*

## TRANSMISSION, TRANSFER CASE, AND POWER TAKE-OFF

mission, transfer case, and power take-off. As this unit is equipped with a magnetic drain plug, clean off any metal particles that may be clinging to bottom of plug before reinstalling.

b. **Remove Floor Plates.** Remove nine bolts, lock washers, and nuts from left-hand floor plate and lift out plate. Remove eight bolts, lock washers, and nuts from right-hand floor plate and lift out plate. Remove two bolts, lock washers, and nuts, and three machine screws from the small section at right-hand front corner of center floor plate. Remove knob from transfer case lever and lift out plate over transfer case and front axle levers. Remove the two side panels and the center floor plate in one section by removing three machine screws with lock washers and nuts from the right-hand side plate and four machine screws with lock washers and nuts from the left-hand side plate; three bolts, lock washers, and nuts at the rear of the floor plate and two bolts, lock washers, and nuts at the front.

c. **Disconnect Speedometer Cable.** Unscrew the round coupling nut on speedometer cable at connection to transfer case. Remove two cap screws and lock washers from two clips which attach speedometer cable to right-hand side of the transmission.

d. **Block Propeller Shaft Brake Operating Lever.** Pull propeller shaft brake to full "ON" position and block the operating lever (fig. 104) to hold the brake disk and assembly in their proper position after removal of rear propeller shaft.

e. **Remove Rear Axle Propeller Shaft.** Refer to paragraph 105.

f. **Disconnect Front Axle and Power Take-off Propeller Shaft.** Refer to paragraphs 104 and 106.

g. **Remove Transmission Case Protector.** Remove four bolts, nuts, and lock washers at each end of transmission case protector where it is secured to the frame side rail brackets and remove protector from brackets. Remove the four bolts, nuts, and lock washers securing the left side rail bracket to the frame and slide the bracket toward the rear to clear the power take-off unit.

h. **Disconnect Radio Bonding Strap.** Remove cap screw and lock washer from transfer case-to-frame bonding strap on transfer case.

i. **Remove Clutch Release Lever.** Disconnect clutch relay shaft lever rod from clutch release shaft lever by removing cotter pin and rod end pin. Loosen the clamp bolt on clutch release shaft lever and pull lever off the clutch shifter shaft.

j. **Remove Transmission Gearshift Lever.** Place lever in neutral and remove four nuts and lock washers which attach gear shifter housing cover to transmission. Lift out lever, housing cover, and gasket.

k. **Remove Power Take-off Lever and Bracket.** Disconnect lever and connecting link at bottom of shift lever by removing cotter pin and rod end pin. Remove the mounting bracket from the transmission and transfer case by removing a cap screw and lock washer from the front end of the bracket, and a nut and lock washer at the rear end. Lift off lever and mounting bracket as a unit.

l. **Remove Hand Lever and Bracket Assembly (Propeller Shaft Brake).** Remove cotter pin and clevis pin from pull rod yoke end and disconnect yoke end from operating lever (fig. 161). Remove two cap

# TM 9-710
## 102
### BASIC HALF-TRACK VEHICLES (WHITE, AUTOCAR, and DIAMOND T)

screws and lock washers from quadrant and pull assembly from transfer case.

m. **Disconnect Shift Levers Connecting Links.** Remove cotter pins and rod end pins from the front axle and transfer case connecting links at the transfer case connection. Lower the shift levers and bind levers and connecting links with wire (fig. 105).

n. **Sling Transmission and Transfer Case Assembly** (fig. 105). Arrange rope in figure eight sling around transmission assembly, making certain the unit will be balanced and fully supported during removal

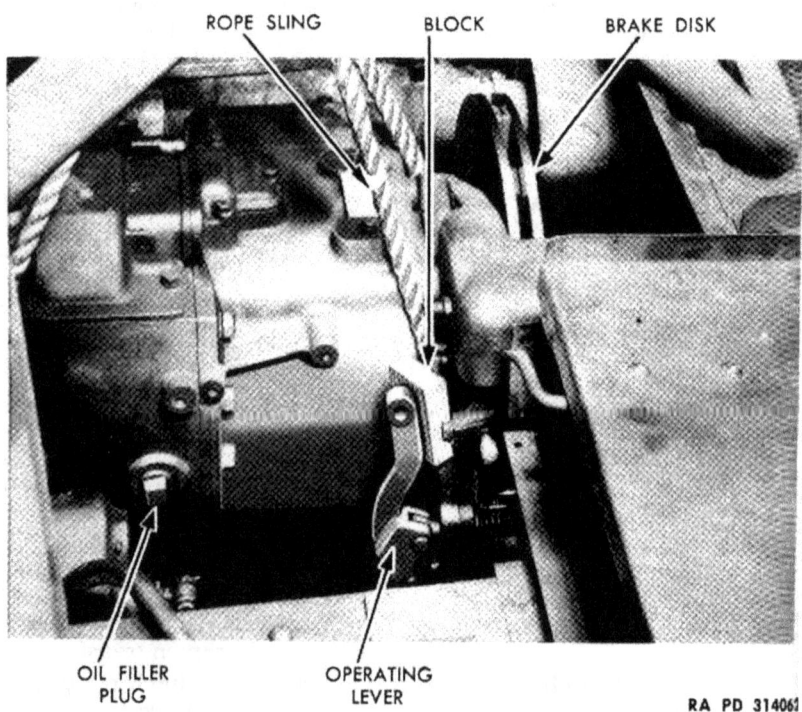

Figure 104—Blocking Propeller Shaft Brake Operating Lever

of the supporting cap screws and spring pressure plate, in order to prevent injury or springing of the transmission splined shaft.

o. **Disconnect Transmission at Flywheel Housing and Spring Pressure Plate.** Remove 12 cap screws and lock washers which secure transmission to flywheel housing. Push battery cable and two clips, which are secured by two of the flywheel housing cap screws, out of the way. Remove two cap screws and lock washers from spring pressure plate and transmission support spring (fig. 103).

p. **Remove Transmission Assembly.** Using the sling to fully support the assembly, pull assembly straight back until transmission splined shaft is clear of clutch splines. Lower the assembly to the floor and slide it out from under the vehicle.

TM 9-710
103

# TRANSMISSION, TRANSFER CASE, AND POWER TAKE-OFF

## 103. INSTALLATION.

a. **Preliminary Procedure.** Before installing transmission and transfer case assembly, remove the clutch ventilator plate cover so that engagement of the splined shaft can be observed as it is being guided into position. After engagement is completed, install the cover.

b. **Position Transmission in Vehicle.** Arrange the rope sling around transmission and transfer case assembly so that it will support and balance the assembly and maintain the alinement of splined shaft and clutch spline as it is engaged. Slide the assembly under vehicle and lift to proper height. Aline splined shaft with clutch spline (it may be necessary to rotate the clutch spline slightly to aline) and engage the two units.

c. **Secure Transmission to Flywheel Housing and Spring Pressure Plate.** Install and tighten 12 cap screws and lock washers to secure transmission to flywheel housing. (Install the two battery cable clips under two of the flywheel housing cap screws.) Install and tighten two lock washers and cap screws through spring pressure plate to secure transfer case to support spring. Remove rope sling.

d. **Connect Clutch Release Lever.** Install the clutch release lever on the clutch shifter shaft and secure with Woodruff key and the half-clamp bolt. Connect the clutch relay shaft lever to the clutch release shaft lever by inserting rod end pin and securing with cotter pin.

e. **Install Speedometer Cable.** Insert end of speedometer cable in connection at transfer case and secure by tightening the round nut. Install the two clips which hold cable to side of transmission and secure with two cap screws.

f. **Connect Front Axle and Winch Propeller Shafts.** Refer to paragraphs 104 and 106.

g. **Install Rear Axle Propeller Shaft.** Refer to paragraph 105.

h. **Install Hand Lever and Bracket Assembly (Propeller Shaft Brake).** Place hand lever and bracket assembly in proper position on transfer case and secure with two cap screws and lock washers. Connect pull rod yoke end and operating lever; insert clevis pin and secure with cotter pin. Remove wood block from behind operating lever.

i. **Install Power Take-off Lever and Bracket.** Place power take-off shift lever and bracket in position over brake quadrant bracket and secure front end of bracket to transfer case with lock washer and cap screw. Secure the rear end of bracket to stud in brake quadrant with lock washer and nut. Install clevis pin to bottom of shift lever and connecting link and secure with cotter pin.

j. **Install Transmission Gearshift Lever.** Install gearshift lever and gear shifter housing cover with new gasket and secure with four lock washers and nuts.

k. **Connect Shift Lever Connecting Links.** Install the transfer case and front axle shift lever connecting links to their transfer case connections and secure with rod end pins and cotter pins.

l. **Install Transmission Case Protector.** Place the left-hand transmission case protector bracket in position on frame side rail and secure with four bolts, lock washers, and nuts. Install the transmission

**BASIC HALF-TRACK VEHICLES (WHITE, AUTOCAR, and DIAMOND T)**

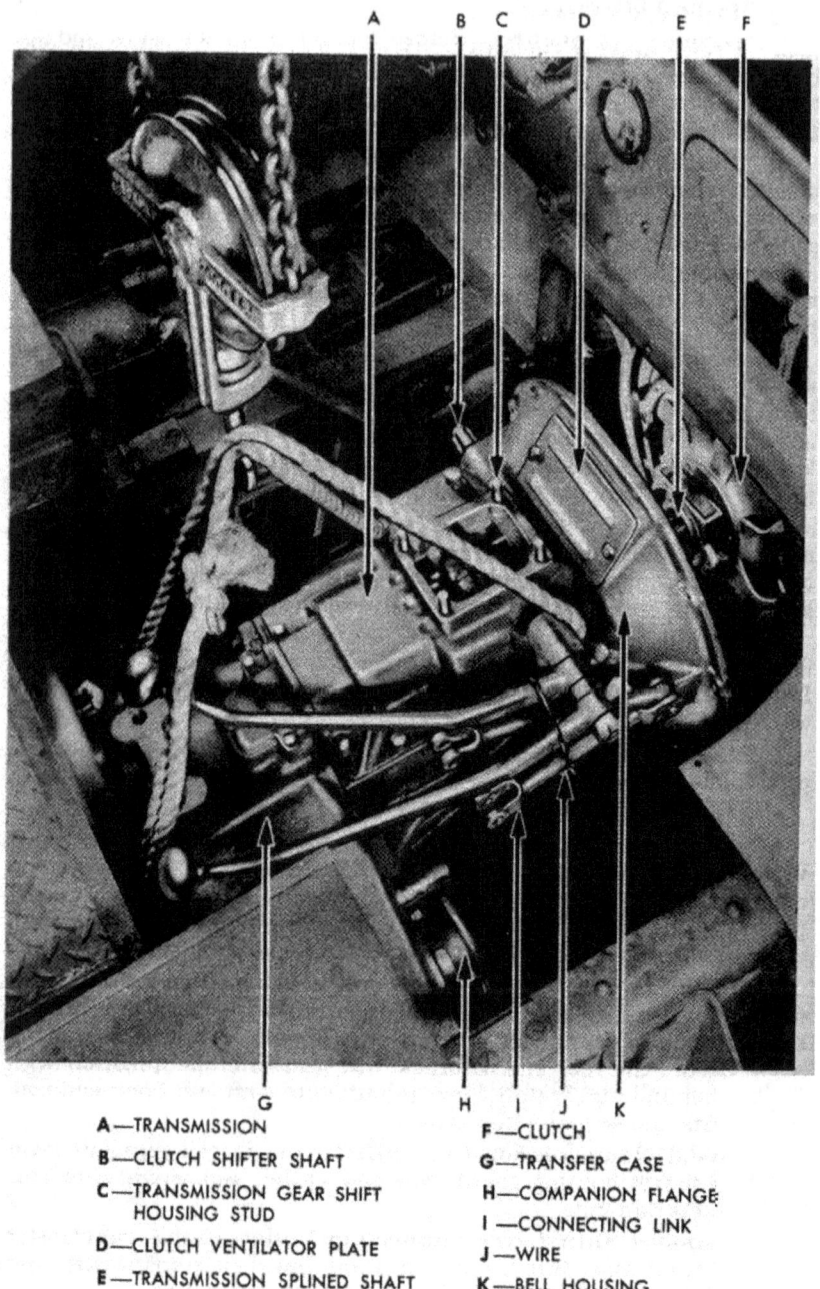

A—TRANSMISSION
B—CLUTCH SHIFTER SHAFT
C—TRANSMISSION GEAR SHIFT HOUSING STUD
D—CLUTCH VENTILATOR PLATE
E—TRANSMISSION SPLINED SHAFT
F—CLUTCH
G—TRANSFER CASE
H—COMPANION FLANGE
I—CONNECTING LINK
J—WIRE
K—BELL HOUSING

RA PD 314063

*Figure 105—Removing Transmission, Transfer Case, and Power Take-off*

# TM 9-710
## 103
### TRANSMISSION, TRANSFER CASE, AND POWER TAKE-OFF

case protector to the side brackets and secure at each end with four bolts, lock washers, and nuts.

m. **Install Radio Bonding Strap.** Install radio bonding strap, lock washer and cap screw, to right side of transfer case.

n. **Install Floor Plates.** Install the two side panels and center floor plate section. Secure the right-hand side panel with three machine screws, lock washers, and nuts and the left-hand side panel with four machine screws, lock washers, and nuts. Secure the front end of floor plate with two bolts, lock washers, and nuts and the rear end with three bolts, lock washers, and nuts. Slip the small section of center plate over the transfer case and front axle levers and secure with two bolts, lock washers, nuts, and three machine screws. Install transfer case lever knob. Place the right-hand and left-hand floor plates in position and secure the right-hand plate with eight bolts, lock washers, and nuts and the left-hand plate with nine bolts, lock washers, and nuts.

o. **Replace Lubricant in Transmission.** Pour nine quarts of the specified grade of lubricant into transmission at filler plug if unit is equipped with power take-off; 7½ quarts if no power take-off is connected to the assembly. Oil filler plug is located on the left-hand side of transmission (fig. 160).

TM 9-710
104

**BASIC HALF-TRACK VEHICLES (WHITE, AUTOCAR, and DIAMOND T)**

Section XXII

## PROPELLER SHAFTS AND UNIVERSAL JOINTS

|  | Paragraph |
|---|---|
| Transfer case to front axle propeller shaft | 104 |
| Transfer case to rear axle (jackshaft) propeller shaft | 105 |
| Power take-off to winch propeller shaft | 106 |

**104. TRANSFER CASE TO FRONT AXLE PROPELLER SHAFT.**

a. Description. The transfer case to front axle propeller shaft consists of two flange-yoke universal joints and a connecting tube welded to these joints (fig. 106). The transfer case end of the con-

*Figure 106—Front Axle and Winch Propeller Shaft Installed*

# TM 9-710
## 104-105

### PROPELLER SHAFTS AND UNIVERSAL JOINTS

necting tube is fitted with a slip joint (splined shaft) to absorb differences in length caused by the flexing of the vehicle springs. The flange yokes on the two universal joints are bolted to companion flanges at the transfer case and front axle.

b. **Removal.** Remove four bolts, nuts, and lock washers at each end of the shaft to disconnect the companion flanges from the shaft universal joint flange yokes. Lower assembly to the floor.

c. **Installation.** Place propeller shaft assembly (fig. 107) in position. Place the slip joint end against the transfer case companion flange

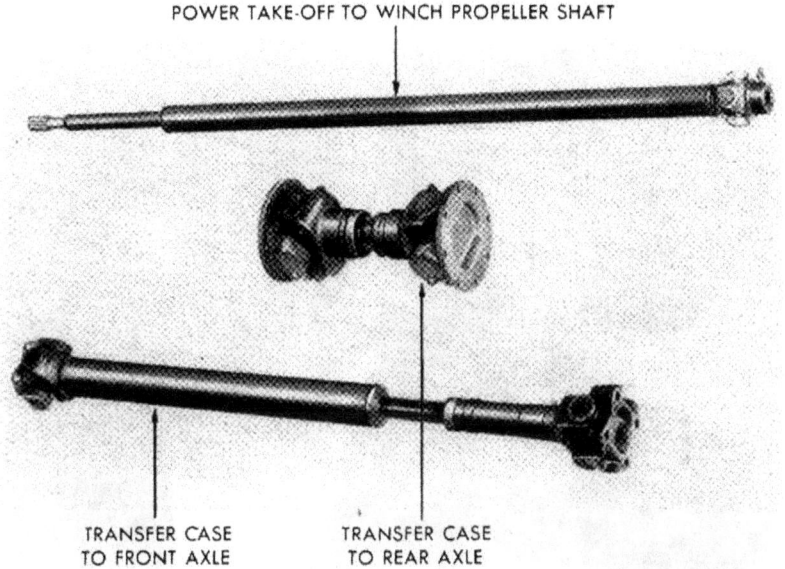

*Figure 107—Propeller Shafts*

and line up the four bolt holes. Insert four bolts through holes in flange yoke and companion flange and secure with four lock washers and nuts. Secure the opposite end of shaft in same manner except to reverse the insertion of the bolts (through the companion flange first).

### 105. TRANSFER CASE TO REAR AXLE (JACKSHAFT) PROPELLER SHAFT.

a. **Description.** The transfer case to rear axle propeller shaft (fig. 108) consists of two flange yoke universal joints connected with a slip joint, which is installed on the transfer case end. This joint absorbs differences in the length of the propeller shaft that are caused by the flexing of the track and bogie assembly.

b. **Removal.** Remove eight cotter pins, castellated nuts, and bolts

# TM 9-710
## 105-106

**BASIC HALF-TRACK VEHICLES (WHITE, AUTOCAR, and DIAMOND T)**

at each end to disconnect the flange yokes on the propeller shaft from the companion flanges. Push the slip joint together by shoving the rear end of propeller shaft toward front and lower assembly to the floor. NOTE: *Disconnect the jackshaft end first, then shift transmission to neutral.* The drive shaft brake disk can be rotated to facilitate removal of the cotter pins, nuts, and bolts at this end.

c. **Installation.** Position propeller shaft flange yoke (with slip joint toward brake disk) to transfer case companion flange and line up bolt holes. Insert eight bolts through holes in companion flange,

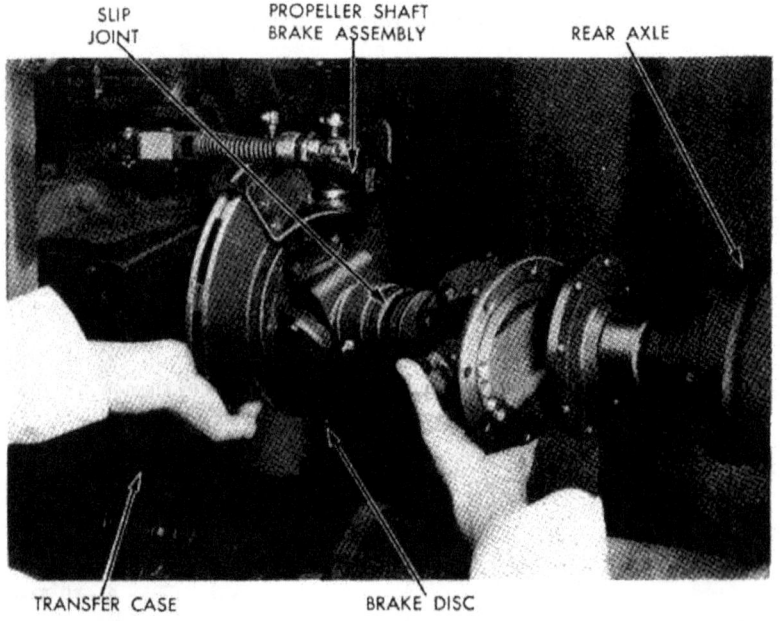

*Figure 108—Removing Transfer Case to Rear Axle Propeller Shaft*

brake disk, and flange yoke, and install and tighten eight castellated nuts. Secure nuts with cotter pins. Secure the opposite end with eight bolts, nuts, and cotter pins.

**106. POWER TAKE-OFF TO WINCH PROPELLER SHAFT.**

a. **Description.** The power take-off to winch propeller shaft consists of two universal joints connected with a tubular shaft having a slip joint at the winch end of the shaft.

b. **Removal.** Unscrew jam nut on the set screw holding the propeller shaft universal joint to the power take-off shaft and back off set screw. Push propeller forward (the slip joint at winch end will allow the rear universal joint to clear the power take-off shaft), then pull pro-

## PROPELLER SHAFTS AND UNIVERSAL JOINTS

peller shaft free of front universal slip joint and remove propeller shaft. NOTE: *If necessary to replace the universal joint on winch worm shaft, remove the cotter pin from shear pin in end yoke and remove shear pin.* Unscrew and remove eight nuts, lock washers, and bolts attaching winch frame to supporting members and slide winch back enough to pull the universal joint from end of winch worm drive shaft. Replace the universal joint on winch drive shaft and install shear pin, securing assembly with cotter pin inserted through shear pin. Install eight bolts, lock washers, and nuts to winch frame and supporting members.

c. **Installation.** Install winch propeller shaft to winch worm drive shaft universal joint by inserting propeller shaft spline end through opening in bottom corner of radiator and armor shield. Pull rear end of winch propeller shaft onto the power take-off shaft and Woodruff key and secure connection with set screw and jam nut.

TM 9-710
107-108

**BASIC HALF-TRACK VEHICLES (WHITE, AUTOCAR, and DIAMOND T)**

Section XXIII

## FRONT AXLE

| | Paragraph |
|---|---|
| Description and tabulated data | 107 |
| Maintenance and adjustment | 108 |
| Tie rod | 109 |
| Removal of front axle assembly | 110 |
| Installation of front axle assembly | 111 |

### 107. DESCRIPTION AND TABULATED DATA.

*a. Description.* The front axle (fig. 109) is of the single-reduction, full-floating type, with a straddle mounted pinion gear and a conventional type differential. The front wheels are driven through constant-velocity type universal joints enclosed within steering knuckles at the outer ends of the axle housing. Boots encircle the joints to prevent lubricant leakage, and these boots are protected by brush guard pins. A tie rod is part of the assembly, transmitting the turning force from the left-hand steering knuckle to the right-hand steering knuckle.

*b. Tabulated Data.*
  Make . . . . . . . . . . . . . . . . . . . . . . . . . . . . . Timken
  Model No. . . . . . . . . . . . . . . . . . . . . . . F-35-HX-1
  Type . . . . . . . . . . . . . single-reduction, full-floating

### 108. MAINTENANCE AND ADJUSTMENT.

*a. Maintenance.* Inspect the axle assembly at regular intervals for evidence of leaks, cracks, or other faulty conditions. Keep all mountings bolts tight. Lubricate regularly as specified (par. 23).

(1) STEERING KNUCKLE BOOT REPLACEMENT.

*(a) Removal.* Block vehicle tracks. Jack up front wheel on side boot is to be replaced and remove wheel. Remove the boot guard (fig 110) by removing four nuts and lock washers from the attaching studs Loosen but do not remove the two remaining nuts at the rear of the plate assembly to provide clearance to remove and install the boot. Remove the outer and inner clamping rings (fig. 111). Sever the steering knuckle boot with a knife and remove. Remove all grease and dirt from the components to which boot was clamped, using dry-cleaning solvent, and wipe all surfaces thoroughly dry.

*(b) Installation.* Open the zipper on the new steering knuckle boot and install around axle housing. Close the zipper fastening (fig. 112). NOTE: *The zipper must be in a horizontal position in front of the axle tube on the left-hand side of the vehicle and on the rearward side of the front axle tube on the right-hand side.* Force the inner edge of the closed boot over the steering knuckle ball joint and aline in the groove. Install the inner clamping ring to the inner edge of boot and tighten. Cut off excess of ring with side cutting pliers and remove. Install outer clamping

## FRONT AXLE

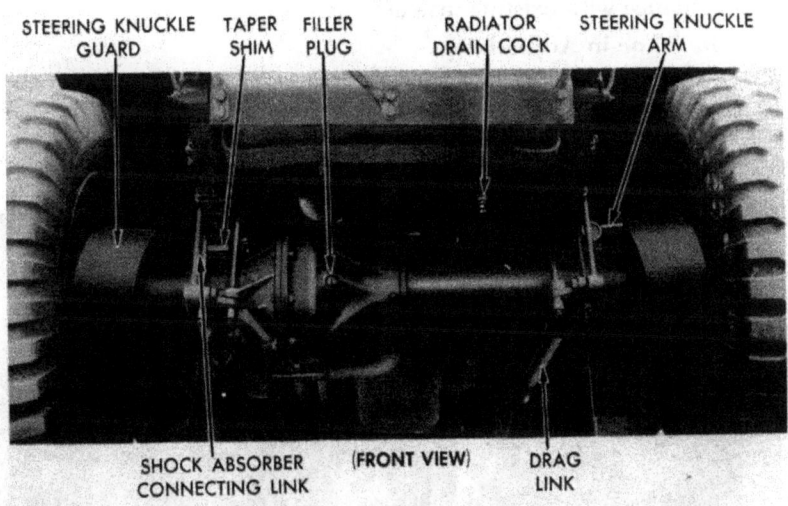

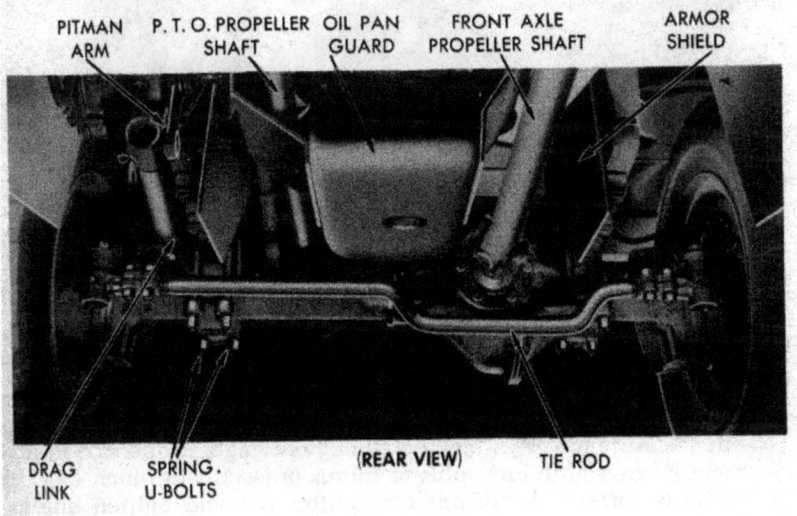

**Figure 109—Front Axle Installed**

## BASIC HALF-TRACK VEHICLES (WHITE, AUTOCAR, and DIAMOND T)

ring to outer edge of boot and tighten. Cut off excess threaded portion of clamping ring. Paint the zipper with rubber tire patching cement. Reassemble the steering knuckle boot guard parts and wheel in reverse order of their removal. Lubricate the steering knuckle assembly in accordance with existing instructions.

b. **Toe-in Adjustment.**

(1) "COARSE" ADJUSTMENT. Remove cotter pin and nut from right end knuckle pin, and tap pin down through bracket. Loosen binder bolts

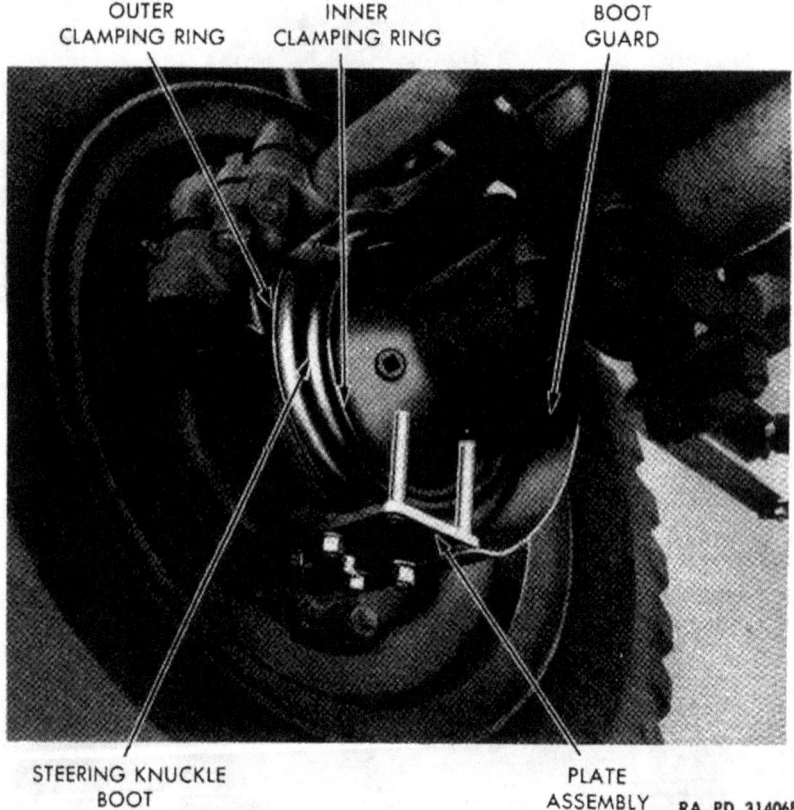

*Figure 110—Steering Knuckle Boot and Guard (Rear View)*

at right-hand end, and turn tie rod end assembly one complete turn, in or out. Install tube end knuckle pin to bracket, and install and tighten nut. Measure toe-in with wheel alinement gage. Proper toe-in measurement is one-eighth inch, plus or minus one-sixteenth inch (fig. 113). If toe-in is correct, secure nut with cotter pin and tighten binder bolts.

(2) "FINE" ADJUSTMENT. Make a fine adjustment by disconnecting left-hand end of the tie rod knuckle pin from its bracket. Loosen the binder bolts on this end, and turn the tie rod end assembly a complete turn, increasing or decreasing the effective length, depending on which

## FRONT AXLE

direction it is rotated. The length should be adjusted to produce the proper toe-in. After correct adjustment has been obtained, install the end removed to the bracket and secure with nut and cotter pin. Tighten the binder bolts.

### 109. TIE ROD.

  **a. Description.** The tie rod consists of a tube, with a double offset to clear the differential and pinion housing, and two end assemblies connecting with the left-hand and right-hand steering knuckles. It also controls the wheel toe-in. The tie rod has finer threads on the left-hand end than on the right-hand end to permit a finer degree of toe-in adjustment.

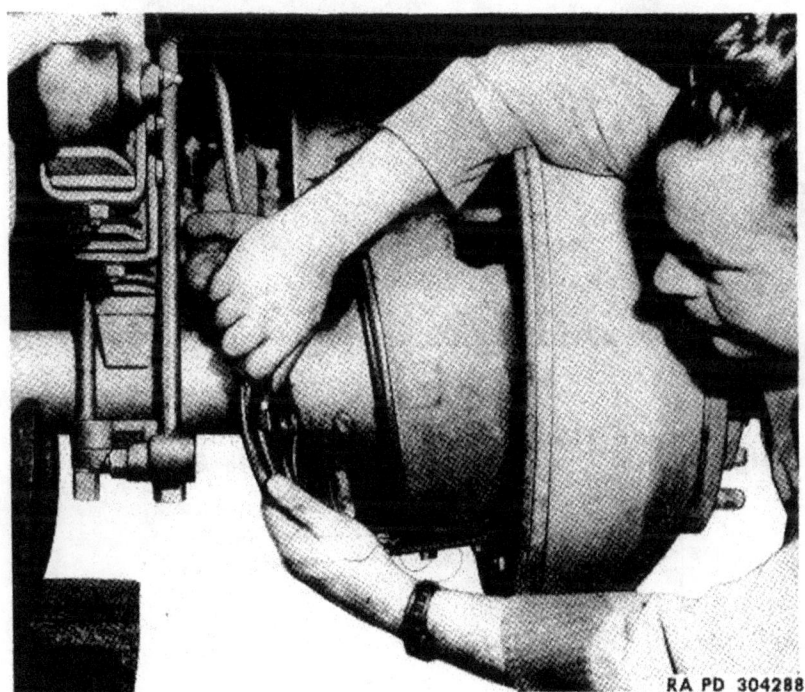

*Figure 111—Removing Clamping Rings*

  **b. Removal.** Remove cotter pin and nut from each end of the tie rod end pins. Loosen end pins from the bracket by hitting side of the end pin bracket a sharp blow with hammer; remove tie rod assembly. A coil wire spring is located between tie rod end pins and bracket.

  **c. Installation.** Place tie rod assembly end pins and spiral wire spring in bracket at each wheel and secure with nut. Adjust front wheel toe-in (par. 108 b). Secure tie rod end pins with cotter pins after adjustment is completed and check tightness of the binder bolts at each end.

# TM 9-710
## 109

**BASIC HALF-TRACK VEHICLES (WHITE, AUTOCAR, and DIAMOND T)**

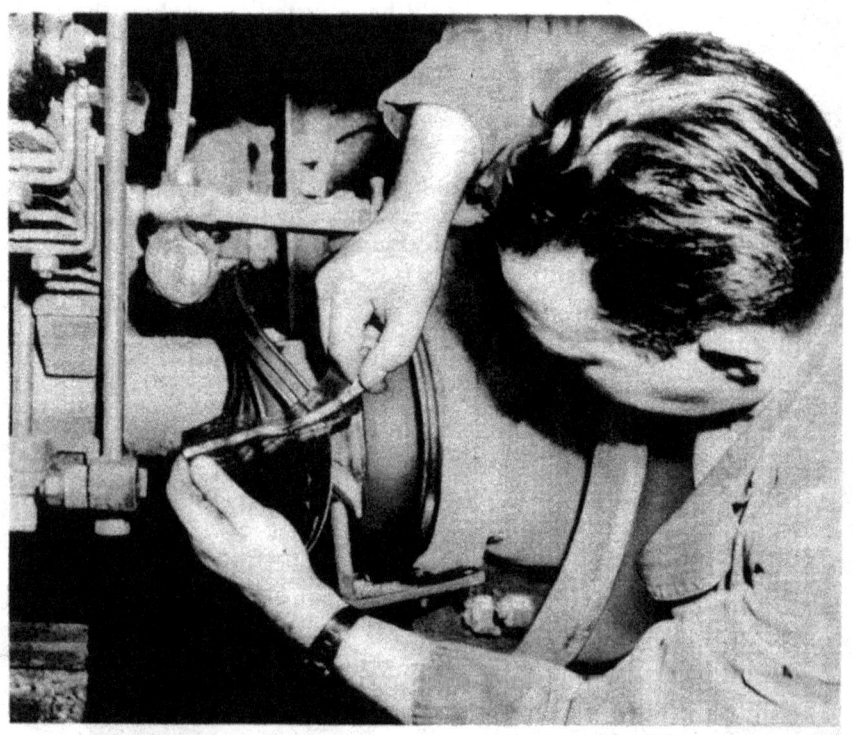

Figure 112—Installing Steering Knuckle Boot

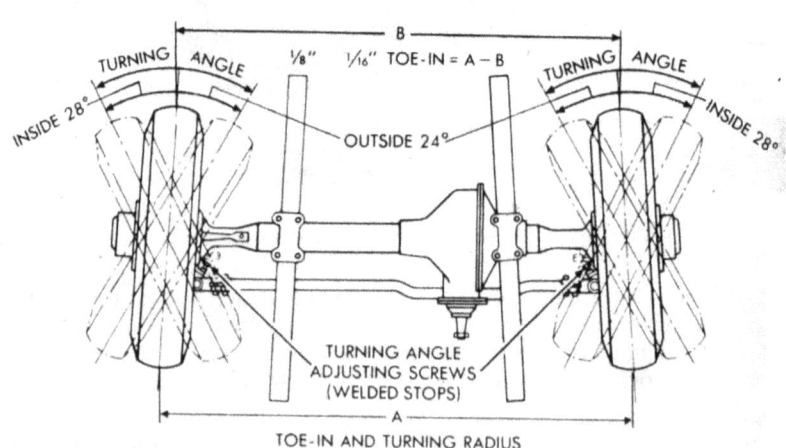

Figure 113—Front Axle Alinement Chart

## FRONT AXLE

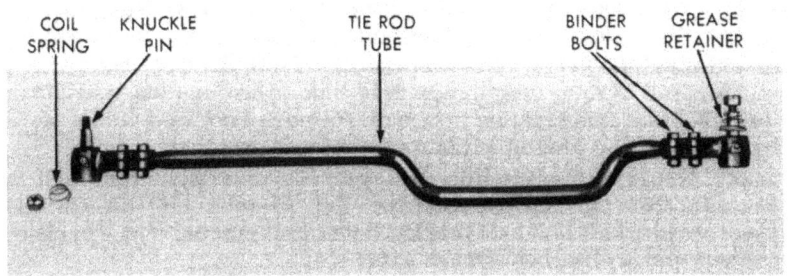

*Figure 114—Tie Rod Assembly*

110. **REMOVAL OF FRONT AXLE ASSEMBLY** (fig. 115).

a. **Remove Engine Armor Side Plates and Raise Vehicle.** Remove four cap screws, and the lock washers which secure engine armor side plates to left and right frame rails, and lower plates to ground. Loosen the six wheel stud nuts on each front wheel. Place jacks under the frame side rails, behind each spring bracket, and raise vehicle until weight is removed from springs and chassis is high enough to permit front axle to be rolled out.

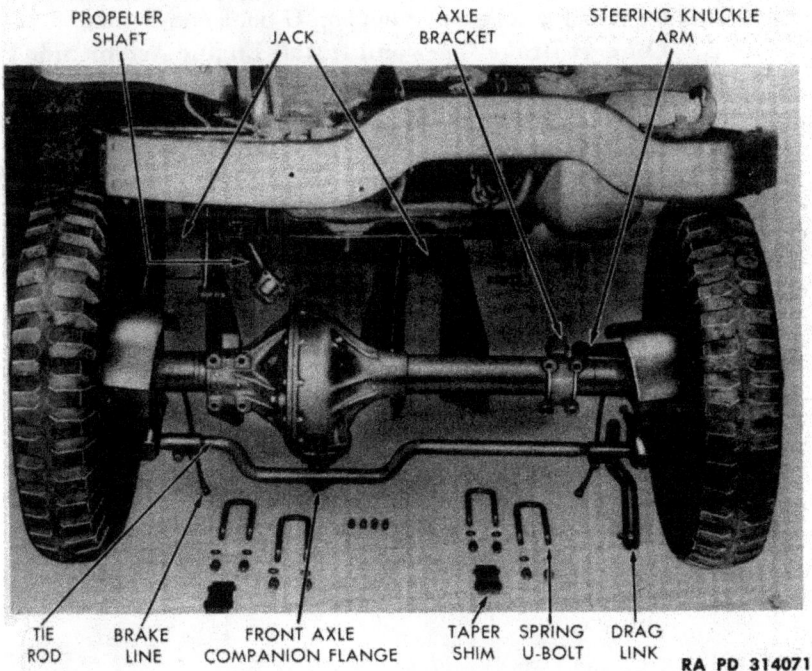

*Figure 115—Front Axle Removal*

## BASIC HALF-TRACK VEHICLES (WHITE, AUTOCAR, and DIAMOND T)

**b. Disconnect Propeller Shaft and Remove Drag Link.** Remove four nuts, lock washers, and bolts which secure propeller shaft to front axle companion flange and lower the shaft. Remove boot and cotter pin at front end of drag link, loosen drag link adjusting plug, and lift drag link off front axle steering arm ball. Remove boot and cotter pin and loosen adjusting plug at Pitman arm. Lower drag link to floor.

**c. Remove Spring Clip U-bolts.** Remove eight nuts and lock washers from spring clip U-bolts. Tap U-bolts up through shock absorber brackets and axle bracket holes and remove. This will also disconnect shock absorber arms at axle.

**d. Disconnect Brake Hose.** Unscrew each wheel brake hose coupling nut from fitting on frame side rails and permit hose to hang free.

**e. Remove Axle.** Guide axle, rolling left wheel forward, and maneuver from under vehicle. Jack up axle, remove six wheel stud nuts from each wheel, and lift off wheels.

## 111. INSTALLATION OF FRONT AXLE ASSEMBLY.

**a. Position Axle under Vehicle.** Place wheels in position, and install and tighten six wheel stud nuts on each wheel. Roll right wheel under vehicle first and then maneuver axle into position under springs.

**b. Install Spring U-bolts.** Lower jacks until springs rest on taper shim pads on axle. Install four U-bolts over springs and through axle brackets. Place shock absorber arm brackets in position on U-bolts. Install eight lock washers and nuts on U-bolts and tighten.

**c. Connect Brake Lines and Install Engine Armor Side Plates.** Connect brake lines at fittings on frame side rail and tighten coupling nuts. Install engine armor side plates and secure each side with four cap screws and lock washers.

**d. Connect Propeller Shaft and Drag Link.** Install propeller shaft at companion flange on axle center. Insert and tighten four bolts, lock washers, and nuts. Place drag link in position on steering arm ball, screw adjusting plug in tight, then back off one turn. Lock with cotter pin and install boot. Install other end of drag link to Pitman arm in the same manner.

**e. Final Adjustments.** Lower vehicle until jacks are free, then remove jacks. Inspect assembly for correct position and tightness of all fittings. Test and adjust toe-in (par. 108 b). Bleed all brake lines (par. 122) and test before operation of vehicle.

TM 9-710
112-113

Section XXIV

# REAR AXLE (JACKSHAFT)

|  | Paragraph |
|---|---|
| Description and tabulated data | 112 |
| Axle shaft removal and installation | 113 |
| Removal | 114 |
| Installation | 115 |

## 112. DESCRIPTION AND TABULATED DATA.

**a. Description.** The rear axle is a single-reduction, full-floating type with a spiral bevel drive gear (fig. 116). The differential and bevel ring gear assembly, and the pinion gear, are mounted in the carrier casting and are assembled as a unit in the banjo type axle housing.

**b. Tabulated Data.**
  Make .......................... Timken
  Model ..................... 56410-BX-67
  Type ............ single-reduction, full-floating

## 113. AXLE SHAFT REMOVAL AND INSTALLATION (fig. 117).

**a. Removal.** Remove 12 flange nuts and toothed lock washers. Tap center of flange to loosen tapered lock washers and remove wash-

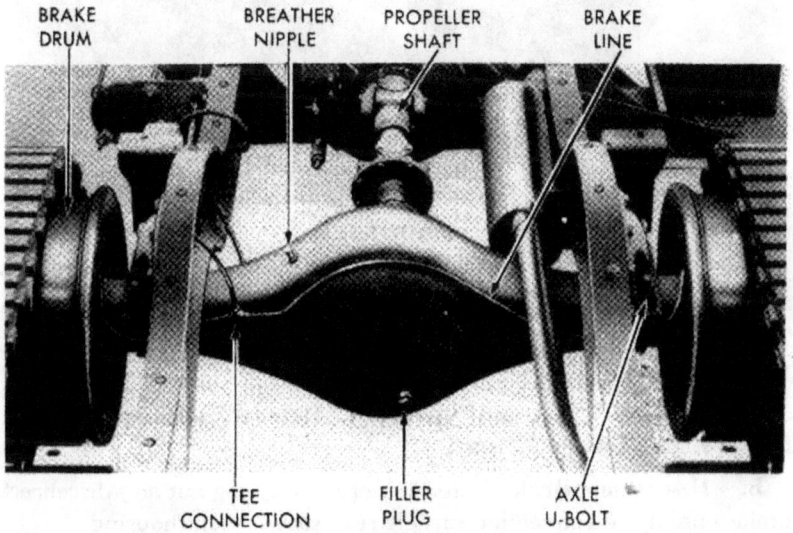

*Figure 116—Rear Axle Installed*

# TM 9-710
113-114

**BASIC HALF-TRACK VEHICLES (WHITE, AUTOCAR, and DIAMOND T)**

ers. Remove locking wire from flange puller screws and screw in puller screws to loosen flange from hub. Pull axle from housing.

**b. Installation.** Unscrew flange puller screws until bottom is even with flange. Push axle through hub and housing and guide splined end into differential side gear splines until flange seats on hub. Install and tighten 12 tapered lock washers, toothed lock washers, and nuts. Secure flange puller screws with locking wire and twist ends of wire together.

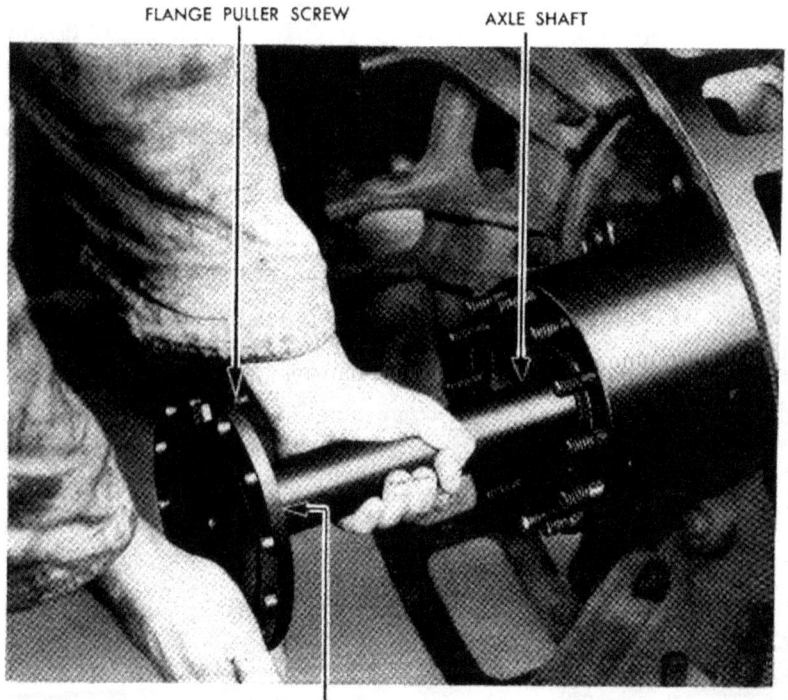

*Figure 117—Removing Rear Axle Drive Shaft*

**114. REMOVAL.**

**a. Remove Track and Sprockets.** Remove track (par. 117 c). Remove sprockets (par. 136).

**b. Disconnect Brake Line.** Unscrew coupling nut and disconnect brake line at tee connection on left rear side of axle housing.

**c. Disconnect Propeller Shaft.** Remove eight cotter pins, castellated nuts, and bolts which secure propeller shaft flange yoke to rear

226

# TM 9-710
114-115

## REAR AXLE (JACKSHAFT)

axle companion flange and lower propeller shaft, permitting it to hang freely.

*d.* **Remove Axle.** Place floor jack under center of axle assembly. Remove four nuts and lock washers from axle U-bolts (fig. 118). Lower axle with floor jack to clear frame and pull out from under vehicle (fig. 119).

## 115. INSTALLATION.

*a.* **Install Axle.** Raise axle into position under frame, install and tighten two U-bolts and four lock washers and nuts.

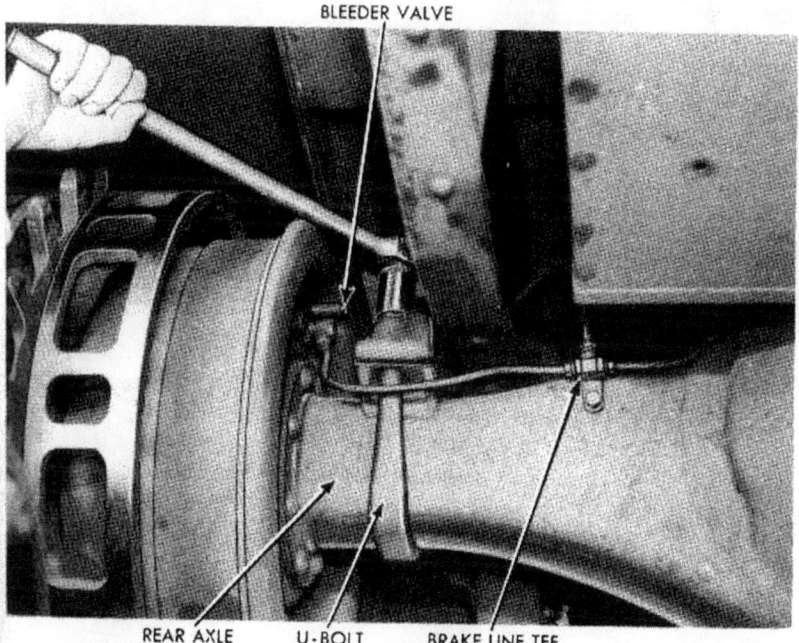

*Figure 118—Removing Rear Axle U-bolts*

*b.* **Connect Propeller Shaft.** Place propeller shaft in position with rear axle companion flange and install and tighten eight bolts and castellated nuts. Secure with cotter pins.

*c.* **Connect Brake Line.** Secure brake line coupling nut to tee at left rear of axle housing.

*d.* **Install Sprockets and Tracks.** Install sprockets (par. 136). Install and adjust track (par. 117). Bleed all brake lines (par. 122). and test brakes before operation of vehicle.

# TM 9-710
**115**

## BASIC HALF-TRACK VEHICLES (WHITE, AUTOCAR, and DIAMOND T)

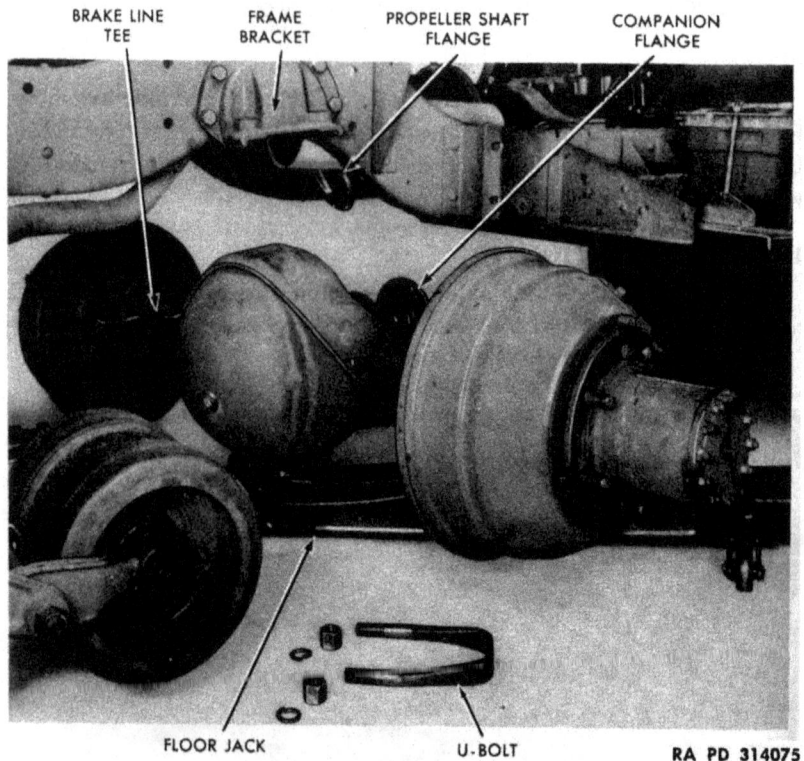

*Figure 119—Rear Axle Removal*

TM 9-710
116-117

Section XXV

# BOGIE SUSPENSION AND TRACK

|  | Paragraph |
|---|---|
| Description | 116 |
| Tracks | 117 |
| Bogie | 118 |
| Idler and adjusting mechanism | 119 |
| Track chains | 120 |

## 116. DESCRIPTION.

**a.** The Half-track derives its name from the type of suspension supporting the rear of the vehicle (fig. 120). Two endless band tracks supported by rollers are driven by sprockets on the rear axle and drive the vehicle. The weight of the rear part of the vehicle is supported by the suspensions on each side called bogies. These bogies have flat spiral springs incorporated in their structure to absorb the vertical movements of the vehicle. The idler wheels at the extreme rear of the vehicle are mounted with a spring-loaded arm designed to maintain proper tension on the tracks.

## 117. TRACKS (fig. 121).

**a. Description.** The tracks are the endless-band type, made of rubber molded to steel cables which extend throughout the track length. Metal guide plates with steel cross members are bolted to the cables along the inside center of the tracks. These serve as contacts for the jackshaft driving sprocket teeth and guides to keep the tracks on the bogie rollers and sprockets. The edges of the track incorporate projections, or tabs, for added traction.

**b. Maintenance and Adjustments.**

(1) SWITCHING TRACKS. Band tracks on vehicles operated over hard surface roads have a tendency to wear faster on the right side of the vehicle (fig. 122). When uneven wear on tracks becomes apparent, they should be changed from one side of the vehicle to the other to equalize wear.

(2) GUIDES. Guides should be kept tight at all times. They should be checked after the first 500 miles on a new vehicle and every 1,000 miles thereafter. Bent guides should be straightened immediately upon discovery by rolling the vehicle until the bent guide engages with the rear idler and then straighten the guide with the crow bar (fig. 123). Broken or missing guides should be replaced as soon as possible to prevent "jumping" of track.

(3) REPLACEMENT. Tracks should be replaced when the following conditions are apparent (fig. 122): rubber on ground side of track is worn completely off the entire length of two steel cross bars; rubber on ground side of track worn completely off half the length of five steel cross bars; rubber on the ground side of the track worn so that five steel cables are exposed at any point.

# TM 9-710

## BASIC HALF-TRACK VEHICLES (WHITE, AUTOCAR, and DIAMOND T)

(4) CHECK TRACK TENSION. (fig. 124).

*(a) General.* Tracks with too much tension have the effect of a braking action on the vehicle and result in additional strains being placed on the entire rear suspension, with consequent misalinement of rear idler, excessive wear on drive sprocket teeth, driving lugs, guides, bogie flanges, idler flange, and the bearings in sprocket, idler, and bogies. It also causes excessive wear on the track treads and sometimes results in broken tracks. Too much slack in the tracks will result in the track being thrown and damage to bogie tires, bogie flanges, track guides, and idler flanges.

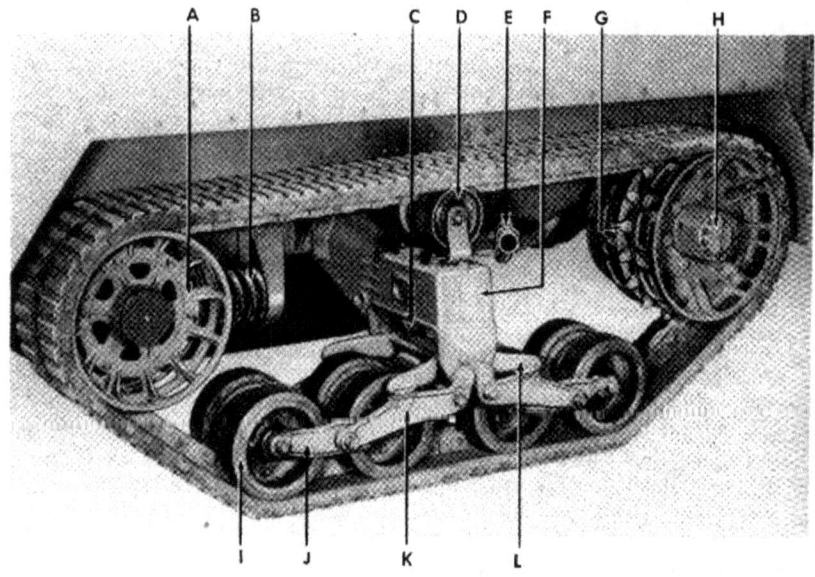

| | |
|---|---|
| A — IDLER WHEEL | E — TAIL PIPE |
| B — IDLER SPRING | F — BOGIE AND FRAME ASSEMBLY |
| C — VOLUTE SPRING | G — TRACK DRIVING SPROCKET |
| D — BOGIE UPPER ROLLER | H — REAR AXLE SHAFT FLANGE |
| I — BOGIE ROLLER | |
| J — BOGIE FRAME | |
| K — BOGIE ARM | |
| L — CRAB | |

RA PD 314076

*Figure 120—Bogie and Track Assembly*

*(b)* Place vehicle on level surface and operate slowly in reverse about half the length of the vehicle, to transfer all slack to the top section of the track.

*(c)* Lay a straightedge between the top roller and the rear idler. This is conveniently accomplished by the use of a piece of string 11½ feet long with a weight, such as a heavy nut, tied to each end. Lay the string on the inner half of the track next to the center edge and let the weights hang over at each end to keep the string taut.

*(d)* Have an average weight man (150 to 175 lb) stand on the outer half of the track, midway between the rear idler and top roller, with his feet spread 6 inches apart. NOTE: *The presence of mine*

## BOGIE SUSPENSION AND TRACK

racks on the sides of the vehicle necessitates holding to side of vehicle with the hands but the weight should rest on the toes, which are placed on the outer half of the track.

(e) Measure the track sag or vertical distance between the straightedge or string and the top center edge of the inner half of the track at a point midway between the feet of the man standing on the track. The correct sag at this point is three-quarter inch minimum, and one inch maximum. NOTE: *A short stick with a one-quarter inch wide mark covering the three-quarter to one inch space measured from one end should be used for measuring. As long as the measurement falls anywhere on the mark, then tension is correct.*

(5) ADJUST TRACK TENSION.

(a) Tension should be adjusted with the vehicle carrying stowage, but without personnel and this tension will be found satisfactory for

*Figure 121—Track Assembly*

normal operation with varying numbers of personnel. In case of excessive overload, the tension should be checked and adjusted after load is applied and again after overload is removed.

(b) Remove cover or protecting wrapping from the threads on the idler adjusting screw. Clean threads and apply oil so that tension adjusting nut can be easily turned.

(c) Check tension and if there is insufficient sag, back off the adjusting nut on the idler adjusting screw. This moves the idler forward and decreases the tension. If sag is excessive, screw the adjusting nut forward which moves idler back and increases the tension. NOTE: *With the single coil spring-loaded idler, the taper-fitted anchor pin must be loosened by backing off the anchor pin nut a couple of turns and tapping on the adjusting screw boss with a hammer to loosen pin before adjusting track tension.* After adjustment is made, retighten anchor pin nut.

## TM 9-710
117

**BASIC HALF-TRACK VEHICLES (WHITE, AUTOCAR, and DIAMOND T)**

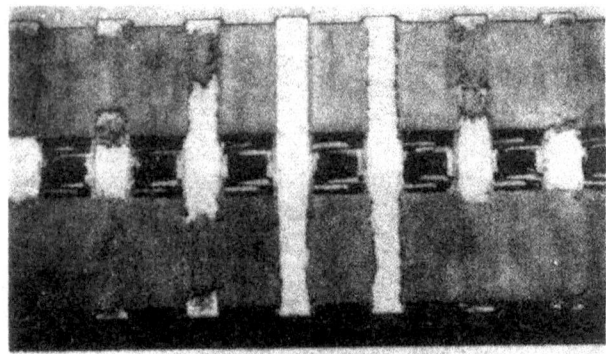
RUBBER WORN FROM FULL LENGTH OF TWO CROSS BARS

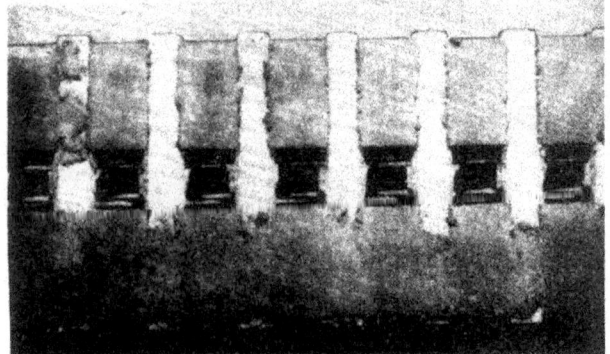
RUBBER WORN FROM HALF LENGTH OF FIVE CROSS BARS

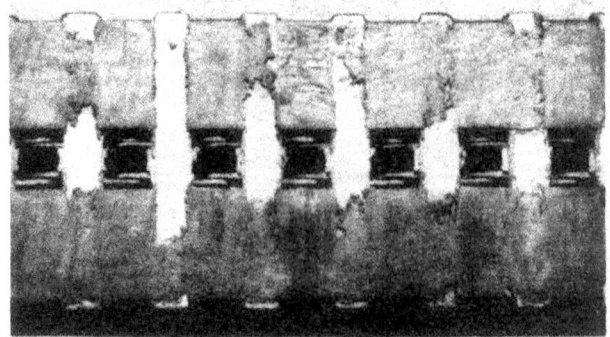
RUBBER WORN FROM FIVE CABLES

*Figure 122—Track Wear*

## BOGIE SUSPENSION AND TRACK

*(d)* After adjusting tension, operate the vehicle over rough ground nd make a final check to be sure tension is correct. Replace tape rapping on idler adjusting screw threads after first applying thin lm rust preventive compound. If not available, use lubricating oil.

*(e)* Adjust idler stop screw till clearance of 1¾ inch to 2 inches ; obtained between end of stop screw and idler shackle (fig. 125).

**c. Removal.**

(1) BLOCK VEHICLE. Park vehicle on firm level ground and stop ngine. Set propeller shaft brake, place transmission in reverse gear, ind place chocks in front and behind the front wheels.

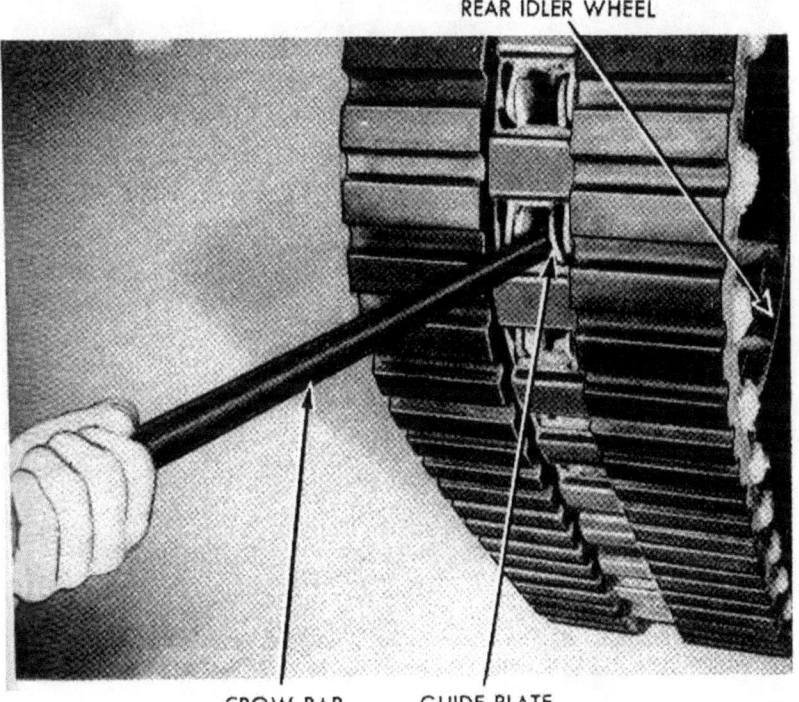

*Figure 123—Straightening Bent Guides*

(2) LOOSEN IDLER FLANGE NUTS AND ADJUSTING NUT. Loosen all idler flange nuts but do not remove them. Remove protecting wrapping from idler adjusting screw and completely back off the adjusting nut.

(3) SLACKEN TRACK. The following procedure is not necessary on vehicles which have a double coil spring loaded idler equipped with full threaded or modified undercut adjusting idler screw. Place hydraulic jack with wood blocks between bogie bracket and rear idler and jack idler back until all sag is out of track and all compression is

## BASIC HALF-TRACK VEHICLES (WHITE, AUTOCAR, and DIAMOND T)

removed from idler spring (fig. 126). Remove nuts from anchor bolt which secures idler adjusting screw to idler shackle and tap out anchor bolt. Remove spring and adjusting screw from bracket and lower to floor (fig. 127). Remove jack, allowing idler to move forward and give ample slack in track.

*Figure 124—Measuring Slack in Track*

(4) INSTALL C-CLAMPS AND RAISE VEHICLE. Install C-clamps or similar equipment over each bogie roller outer arm and crab (figs. 128 and 129). Place jack on block directly under end of bogie bracket cross tube and raise vehicle until bogie rollers clear track guides.

(5) REMOVE IDLER FLANGE. Remove the six nuts and lock washers which secure idler flange to idler and pull off flange.

(6) REMOVE TRACK. Pry track from rear idler inner flange and top supporting roller. Then pry track from drive sprocket and lower it to floor.

## BOGIE SUSPENSION AND TRACK

**d. Installation.**

(1) INSTALL TRACK. Place track close beside vehicle, making certain that outside wings of guides on bottom part of track are toward front of vehicle. Lift track and place inside edge of track on drive sprocket outer flange. Then lift track into position on top supporting roller and slide lower part of track under bogie rollers until it lines up with top part of track. Pry track onto drive sprocket until guides engage sprocket teeth. Pull all slack in track to the rear and then lift track onto hub of idler. Insert pry bar into an opening in idler wheel

*Figure 125—Adjusting Idler Stop Screw*

directly back of hub and pry track backwards and upwards until inside edge rests upon idler inner flange.

(2) INSTALL IDLER OUTER FLANGE AND REMOVE C-CLAMPS. Place outer flange in position and secure with nuts and lock washers. Lower vehicle onto track and remove jack and C-clamps.

(3) If idler anchor pin was removed to slacken track for ease of removal, place wood blocks and jack between bogie bracket and idler and force idler back as far as possible (fig. 126). Place idler spring and adjusting screw in position and secure with anchor pin and nuts. Remove jack and wood blocks.

(4) ADJUST TRACK. See paragraph 117 b (5).

**118. BOGIE.**

**a. Description.** The rear of the vehicle is supported by the two bogie suspensions which are connected to the frame. These are held

# TM 9-710

## BASIC HALF-TRACK VEHICLES (WHITE, AUTOCAR, and DIAMOND T)

in alinement by a tubular cross support which connects to the bogie frame brackets. Each suspension is supported by dual volute springs and four rubber-tired roller assemblies running on an endless rubber track. Shocks or vertical movements of the rollers are transferred to the carrying arms and levers and absorbed by the volute springs.

**b. Bogie Upper Roller** (fig. 130).

(1) DESCRIPTION. A steel roller mounted on a bracket is secured to the top of each bogie frame bracket. It supports and guides the returning track.

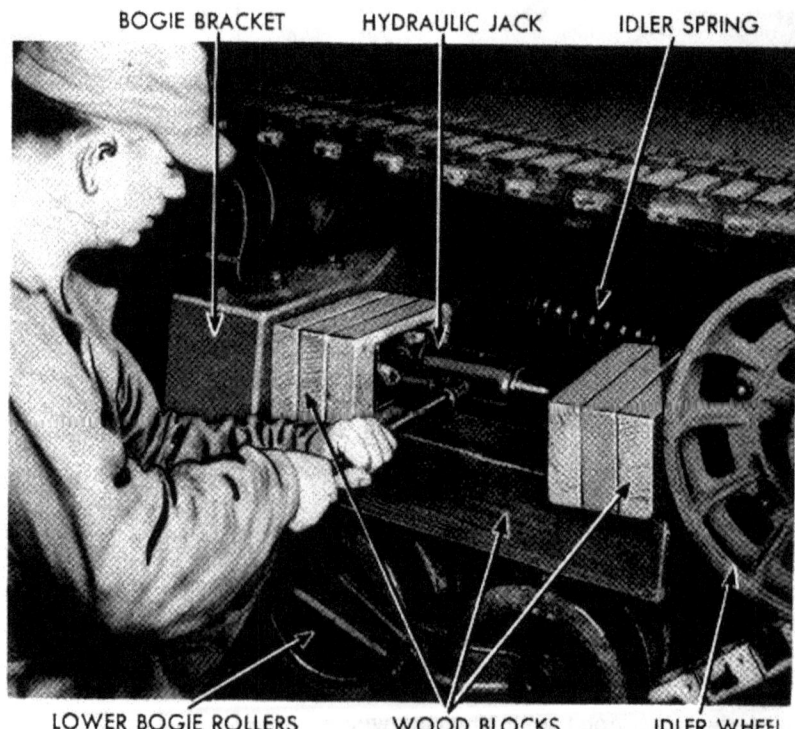

*Figure 126—Removing Tension from Single Coil Idler Spring*

(2) REMOVAL. Loosen idler tension (par. 117 c (3)). Prop up the slack obtained in track above upper roller. Remove four cap screws and lock washers which secure roller bracket to top of bogie frame bracket and lift off assembly. On tail pipe side, remove tail pipe bracket also.

(3) MAINTENANCE.

*(a) Remove Bearings, Oil Seals, Gudgeon.* Remove gudgeon nut. Press or drive out gudgeon with brass drift. Remove end brackets. Remove grease seals and bearings with a bearing puller or by knocking out with a brass drift.

**TM 9-710**
**118**

## BOGIE SUSPENSION AND TRACK

(b) *Install Bearings, Oil Seals, Gudgeon.* Install new bearings, and if oil seals have been damaged in removal, replace with new ones. NOTE: *Install oil seals, with open end of seal lips away from the bearing.*

(4) INSTALLATION. Install roller assembly in brackets and secure with gudgeon and nut. Secure roller and bracket assembly to top of bogie frame bracket with four cap screws and lock washers. Lower track into roller groove and adjust track to proper tension (par. 117 b (5)).

c. **Bogie Lower Roller Assembly** (fig. 131).

(1) DESCRIPTION. The bogie roller wheels are the supporting and

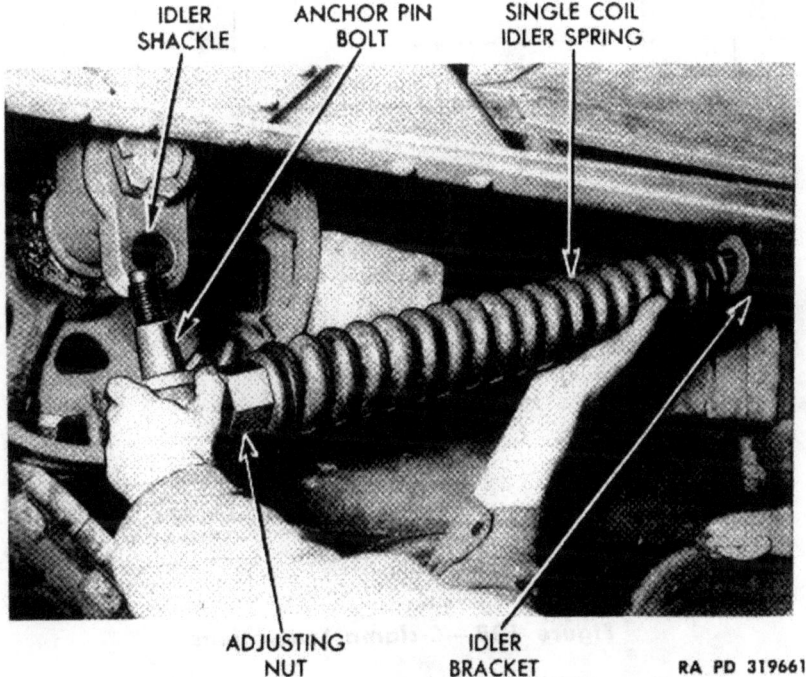

*Figure 127—Removing Single Coil Idler Spring*

conveying units for the rear of the vehicle. Four steel wheels with solid rubber tires are located on each side of the vehicle. They rest on the revolving endless rubber track and press the track down to follow the contour of the terrain.

(2) REMOVAL OF BOGIE LOWER ROLLER ASSEMBLY.

(a) *Remove Bogie Upper Roller.* Refer to paragraph 118 b.

(b) *Compress Volute Springs.* Use bogie volute spring compressor (Special Tool List, fig. 46), or install two 7/8-inch screws 12 inches long, with nuts to fit screws, into the spring block (fig. 136) through holes in top of bogie frame bracket, and compress springs by holding screws stationary and tightening the screw nuts until crab no longer rests on the carrying arms.

# TM 9-710

## BASIC HALF-TRACK VEHICLES (WHITE, AUTOCAR, and DIAMOND T)

(c) *Remove Side Carrying Arms.* Jack up vehicle and place blocks under the bogie lower rollers (fig. 131). NOTE: *The track does not have to be removed as is shown in this picture.* Remove the safety nuts on the tie bolt and tie bar at each side of the lower bogie roller assembly and remove the outside, inside, and carrying arms. Remove the tie bar.

(d) *Remove Side Frames.* Remove bogie roller gudgeon nuts and pull the side frames off the tie bolt and gudgeons.

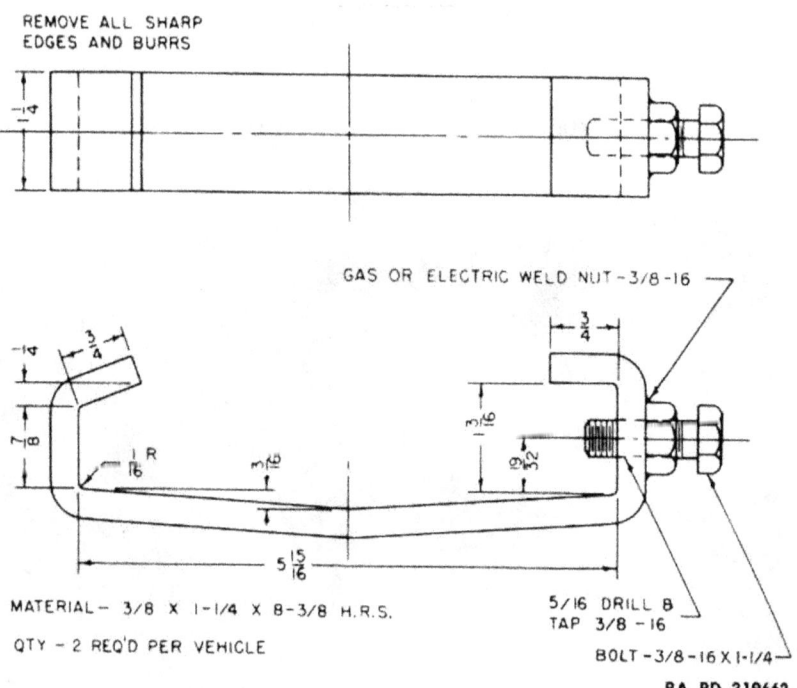

*Figure 128—C-clamp Dimensions*

(3) MAINTENANCE.

(a) *Limit of Service for Bogie Rollers.* Bogie rollers will be continued in service until one or more of the following conditions occur:

1. The average over-all width "W" of the tread, determined by measuring the tread width at six equally spaced points, is less than 2½ inches (fig. 132).

2. The average outside diameter "D" of the roller tread is less than 11⅞ inches.

3. The tread has pulled loose from the base band in such a manner as to permit sand, fine gravel, or other foreign material to enter and become lodged between the rubber tread and the base band for a distance, "S", equal to, or greater than, ⅝ inch measured inward from the edge of the existing tread.

## BOGIE SUSPENSION AND TRACK

*(b) Replacement of Bogie Rubber Roller.* Remove six safety nuts from wheel hub studs and lift rubber tire assembly from hub. Replace with new tire assembly and secure to hub studs with six safety nuts.

*(c) Replacement of Bogie Roller Bearing.* Press or drive out gudgeon with brass drift. Remove the grease seals and bearings with a bearing puller. Drive new bearings into hubs (fig. 133) and if seals have been damaged in removal, replace with new ones (fig. 134). NOTE: *Insert the oil seals with the open end of lip away from the bearing.*

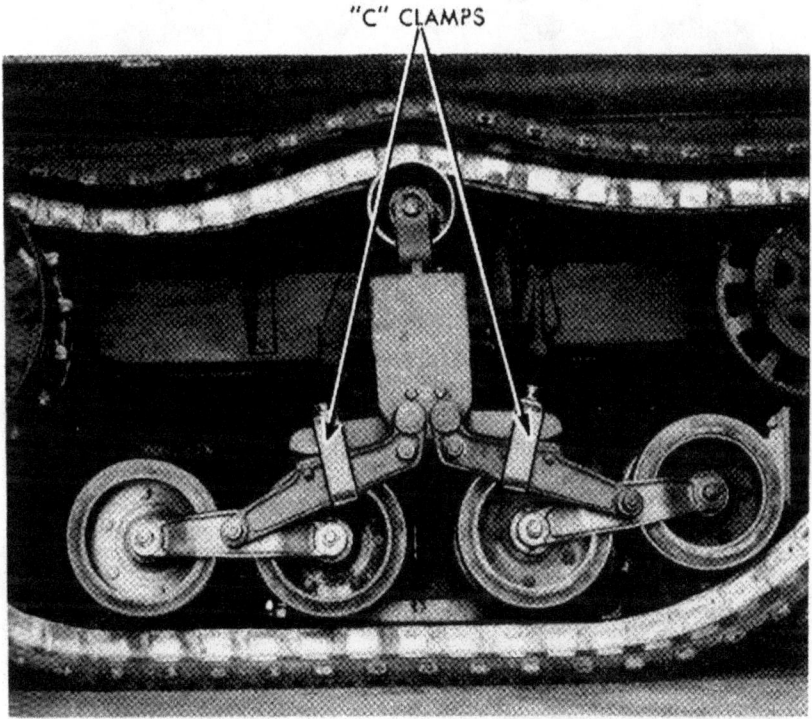

*Figure 129—C-clamps Installed*

(4) INSTALLATION OF BOGIE LOWER ROLLER ASSEMBLY.

*(a) Install Side Frames.* Place the side frames and tie bolt in position on the two gudgeons and wheels and secure the frames with the gudgeon safety nuts.

*(b) Install Side Carrying Arms.* Place the lower roller assembly of wheels and side frames in position to install the side carrying arms. Place the side carrying arms in position on the tie bolt, tie bar, and bogie frame bracket and secure the tie bolt and tie bar with safety nuts.

*(c) Release Volute Spring Tension.* Remove the blocks supporting the bogie lower rollers and release the volute spring tension by re-

## BASIC HALF-TRACK VEHICLES (WHITE, AUTOCAR, and DIAMOND T)

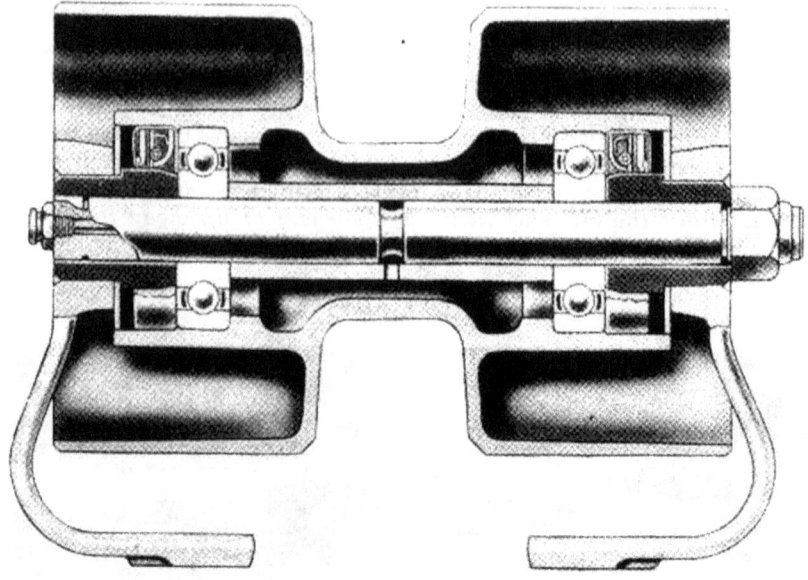

*Figure 130—Bogie Upper Roller (Sectional View)*

moving the spring compressing bolts. NOTE: *If track has been removed, install track (par. 117 d) before releasing the volute spring tension.*

(d) *Install Bogie Upper Roller.* Place roller assembly and bracket in proper position on top of bogie frame bracket and secure with four cap screws and lock washers. Adjust track tension (par. 117 b (5)).

*Figure 131—Bogie Lower Roller Removal*

# TM 9-710
118

## BOGIE SUSPENSION AND TRACK

d. **Volute Spring and Crab.**

(1) REMOVAL.

*(a) Remove Bogie Lower Roller Assembly.* Refer to paragraph 118 c.

*(b) Release Volute Spring Tension.* Unscrew the nuts on volute spring compression bolts and remove bolts from spring blocks. Lower the crab and springs.

*(c) Spring and Crab Disassembly.* Lift volute springs from crab assembly. Crab disassembly is accomplished by punching out the small tapered pins holding the crab slide blocks to the ends of the crab shaft, removing the small slide blocks, and pulling out the shaft.

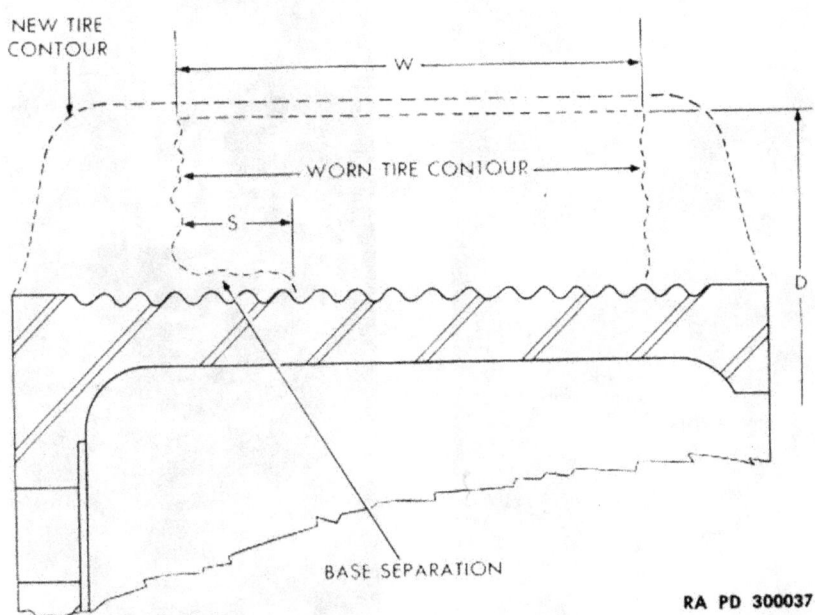

*Figure 132—Limit of Bogie Roller Tread Wear*

*(d) Crab Slide Blocks Replacement.* Bend away the edges of the locking strip and remove the two cap screws holding the guide slide blocks to each bogie frame bracket and lift blocks from frame bracket. Replace blocks and secure with cap screws and bend locking strip against head of cap screws.

(2) INSTALLATION.

*(a) Install Springs and Crab.* Assemble crab block, shaft, and install small blocks to ends of crab shaft, securing with taper pins. Place volute springs on crab spring blocks, slide assembly into place in bogie frame bracket. Compress volute springs into volute spring compression tool or bolts.

*(b) Install Lower Bogie Assembly.* Refer to paragraph 118 c (4).

241

**TM 9-710**
118

**BASIC HALF-TRACK VEHICLES (WHITE, AUTOCAR, and DIAMOND T)**

RA PD 3608

*Figure 133—Installing Bogie Lower Roller Bearing*

RA PD 3609

*Figure 134—Installing Bogie Lower Roller Bearing Seal*

    e. Bogie Assembly (fig. 136).
      (1) REMOVAL.
      (a) *Remove Upper Roller Assembly.* Refer to paragraph 118 c (2) (b).
      (b) *Compress Volute Springs.* Refer to paragraph 118 c (2) (b).
      (c) *Remove Tracks.* Refer to paragraph 117 c.

**TM 9-710**
**118**

**BOGIE SUSPENSION AND TRACK**

*(d) Remove Bogie Assembly.* Lower vehicle until bogie assembly is resting on ground. Remove six bolts, nuts, and lock washers at sides of bogie frame bracket and chassis frame. Remove two bolts, nuts, and lock washers at underneath side of bogie frame bracket to chassis frame. Remove one bolt, nut, and lock washer from each end of tubular cross support. Use hoist and rope sling to remove one side of bogie assembly and repeat process for the other side.

RA PD 43394

*Figure 135—Bogie Volute Spring Removal*

(2) INSTALLATION.

*(a) Install Bogie Assembly.* Lift one side of bogie assembly with rope sling and hoist, maneuver it into proper position to attach frame bracket to chassis frame. Install and tighten six bolts, lock washers, and nuts to side of bogie frame bracket, and two bolts, nuts, and lock washers to underside of frame bracket and frame. Place tubular cross support in assembly and maneuver other side of bogie assembly into position and secure to chassis frame with eight bolts, lock washers, and nuts. Secure tubular cross support at each end with bolt, lock washer, and nut.

**TM 9-710**
**BASIC HALF-TRACK VEHICLES (WHITE, AUTOCAR, and DIAMOND T)**

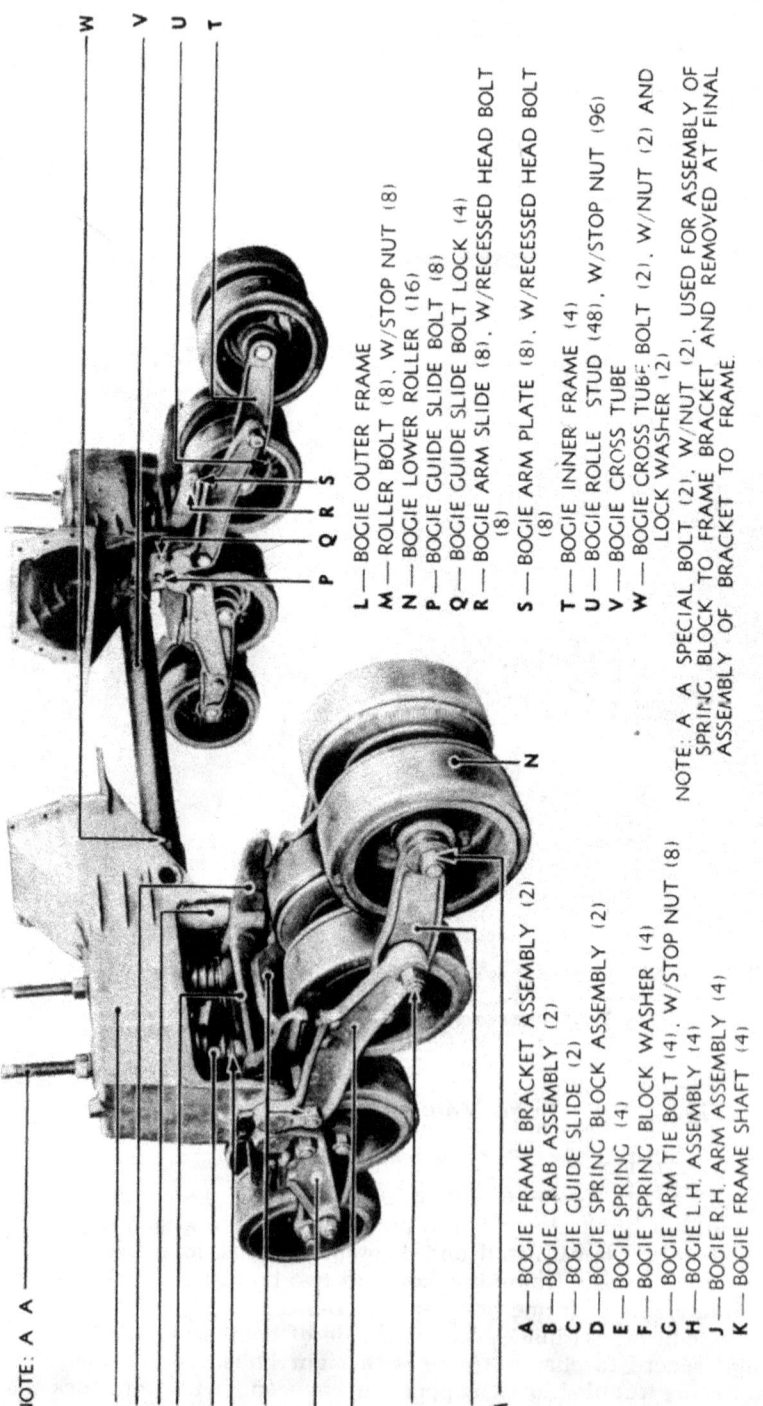

A — BOGIE FRAME BRACKET ASSEMBLY (2)
B — BOGIE CRAB ASSEMBLY (2)
C — BOGIE GUIDE SLIDE (2)
D — BOGIE SPRING BLOCK ASSEMBLY (2)
E — BOGIE SPRING (4)
F — BOGIE SPRING BLOCK WASHER (4)
G — BOGIE ARM TIE BOLT (4), W/STOP NUT (8)
H — BOGIE L.H. ARM ASSEMBLY (4)
J — BOGIE R.H. ARM ASSEMBLY (4)
K — BOGIE FRAME SHAFT (4)
L — BOGIE OUTER FRAME
M — ROLLER BOLT (8), W/STOP NUT (8)
N — BOGIE LOWER ROLLER (16)
P — BOGIE GUIDE SLIDE BOLT (8)
Q — BOGIE GUIDE SLIDE BOLT LOCK (4)
R — BOGIE ARM SLIDE (8), W/RECESSED HEAD BOLT (8)
S — BOGIE ARM PLATE (8), W/RECESSED HEAD BOLT (8)
T — BOGIE INNER FRAME (4)
U — BOGIE ROLLER STUD (48), W/STOP NUT (96)
V — BOGIE CROSS TUBE
W — BOGIE CROSS TUBE BOLT (2), W/NUT (2) AND LOCK WASHER (2)

NOTE: A A SPECIAL BOLT (2), W/NUT (2), USED FOR ASSEMBLY OF SPRING BLOCK TO FRAME BRACKET AND REMOVED AT FINAL ASSEMBLY OF BRACKET TO FRAME.

RA PD 3524A

*Figure 136 — Bogie Assembly*

**TM 9-710**

## BOGIE SUSPENSION AND TRACK

A — IDLER SPRING BRACKET
B — IDLER POST BRACKET
C — IDLER POST
D — IDLER SPRING
E — ADJUSTING NUT
F — JAM NUT
G — IDLER ADJUSTING SCREW
H — ANCHOR PIN BOLT
I — IDLER STOP SCREW
J — IDLER POST BRACE
K — IDLER WHEEL SHAFT
L — IDLER SHACKLE
M — STOP SCREW BRACKET

RA PD 319664

*Figure 137—Idler Post Assembly Installed*

# TM 9-710
118-119

## BASIC HALF-TRACK VEHICLES (WHITE, AUTOCAR, and DIAMOND T)

   *(b)* *Install Tracks.* Raise vehicle until bogie rollers will clear ground enough to install the track. Refer to paragraph 117 d.

   *(c)* *Release Volute Springs.* Refer to paragraph 118 c (4) *(b)*.

   *(d)* *Install Upper Roller Assembly.* Refer to paragraph 118 b (4).

   *(e)* *Adjust Tracks.* Refer to paragraph 117 h (5).

119. **IDLER AND ADJUSTING MECHANISM.**

   a. **Description.** Steel idler wheels are mounted on each side of the frame near the rear of the vehicle (fig. 137). These idler wheels support the rear end of the endless rubber track. Each idler wheel is mounted on an idler shaft that is carried in an idler shackle which is

*Figure 138—Removing Track Adjusting Idler Bearing Nut*

mounted on an idler post secured to the frame and further supported by an idler brace. This unit as now installed, provides a two-way action for the idler wheel by having it work against a double coil spring. This keeps the track under tension but will allow the idler wheel to move forward to ease unusual strain on the track, or to move backward to take up any extra slack created momentarily. This relieves strain on both the track and idler post.

   b. **Removal of Idler Wheel and Bearing.**

   (1) REMOVE TRACK. Refer to paragraph 117 c.

   (2) REMOVE HUB COVER. Remove six hub stud nuts. Tap cap lightly to loosen it on studs and pull it off with its gasket.

246

## BOGIE SUSPENSION AND TRACK

(3) REMOVE IDLER WHEEL AND BEARINGS. Remove idler bearing nut and lock washer (fig. 138), using a long-nosed chisel and screwdriver in the manner illustrated. Remove idler wheel and bearings, using a wheel puller (fig. 139) or similar equipment.

c. **Replacement of Bearing.**

(1) REMOVAL. Drive out seal and bearings with a brass drift and hammer.

(2) INSTALLATION. Drive new bearings into the idler and if grease seal has been damaged, replace with new seal. Install seal with the lips or open ends away from the bearings.

*Figure 139—Track Idler Inner Flange Removal*

d. **Installation of Idler Wheel and Bearings.**

(1) INSTALL INNER IDLER WHEEL ASSEMBLY. Place idler wheel with bearing spacer, bearings, and oil seals installed in idler wheel hub on idler shaft and secure to shaft with idler bearing nut and lock washer. Place hub cover and gasket in position on hub studs and secure with six hub stud nuts.

e. **Removal of Idler and Track Tension Mechanism.**

(1) REMOVE TRACK. Refer to paragraph 117 c.

(2) REMOVE INNER IDLER WHEEL ASSEMBLY. Refer to paragraph 119 b.

(3) REMOVE COIL SPRINGS AND TENSION SCREW. Release tension on coil springs and tension screw. Remove coil springs and tension

# TM 9-710

**BASIC HALF-TRACK VEHICLES (WHITE, AUTOCAR, and DIAMOND T)**

screw from shackle by removing nut from anchor pin on coil spring tension screw and punching anchor pin from shackle.

(4) REMOVE IDLER POST BRACE. Remove cotter pin and castellated nut which secure idler post brace to idler post; remove four nuts, lock washers, and bolts holding idler post brace to frame and pull idler post brace from assembly.

(5) REMOVE IDLER POST AND SHACKLE. Remove cotter pin and castellated nut from end of idler post on inside of frame and pull idler post and shackle from idler post outer bracket.

(6) REMOVE IDLER POST OUTER BRACKET AND STOP SCREW BRACKET. Remove four nuts, lock washers, and bolts from idler post outer bracket and remove from frame. Remove three nuts, lock wash-

RA PD 319666

*Figure 140—Track Chain Installed*

ers, and bolts from stop screw bracket and remove bracket and stop screw assembly from frame.

**f. Installation of Idler and Track Tension Mechanism.**

(1) INSTALL IDLER POST OUTER BRACKET AND STOP SCREW BRACKET. Install idler post outer bracket to proper position on frame and secure with four bolts, lock washers, and nuts. Install stop screw bracket assembly to proper position on frame and secure with three bolts, lock washers, and nuts.

(2) INSTALL IDLER POST AND SHACKLE. Install idler post and shackle to idler post outer bracket, and secure assembly with castellated nut and cotter pin to end of idler post inside of frame.

(3) INSTALL IDLER POST BRACE. Install idler post brace to idler

248

## BOGIE SUSPENSION AND TRACK

post and frame using castellated nut and cotter pin on outer end of idler post and four bolts, lock washers, and nuts to connection at frame.

(4) INSTALL COIL SPRINGS AND TENSION SCREW. Place idler adjusting screw and tension springs assembly in position in idler spring frame bracket and install anchor pin bolt in idler shackle and secure with nut. Tighten idler stop screw to compress idler spring tension.

(5) INSTALL IDLER WHEEL AND BEARINGS. Refer to paragraph 119 d.

(6) INSTALL AND ADJUST TRACK. Refer to paragraph 117 d.

### 120. TRACK CHAINS (fig. 140).

*a. Description.* The chains used on the bogie track are of conventional design and are constructed of standard tire chain materials. A shackle and screw pin joiner are used on the side chains to lock them in position or to provide necessary adjustment. NOTE: *Chains should be applied as tightly as possible by hand.* If driving continually, check chains occasionally and take up any excess slack in side chains.

*b. Maintenance.*

(1) Repair broken or damaged track links immediately, using repair links which are carried on vehicle.

(2) Dip chains in used crankcase oil before stowing on vehicle after each chain application.

*c. Installation.*

(1) INSTALL ONE END OF CHAIN ON TRACK. Lay out each chain directly behind tracks with ends having four free links nearest vehicle. Lift end nearest vehicle onto track and place half way between top support roller and rear idler. Hook male half of clip with long side up, through third link of inner side-chain and slide clip onto inner band of track with long end on top of track. Hook female half of clip, long side up, through third link of outer side-chain, slide clip onto outer band of track directly opposite male clip, and push two halves of clip firmly together (fig. 141).

(2) SECURE CHAIN TO TRACK. Drive vehicle slowly forward and feed chain evenly onto track, taking care not to become entangled in chain since it moves forward faster than vehicle. Stop vehicle when clips are centered between rear bogie wheels and rear idler. Remove clip and fasten side chain ends together with the screw pin joiner shackles and tighten shackle screws (fig. 142). NOTE: *Drive vehicle slowly and observe chains until it is certain that there is adequate clearance.* Check chains, and adjust, if necessary, after ten miles of operation, and at frequent intervals thereafter.

*d. Removal.*

(1) REMOVE CHAINS. Stop vehicle with chain ends located between rear bogie rollers and idler. Remove screw pin joiner shackles and drive vehicle forward off chains.

(2) STOW CHAINS IN VEHICLE. Fold chain so that ends are together and fasten ends with screw joiner shackles so they will not become entangled. Clean chains and dip them in oil. Then place chains in bag with attachment clips and stow in vehicle.

**TM 9-710**

**BASIC HALF-TRACK VEHICLES (WHITE, AUTOCAR, and DIAMOND T)**

*Figure 141—Installing Chain Applier*

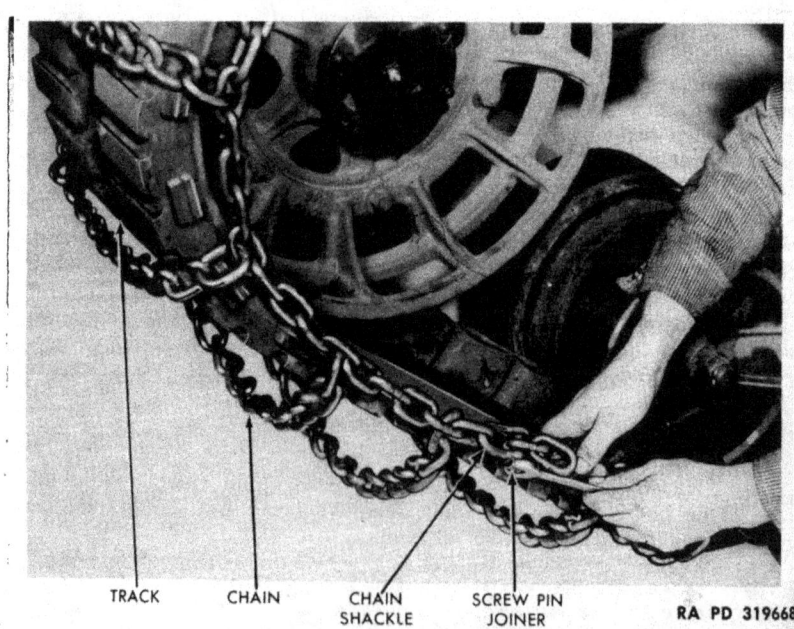

*Figure 142—Installing Screw Pin Joiners at Chain Shackles*

TM 9-710

Section XXVI

# BRAKE SYSTEM

| | Paragraph |
|---|---|
| Description and tabulated data | 121 |
| Bleeding the hydraulic system | 122 |
| Brake pedal and linkage (vacuum booster) | 123 |
| Brake booster (vacuum) | 124 |
| Brake pedal and linkage (Hydrovac) | 125 |
| Brake booster (Hydrovac) | 126 |
| Brake booster air cleaner | 127 |
| Brake booster check valve | 128 |
| Master cylinder | 129 |
| Front and rear wheel cylinders | 130 |
| Hose, lines, and fittings | 131 |
| Service brake shoes | 132 |
| Propeller shaft (parking) brake | 133 |
| Electric trailer brake controller and linkage | 134 |

## 121. DESCRIPTION AND TABULATED DATA.

a. **Description.** The service brakes are four-wheel hydraulic. Two types of vacuum power booster units have been used on these vehicles. These units provide greater pressure to the hydraulic system than could be exerted by foot pressure alone. On the vacuum power type (fig. 143), fluid pressure is transmitted directly from the master cylinder to the wheel cylinders. Pressure applied to the foot pedal actuates the master cylinder piston, which in turn actuates the wheel cylinders through hydraulic lines, thus applying the brakes. This booster is connected mechanically to the master cylinder piston rod and through application of engine vacuum, augments the pressure applied by the brake pedal to the master cylinder piston. The Hydrovac-type booster (fig. 144) augments the pressure applied by the brake pedal also, but acts directly on the hydraulic fluid leading to the brake cylinders rather than on the master cylinder piston. Internal expanding shoes for both front wheels and rear driving sprockets are actuated by opposed pistons acting in a cylinder and operating directly on each shoe. The hand brake for parking is a mechanical type and consists of two shoes operating against a disk mounted on the companion flange of the propeller shaft. An electric trailer brake controller, governed by a rheostat located on the instrument panel, is provided to control the electric brakes as used on the trailer brake system.

b. **Tabulated Data.**
   (1) HYDROVAC UNIT.
      Make .......................... Bendix Products
      Model ................................. 373000
      Type ................................... vacuum

TM 9-710
121

**BASIC HALF-TRACK VEHICLES (WHITE, AUTOCAR, and DIAMOND T)**

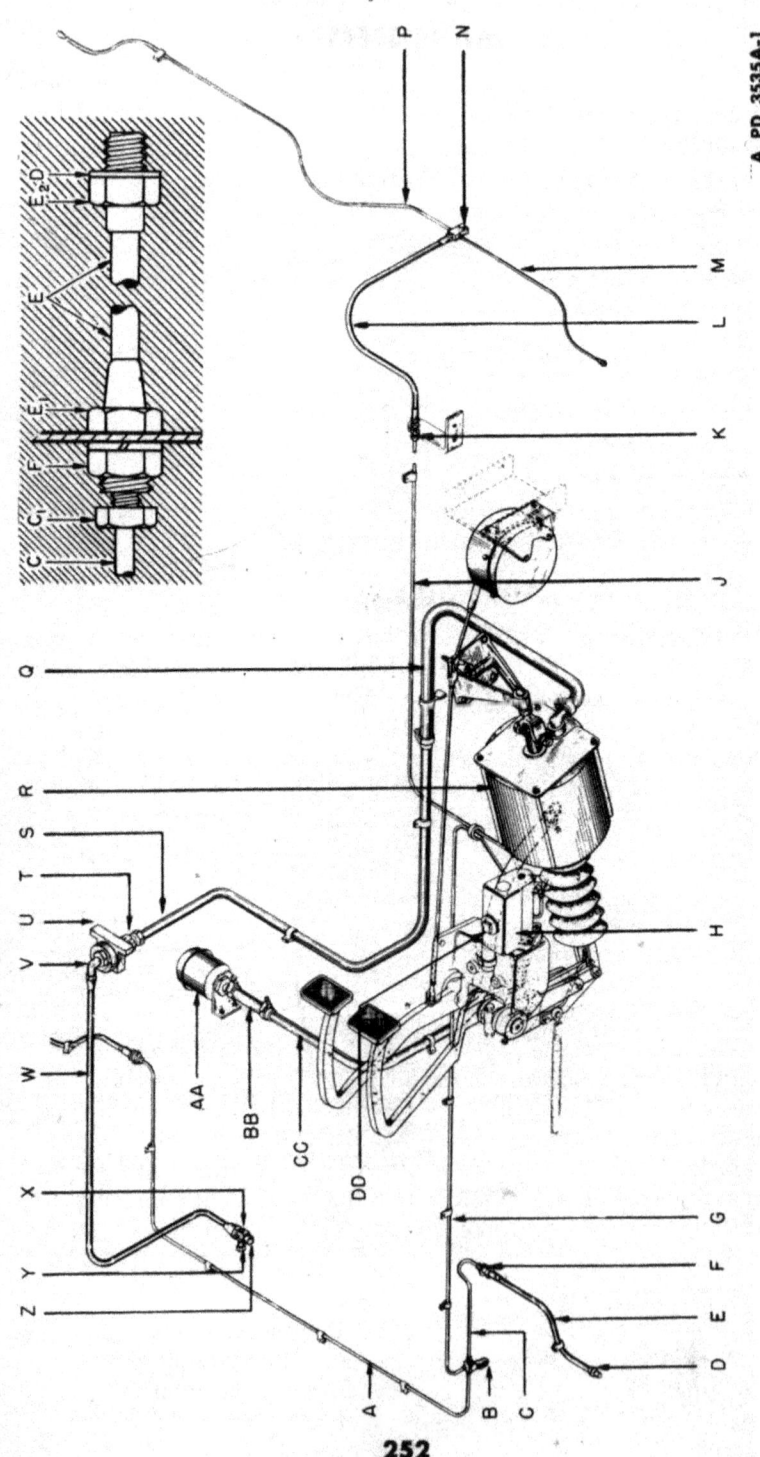

Figure 143—Hydraulic Brake System with Original Type Vacuum Booster (Schematic)

## BRAKE SYSTEM

**HYDRAULIC LINES (TO FRONT WHEEL BRAKES)**
- A — PIPE ASS'Y - TEE TO RIGHT WHEEL BRAKE CYLINDER
- B — TEE, W/SCREW, NUT, AND LOCK WASHER
- C — PIPE ASS'Y - TEE TO LEFT WHEEL BRAKE CYLINDER
- C1 — NUT - COUPLING PIPE ASS'Y TO HOSE
- D — GASKET - HOSE TO CYLINDER
- E — HOSE - PIPE ASS'Y TO WHEEL BRAKE CYLINDER
- E1 — RIGID NUT - ON PIPE ASS'Y AT FRAME
- E2 — RIGID NUT - ON PIPE ASS'Y AT WHEEL CYLINDER
- F — NUT. W/LOCK WASHER - SECURING HOSE TO FRAME
- G — PIPE ASS'Y - MASTER CYLINDER TO TEE
- H — MASTER CYLINDER ASSEMBLY
- J — PIPE ASS'Y - MASTER CYLINDER TO ADAPTER

**HYDRAULIC LINES (TO REAR WHEEL BRAKES)**
- K — ADAPTER, W/NUT AND LOCK WASHER PIPE ASS'Y TO HOSE
- L — HOSE - ADAPTER TO TEE
- M — PIPE ASS'Y - TEE TO LEFT WHEEL BRAKE CYLINDER
- N — TEE, W/SCREW AND WASHERS - HOSE TO PIPE ASS'Y
- P — PIPE ASS'Y - TEE TO RIGHT WHEEL BRAKE CYLINDER
- Q — HOSE - CHECK VALVE TO POWER CYLINDER
- R — POWER CYLINDER ASSEMBLY
- S — PIPE ASS'Y - CHECK VALVE TO POWER CYLINDER

**VACUUM LINES (MANIFOLD TO BOOSTER)**
- T — NIPPLE - BOTTOM OF CHECK VALVE
- U — CHECK VALVE ASS'Y
- V — ELBOW - TOP OF CHECK VALVE
- W — PIPE ASS'Y - MANIFOLD TO CHECK VALVE
- X — PLUG - MANIFOLD NIPPLE
- Y — CONNECTOR - TO VACUUM PUMP
- Z — NIPPLE - TO MANIFOLD
- AA — AIR CLEANER ASS'Y

**VACUUM LINES (AIR CLEANER TO BOOSTER)**
- BB — HOSE. W/CLAMP - AIR CLEANER TO PIPE ASS'Y
- CC — PIPE ASS'Y - AIR CLEANER TO POWER CYLINDER
- DD — HOSE - PIPE ASS'Y TO POWER CYLINDER

RA PD 3535B

*Legend for Figure 143—Hydraulic Brake System with Original Type Vacuum Booster (Schematic)*

**TM 9-710**

**BASIC HALF-TRACK VEHICLES (WHITE, AUTOCAR, and DIAMOND T)**

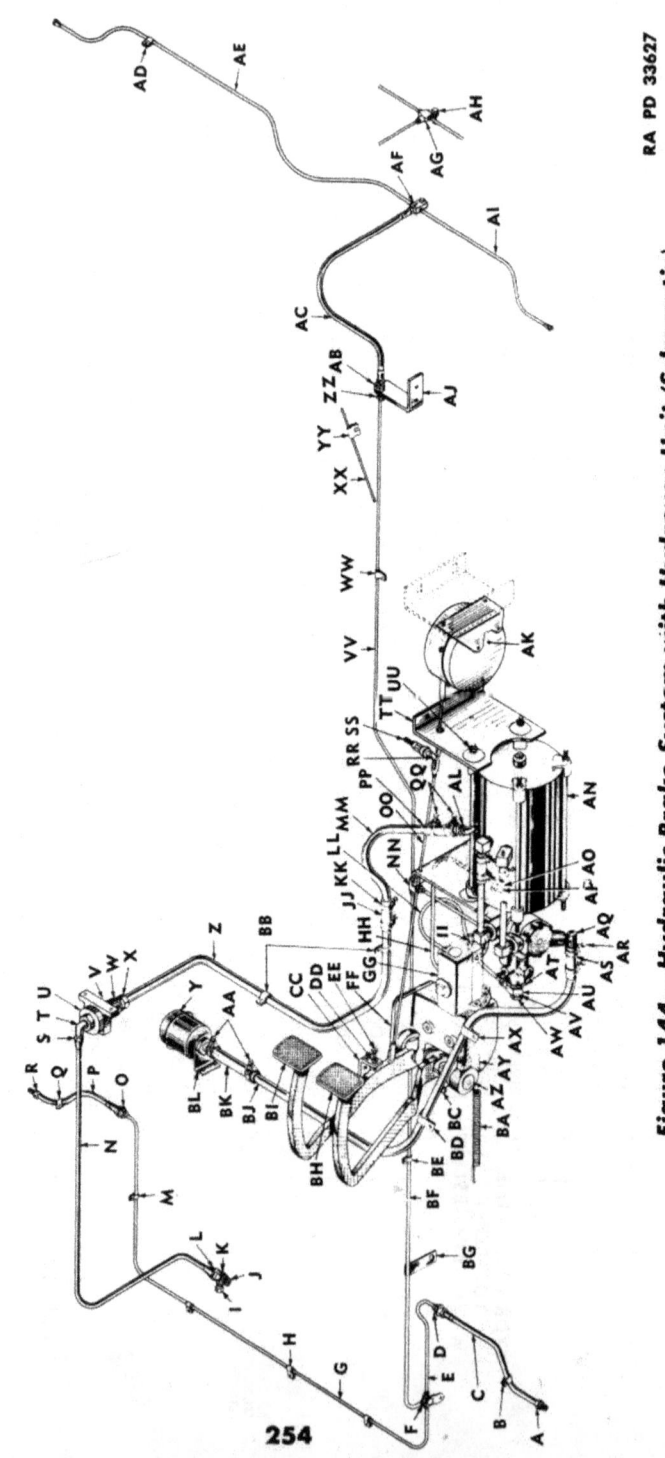

Figure 144—Hydraulic Brake System with Hydrovac Unit (Schematic)

## BRAKE SYSTEM

A — GASKET
B — TUBE CLIP
C — HYDRAULIC HOSE
D — NUT
E — HYDRAULIC LINE TO LEFT FRONT BRAKE
F — HYDRAULIC BRAKE LINE TEE
G — HYDRAULIC LINE TO RIGHT FRONT BRAKE
H — TUBE CLIP
I — WINDSHIELD WIPER LINES CONNECTOR; PLUG USED INSTEAD FOR 75 - M3
J — FITTING
K — PLUG
L — FLARED TUBE NUT
M — TUBE CLIP
N — VACUUM LINE FROM MANIFOLD TO CHECK VALVE
O — NUT
P — HYDRAULIC HOSE
Q — TUBE CLIP
R — GASKET
S — FLARED TUBE NUT
T — ELBOW
U — CHECK VALVE ASSEMBLY
V — PLUG
W — FITTING
X — FLARED TUBE NUT
Y — AIR CLEANER ASSEMBLY
Z — VACUUM LINE ASSEMBLY FROM CHECK VALVE TO HYDROVAC
AA — HOSE CLAMP
BB — TUBE CLIP
CC — BRAKE PEDAL STOP
DD — NUT
EE — CAP SCREW
FF — CLUTCH AND BRAKE PEDAL SUPPORT BRACKET
GG — MASTER CYLINDER ASSEMBLY
HH — HYDRAULIC LINE ASSEMBLY FROM MASTER CYLINDER TO HYDRAULIC CYL.
II — STOP LIGHT HYDRAULIC SWITCH
JJ — HOSE
KK — HOSE CLAMP
LL — HYDRAULIC LINE ASSEMBLY FROM HYDRAULIC CYLINDER TO TUBING TEE AT FRAME RAIL
MM — VACUUM TUBE
NN — HYDRAULIC BRAKE LINES TEE
OO — ELECTRIC BRAKE CONTROLLER ROD
PP — HOSE
QQ — HOSE CLAMP
RR — ELECTRIC BRAKE CONTROLLER ROD RELAY LEVER
SS — ELECTRIC BRAKE CONTROLLER ROD SHAFT AND SPACER
TT — HYDROVAC REAR MOUNTING BRACKET
UU — HYDROVAC STUD NUT AND WASHER
VV — HYDRAULIC LINE ASSEMBLY TO REAR BRAKE CONNECTION†
WW — TUBE CLIP
XX — HYDRAULIC LINE ASSEMBLY TO REAR BRAKE CONNECTION*
YY — TUBE CLIP
ZZ — UNION†
AB — NUT*
AC — HOSE†
AD — CLIP
AE — HYDRAULIC LINE TO RIGHT REAR BRAKE
AF — HYDRAULIC BRAKE LINE TEE†
AG — HYDRAULIC BRAKE LINE TEE*
AH — CAP SCREW AND WASHER*
AI — HYDRAULIC LINE TO LEFT REAR BRAKE
AJ — FRAME BRACKET†
AK — ELECTRIC BRAKE CONTROLLER ASSEMBLY
AN — HOSE NIPPLE
AO — HYDROVAC
AP — WASHER
AQ — CONNECTOR
AR — HOSE ELBOW
AS — HOSE CLAMP
AT — HOSE
AU — GASKET
AV — FITTING
AW — GASKET
AX — BOLT
AY — TUBE CLIP
AZ — MASTER CYLINDER ROD END YOKE
BA — CLUTCH AND BRAKE PEDAL SHAFT
BC — BRAKE PEDAL RETURN SPRING
BD — MASTER CYLINDER OPERATING LEVER
BE — TUBE CLIP
BF — TUBE CLIP
BG — HYDRAULIC LINE ASSEMBLY TO FRONT BRAKE LINE TEE
BH — TUBE CLIP
BI — CLUTCH PEDAL
BJ — BRAKE PEDAL
BK — ATMOSPHERIC TUBE ASSEMBLY FROM AIR CLEANER TO HYDROVAC
BL — HOSE
NOTE: OMIT † WHEN * ARE USED AIR CLEANER MOUNTING BRACKET

RA PD 33627B

**Legend for Figure 144—Hydraulic Brake System with Hydrovac Unit (Schematic)**

# TM 9-710
## 121-122
**BASIC HALF-TRACK VEHICLES (WHITE, AUTOCAR, and DIAMOND T)**

    (2) MASTER CYLINDER.
        Make .................... Wagner Electric
        Size ............................ 1½ in.
        Type ............................ hydraulic
    (3) WHEEL CYLINDERS.
        Make .................... Wagner Electric
        Model ......................... FD-7169
        Type ............................ hydraulic
        Size (front) ..................... 1⅜ in.
        Size (rear) ...................... 1¾ in.
    (4) BRAKE SHOES.
        Size (front) ................ 16 x 2¼ in.
        Size (rear) ................. 16 x 3½ in.

*Figure 145—Fluid Replacement at Master Cylinder*

**122. BLEEDING THE HYDRAULIC SYSTEM.**

    **a. General.** Bleeding the hydraulic system displaces any air in the system with hydraulic brake fluid. Forcing the fluid through the lines by depressing the brake pedal until it flows from the opened bleeder valve in a solid stream, indicates that the air has been displaced with fluid. Three bleeder valves are located at the hydrovac slave cylinder and one at each of the four wheel cylinders. The hydrovac unit must be bled first and then the wheel cylinders. Bleeding the system is necessary only when some part of the system has been disconnected or when the fluid level in the master cylinder has become too low.

## BRAKE SYSTEM

NOTE: *It is necessary to bleed the wheel cylinders only on vehicles which do not have a hydrovac unit.*

b. **Procedure.**

(1) INSTALL BRAKE FLUID REFILLER. Remove the two screws and lock washers which secure the left-hand floor plate in the driver's compartment above the master cylinder, and remove plate. Unscrew filler plug from top of master cylinder and install fluid refiller (fig. 145). NOTE: *The master cylinder must be kept filled as the bleeding progresses to prevent additional air from entering the system.*

(2) DISCONNECT HYDROVAC VACUUM LINE. Unscrew flared tube nut on vacuum pipe at bottom of check valve on dash and disconnect

*Figure 146—Bleeding Wheel Cylinders*

pipe. NOTE: *This operation is not necessary for vehicles which do not have a hydrovac unit.*

(3) BLEED HYDROVAC UNIT. (fig. 149). Remove cap screw and lock washer from bleeder valve nearest vacuum cylinder and install bleeder tube. Insert free end of bleeder tube in a clean one-pint glass jar containing enough fluid to cover end of tube (fig. 146). Unscrew bleeder valve three-fourths turn. Depress brake pedal slowly by hand and allow pedal to return slowly to its normal position. Continue this pumping action until fluid comes out end of tube in a solid stream and no more air is expelled as indicated by lack of bubbles. Tighten bleeder valve and remove bleeder tube. Install bleeder valve cap screw and

TM 9-710
122

**BASIC HALF-TRACK VEHICLES (WHITE, AUTOCAR, and DIAMOND T)**

A—BRAKE PEDAL, WITH KEY
B—BRAKE PEDAL ROD END PIN, WITH COTTER PIN
C—OPERATING LEVER LOCKING BOLT, WITH LOCK WASHER AND NUT
D—BRAKE PEDAL LOCKING BOLT, WITH LOCK WASHER AND NUT
E—OPERATING LEVER ADJUSTING SCREW, WITH NUT
F—OPERATING LEVER, WITH KEY
G—BRAKE PEDAL PULL BACK SPRING
H—MASTER CYLINDER PISTON ROD CLEVIS PIN, WITH COTTER PIN
J—OPERATING FORK RETAINING SCREW (2), WITH LOCK WASHER (2) AND HOOK WASHER
K—POWER CYLINDER VALVE OPERATING FORK
L—MASTER CYLINDER INNER RELAY LEVER
M—POWER CYLINDER PISTON ROD CLEVIS PIN, WITH COTTER PIN
N—MASTER CYLINDER OUTER RELAY LEVER
P—RELAY LEVER ROD END PIN, WITH COTTER PIN
Q—POWER LEVER
R—PEDAL SHAFT LUBRICATOR
S—BRAKE AND CLUTCH PEDAL SHAFT
T—BRAKE PEDAL ROD, WITH JAM NUTS (2)
U—STUD RETAINING NUT AND LOCK WASHER
V—RELAY LEVER SHOULDER STUD, WITH PLAIN WASHER AND COTTER PIN
W—RELAY LEVER ASSEMBLY
X—ELECTRIC BRAKE CONTROL OVERTRAVEL ASSEMBLY

RA PD 43399

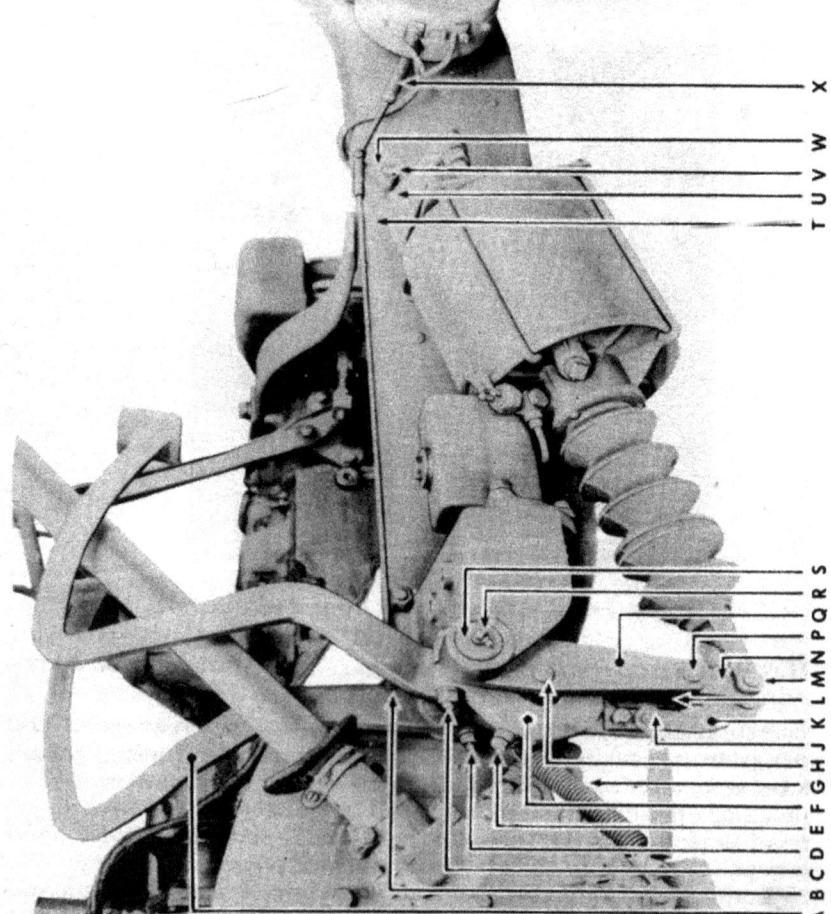

Figure 147—Service Brake Pedal and Linkage Installed (Vacuum Booster)

## BRAKE SYSTEM

lock washer. Bleed the remaining two bleeder valves, working toward outer end of slave cylinder.

(4) BLEED WHEEL CYLINDERS. Bleed each of the four wheel cylinders in the same manner as used for each hydrovac bleeder valve above, starting with wheel cylinder farthest from master cylinder and working around vehicle to nearest wheel cylinder.

(5) CONNECT VACUUM LINE. Install vacuum inlet pipe to bottom connection of check valve on dash and secure with flared tube nut.

(6) CHECK FLUID LEVEL IN MASTER CYLINDER. When bleeding has been completed, remove the fluid refiller from the master cylinder. Fluid must be one-half inch below the top. Install and tighten the filler plug. NOTE: *Fluid withdrawn in the bleeding operation should not be used again.*

(7) INSTALL FLOOR PLATE. Remove fluid refiller. Install floor plate on left-hand side of cab and secure plate with screws and lock washers.

### 123. BRAKE PEDAL AND LINKAGE (VACUUM BOOSTER).

a. **Description.** The service brake pedal and its linkage are located on the outer left side of the frame directly behind the steering gear (fig. 147). The pedal is connected by two piston rods to the master cylinder and the power booster cylinder. The power cylinder piston rod acts in direct leverage on the brake pedal linkage to assist the operator in applying the brakes.

b. **Maintenance.** The clamp bolts for the brake pedal and its associated linkage must be kept tight; loose leverage will adversely affect the operation of the brakes. Replace return spring when it is weak or broken. Renew worn clevis pins connecting brake levers to master cylinder piston rod, and power cylinder piston and valve rod.

c. **Pedal Linkage Adjustment** (figs. 147 and 148). Improper adjustments will affect the application and operation of the brakes, especially where the vacuum booster is concerned. The valve operating fork is attached to the brake pedal extension lever by screws in elongated holes to facilitate adjustment. Check the adjustments in the following manner:

(1) Loosen valve operating fork anchor screws (C, fig. 148), and remove master cylinder and power piston rod clevis pins.

(2) Be sure that the leverage system is clean, in correct alinement, and not binding.

(3) Block brake pedal in release position.

(4) Adjust master cylinder clevis to permit about $\frac{1}{32}$-inch lost motion in the master cylinder piston rod; insert clevis pin and secure with cotter pin.

(5) Pull out power cylinder piston rod until the piston bottoms. Aline piston rod clevis with power lever eye by turning mounting yoke in the frame mounting bracket.

(6) Check to see that the piston rod clevis pin (F, fig. 148) is against the rear side wall of the valve rod link bushing with no clear-

## BASIC HALF-TRACK VEHICLES (WHITE, AUTOCAR, and DIAMOND T)

ance at "G," and about $\frac{7}{64}$-inch clearance at "K." If clearance at "G" is incorrect, release adjustment screws "C," exercising care not to disturb position of the valve rod. Adjust valve operating fork "D" in elongated holes at "C" as needed, and tighten screws "C." Be sure valve operating fork is centrally and squarely located on the valve rod link bushing to avoid binding.

(7) Check that clearance at "K," between set screw "A" and master

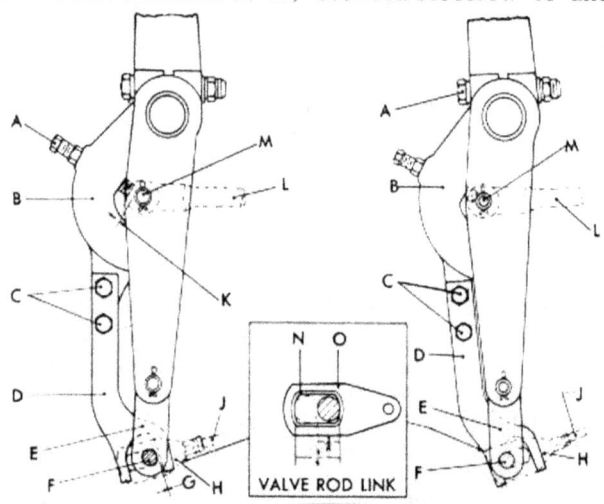

VALVE OPERATING FORK AND LINK IN CLOSED POSITION

VALVE OPERATING FORK AND LINK IN OPEN POSITION

A — ADJUSTING SET SCREW, W/NUT
B — BRAKE PEDESTAL EXTENSION LEVER
C — VALVE OPERATING FORK ANCHOR SCREW (2)
D — VALVE OPERATING FORK
E — POWER LEVER
F — POWER CYLINDER PISTON CLEVIS PIN
G — { CLEARANCE FOR PIN AND VALVE LINK BUSHING SIDE WALL
H — VALVE ROD LINK W/BUSHING
J — POWER CYLINDER VALVE ROD
K — CLEARANCE FOR SET SCREW AND PIN
L — MASTER CYLINDER PISTON CLEVIS PIN
M — MASTER CYLINDER PISTON ROD CLEVIS PIN
N — PISTON ROD LINK
O — PISTON ROD LINK BUSHING

RA PD 319669

*Figure 148—Hydraulic Brake Pedal Linkage (Vacuum Booster)*

cylinder clevis pin "M," is such that $\frac{3}{8}$-inch travel of the valve operating fork at "G" is obtained.

(8) If adjustment has been made correctly, all clearance at "B" will be taken up and the power cylinder valve rod will move inward about three-eighths inch when the brake pedal is moved by hand, with the engine shut off.

(9) As a further check, the power cylinder valve rod should move about $\frac{3}{16}$-inch inward before any movement of the power lever occurs when the brake pedal is moved by hand with the engine running.

**BRAKE SYSTEM**

(10) Check for insertion of cotter pins and for tightness of lock nuts and cap screws.

## 124. BRAKE BOOSTER (VACUUM).

**a. Description.** The vacuum power cylinder unit is mechanically connected to the brake linkage by means of a piston rod and piston. The piston is housed in a cylinder and is actuated by the force of the engine vacuum. It acts as a power booster complement for the brake pedal, to actuate the master cylinder, thereby reducing the amount of physical effort required to apply the brakes. The cylinder is connected to the engine intake manifold through a check valve and tubing. Outside atmospheric pressure is admitted to the cylinder through an air cleaner. Protection against damage of the vacuum power booster cylinder and brake linkage is afforded by a steel booster lever guard which is bolted to the left frame rail and to the left side body plate.

**b. Removal (Vacuum Booster).** Disconnect the vacuum line at rear of booster cylinder by loosening the hose clamp and pulling hose from the nipple. Disconnect the air cleaner line by loosening the hose clamp at front end of booster cylinder and pulling the hose from the nipple. Remove the cotter pin and rod-end pin at the bracket end of the cylinder and lower end of cylinder. Remove the cotter pin and rod-end pin from the brake linkage and remove booster assembly.

**c. Installation (Vacuum Booster).** Place the booster assembly in position and install the rod-end pin and cotter pin at the brake linkage end. Install the cotter pin and rod-end pin at the bracket end. Connect the air cleaner line by installing it on the nipple at the front end of cylinder and tightening the host clamp. Connect the vacuum line at the rear of the cylinder by installing it on the nipple of the booster and tightening the hose clamp. Check adjustments on pedal linkage. (par. 123).

**d. Emergency Measures.** (These measures are for vehicles not equipped with hydrovac system). In case of failure of the brake system because of punctures of the booster cylinder, fracture of the cylinder head, or any other reason, and a replacement unit is not immediately available, proceed as follows:

(1) Disconnect the vacuum line at the cylinder and plug it up with the plug which can be obtained from the front cylinder end plate. Hold plug in end of hose by tightening the host clamp.

(2) Disconnect the vacuum line at cylinder by loosening clamps and tie up end of line to clear road obstructions.

(3) Remove the vacuum booster completely from the vehicle by first removing the rod-end pins as described in subparagraph b above. *CAUTION: Since braking is less effective after the vacuum booster has been removed, be extremely careful in operating the vehicle.* The proper complete repair and replacement of the unit should be made as soon as possible.

TM 9-710
125

**BASIC HALF-TRACK VEHICLES (WHITE, AUTOCAR, and DIAMOND T)**

## 125. BRAKE PEDAL AND LINKAGE (HYDROVAC).

a. **Description.** The brake pedal and its linkage are located on the outer left side of the frame directly behind the steering gear and operate the hydraulic master cylinder piston only. A return spring brings the pedal and its connecting parts back to normal position when pressure on the pedal is released. This type of booster unit is different in the application of the power, acting directly on the hydraulic fluid instead of the brake pedal as in the vacuum booster.

b. **Maintenance.** The clamp bolts for the brake pedal and its associated linkage must be kept tight. Replace return spring when it is weak or broken. Renew worn clevis pins connecting brake lever to master cylinder piston rod. Lubricate pedal linkage at regular specified intervals.

c. **Removal.**

(1) UNHOOK RETURN SPRINGS. Unhook the two pedal return springs from hook washer on the steering housing.

(2) DISCONNECT MASTER CYLINDER HOUSING. Remove three cap screws and lock washers which secure the master cylinder housing to the pedal frame bracket.

(3) DISCONNECT CLEVIS YOKES. Remove cotter pin and clevis pin at bottom connection of clutch pedal yoke. Remove cotter pin and clevis pin from yoke on master cylinder and bottom of brake pedal.

(4) REMOVE TOE PLATES. Remove bolts, nuts, and lock washers from the two toe plates around clutch and brake pedals and steering column. Pull accelerator pedal from throttle rod ball and remove toe plates.

(5) DISCONNECT ELECTRIC BRAKE CONTROLLER ROD. Disconnect brake controller rod from yoke connection of the brake pedal at brake pedal end.

(6) REMOVE PEDAL BRACKET. Remove four bolts, nuts, and lock washers securing pedal bracket to frame. Remove two cap screws and lock washers at top of bracket, and pull the bracket forward off the master cylinder. Lower assembly until it is supported by the foot pedals hanging on the frame and steering column.

(7) REMOVE BRAKE PEDAL. Loosen the binder bolt, nut, and lock washer securing brake pedal to shaft and Woodruff key. Remove brake pedal.

(8) DISASSEMBLE PEDAL BRACKET. Lower assembly and remove to arbor press. Loosen binder bolt on brake shaft lever, and use arbor press to remove pedal shaft from pedal bracket. Press shaft and bushing, out of bushing end of pedal bracket, and disassemble clutch pedal, brake shaft lever with Woodruff key, and pedal bracket bushing.

d. **Installation.**

(1) INSTALL BRAKE PEDAL. Push the pedal bracket assembly (minus the brake pedal) into position to install the brake pedal. Put the brake pedal in from above the assembly and install it on shaft and Woodruff key. Tighten the binder bolt, lock washer, and nut.

## BRAKE SYSTEM

(2) INSTALL PEDAL BRACKET. Place bracket in proper position on frame and master cylinder and secure bracket to side of frame with four bolts, lock washers, and nuts. Install and tighten two cap screws with lock washers through the bracket at top of pedal bracket.

(3) CONNECT MASTER CYLINDER HOUSING. Install three cap screws and lock washers to attach the master cylinder housing to the pedal frame bracket.

(4) CONNECT CLEVIS YOKES. Install clevis pin and cotter pin to connection with yoke on clutch pedal linkage. Install clevis pin and cotter pin to yoke on master cylinder and bottom connection of brake pedal.

(5) HOOK UP RETURN SPRINGS. Hook the two pedal return springs to hook washer on steering gear housing.

(6) CONNECT ELECTRIC CONTROLLER ROD YOKE TO BRAKE PEDAL. Install end of the electric controller rod to yoke end on brake pedal and tighten locking nut.

(7) INSTALL TOE PLATES. Place toe plates in proper position around pedals and steering column and secure with bolts, lock washers, and nuts. Press accelerator pedal onto accelerator rod ball.

## 126. BRAKE BOOSTER (HYDROVAC).

a. Description. The Hydrovac unit (fig. 149) consists of a hydraulic slave cylinder, relay valve, and a power cylinder. The power cylinder is divided in two parts by a stationary center plate and encloses two pistons connected to the same piston rod. The relay valve and hydraulic slave cylinder are located on the front end of the cylinder. The assembly is connected by a hydraulic line from the master cylinder to the rear of the relay valve. The relay valve connects to the hydraulic slave cylinder and brake lines. An air line with a check valve connects the intake manifold to the center plate on the Hydrovac unit, utilizing the intake manifold suction to operate the unit. Outside air is admitted to the system through an air cleaner and tube connected to the relay valve. This type of booster acts directly on the hydraulic fluid leading to the brake cylinders from the slave cylinder rather than the master brake cylinder as applied to earlier models of brake boosters.

b. Tests and Maintenance.

(1) TEST HYDROVAC SYSTEM FOR LEAKS. Insert one vacuum gage in line running from the check valve to vacuum inlet elbow at hydrovac, and another vacuum gage in the pipe plug hole at rear end of cylinder. Start the engine and note gage reading which should show a vacuum of 17 to 20 inches. Stop the engine and note whether or not the vacuum is retained for a reasonable length of time. If gage shows a rapid decrease (more than 10 inches in ten seconds), a leak is indicated in the cylinder, line, check valve, or inlet manifold connection.

(a) *Leak in Hydrovac.* Start the engine and build up vacuum in hydrovac. Both gages should read manifold vacuum. If either gage drops in reading or does not attain manifold vacuum reading, there is a leak in the hydrovac.

# TM 9-710

**BASIC HALF-TRACK VEHICLES (WHITE, AUTOCAR, and DIAMOND T)**

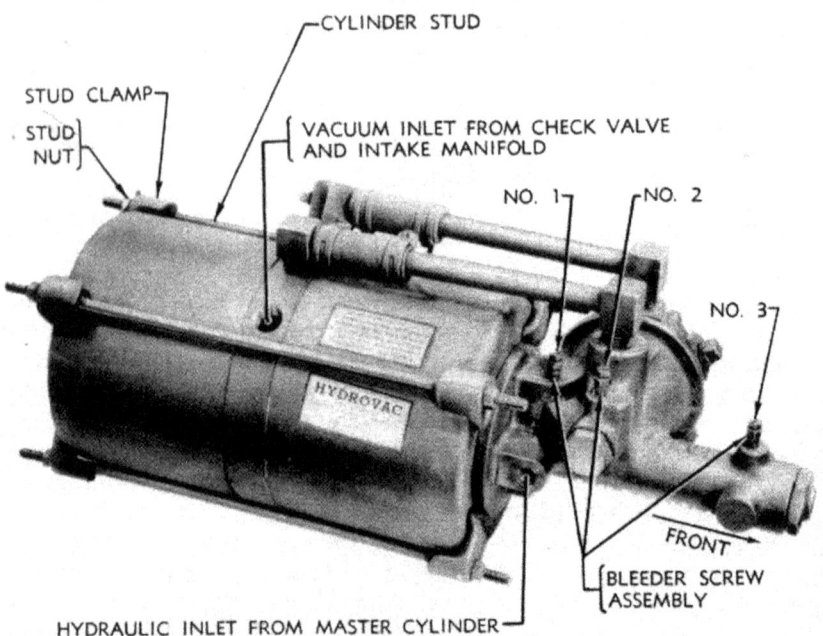

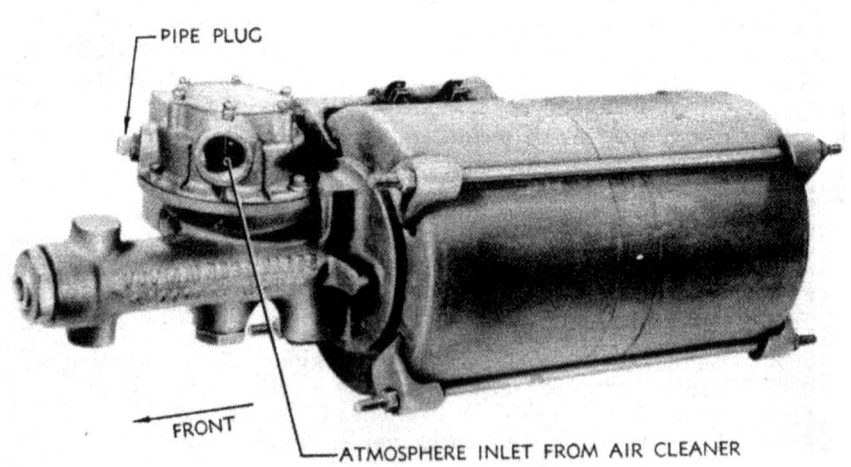

*Figure 149—Hydrovac Assembly*

## BRAKE SYSTEM

*(b) Leak in Check Valve.* Remove line from vacuum inlet elbow with gage connected to it, and cover end of line with thumb. Start engine and then stop it. The vacuum reading on the gage should remain constant after engine is stopped, if there is no leak in the check valve.

(2) BRAKE PERFORMANCE TEST. The following tests should be made at regular intervals to check the condition of the vehicle brakes:

*(a) With Engine Stopped.* Depress brake pedal and hold foot pressure. If the brake pedal gradually "falls away" under foot pressure, the hydraulic brake system is leaking and an immediate check and correction must be made. If the brake pedal travels to within 2 inches of the floor board, there is not enough brake pedal reserve, and a brake adjustment is required (par. 132).

*(b) With Engine Running.* While still holding foot on the brake pedal, as explained in the preceding paragraph, start the engine. The brake pedal should tend to move down slightly under the foot. If not, the vacuum system is not working correctly and a test should be made.

*(c) Road Test.* Road test the vehicle by making a brake application at about 20 miles per hour, noting whether or not the vehicle stops evenly and quickly. If the brake pedal has a spongy feel when the brakes are applied, there is air in the hydraulic system. Bleed the brakes as described in paragraph 122. If the brakes operate satisfactorily when tested at temperatures above freezing, but are ineffective and do not release properly at temperatures below freezing, report this condition to higher authority, as water may have entered the vacuum system where it may later cause more serious difficulty.

(3) MAINTENANCE. Every 20,000 miles or each six months, whichever occurs first, the hydrovac power cylinder should be lubricated with vacuum cylinder oil. Remove the pipe plug from rear end of hydrovac cylinder and the pipe plug on the atmosphere control line at the center plate and inject one-half ounce of vacuum cylinder oil at each plug opening. Install and tighten plugs. NOTE: *Leakage in the power cylinder may often be corrected by a thorough lubrication of the unit.*

c. **Removal.**

(1) DISCONNECT VACUUM LINE. Loosen screw in hose clamp, holding hose to nipple in hydrovac center plate. Pull hose off nipple, disconnecting vacuum line.

(2) DISCONNECT MASTER CYLINDER TO HYDROVAC INLET LINE. Remove the flared tube nut from the fitting in the hydraulic slave cylinder. Pull line and flared tube nut from fitting.

(3) DISCONNECT ATMOSPHERIC INLET TUBE AT RELAY VALVE. Loosen hose clamp screw on tube from air cleaner to atmospheric inlet connection at relay valve and pull hose off elbow in relay valve.

(4) DISCONNECT HYDRAULIC OUTLET LINE AT FRONT END OF SLAVE CYLINDER. Remove bolt holding fitting to front end of hydraulic slave cylinder and remove fitting and brake line.

(5) REMOVE HYDROVAC. Remove four nuts and lock washers from the two long studs holding hydrovac to the two frame brackets. Loosen

## BASIC HALF-TRACK VEHICLES (WHITE, AUTOCAR, and DIAMOND T)

two bolts, nuts, and lock washers holding the rear frame bracket to the frame. Slip rear bracket off ends of long studs on hydrovac. Pull hydrovac and other end of long studs free of the front frame bracket and remove hydrovac.

d. Installation.

(1) INSTALL HYDROVAC. Set hydrovac in position, with hydraulic slave cylinder toward front of the vehicle. Insert front end of two long studs in front frame bracket holes. Install rear frame bracket on rear end of the two long studs and tighten two bolts, lock washers, and nuts securing rear frame bracket to the frame. Install and tighten four lock washers and nuts to ends of the two long studs through the front and rear frame brackets.

(2) CONNECT VACUUM LINE. Slip hose, on end of vacuum line, over the nipple in hydrovac center plate and tighten hose clamp screw.

(3) CONNECT MASTER CYLINDER TO HYDRAULIC INLET LINE. Install line from master cylinder to hydraulic inlet connection at rear of slave cylinder and secure line to fitting with flared tube nut.

(4) CONNECT ATMOSPHERIC INLET TUBE TO RELAY VALVE. Slip hose on atmospheric inlet tube over elbow on relay valve and tighten hose clamp screw.

(5) INSTALL HYDRAULIC OUTLET LINE TO SLAVE CYLINDER. Install line and fitting to front end of hydraulic slave cylinder and secure fitting with bolt.

### 127. BRAKE BOOSTER AIR CLEANER.

a. Description. A small air cleaner unit to filter the air taken into the hydrovac through a connecting pipe at the atmospheric intake on the relay valve is located underneath the generator regulator bracket. The air is filtered by means of an oil-treated, curled-hair element located inside the air cleaner.

b. Removal. Remove one screw and lock washer from the center of the lid on the air cleaner and pull the complete assembly from the end of the atmospheric inlet pipe.

c. Maintenance. The air cleaner should be examined and cleaned at regular maintenance intervals. Remove the hair, wash it thoroughly in dry-cleaning solvent, dry, and then saturate with light machine oil. Install hair in body of air cleaner and reassemble. Clean off all dirt around the front plate holes and body of cleaner.

d. Installation. Push air cleaner over end of inlet pipe and secure with one screw and lock washer through the center of the lid on air cleaner.

### 128. BRAKE BOOSTER CHECK VALVE.

a. Description. The brake booster check valve (fig. 150) is mounted in a rubber bracket under the hood on the right front side of dash. A line from the intake manifold is connected to the top of the check valve and the line at the bottom of the valve connects to the center plate (vacuum inlet hole) on the hydrovac. The check valve closes automatically when the engine is shut off. This seals the vacuum

TM 9-710
128-129

## BRAKE SYSTEM

n the hydrovac unit and lines after the engine has been stopped, providing sufficient vacuum for a complete brake application.

b. **Removal.** Unscrew the flared tube nut connection of intake manifold tubing to check valve, and disconnect tubing from check valve. Unscrew the fitting on tubing connection at bottom of check valve and disconnect tubing. Remove two bolts, nuts, and four washers from check valve rubber mounting bracket and pull check valve and bracket from dash.

c. **Installation.** Place check valve and rubber bracket in proper position on dash, elbow nipple up. Secure rubber bracket to dash with

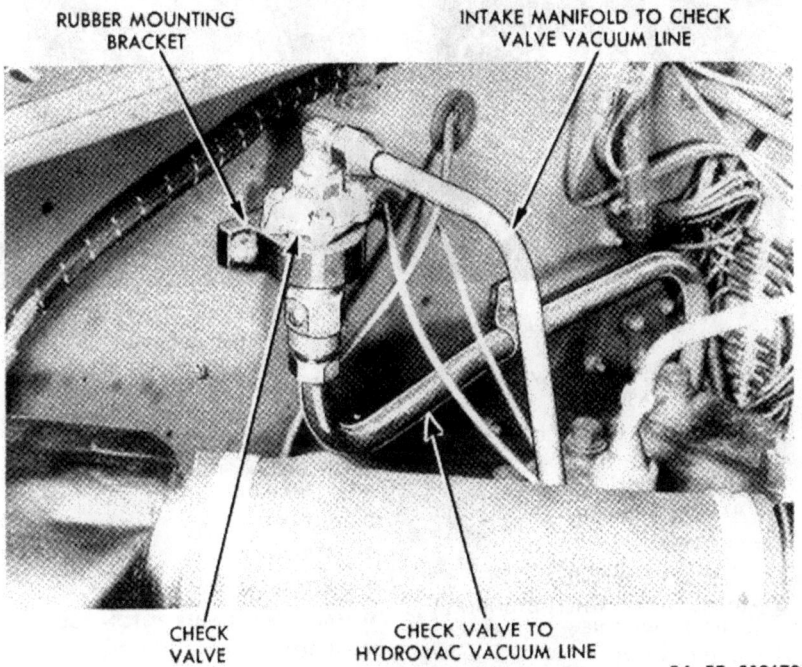

*Figure 150—Check Valve Installed*

two bolts, four washers (one plain and one lock washer on each bolt), and two nuts. Connect tubing from hydrovac vacuum inlet to bottom of check valve and secure fitting. Connect tubing from intake manifold to top of check valve and secure with flared tube nut.

### 129. MASTER CYLINDER.

a. **Description.** The master cylinder (fig. 151) consists of a storage tank for hydraulic fluid, and a piston and cylinder assembly to set up pressure in the system to operate the brakes. The storage tank automatically maintains a constant volume of fluid in the system, compensates for expansion or contraction of the fluid caused by temperature changes, and replenishes any loss of fluid from slight leaks.

# TM 9-710
## BASIC HALF-TRACK VEHICLES (WHITE, AUTOCAR, and DIAMOND T)

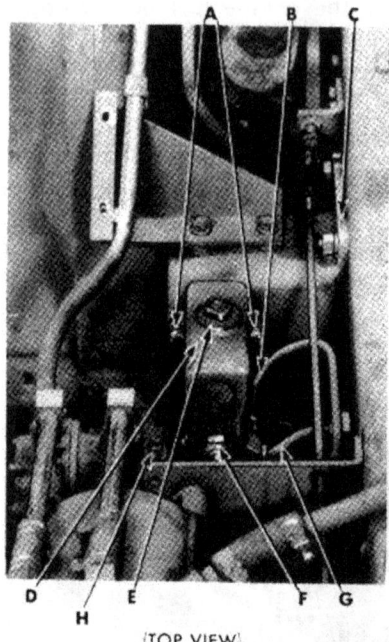 

(TOP VIEW)

A — MOUNTING CAP SCREWS WITH LOCK WASHERS
B — MASTER CYLINDER TO HYDROVAC HYDRAULIC LINE
C — PEDAL BRACKET
D — MASTER CYLINDER
E — FILLER CAP
F — STOP LIGHT SWITCH
G — HYDROVAC TO WHEEL CYLINDERS HYDRAULIC LINE
H — BLEEDER VALVE

(BOTTOM VIEW)

A — STOP LIGHT SWITCH
B — MASTER CYLINDER TO HYDROVAC HYDRAULIC LINE
C — HYDROVAC TO WHEEL CYLINDERS HYDRAULIC LINE
D — CLEVIS PIN
E — SPRING PLATE
F — RETURN SPRING
G — MASTER CYLINDER PISTON ROD
H — BOOT

RA PD 319671

*Figure 151—Master Cylinder Installed*

b. **Maintenance.** Remove the inspection plate on the left-hand floor plate to inspect fluid level in master cylinder. Unscrew and remove filler cap. Proper fluid level is one-half inch below the top of supply tank. Use only genuine hydraulic fluid. Inspect fluid level at regular maintenance intervals. There is practically no loss of fluid in the operation of the brakes. Any noticeable loss indicates a leak in the system, which must be located and stopped. If tank becomes more than half empty, air is pumped into the system. System will then have to be bled to put it back into proper operating condition. (Refer to paragraph 122.)

## BRAKE SYSTEM

c. **Removal.**

(1) DISCONNECT BRAKE PEDAL ROD AND RETURN SPRING. Pull brake return spring loose from hook washer on steering housing. Remove cotter pin, spring plate and spring, and clevis pin connecting brake pedal rod and clevis yoke on master cylinder piston rod.

(2) DISCONNECT STOP LIGHT SWITCH TERMINALS. Unscrew locking nuts on two wires at terminals of stop light switch at rear end of master cylinder, and disconnect.

(3) DISCONNECT HYDRAULIC LINE. Unscrew bolt on hydraulic line fitting at master cylinder and disconnect line.

(4) REMOVE MASTER CYLINDER. Remove three cap screws and lock washers securing the master cylinder housing to brake pedal bracket and pull complete assembly from bracket.

d. **Installation.**

(1) INSTALL MASTER CYLINDER. Insert piston rod end of master cylinder through hole in pedal bracket and secure master cylinder to bracket with three cap screws and lock washers.

(2) CONNECT HYDRAULIC LINE. Install hydraulic line to master cylinder and secure with bolt.

(3) CONNECT STOP LIGHT TERMINALS. Install two wires of stop light switch to terminals and secure wires with locking nuts.

(4) INSTALL PEDAL ROD AND RETURN SPRING. Insert clevis pin through spring plate with spring and connect to yoke of master cylinder piston rod and brake pedal shaft lever. Secure with cotter pin. Stretch the return spring and install it to the hook washer on the steering column.

(5) BLEED THE BRAKE SYSTEM. Fill the master cylinder with hydraulic brake fluid and proceed to bleed the brake system as outlined in paragraph 122.

## 130. FRONT AND REAR WHEEL CYLINDERS.

a. **Description.** One wheel cylinder is mounted on each wheel brake backing plate. The open ends of the cylinders are protected by rubber boots which prevent the entrance of dust and grit. The brake fluid enters the cylinder between two pistons enclosed in the cylinder, forcing them apart and expanding the brake shoes in the brake drum.

b. **Removal.**

(1) REMOVE HUB AND DRUM. If a front wheel cylinder is to be removed, remove front wheel and brake drum (pars. 135 and 137). If a rear wheel cylinder is to be removed, remove the track, driving sprocket, and brake drum (par. 117 and 137).

(2) BLOCK BRAKE PEDAL. Block or tie the brake pedal in released position to prevent any movement of pedal.

(3) INSTALL WHEEL BRAKE CYLINDER CLAMP (fig. 152). Clamp the ends of the wheel cylinder with a wheel brake cylinder spring clamp.

(4) REMOVE BRAKE SHOE RETURN SPRING (fig. 153). Use a pair of special brake spring pliers to release one end of brake shoe return spring, and remove spring.

# TM 9-710

## BASIC HALF-TRACK VEHICLES (WHITE, AUTOCAR, and DIAMOND T)

(5) DISCONNECT BRAKE HOSE (FRONT WHEEL). Remove the protecting armor side plates attached to the frame at each side of the engine, and disconnect the hydraulic brake hose at the frame. After disconnecting hose line at frame connection, loosen steering knuckle bearing plate nuts holding hose clips, so that hose can turn in its clips. Disconnect hose at wheel cylinder. NOTE: *Rear wheel cylinder brake tube can be disconnected without any preliminary steps.*

(6) REMOVE WHEEL CYLINDERS. Remove bleeder valve and two cap screws and lock washers securing wheel cylinders to backing plate.

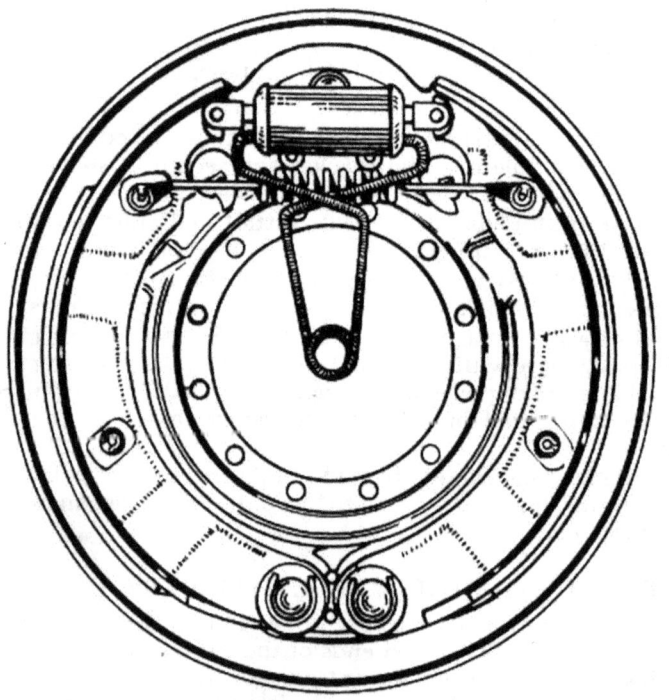

RA PD 3503A

*Figure 152—Wheel Brake Cylinder Clamp Installed*

Push brake shoes apart and lift wheel cylinder assembly and clamp from brake shoes and backing plate.

c. **Installation.**

(1) INSTALL WHEEL CYLINDER. Place wheel cylinder, with clamp spring holding ends in place, in position on backing plate with cylinder links set in the brake shoe recesses. Secure by installing and tightening the bleeder valve, two cap screws and lock washers.

(2) INSTALL BRAKE HOSE. Install brake hose to wheel cylinder connection and tighten. If front wheel, install and tighten other end to connection at frame, tighten hose clips, and install protecting armor side plates.

## BRAKE SYSTEM

(3) INSTALL BRAKE SHOE SPRING. Slip one end of spring into upper guide pin slot of forward shoe. Stretch spring with special spring pliers and hook the other end into guide slot of the other shoe. Remove wheel cylinder clamp.

(4) INSTALL HUB AND DRUM. Install front hub and brake drum and wheel (pars. 135 and 137). Install rear hub and drum, sprocket, and track (pars. 117 and 137).

(5) BLEED BRAKE SYSTEM. Refer to paragraph 122.

RA PD 3543A

*Figure 153—Removing Brake Shoe Return Spring*

131. **HOSE, LINES, AND FITTINGS** (fig. 144).

a. **Description.** One main line for the hydraulic service brake system is connected to the front end of the slave cylinder located on the front end of the hydrovac. This main line connects to a brake line tee (**NN**, fig. 144). This tee has two connecting lines attached to it (VV-hydraulic line to rear brake connection and BF-hydraulic line to front brake). These solid lines (tubing) run along the inside of the frame until they are approximately opposite the wheel cylinders, at which point they are connected to the wheel cylinders' flexible hose fittings. Clips secure the lines to the frame.

# TM 9-710
131

**BASIC HALF-TRACK VEHICLES (WHITE, AUTOCAR, and DIAMOND T)**

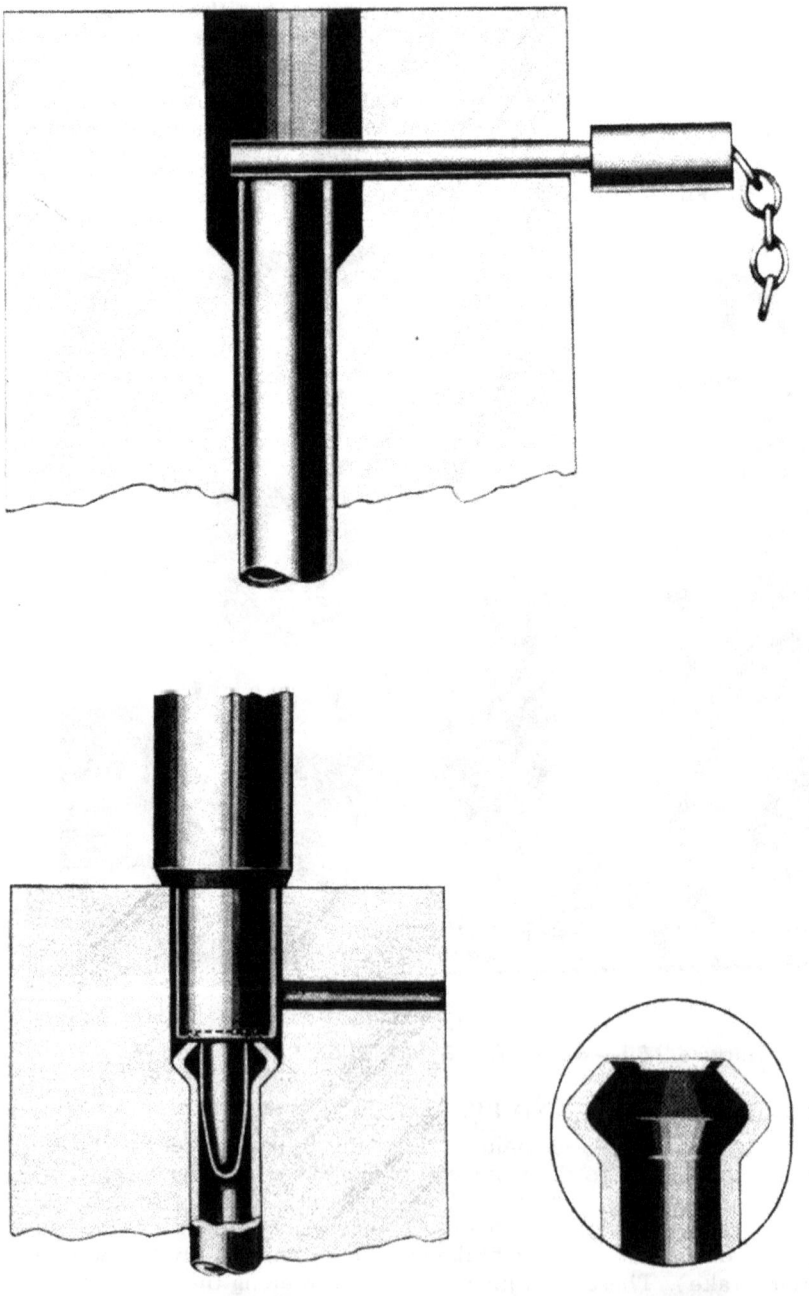

RA PD 330826

*Figure 155—First Flaring Operation*

**TM 9-710**

## BRAKE SYSTEM

b. **Removal of Hose and Line Assemblies.**

(1) REMOVE FRONT WHEEL CYLINDER HOSE ASSEMBLIES. Remove protecting armor side plates attached to inner side of frame at each side of engine. Disconnect flared tube nuts at frame end of hose. Disconnect each hose fitting from frame by removing holding nut and lock washer. Free hose clips at steering knuckle. Unscrew hose assemblies from wheel cylinder inlet fittings, and remove.

(2) REMOVE LINE ASSEMBLY (FRONT TEE TO LEFT-HAND WHEEL). Disconnect inverted flared tube nut at tee, and remove line assembly.

(3) REMOVE LINE ASSEMBLY (FRONT TEE TO RIGHT-HAND WHEEL). Disconnect inverted flared tube nut at tee. Detach clips holding line assembly to frame and remove line assembly.

(4) REMOVE LINE ASSEMBLY (INTERMEDIATE TEE TO FRONT TEE). Disconnect inverted flared tube nuts at both tees. Detach clips from frame and drop line assembly.

(5) REMOVE FRONT TEE. Remove bolt, nut, and lock washer holding tee to front left-hand side of frame and lift out tee.

(6) REMOVE LINE ASSEMBLY (SLAVE CYLINDER HYDRAULIC OUTLET TO INTERMEDIATE TEE). Remove bolt from fitting on line at slave cylinder and inverted flared tube nut at intermediate tee, and remove line assembly.

(7) REMOVE LINE ASSEMBLY (MASTER CYLINDER TO SLAVE CYLINDER INLET). Remove bolt securing master cylinder outlet fitting, remove inverted flared tube nut at inlet of slave cylinder, and lift out line assembly.

(8) REMOVE LINE ASSEMBLY (INTERMEDIATE TEE TO UNION OF REAR HOSE). Remove inverted flared tube nuts at intermediate tee and at union of rear brake line connecting hose. Detach clips holding line assembly to frame and remove assembly.

(9) REMOVE HOSE ASSEMBLY (REAR CONNECTION TO AXLE TEE). Remove nut and lock washer holding hose fitting to bracket. Unscrew flared tube nut on hose at tee, and remove assembly.

(10) LINE ASSEMBLY (REAR AXLE TEE TO LEFT-HAND WHEEL). Disconnect inverted flared tube nut at tee and flared tube nut at wheel cylinder, and remove line assembly.

(11) LINE ASSEMBLY (REAR AXLE TO RIGHT-HAND WHEEL). Disconnect inverted flared tube nut at tee and flared tube nut at wheel cylinder. Remove cap screw and lock washer holding line clip to axle housing, and remove line assembly.

(12) REMOVE REAR TEE. Remove cap screw and lock washer holding tee to housing and lift off tee.

c. **Maintenance.**

(1) Very little maintenance is necessary on hydraulic lines, since damaged parts can usually be replaced as assemblies. However, an assembly can be made from a piece of tubing as follows:

## TM 9-710
### 131
**BASIC HALF-TRACK VEHICLES (WHITE, AUTOCAR, and DIAMOND T)**

(a) Cut tubing to desired length with tube cutter. Square ends with a fine cut mill file, then ream the sharp edges with reamer blade provided on cutter.

(b) Install new compression coupling nuts on tubing. Dip end of tubing to be flared in hydraulic brake fluid. This type of lubrication results in a better formation of the flare. Loosen clamping nuts on flaring tool. Insert tubing in channel of the die until it bears against stop (fig. 154). Tighten clamp nuts on tool by hand, then place tool in a bench vise. Proceed to tighten clamping nuts securely with a wrench and remove stop pin from tool. The tubing is now ready for first flaring operation.

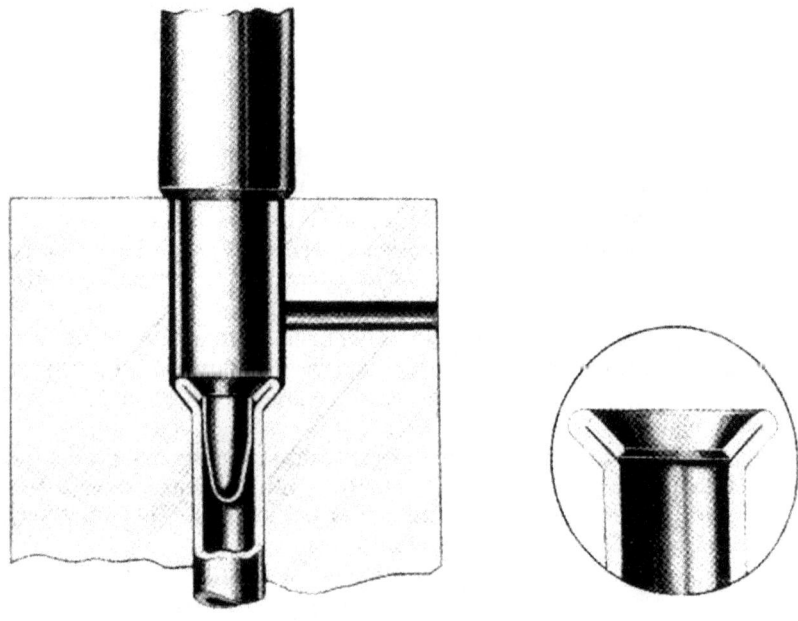

RA PD 330827

*Figure 156—Final Flaring Operation*

(c) Insert flare-forming tool having concave end in die containing tubing, then strike tool firmly with a hammer until shoulder of tool contacts top of die (fig. 155).

(d) Install flare-forming tool with a forty-five degree convex end in die containing tubing (fig. 156). Strike tool firmly with a hammer until tool bottoms on die.

(e) Loosen clamping nuts, remove die from vise, then remove tubing from die. Examine flare in tubing, and make certain that flare is properly formed.

(2) Replace the flexible hose at the end of two years' service. Keep all connections tight and inspect frequently for leaks.

## BRAKE SYSTEM

*Figure 157—Front Brake Shoe Installed*

(3) Bleeding the brake system becomes necessary when some part of the hydraulic mechanism has been disconnected or when the fluid in the supply tank has become too low. See paragraph 122 for bleeding operations.

d. **Installation of Hose and Line Assemblies.**

(1) INSTALL REAR AXLE TEE. Secure tee to rear axle housing with lock washer and cap screw.

(2) INSTALL LINE ASSEMBLIES TO REAR WHEEL BRAKE CYLINDERS. Secure proper end of each assembly to rear tee with inverted flared tube nut. Secure opposite ends to wheel cylinder fittings with flared tube nut. Fasten right-hand line clip to frame with cap screw and lock washer.

(3) INSTALL HOSE ASSEMBLY (AXLE TEE TO REAR TUBE CONNECTION). Secure hose to tube fitting at bracket with lock washer and nut. Screw flared tube nut securely into tee at rear axle.

# TM 9-710

## BASIC HALF-TRACK VEHICLES (WHITE, AUTOCAR, and DIAMOND T)

(4) INSTALL LINE ASSEMBLY (INTERMEDIATE TEE TO UNION OF REAR HOSE). Place line in position and secure ends with flared tube nuts to intermediate tee and rear hose union. Secure line clips to frame with cap screws and lock washers.

(5) INSTALL LINE ASSEMBLY (MASTER CYLINDER TO INLET OF SLAVE CYLINDER). Secure fitting to master cylinder outlet with bolt and secure opposite end of line to slave cylinder inlet with flared tube nut.

(6) INSTALL ASSEMBLY (SLAVE CYLINDER HYDRAULIC OUTLET TO INTERMEDIATE TEE). Secure line fitting to slave cylinder outlet with

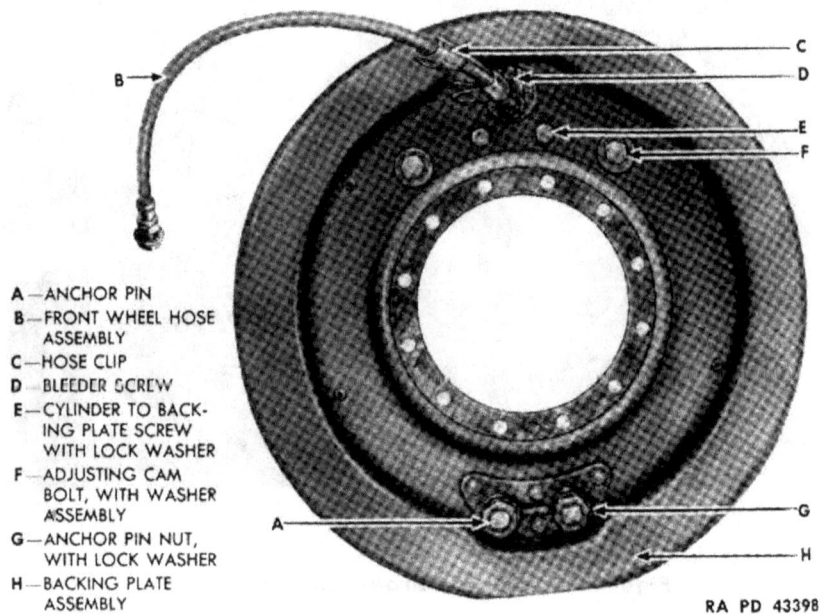

A—ANCHOR PIN
B—FRONT WHEEL HOSE ASSEMBLY
C—HOSE CLIP
D—BLEEDER SCREW
E—CYLINDER TO BACKING PLATE SCREW WITH LOCK WASHER
F—ADJUSTING CAM BOLT, WITH WASHER ASSEMBLY
G—ANCHOR PIN NUT, WITH LOCK WASHER
H—BACKING PLATE ASSEMBLY

RA PD 43398

*Figure 158—Brake Shoe Adjusting Cams*

bolt. Install opposite end of line in intermediate tee and secure with inverted flared tube nut.

(7) INSTALL FRONT TEE. Secure tee to proper position on front left-hand side of frame with bolt, lock washer, and nut.

(8) INSTALL LINE ASSEMBLY (INTERMEDIATE TEE TO FRONT TEE). Place line assembly in position and secure one end to intermediate tee and the opposite end to front tee with inverted flared tube nuts. Secure tube clips to frame with lock washers and cap screws.

(9) INSTALL FRONT WHEEL CYLINDER HOSE ASSEMBLIES. Place hose in position and secure one end to wheel brake cylinder inlet fitting. Tighten hose clips at steering knuckle. Connect hose fitting at frame end of hose and tighten flared tube nuts. Install engine protecting armor side plates to frame sides.

## BRAKE SYSTEM

(10) INSTALL LINE ASSEMBLY (FRONT TEE TO LEFT AND RIGHT-HAND WHEEL). Install proper end of each assembly to tee, and secure with inverted flared tube nut. Install opposite end of each assembly to wheel cylinders' hose connections at frame, and secure with flared tube nuts.

### 132. SERVICE BRAKE SHOES.

a. **Description.** The service brakes proper consist of a combination of two internal-expanding shoes, a brake drum, and a wheel cylinder for each front wheel and rear drive sprocket (fig. 157). The shoes, lined with molded brake lining, are supported at the lower ends by adjustable eccentric anchor pins, and connected at the top to a wheel cylinder. The shoes are expanded against the brake drums by opposed pistons acting in the wheel cylinder operating directly on each shoe.

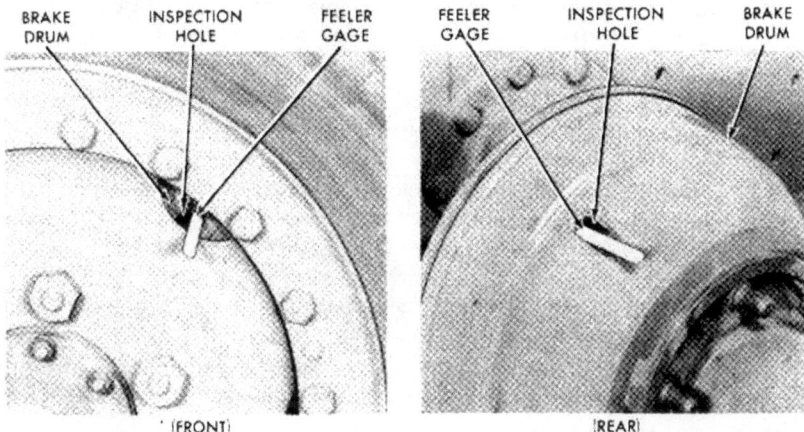

*Figure 159—Using Feeler Gage to Adjust Brake Lining Clearance*

b. **Adjustment.**

(1) MINOR ADJUSTMENT. To take up wear on the lining, only a minor adjustment is necessary. To adjust front brakes, jack up the vehicle until wheels are free of ground. Adjust one shoe at a time by turning adjusting cam (fig. 158) in the direction of the forward rotation of the wheel until the lining is pressed firmly against the drum. Back off this adjustment slightly until the wheel rotates freely without drag. Adjust all eight brake shoes in this manner. These cams are automatically locked in position by friction springs. Lower vehicle to ground and remove jack. NOTE: *Before attempting to make adjustment of brakes, it is important to see that all wheel bearings are properly adjusted and that the brake pedal arm stop screw is set to provide ½-inch clearance between the brake pedal arm and the underside of the toe board.*

(2) MAJOR ADJUSTMENT. Major adjustments are not ordinarily necessary except after relining brakes, grinding drums, or in case of displaced anchor pins.

## BASIC HALF-TRACK VEHICLES (WHITE, AUTOCAR, and DIAMOND T)

*(a) Jack Up Vehicle.* Leave wheels and drums in place and raise the vehicle until wheels are free of ground.

*(b) Adjust Heel of Brake Shoe.* Remove inspection hole cover, and position the hole one inch from the "heel" of lining on lower end of brake shoe being adjusted. Loosen the proper eccentric anchor pin nut at the rear of the backing plate and insert a feeler gage in the inspection plate hole between the brake lining and drum (fig. 159). Set this clearance to 0.005 inch by turning eccentric anchor pin. Lock anchor pin with its locking nut, and recheck setting.

*(c) Adjust Toe of Brake Shoe.* Turn the inspection plate hole on brake drum until it is 1 inch from the "toe" or upper end of the brake shoe lining. Insert a feeler gage in the inspection plate hole between the lining and brake drum. Turn the adjusting cam bolt (fig. 158) until the clearance is 0.010 inch. Pull out feeler gage and install inspection plate. Adjust all eight brake shoes in this manner. NOTE: *The rear driving sprocket drum inspection holes are practically inaccessible unless sprockets are dismounted.*

*(d) Check Pedal Travel.* Secure all locking nuts on anchor bolt eccentrics and try pedal travel and brake action.

c. **Removal.**

(1) REMOVE WHEEL (OR SPROCKET) AND BRAKE DRUM. To remove front wheel and drum, refer to paragraphs 135 and 137. To remove driving sprocket and brake drum, refer to paragraphs 117 and 137.

(2) BLOCK BRAKE PEDAL. Block or tie the brake pedal in released position to prevent any movement of pedal.

(3) INSTALL WHEEL BRAKE CYLINDER CLAMP. Clamp the ends of the wheel cylinder with a wheel brake cylinder spring clamp (fig. 152).

(4) REMOVE BRAKE SHOE SPRING. Use a pair of special brake spring pliers to release one end of brake shoe retracting spring and remove spring (fig. 153).

(5) REMOVE GUIDE PIN WASHERS. Remove the "C" washers by placing a screwdriver against the tang end and driving them off. Lift off the plain washers.

(6) REMOVE BRAKE SHOE. Remove anchor pin "C" washers by forcing a screwdriver under end of washer and twisting. Remove the spacer washers. Pull brake shoe off anchor pin at the heel end of shoe and slip the recessed hole in toe end, off the wheel cylinder link.

d. **Installation.**

(1) INSTALL BRAKE SHOES. Place brake shoes in proper position on anchor pins, guide pins and wheel cylinder link. Install the plain spacer washers and lock them in place with the "C" washers on both guide pins and anchor pins.

(2) INSTALL BRAKE SHOE SPRING. Slip one end of retracting spring into upper guide slot of forward shoe, stretch spring with the special pliers, and slip other end of spring into upper guide slot of reverse shoe. Remove brake wheel cylinder clamp.

## BRAKE SYSTEM

A — HAND BRAKE LEVER
B — BRAKE SHOE ADJUSTING SET SCREWS
C — BRAKE DISC
D — REAR BRAKE LEVER ARM
E — P. T. O. SHIFT LEVER
F — PULL ROD
G — OPERATING LEVER
H — FRONT BRAKE LEVER ARM
I — BRAKE SHOE SPRING
J — LEVER ARM RELEASE SPRING
K — SPHERICAL ADJUSTING NUT

RA PD 319674

*Figure 160 — Propeller Shaft Brake Installed*

**TM 9-710**
**132**

**BASIC HALF-TRACK VEHICLES (WHITE, AUTOCAR, and DIAMOND T)**

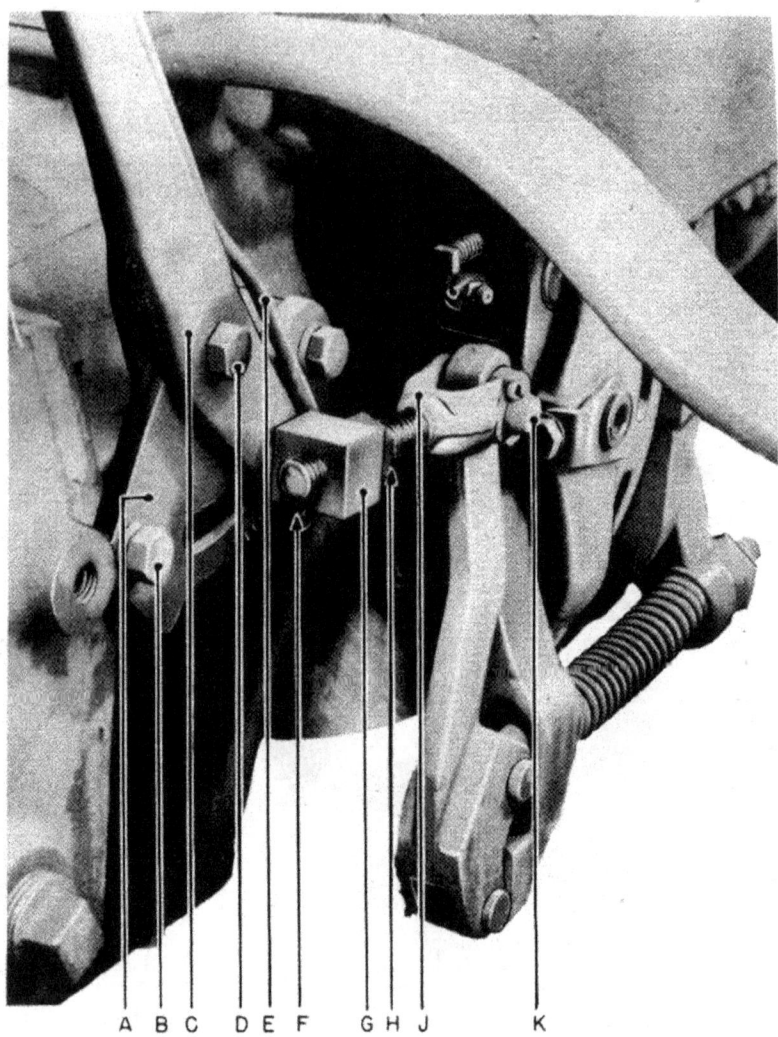

- A. HAND BRAKE LEVER QUADRANT
- B. QUADRANT TO CASE SCREWS (2) W/LOCK WASHERS (2)
- C. HAND BRAKE LEVER ASSEMBLY
- D. HAND BRAKE TO QUADRANT SCREW, W/NUT AND COTTER PIN
- E. HAND BRAKE LEVER PAWL ROD
- F. HAND BRAKE LEVER CLEVIS PIN, W/PAWL AND COTTER PIN
- G. HAND BRAKE LEVER BLOCK, W/WASHER AND COTTER PIN
- H. PULL ROD LOCK NUT
- J. DRIVE SHAFT BRAKE YOKE END PULL ROD
- K. PULL ROD CLEVIS PIN, W/COTTER PIN

RA PD 3545

*Figure 161—Propeller Shaft Brake Linkage Installed*

**BRAKE SYSTEM**

(3) INSTALL FRONT BRAKE DRUMS AND WHEELS. Refer to paragraphs 135 and 137.

(4) INSTALL REAR BRAKE DRUMS. Refer to paragraphs 137 and 117.

(5) ADJUSTMENT OF BRAKES AFTER RELINING. Follow procedure outlined in paragraph 132. The rear brakes are adjusted before the installation of the driving sprocket and track.

(6) INSTALL SPROCKET AND TRACK. Refer to paragraphs 136 and 117.

## 133. PROPELLER SHAFT (PARKING) BRAKE.

a. **Description.** The propeller shaft brake (fig. 160) is composed of a ventilated disk, mounted on the propeller shaft between the transmission and jackshaft. Two brake shoes bear on the disk when actuated by the brake lever and linkage. A pawl and ratchet on the hand lever lock it in the desired position. The brake is set after the vehicle is stopped and should only be used as a parking brake.

b. **Adjustment.** Brake shoes normally must be parallel to, but not touching the disk when the brake is in the released position. When linings wear so the brake will not hold, adjustment is necessary.

(1) RELEASE HAND BRAKE LEVER. Press down the release button on the hand brake lever, and push the hand brake forward to released position.

(2) REMOVE HAND LEVER PULL ROD CLEVIS PIN (fig. 161). Remove cotter pin from pull rod clevis pin and disconnect pull rod from the brake operating lever.

(3) TIGHTEN SPRING TENSION. Loosen locking nut on spherical adjusting nut. Screw in on spherical adjusting nut until the lever arm release spring on the tie rod draws the operating lever firmly against the front brake lever arm.

(4) ADJUST FRONT SHOE CLEARANCE. Insert a $\frac{1}{32}$-inch shim or feeler gage between the front shoe lining and brake disk. Adjust the hand lever pull rod to maintain this clearance, and install clevis pin and secure with cotter pin.

(5) ADJUST REAR SHOE CLEARANCE. Adjust rear shoe to the same clearance with disk using the spherical nut on the tie rod to get this setting. Secure setting by tightening locking nut against the spherical nut.

(6) ADJUST SHOES PARALLEL. See that the brake shoe spring which connects the lower ends of brake shoes is in place. Loosen locking nuts, and adjust the top screws at the front and rear of the bracket to make shoes parallel to the disk. Secure setting of adjusting screws with locking nuts.

c. **Removal of Brake Shoe Assembly.**

(1) RELEASE HAND BRAKE LEVER. Press down the release button on the hand brake lever and push the lever forward to released position.

**TM 9-710**

**BASIC HALF-TRACK VEHICLES (WHITE, AUTOCAR, and DIAMOND T)**

(2) REMOVE OPERATING LEVER TIE ROD. Unscrew the locking nut and spherical nut from tie rod. Remove cotter pin and clevis pin from opposite end of tie rod and remove rod, spring, and two washers.

(3) REMOVE BRAKE SHOES. Loosen the parallel adjustment screws at top of anchor bracket. Remove two cap screws and lock washers from the brake shoe pivot pin retainers and remove retainers and pivot pins. Remove brake shoes and take off the small spring connecting them at their lower end.

d. **Installation of Brake Shoe Assembly.**

(1) INSTALL BRAKE SHOES. Slip brake shoe assembly up into proper position and line up holes in shoe with hole in arm, and install the pivot pin. Secure pivot pin by installing retainer with lock washer and cap screw. Install small spring, connecting brake shoes at bottom of shoes.

(2) INSTALL OPERATING LEVER TIE ROD. Place operating lever rod in proper position in operating levers with washers and spring. Secure with clevis pin and cotter pin at front end and spherical nut and locking nut at the rear.

(3) ADJUST BRAKE SHOES. Refer to paragraph 132.

e. **Removal of Brake Disk.**

(1) REMOVE PROPELLER SHAFT. Remove eight cotter pins, nuts, and bolts from jackshaft end of the propeller shaft. Remove eight cotter pins and nuts from the brake disk end of propeller shaft, and lower the propeller shaft to the floor.

(2) REMOVE BRAKE DISK. Release brake shoes from disk by pushing hand brake lever forward to off position. Place transmission in neutral and brake disk can then be rotated and the bolts taken out of transfer case companion flange and brake disk. Lower disk to floor.

f. **Installation of Brake Disk.**

(1) INSTALL DISK. Slip disk between brake shoes and hold it in its normal running position. Place propeller shaft in position with the slip joint end to the brake disk and insert eight bolts through the companion flange of transfer case, brake disk, and propeller shaft flange. Secure bolts with eight nuts and cotter pins. Secure opposite end of propeller shaft to companion flange on the jackshaft.

(2) CHECK PARKING BRAKE SHOE ADJUSTMENT. Refer to paragraph 133.

g. **Removal of Brake Hand Lever and Brake Assembly.**

(1) REMOVE POWER TAKE-OFF SHIFT LEVER. Disconnect lever and connecting link at bottom of shift lever by removing cotter pin and clevis pin. Remove cap screw and lock washer from front end of shift lever mounting bracket, and nut and lock washer at rear end; remove bracket with shift lever attached. NOTE: *These instructions regarding the power take-off can be ignored if vehicle is not equipped with a winch.*

(2) REMOVE HAND BRAKE LEVER AND QUADRANT. Remove cotter pin and clevis pin from pull rod yoke end and disconnect yoke end from operating lever (fig. 160). Remove two cap screws and lock washers from quadrant, and lower assembly from transfer case.

**TM 9-710**
**133-134**

## BRAKE SYSTEM

(3) REMOVE PROPELLER SHAFT AND BRAKE DISK. Follow steps (1) and (2) in e of this paragraph.

(4) REMOVE ANCHOR BRACKET ASSEMBLY. Remove one long cap screw and two short cap screws holding bracket to transfer case, and lower anchor bracket assembly to floor.

h. **Installation of Brake Hand Lever and Brake Assembly.**

(1) INSTALL ANCHOR BRACKET ASSEMBLY. Lift anchor bracket assembly to proper position at rear of transfer case and secure it with three cap screws and lock washers.

(2) INSTALL BRAKE DISK. Follow step (1) in f of this paragraph.

(3) INSTALL HAND BRAKE LEVER AND QUADRANT. Place hand brake lever and quadrant in proper position on transfer case and secure with two cap screws and lock washers. Connect pull rod yoke end and operating lever (fig. 161); insert clevis pin and secure with cotter pin.

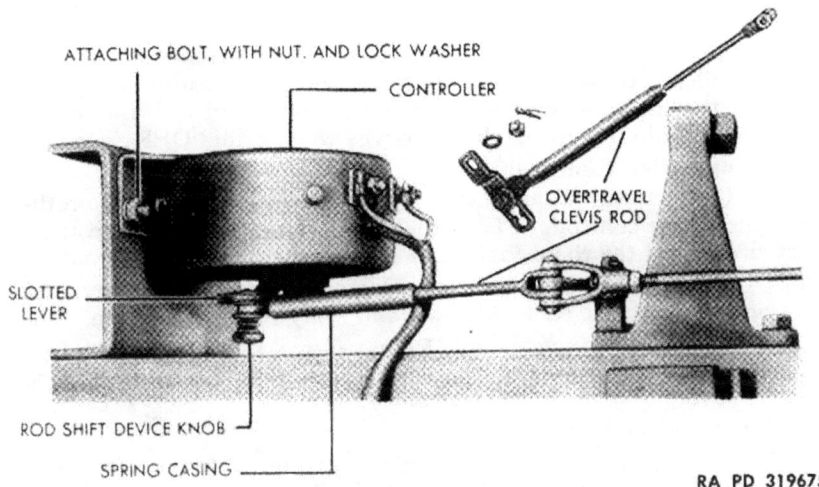

*Figure 162—Trailer Brake Controller*

(4) INSTALL POWER TAKE-OFF SHIFT LEVER. Place power take-off lever and bracket in position on brake quadrant and secure front end of bracket to transfer case with cap screw and lock washer. Secure the rear end of bracket to stud in brake quadrant with lock washer and nut. Install clevis pin to bottom of shift lever and connecting link and secure with cotter pin.

(5) CHECK PROPELLER SHAFT BRAKE SHOE ADJUSTMENT. Follow steps under h in this paragraph.

134. **ELECTRIC TRAILER BRAKE CONTROLLER AND LINKAGE.**

a. **Description.** A manually operated electric trailer brake controller is connected by means of adjustable linkage to the foot-brake pedal (fig. 162). The device provides for application of electric trailer

**BASIC HALF-TRACK VEHICLES (WHITE, AUTOCAR, and DIAMOND T)**

brakes at the same time and in proportion to the braking effort of the towing vehicle. The intensity of application may be adjusted by means of the rheostat control on the instrument panel. It is mounted on the outer left side of the frame just ahead of the driving sprocket.

b. **Adjustment.**

(1) ADJUSTMENT OF SLOTTED LEVER. The slotted lever on the controller has three positions which may be used to shorten or increase the movement of the slotted lever in conjunction with the movement of the brake pedal and the connecting rod on the controller. The shift is made by pushing the knob in, toward the controller housing, until the mechanism can be moved to other positions within the lever slot. If the service brake pedal has very little movement to apply the service brakes, the rod shift knob should be set in the slotted lever hole nearest its axis. Ordinarily, the center hole in the slotted lever will be correct for the rod motion.

(2) ADJUSTMENT OF ROD CLEVIS. Set the rod clevis on the brake pedal rod so there will be from $\frac{1}{8}$- to $\frac{3}{16}$-inch compression of the rear overtravel spring with the foot pedal in a fully released position and the controller lever in its full "OFF" position. Measure setting by watching the movement of the overtravel clevis rod into the spring casing just as the controller lever moves to the full "OFF" position.

c. **Controller Removal.**

(1) DISCONNECT TERMINALS. Disconnect the two wires from the terminals on the controller. Tape the ends so that they cannot cause a short circuit and tag them for installation to their proper terminals.

(2) DISCONNECT CLEVIS YOKE. Remove cotter pin and clevis pin from brake rod clevis, controller rod, and relay lever connection.

(3) REMOVE CONTROLLER. Remove two bolts, nut, and lock washers securing controller to frame bracket and remove controller and overtravel rod.

d. **Controller Installation.**

(1) INSTALL CONTROLLER. Install controller to frame bracket, in proper position, and secure with two bolts, lock washers, and nuts.

(2) CONNECT CLEVIS YOKE. Connect overtravel rod to brake rod clevis and relay lever connection and secure with clevis pin and cotter pin.

(3) CONNECT TERMINALS. Remove tape from ends of wires and connect the two wires to proper terminals, securing with lock washers and nuts.

e. **Linkage Removal.** Remove cotter pin, castellated nut, and washer from connection of controller lever to controller box and pull slotted lever and overtravel rod from controller. Disconnect clevis yokes and relay lever by removing cotter pin and clevis pin at bottom of relay lever. Unscrew locking nut on brake controller rod at brake pedal, and unscrew rod from clevis yoke and remove.

f. **Linkage Installation.** Install slotted lever, with overtravel rod connected (fig. 162), on controller box shaft and secure with washer, castellated nut, and cotter pin. Screw brake controller rod into yoke on brake pedal and secure with locking nut. Connect yokes of over-

TM 9-710
134

**BRAKE SYSTEM**

travel rod and brake rod to connection at bottom of relay shaft and secure with clevis pin and cotter pin. Adjust linkage (par. 134 b).

    g. **Control Rheostat Removal.** Remove bottom inspection plate on instrument panel by removing thumb screw and lock washer at each end of plate. Remove knob on rheostat by loosening set screw in knob and pulling knob from shaft. Unscrew the nut uncovered by the removal of the knob, and lift nut and dial of rheostat from assembly. Slip rheostat out of hole in panel, from rear of panel, far enough to disconnect the two wires from the rheostat terminals and remove rheostat. Tag the wires for identification when reinstalling.

    h. **Control Rheostat Installation.** Push the control rheostat up to approximate position to install in instrument panel, from the rear of panel, and connect the two wires to their proper terminals. Place shaft of rheostat through hole in instrument panel and position properly. Install dial face correctly and secure rheostat and dial to instrument panel with nut on shaft bushing. Install knob and tighten set screw on the flat surface of shaft. Install inspection plate to bottom of instrument panel, and secure with two thumb screws and lock washers.

TM 9-710
135-136

**BASIC HALF-TRACK VEHICLES (WHITE, AUTOCAR, and DIAMOND T)**

Section XXVII

# WHEELS, SPROCKETS, HUBS AND BEARINGS, TIRES, AND CHAINS

|  | Paragraph |
|---|---|
| Wheels | 135 |
| Jackshaft sprocket | 136 |
| Hubs and bearings | 137 |
| Tires and tubes | 138 |

## 135. WHEELS.

**a. Description and Data.**

(1) DESCRIPTION. The front wheels are 20 x 7 ventilated steel-disk type. Each has six mounting holes and is secured to the hub wheel studs with tapered nuts. The right wheel stud nuts have a left-hand thread and the left wheel nuts have a right-hand thread. The tires and tubes are mounted on the wheel rims.

(2) DATA.
  Make .............................. Budd
  Model ........................... D45550
  Type ................... ventilated steel disk

**b. Removal.** Place jack under axle close to wheel to be removed and raise wheel until tire is just free of ground. Slip a greased board under tire to facilitate wheel removal. Remove the six wheel stud nuts, and pull wheel and tire assembly off studs along greased board, being careful not to damage threads of wheel studs.

**c. Installation.** Slide wheel and tire assembly along greased board and guide wheel onto studs. Install stud nuts and tighten securely. Lower wheel to ground and remove jack.

## 136. JACKSHAFT SPROCKET.

**a. Description.** This all-steel sprocket wheel consists of an inner flange, a flat sprocket, and an outer flange, bolted together to form the sprocket assembly. The center sprocket wheel drives the track. The inner and outer flanges are designed with sockets which act as guides for the track guide plates, and in conjunction with the scallops on these plates, give added sprocket drive to the track.

**b. Removal.**

(1) REMOVE TRACK. See paragraph 117 c.

(2) REMOVE SPROCKET. Unscrew and remove six nuts holding sprocket wheel to hub studs. Pull sprocket assembly off studs and hub, being careful not to damage threads of studs.

**c. Installation.**

(1) INSTALL SPROCKET. Place sprocket assembly in position on hub flange studs. Install and tighten six stud nuts.

(2) INSTALL AND ADJUST TRACK. See paragraph 117.

TM 9-710

## WHEELS, SPROCKETS, HUBS AND BEARINGS, TIRES, AND CHAINS

### 137. HUBS AND BEARINGS.

**a. Description and Data.**

(1) FRONT WHEEL HUBS AND BEARINGS. Each hub and bearing assembly consists of a hub which rotates on two opposed tapered roller bearings, and which is secured by means of a bearing adjusting nut, lock washer, and lock nut. An oil seal on the inner side of the inner bearing prevents lubricant from leaking out of the hub. The drive flange is secured to the hub with eight studs, lock washers, and nuts; it is splined to axle shaft and secured with an axle nut and cotter pin. The shaft and drive flange drive the hub.

(2) JACKSHAFT SPROCKET HUBS AND BEARINGS. Each hub and bearing assembly consists of a hub which rotates upon two opposed tapered roller bearings, and which is secured by means of a bearing adjusting nut, lock washer, and lock nut. An oil seal on the inner side of the inner bearing prevents lubricant from leaking out of the hub. The hub is driven by the axle shaft and drive flange assembly which is bolted to it.

(3) DATA.

(a) *Front Wheel Bearings.*
  Make .......................... Timken
  Type ........................ tapered roller

(b) *Drive Sprocket Bearings.*
  Make .......................... Timken
  Type ........................ tapered roller

**b. Front Wheel Bearing Adjustment** (fig. 163).

(1) REMOVE HUB CAP AND DRIVE FLANGE. Jack up wheel to be adjusted. Unscrew and remove eight cap screws and lock washers. Remove cotter pin; unscrew and remove axle nut. Pull drive flange from shaft, tightening alternately the square head cap screws one-quarter turn. NOTE: *If the flange will not pull off using the cap screws, use a puller or similar equipment to remove.* Unscrew and remove lock nut and lock washer.

(2) ADJUST BEARING. Tighten adjusting nut until wheel binds, then loosen one-eighth turn. Place small finger of either hand past the adjusting nut and against the surface of the bearing cone and cup. Use a large pinch bar to pry the wheel assembly up and down, and sideways (fig. 164). A very slight movement between the bearing cup and cone indicates correct adjustment. If proper looseness is felt and the wheel revolves without binding, install lock washer and lock nut and tighten. Test again for looseness or wheel binding. If adjustment of bearings is correct, proceed with step (3).

(3) INSTALL DRIVE FLANGE AND HUB CAP. Place drive flange on shaft splines and hub studs, and secure with the axle nut and cotter pin. Install hub cap gasket and cap, and insert and tighten eight cap screws. Lower jack and wheel to ground.

**c. Front Wheel Hubs and Bearings Removal.**

(1) REMOVE HUB CAP AND DRIVE FLANGE. Refer to subparagraph b (1) above.

**BASIC HALF-TRACK VEHICLES (WHITE, AUTOCAR, and DIAMOND T)**

(2) REMOVE HUB, OUTER BEARING CUP AND CONE, AND INNER CUP. Unscrew and remove lock nut, lock washer, and adjusting nut. Pull tire, wheel, and hub assembly from axle housing. Pull inner bearing cone from axle housing with a bearing puller.

(3) REMOVE INNER BEARING CUP AND OUTER BEARING. Tap inner bearing cup from inside hub with a hammer and soft-nosed drift. Tap outer bearing cup and cone from inside hub. Unscrew and remove six nuts holding hub to drum assembly and remove hub.

d. **Front Wheel Hubs and Bearings Maintenance.** When bearing cups and cones have been removed from the hub, clean, inspect,

*Figure 163—Adjusting Front Wheel Bearing, Using Wrench 41-W-2612-25*

and lubricate before installation. Place units in dry-cleaning solvent for a few minutes to dissolve old lubricant. Holding bearing cone in the hand, tap the large side of the cone on a wood board or block to jar out old lubricant. Scrub the cone assembly with dry-cleaning solvent and a stiff brush. Dry with compressed air or soft, clean cloth. Repeat this procedure for cups. Inspect cups and cones for evidence of cracks or other damage. Clean hub and flange and inspect for breaks or cracks. If bearings and cones are in good condition, lubricate with a bearing lubricator or by hand before installing.

e. **Front Wheel Hubs and Bearings Installation.**

(1) INSTALL HUB AND BEARINGS. Press inner bearing cone into position on axle shaft. Tap inner bearing cup into position against flange on inside of hub. Place wheel and hub assembly in position on

# TM 9-710
## 137
### WHEELS, SPROCKETS, HUBS AND BEARINGS, TIRES, AND CHAINS

axle shaft. Push outer bearing cone and cup in place on shaft and in hub.

(2) ADJUST BEARINGS. See subparagraph b (2) above.

(3) INSTALL DRIVE FLANGE AND HUB CAP. See subparagraph b (3) above.

**f. Drive Sprocket Bearing Adustment.**

(1) REMOVE TRACK. See paragraph 117 c.

(2) REMOVE DRIVE FLANGE AND AXLE SHAFT. Unscrew and remove 12 nuts and lock washers from driving flange studs. Tap drive

RA PD 319677

*Figure 164—Testing Wheel Bearing Adjustment*

flange with a heavy soft-nosed hammer to loosen tapered lock washers on flange studs, and remove tapered lock washers. Tighten square head cap screws to pry flange and shaft from housing and remove. Unscrew and remove lock nut and lock washer from axle housing.

(3) ADJUST BEARINGS. Tighten bearing adjusting nut until sprocket wheel binds when rotated by hand. Back off adjusting nut one-eighth turn. Wheel should rotate freely. Place a pinch bar in the top of the sprocket; place small finger past adjusting nut and against bearing cup and cone. Pull and push wheel to check tightness of bearing fit (fig. 165). A very slight movement should be felt.

(4) INSTALL LOCK WASHER, LOCK NUT, AND DRIVE FLANGE. Install and tighten lock washer and lock nut. Test wheel for freedom

**BASIC HALF-TRACK VEHICLES (WHITE, AUTOCAR, and DIAMOND T)**

of movement by rotating with hand. Push shaft and drive flange into position in housing. Install and tighten 12 tapered dowels and flange nuts.

(5) INSTALL TRACK. See paragraph 117 d.

g. **Drive Sprocket Hubs and Bearings Removal.**

(1) REMOVE TRACK. See paragraph 117 c.

(2) REMOVE DRIVE FLANGE AND AXLE SHAFT. See subparagraph f (2) above.

RA PD 319678

*Figure 165—Testing Sprocket Wheel Bearing Adjustment*

(3) REMOVE SPROCKET WHEEL AND HUB AND DRUM ASSEMBLY. Unscrew and remove six wheel stud nuts and pull sprocket from hub and drum assembly. Pull hub and drum assembly from axle housing. Unscrew six drum stud nuts (inside drum) and pull hub from drum.

(4) REMOVE BEARINGS FROM SHAFT AND HUB. Lift outer bearing cone from inside hub. Tap out outer bearing cup with a hammer and soft-nosed drift. Tap out inner bearing cup in the same manner. Pull inner bearing cone from housing with a bearing puller.

h. **Drive Sprocket Hubs and Bearings Maintenance.** See subparagraph f above.

i. **Drive Sprocket Hubs and Bearings Installation.**

(1) INSTALL INNER BEARING AND DRUM. Press inner bearing

# TM 9-710
### 137-138

## WHEELS, SPROCKETS, HUBS AND BEARINGS, TIRES, AND CHAINS

cone into position on axle housing flange. Tap inner bearing cup into position in hub. Place drum on six hub studs and install and tighten stud nuts.

(2) INSTALL HUB AND DRUM ASSEMBLY ON HOUSING. Push drum and hub assembly into position on housing and inner bearing. Place outer bearing cup and cone in position in hub, and install adjusting nut.

(3) INSTALL SPROCKET WHEEL AND ADJUST BEARINGS. Place wheel over hub studs and install and tighten six wheel nuts. Adjust bearings. (See subparagraph f (3) above.)

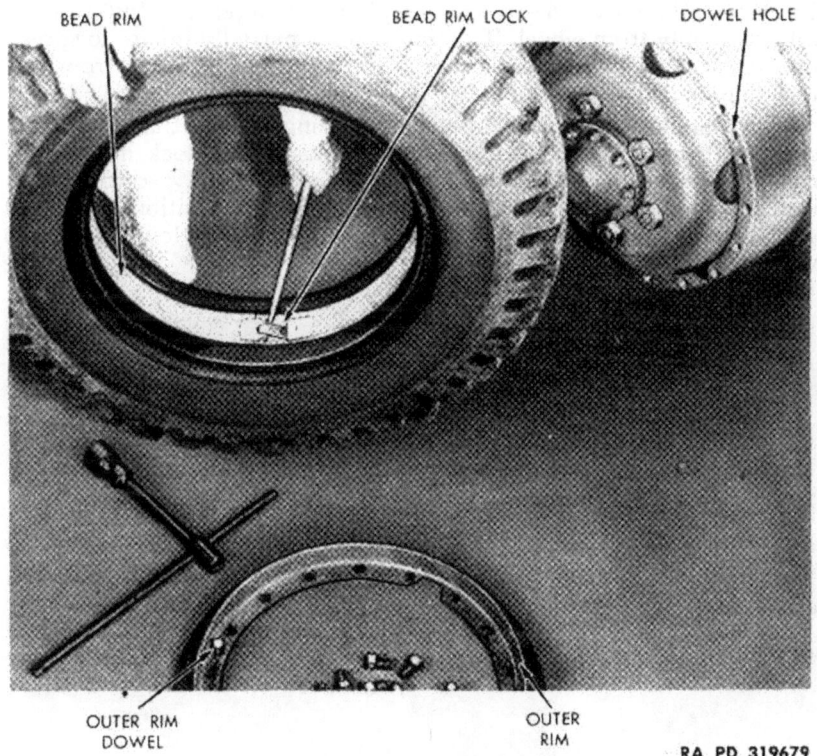

*Figure 166—Removing Bead Rim*

(4) INSTALL LOCK WASHER, LOCK NUT, AND AXLE DRIVE FLANGE ASSEMBLY. Install and tighten lock washer and lock nut. Push axle into housing until drive flange is seated over hub studs. Place tapered lock washers in position, and install and tighten 12 nuts.

(5) INSTALL TRACK. See paragraph 117 d.

## 138. TIRES AND TUBES.

a. Description and Data.

(1) DESCRIPTION. The tires used are "combat" tires, of 12-ply

## BASIC HALF-TRACK VEHICLES (WHITE, AUTOCAR, and DIAMOND T)

construction, and are equipped with bullet-sealing tubes, flaps, and flexible metal bead locks. The tires are mounted on split rims which are held together with cap screws (fig. 166).

(2) DATA.

```
Make................Goodyear, General, Goodrich,
                                Firestone, Seiberling
Type.........................combat, mud and
                                       snow tread
Size ................................. 8.25 x 20
```

    *b.* **Removal.** Jack up wheel and tire to be removed. Deflate tire. Unscrew and remove 18 cap screws and pull off outer rim. Pull tire and tube assembly from wheel. To remove tube, partially inflate to spread tire beads. Pry lock loose on metal bead rim and pull rim from tire. Pull flap and tube from tire.

    *c.* **Installation.** Place tube in tire casing and partially inflate to separate beads. Install flap on tube and install and lock metal bead rim. Place tire and tube assembly on inner rim carefully, so valve stem is in proper position. Place outer rim and dowels in position and install and tighten 18 cap screws. Inflate tire to 55 pounds, lower jack and wheel to ground.

TM 9-710
139

Section XXVIII

## SPRINGS AND SHOCK ABSORBERS

|  | Paragraph |
|---|---|
| Springs and shackles | 139 |
| Shock absorbers and linkage | 140 |

### 139. SPRINGS AND SHACKLES.

a. **Description.** Two springs are mounted to the front axle and frame. They are anchored at the front and shackled at the rear. Each spring is secured to the axle bracket with two inverted U-bolts.

b. **Removal.**

(1) DISCONNECT SHACKLES (SINGLE SPRING). Place jack under frame just back of spring to be removed and raise vehicle, until all

A — SHACKLE
B — REAR ANCHOR BRACKET
C   SHACKLE PINS
D — ADJUSTING INDICATOR
E   SHOCK ABSORBER
F — FILLER PLUG
G — SPRING BUMPER BLOCK
H — CONNECTING LINK
I — FRONT SHACKLE BRACKET
J   U-BOLTS
K — FRONT AXLE BRACKET
L — TAPERED SHIM

RA PD 319680

*Figure 167—Front Spring and Shock Absorber Installed*

293

## TM 9-710

### BASIC HALF-TRACK VEHICLES (WHITE, AUTOCAR, and DIAMOND T)

weight is removed from spring. Remove cotter pin from spring pin nut (front of spring), and remove nut. Tap out spring pin. Remove cotter pin from shackle pin nut (rear of spring), and remove nut, and tap out shackle pin (fig. 167).

(2) REMOVE SPRING (fig. 168). Remove four nuts and lock washers from U-bolts, tap U-bolts up through axle bracket holes and shock absorber bracket and remove. Lift spring bumper block from top of spring. Lift spring and tapered shim from axle.

*Figure 168—Front Spring Removal*

c. **Installation.**

(1) INSTALL SPRING. Place tapered shim (with thick end to front) and spring in position on axle. Install spring bumper pad. Install U-bolts over pad and spring, through axle bracket holes, and shock absorber bracket. Install and tighten four lock washers and nuts on U-bolts.

(2) INSTALL SHACKLES. Lower vehicle until spring pins can be installed. Tap front spring pin through anchor and spring eye. Install and tighten spring pin nut and secure with a cotter pin. Install rear spring shackle pin through shackle and spring and secure with shackle

## SPRINGS AND SHOCK ABSORBERS

pin nut and cotter pin. Lower front of vehicle and remove jack. Inspect all parts for position and tightness.

### 140. SHOCK ABSORBERS AND LINKAGE.

**a. Description and Tabulated Data.**

(1) DESCRIPTION. The shock absorbers are hydraulic, double acting, rotary type and are adjustable. One is mounted to each side rail above the front axle and connected to the axle bracket by a linkage and connecting link plate (fig. 167).

(2) TABULATED DATA.

Make .................................... Houdaille
Model ............... A 10469-R.H.   A 10468-L.H.
Type ........................... double-acting

**b. Maintenance and Adjustments.**

(1) MAINTENANCE. The unit should be inspected at regular intervals for the amount of fluid in the body. The fluid level should be kept up to the bottom of the filler plug. To fill, remove filler plug, disconnect link at axle, and move link up and down slowly while filling housing with shock absorber fluid. Replace filler plug and connect link at axle. NOTE: *Always clean area around filler plug before removing to prevent any dirt getting into shock absorber.*

(2) ADJUSTMENTS. Rotate indicator on the face of unit clockwise to increase resistance of shock absorber, counterclockwise to decrease resistance. NOTE: *Do not turn the indicator more than ⅛ inch at a time until desired control is obtained.*

**c. Removal.** Unscrew and remove two U-bolt nuts and lock washers holding shock absorber arm plate. Pull connecting link down and remove plate from spring clips. Unscrew two nuts, lock washers, and bolts holding unit to frame and lift off unit.

**d. Installation.** Place shock absorber in position on frame, install and tighten two bolts, lock washers, and nuts. Place arm bracket on spring U-bolts and install and tighten two U-bolt lock washers and nuts.

TM 9-710
141

**BASIC HALF-TRACK VEHICLES (WHITE, AUTOCAR, and DIAMOND T)**

Section XXIX

## STEERING GEAR AND DRAG LINK

|  | Paragraph |
|---|---|
| Steering gear............................................... | 141 |
| Drag link.................................................... | 142 |

**141. STEERING GEAR.**

a. **Description and Tabulated Data.**

(1) DESCRIPTION. The steering gear (fig. 170) is the cam and twin lever type. The cam, lever, and shaft are mounted in an oiltight case with full provision for the adjustment of both cam and cam follower. The case is bracket mounted to the frame, and is adjustable. The steering wheel is designed with three spokes and is eighteen inches

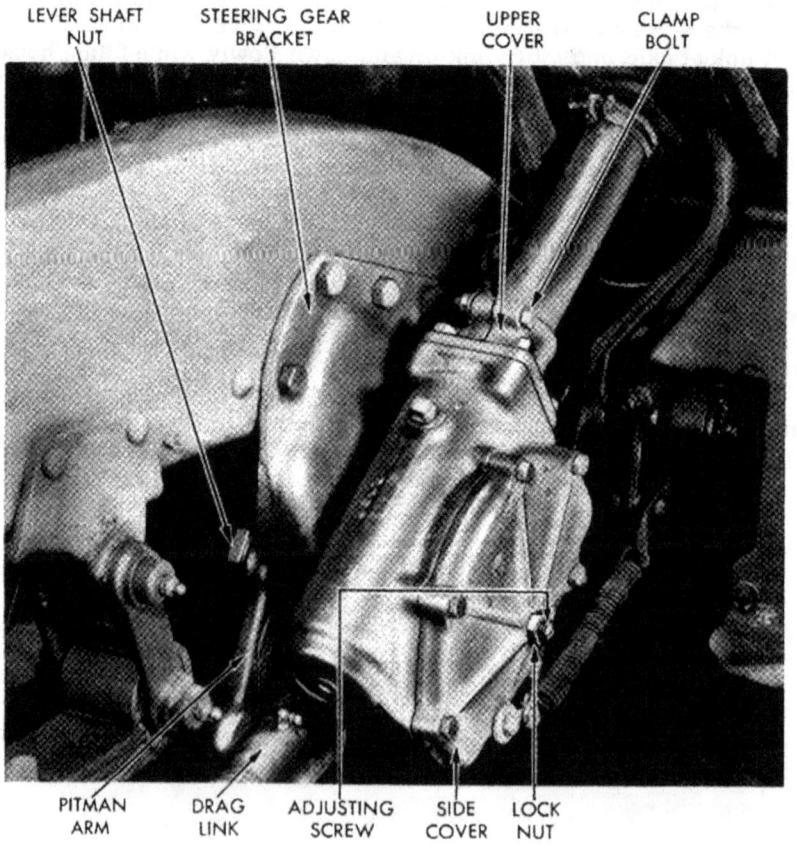

Figure 169—Steering Gear Installed

296

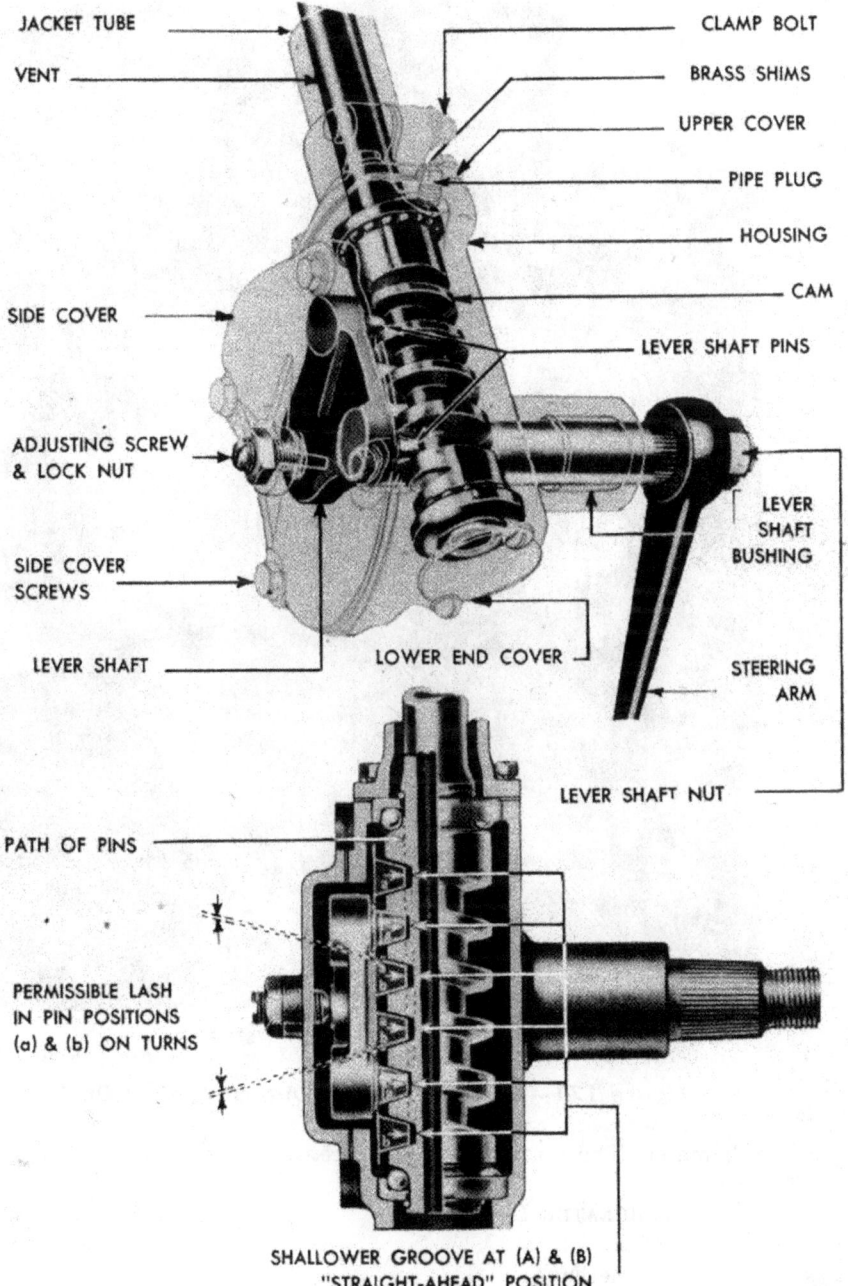

Figure 170—Phantom View of Steering Gear

## TM 9-710
### 141
**BASIC HALF-TRACK VEHICLES (WHITE, AUTOCAR, and DIAMOND T)**

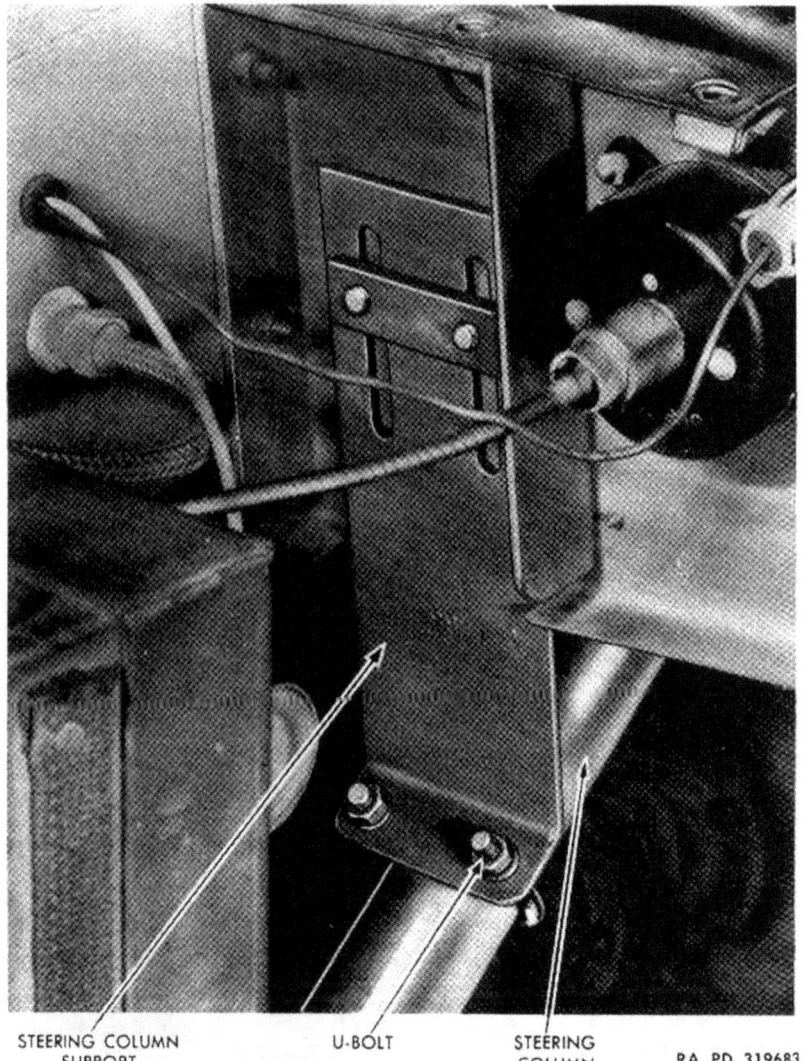

*Figure 171—Steering Column Adjustment at Dash*

in diameter. The horn button is located at the center of the steering wheel.

(2) TABULATED DATA.
Make ............................... Ross
Model No. ........................... TA 26
Type ............................. twin-lever

**b. Adjustments.** When making adjustments, first disconnect the drag link from the steering gear arm, loosen the instrument panel

298

## STEERING GEAR AND DRAG LINK

bracket U-bolt which secures the steering gear jacket tube in place (fig. 171), and proceed as follows:

(1) CAM END PLAY. Adjust ball thrust bearings to take up end play of cam (which shows up as play in the steering wheel) as follows:

*(a) Remove Shims.* Loosen clamp bolt on upper cover. Unscrew and remove four cap screws and lock washers from the upper cover (fig. 170), and raise cover about ¼ inch to permit removal of shims. (A combination of 0.002 inch, 0.003 inch, and 0.010 inch shims are used.) Clip and remove one or more 0.002 inch shims, as required. Install the upper cover and tighten the four cap screws and lock washers. Tighten upper cover clamp bolt.

*(b) Test Adjustment.* Test wheel for play, and if it is excessive, remove or replace shims until adjustment is correct. This adjustment should be an eight ounce pull at the rim of the wheel.

(2) LEVER SHAFT END PLAY. Backlash of the tapered cam studs shows up as end play of the lever shaft (fig. 170) and as backlash at the steering wheel and the ball of the steering arm. Adjustment must be made within the "high" range through the mid-position of the stud travel (fig. 170). This position corresponds to straight ahead position of wheels. Do not adjust in positions off straight ahead. Backlash at these turn positions is not objectionable. Proceed as follows:

*(a) Adjust Side Cover Adjusting Screw.* Tighten the side cover adjusting screw until a very slight drag is felt through the mid-position ("high" range) when turning the steering wheel slowly from one extreme to the other. CAUTION: *The gear must not bind at any place.* Only a very slight drag should be felt. A closer adjustment will not correct any steering condition, but will damage and wear the steering gear parts and impair operation.

*(b) Tighten Lock Nut.* When proper adjustment has been made, tighten the lock nut and give the gear a final test.

*(c) Inspect Steering Connection.* Make sure the steering gear ball arm is tight on the splined shaft and that the lock washer and nut are also tight. CAUTION: *Always adjust the cam end play first.* Do not attempt to cure wander, shimmy, or road shock by tightening the steering gear. Adjust steering gear only to remove play in it.

(3) COLUMN ALINEMENT. Tighten the U-bolt at the instrument panel steering column support. Turn the steering wheel to check if stiffness or binding exists. If so, the gear has been adjusted too tightly or the steering column is out of alinement. The steering column must not be sprung in any direction. Check the steering gear frame bracket for tightness to the frame, so that it rigidly holds the gear assembly and does not spring when the wheel is turned after steering drag link is installed and the wheels are on the ground.

c. Pitman Arm Replacement (fig. 172).

(1) REMOVAL. Remove the drag link at the connection to Pitman arm (par. 142). Remove the lever shaft nut and lock washer and pull Pitman arm from lever shaft.

(2) INSTALLATION. Turn the steering wheel as far to the right as possible. Rotate the wheel in the opposite direction as far as possible

## BASIC HALF-TRACK VEHICLES (WHITE, AUTOCAR, and DIAMOND T)

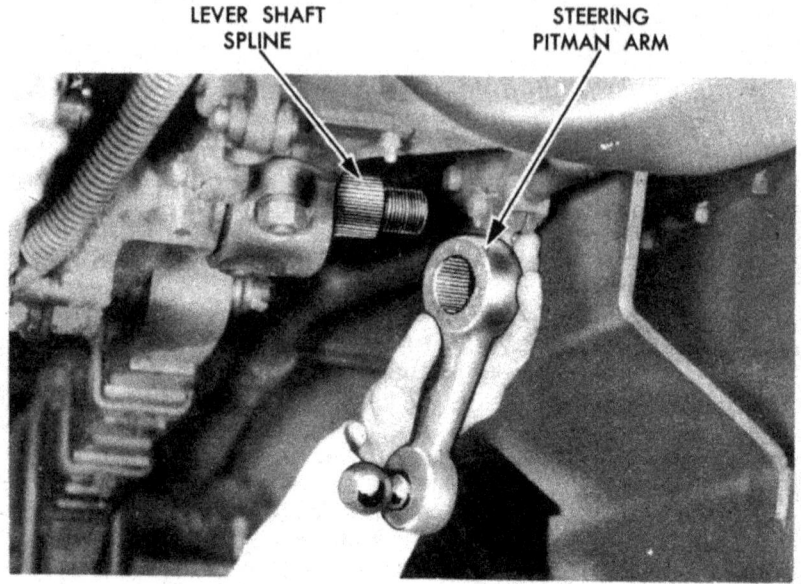

Figure 172—Removing Steering Pitman Arm

Figure 173—Drag Link Installed

**TM 9-710**

## STEERING GEAR AND DRAG LINK

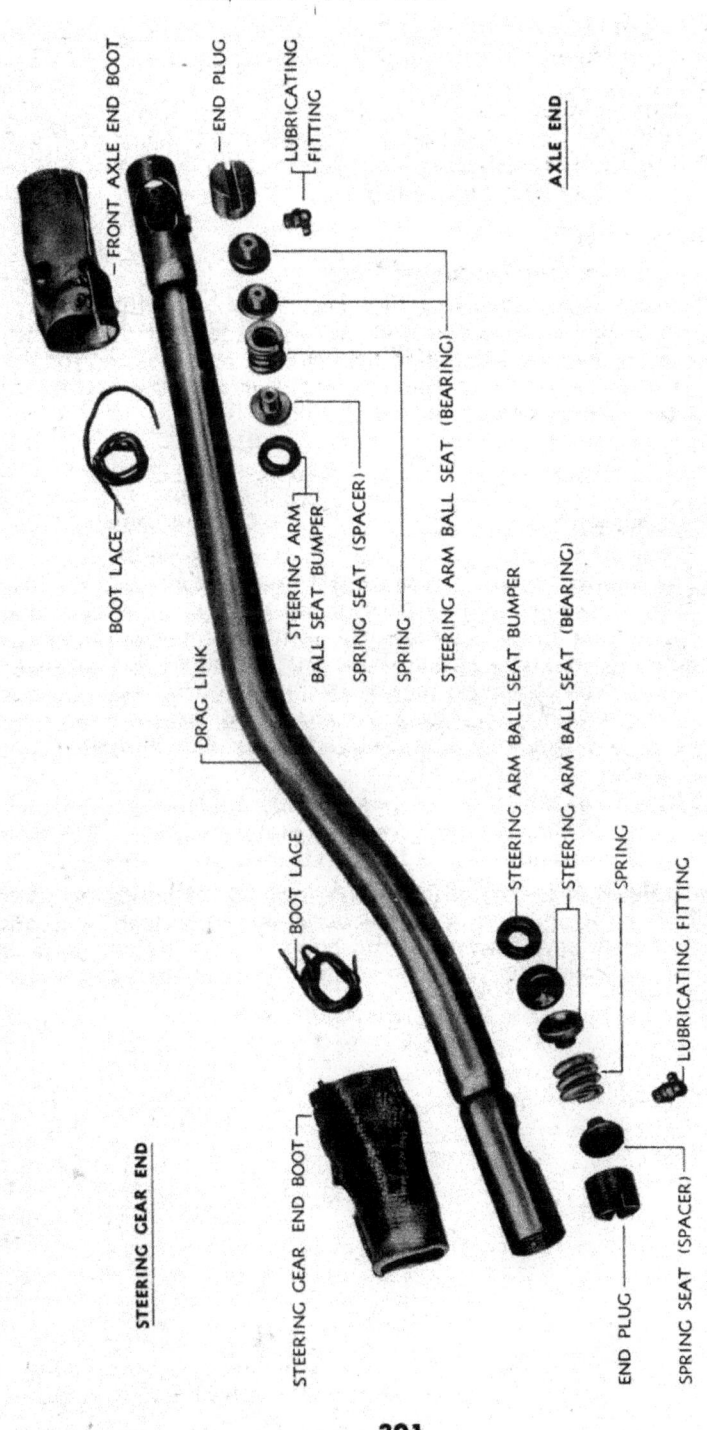

*Figure 174—Drag Link Disassembled*

## BASIC HALF-TRACK VEHICLES (WHITE, AUTOCAR, and DIAMOND T)

and note the total number of turns. Turn the wheel back just one-half of this total movement, thereby placing the gear in mid-position. Place the wheels in position for straight driving. Place the Pitman arm on the lever shaft spline so it and drag link connections can be installed without moving the lever shaft. Secure Pitman arm to lever shaft with lock washer and nut. Install drag link connection to bottom of Pitman arm and adjust drag link (par. 142).

### 142. DRAG LINK.

**a. Description and Tabulated Data.**

(1) DESCRIPTION. The drag link (fig. 173) is the tubular type, with adjustable ball sockets which are spring loaded. At the axle end the spring and spacer are assembled between the ball seat and rod end (bottom of socket), while at the steering gear end, the spring and spacer are between the ball seat and end plug.

(2) TABULATED DATA.
    Make..................Thompson Products Company
    Model No........................20-D-248
    Type..........................spring-loaded

**b. Adjustment.** Unlace and remove boots at each end of the drag link. Remove cotter pin and turn adjusting plug in until tight, then back off approximately one-half turn, or until a new cotter pin of correct size will enter the slot and holes in the end plug being adjusted. Install cotter pin and spread the ends to lock it. Install boots and secure with lacing. NOTE: *The end plugs should not be adjusted too tight. The spring is located to accommodate wear and not intended as a shock absorber.*

**c. Removal** (fig. 174). Remove boots. Remove cotter pins, locking end plugs in place, and unscrew the plugs. Remove drag link from steering Pitman arm ball and front axle steering arm ball stud.

**d. Installation.** Install drag link on front axle steering arm ball stud and steering Pitman arm ball. Screw in and adjust end plugs and secure with cotter pins. Install the boots and secure lacing. Jack up front end of vehicle and turn steering wheel to both extremes to test adjustment.

Section XXX

# BODY AND FRAME

| | Paragraph |
|---|---|
| Description | 143 |
| Roller | 144 |
| Floors, hood, doors, running boards, and mud guards | 145 |
| Seats | 146 |
| Top and bows | 147 |
| Windshield and windshield wipers | 148 |
| Pintle and tow hooks | 149 |
| Frame | 150 |
| Bumpers | 151 |

## 143. DESCRIPTION.

*a. General.* The bodies mounted on the basic half-track chassis vary in design to meet certain specific needs (par. 3). All bodies, with the exception of the multiple gun motor carriage, have full armor plate at the front, sides, and rear. Component units are welded together at all possible points. Specific description of component parts will be given in their respective paragraphs, which follow.

## 144. ROLLER.

*a. Description.* Some vehicles are equipped with a roller mounted to the front bumper (fig. 175). It is used as an aid in maneuvering the vehicle through ditches and holes. It is equipped with a compression spring at each side, mounted on the roller support. These springs absorb shocks encountered when striking banks or high objects and aid the vehicle in rolling through ditches and banks.

*b. Roller Removal.*

(1) REMOVE ROLLER SHAFT TAPER PINS. Drive out one taper pin from each end of roller shaft, using hammer and pin punch.

(2) REMOVE ROLLER. Use two "C" clamps to compress roller springs until all pressure is removed from roller shaft. Place jacks under roller for support and drive roller shaft from roller. Lower roller assembly to ground.

*c. Roller Installation.* Raise roller to proper position with jacks. Insert roller shaft and line up taper pin holes. Install taper pins and drive in securely. Remove spring compressing clamps and jacks.

## 145. FLOORS, HOOD, DOORS, RUNNING BOARDS, AND MUD GUARDS.

*a. Floors.* The floors are of all-steel construction with safety-tread design. In most cases, they are bolted to the frame assembly with screw head bolts, lock washers, and nuts.

*b. Hood.*

(1) DESCRIPTION. The engine and radiator are protected by the armor plate hood and louvers. The shutters of the louvers are operated

# TM 9-710
145

## BASIC HALF-TRACK VEHICLES (WHITE, AUTOCAR, and DIAMOND T)

by a control lever at the right side of the driver's compartment, with three intermediate positions between fully open and fully closed louvers. The hood is made of two double panels hinged together to aid in opening. Two spring latches on each side secure the closed hood.

(2) REMOVAL. Unfasten hood latches. Remove three screw-head bolts and safety nuts from the front and three from the rear of the center panel. Place a rope sling as shown in figure 65, and remove hood from vehicle with a hoist.

(3) INSTALLATION. To install hood, use a hoist and rope sling to place hood in position on vehicle. Install and tighten three screw-

RA PD 18480

*Figure 175—Roller Installed*

head bolts and safety nuts at front and three at rear of center panel. Close hood and fasten latches.

c. Doors.

(1) DESCRIPTION. The vehicle is equipped with doors at each side of the driver's compartment, each door being supported by two hinges screw bolted to the body. Each door is equipped with internal and external door handles. Additional armor plate is hinged to the top of each door. This may be raised and latched to the top frame of the driver's compartment in combat operation. Each of these upper panels is provided with an adjustable view hole.

(2) REMOVAL. Close the door, lower the upper section and lock in lowered position. Remove four screw-head bolts, lock washers, and nuts from door side of hinges. Open door slowly and lift off.

## BODY AND FRAME

(3) INSTALLATION. To install, place door in position on vehicle and close. Install and tighten four screw-head bolts, lock washers and nuts.

d. **Running Boards.**

(1) DESCRIPTION. The vehicle is equipped with safety-tread, all-steel running boards on each side of the driver's compartment.

(2) REMOVAL.

*(a) Remove Right Running Board.* Remove four nuts, lock washers, and bolts, and lift from vehicle.

*(b) Remove Left Running Board.* Remove seven nuts, lock washers, and bolts, and lift from vehicle.

(3) INSTALLATION.

*(a) Install Right Running Board.* Place right-hand running board in position and secure with four bolts, lock washers, and nuts.

*(b) Install Left Running Board.* Place left-hand running board in position and secure with seven bolts, lock washers, and nuts.

e. **Mud Guards.**

(1) DESCRIPTION. Each front wheel is protected with a mud guard (fender) (fig. 176), which is mounted to the side of the body. A mud and stone guard of heavy treated canvas is suspended from the rear of the body in line with each track.

(2) REMOVAL. Remove two nuts, lock washers, and bolts holding forward brace to frame. Remove two nuts, lock washers, and bolts holding rear brace to rear engine armor plate. Remove three nuts, lock washers, and bolts at running board brace. Remove nine nuts, lock washers, and bolts holding fender to side panel. Disconnect headlight cable at terminal on frame and pull cable through fender. Lift fender from vehicle.

(3) INSTALLATION. Place fender in position. Install and tighten nine bolts, lock washers, and nuts holding fender to side panel. Install and tighten three bolts, nuts, and lock washers at running board brace. Install and tighten two bolts, nuts, and lock washers holding rear brace to rear engine armor plate. Install two bolts, nuts, and lock washers holding forward brace to frame. Run headlight cable through fender and install on terminal on frame.

(4) REAR STONE GUARD REPLACEMENT. Remove three bolts, lock washers, and nuts holding guard to rear of body, and lift off. To install, place guard in position and secure with three bolts, lock washers, and nuts.

## 146. SEATS.

a. **Description.** The driver's compartment is equipped with three seats. The driver's seat is adjustable. The other two seats are hinged and can be folded. Loose seat cushions are provided for all seats. These cushions may be opened by slide fasteners, and blankets may be inserted. Other seating facilities in various models are covered in paragraph 3.

## TM 9-710
### 146
## BASIC HALF-TRACK VEHICLES (WHITE, AUTOCAR, and DIAMOND T)

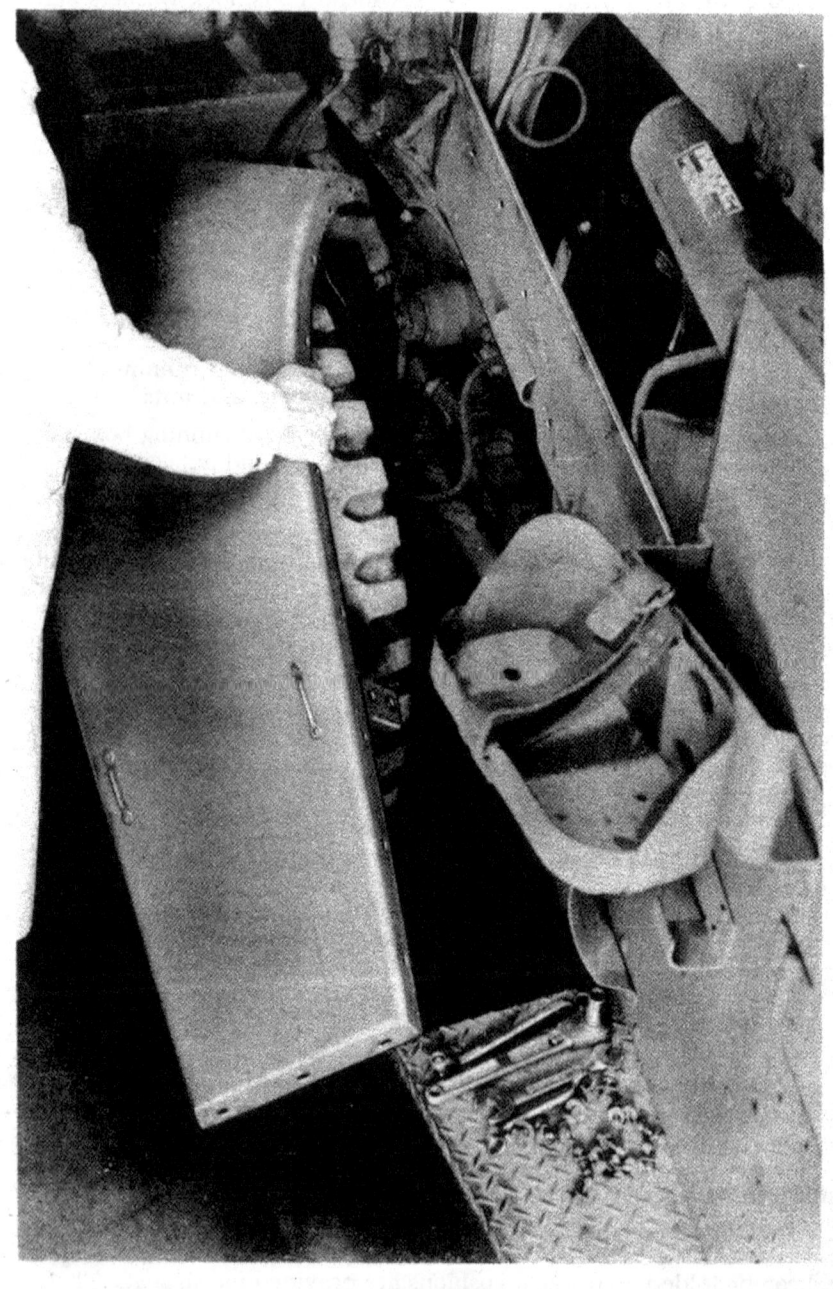

Figure 176—Removing Fender

## BODY AND FRAME

**b. Removal.**

(1) REMOVE RIGHT SEAT. To remove seat, raise into combat position, remove four nuts, lock washers, and bolts from hinges, and one nut, lock washer, and bolt from locking bracket and lift seat from vehicle.

(2) REMOVE LEFT SEAT. Remove four bolts from underside of chassis and lift off seat.

**c. Installation.**

(1) INSTALL RIGHT SEAT. Place seat in position and install and tighten four bolts, lock washers, and nuts into seat hinges. Lower seat into riding position.

(2) INSTALL LEFT SEAT. Place seat in position, install and tighten four bolts into nuts which are welded to the seat rails.

## 147. TOP AND BOWS.

**a. Description.** The detachable canvas top is supported on some models by three removable metal bows and the windshield frame. The top is secured by a series of strap fasteners that attach to footman loops around the sides of the body.

## 148. WINDSHIELD AND WINDSHIELD WIPERS.

**a. Description.** The shatter-proof glass windshield is divided into two sections, each held in position by six half clamps and one full clamp. A protective shield of ½-inch armor plate is hinged to the top of the windshield support frame, and is held in position by three support rods. Before the windshield armor plate can be lowered into closed position, the glass windshield and windshield wiper plates must be removed. The vehicle is equipped with dual windshield wipers which are secured to the body at the base of the windshield frame.

**b. Windshield Removal.** Remove wing nuts at top center, left, and right sides, and bottom left and right. Pull clamps and windshield from frame.

**c. Windshield Installation.** Place windshield in position, install clamps and wing nuts and tighten.

**d. Windshield Wiper Removal.** Compress spring and lift wiper arm from wiper mechanism. Remove nut and washer on wiper shaft and pull wiper mechanism from base of windshield.

**e. Windshield Wiper Installation.** Push shaft through windshield and install and tighten nut. Install wiper arm.

## 149. PINTLE AND TOW HOOKS.

**a. Description.** Two tow hooks are mounted on the front bumper of the frame, and a pintle hook is mounted in the center of the frame rear cross member.

**b. Pintle Hook Removal** (fig. 177). Remove cotter pin, nut, and washer from hook shaft. Pull hook and shaft from hanger. Remove four nuts, lock washers, and bolts holding hanger to frame. Remove hanger and pintle spring.

**TM 9-710**
**149-151**

**BASIC HALF-TRACK VEHICLES (WHITE, AUTOCAR, and DIAMOND T)**

 c. **Pintle Hook Installation.** Place hanger in position and secure to frame with four bolts, lock washers, and nuts. Push hook and shaft through hanger, install spring and washer. Install and tighten nut and secure with lock washer.

 d. **Tow Hook Removal.** Remove two nuts, lock washers, and bolts holding hook to front bumper, and lift hook from bumper.

 e. **Tow Hook Installation.** Place hook in position (pointing toward outside of vehicle), and secure to bumper with two bolts, lock washers, and nuts.

RA PD 319688

*Figure 177—Pintle Hook and Bumperettes Installed*

**150. FRAME.**

 a. **Description.** The chassis frame consists of reinforced channel side rails, braced with reinforced pressed steel cross members. There is some variance in length of the frame to meet specific requirements for units mounted thereon.

**151. BUMPERS.**

 a. **Description.** Two bumperettes made of channel steel are provided for the front end of the vehicle and are located to the left and right of the front bumper roller. Each bumperette is riveted to the frame rail and stiffened with gussets at the corners. The upper gussets are riveted to both the bumperettes and frame rails. The lower gussets are riveted to the bumperettes and bolted to the frame rails. No maintenance is required unless the bumperettes are badly damaged, at which

## BODY AND FRAME

time they should be replaced or straightened and new gusset plates substituted. On vehicles equipped with a winch, the front bumper, of conventional channel design, is bolted to the frame side rails at the front of the vehicle. The rear bumperettes are of standard channel design with the flat side bolted to the rear of the vehicle body.

b. **Front Bumper Removal.** On winch equipped vehicles, remove five nuts, lock washers, and bolts holding each side of bumper to frame member. Remove two nuts, lock washers, and bolts from winch gear box guard (inside bumper channel). Remove four nuts, lock washers, and bolts from each side of bumper and lift off.

c. **Front Bumper Installation.** Place bumper in position and install and tighten four bolts, lock washers, and nuts on each side. Install and tighten two bolts, lock washers, and nuts holding unit to winch guard. Install and tighten five bolts, lock washers, and nuts holding each side to the frame member.

d. **Rear Bumperette Removal.** Remove nuts, lock washers, and bolts holding unit to body and lift off.

e. **Rear Bumperette Installation.** Place unit in position and install and tighten bolts, lock washers, and nuts holding it to body.

# TM 9-710
## 152-153
## BASIC HALF-TRACK VEHICLES (WHITE, AUTOCAR, and DIAMOND T)

### Section XXXI

## BATTERY AND LIGHTING SYSTEM

| | Paragraph |
|---|---|
| Description of system and data | 152 |
| Battery | 153 |
| Headlights and marker lights | 154 |
| Taillights | 155 |
| Terminal block | 156 |
| Terminal box | 157 |
| Fuses and circuit breakers | 158 |
| Horns | 159 |

### 152. DESCRIPTION OF SYSTEM AND DATA.

**a. Description of System.** The 12-volt system (direct current) is single-wire, ground-return type, energized by a storage battery whose negative terminal is grounded to the frame. The battery and lighting system is illustrated in figure 180. The battery and lighting system are interrelated with the starting and generating system and other electrical equipment of the vehicle. (fig. 178).

**b. Data.**

| | Make | Model No. | Volts |
|---|---|---|---|
| Service headlight | Guide L. | 1020-B | 12-16 |
| Blackout driving headlight | | 1020-D | 6-8 |
| Blackout marker light (on headlight) | | 5513-E | 12-16 |
| Blackout taillight (left upper unit) | | 5933305 | 12 |
| Service taillight and stop light (left lower unit) | Guide L. | 593302 | 12 |
| Blackout taillight (right upper unit) | Guide L. | 5933305 | 12 |
| Blackout stop light (right lower unit) | Guide L. | 5933308 | 12 |

### 153. BATTERY.

**a. Description.** The battery (fig. 179) is a 12-volt, 6-cell, 25-plate, lead-acid, safety-fill vent type and rated at 168 ampere-hours, at 20-hour rate. It is located in a compartment at the side of the frame below the right front door and is fully enclosed.

**b. Maintenance.**

(1) CLEANING. Inspect battery at regular intervals for battery fluid level. Maintain this level at ½ inch above battery plates. Keep battery top and terminals clean and dry. Clean with a solution of ordinary baking soda (one pound of soda to one gallon of water), or

## BATTERY AND LIGHTING SYSTEM

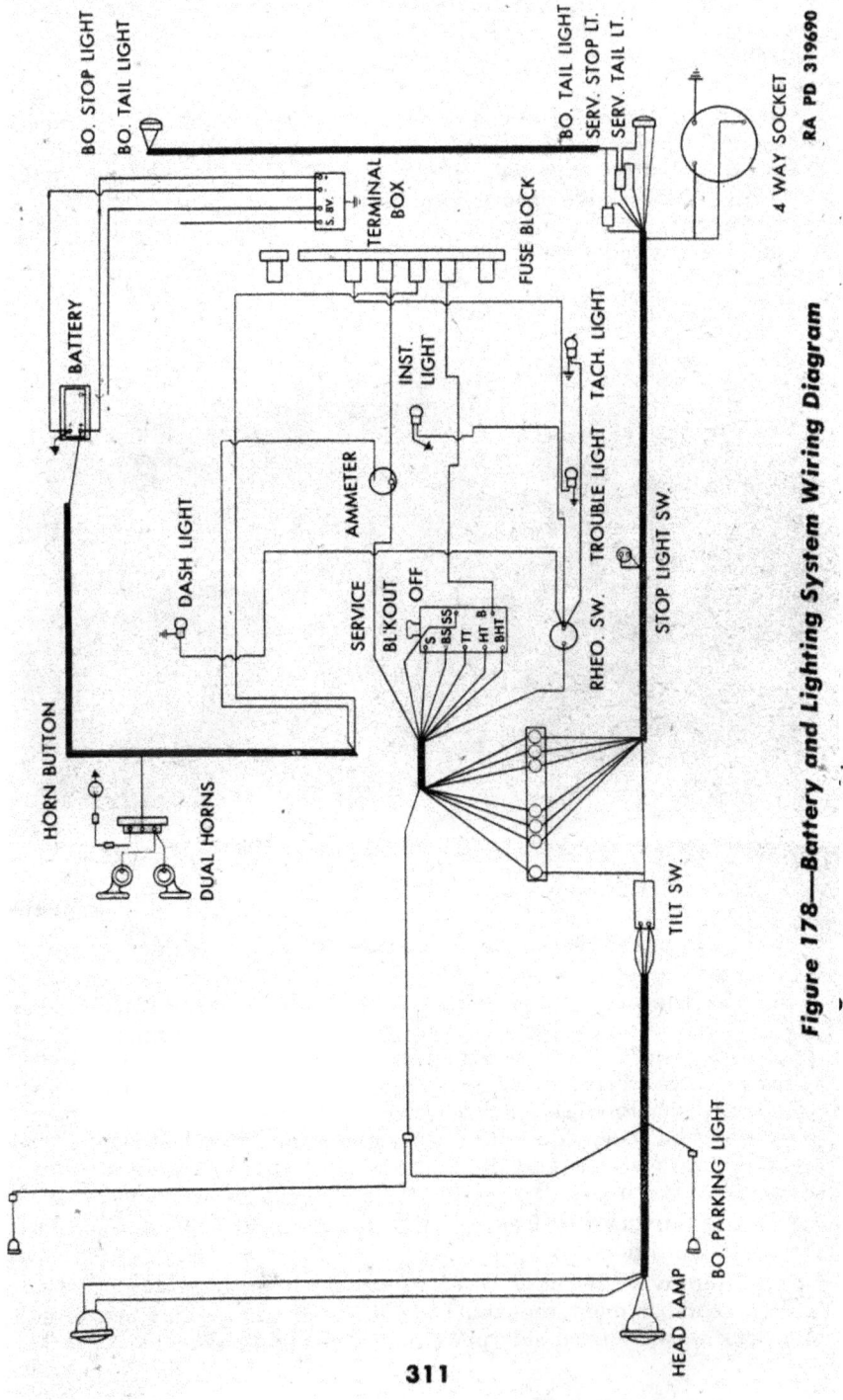

Figure 178—Battery and Lighting System Wiring Diagram

# TM 9-710
## BASIC HALF-TRACK VEHICLES (WHITE, AUTOCAR, and DIAMOND T)

weak ammonia solution. After cleaning with either of these solutions, rinse surface with fresh water, and dry. Keep cables and terminals tight and clean. After cleaning with wire brush, coat terminals with petrolatum.

(2) VOLTMETER CHECK. A direct current voltmeter may be used to indicate to some degree the battery's condition as far as its capacity to supply current is concerned. With the engine shut down and no load on the battery, the open circuit reading should be approximately 12 volts. An excessive drop (more than 2 or 3 volts) in voltage under heavy load (cranking motor engaged, for example) will indicate that something is wrong with the battery or its connections.

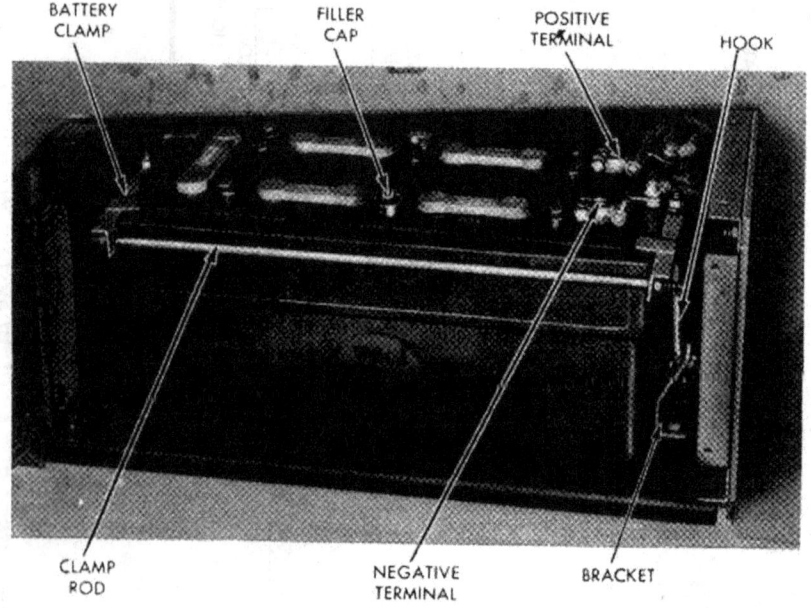

*Figure 179—Battery Installed (Without Cover)*

(3) HYDROMETER TEST. The specific gravity should be maintained above 1.250. A reading of 1.270 to 1.290 should be maintained when the temperature of the battery fluid is 80°F. A reading of 1.220 indicates a half charged battery and a reading of 1.150 or lower indicates complete discharge. Tests with a battery hydrometer made immediately after water has been added will not register correctly. Tests should be made before water is added, or after battery has been on charge, or in use for a few hours.

(4) TEMPERATURE EFFECTS. Refer to section V, "Operating Under Unusual Conditions."

c. **Removal.** Remove three cap screws and lock washers from battery compartment top and lift off top. Remove four cap screws and lock washers from side plate and lower plate. Remove nuts and

## BATTERY AND LIGHTING SYSTEM

lock washers on battery hold-down hooks at each end of the battery and loosen horizontal clamp rod nuts. Loosen and remove terminals of battery cables on battery, removing ground lead first and taping terminal. Lift off battery clamp bracket. Lift battery from vehicle.

d. **Installation.** Place battery in battery compartment on right-hand running board. Install battery clamp bracket and tighten nuts on horizontal clamp rod. Install and tighten lock washers and nuts on hold-down hook at each end of battery. Install terminals and tighten

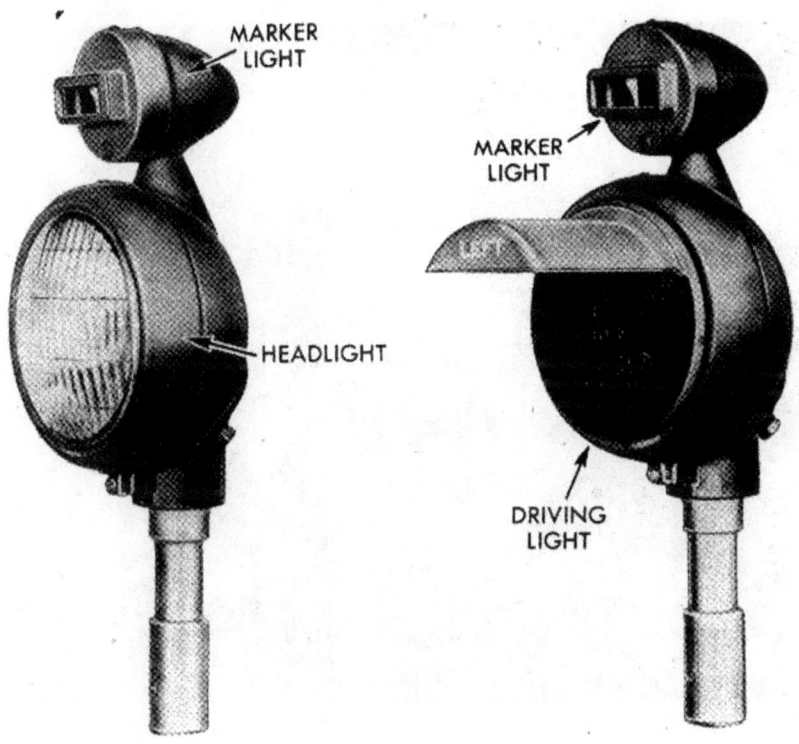

RA PD 319692

*Figure 180—Service Headlight and Marker Light, Blackout Driving Light and Marker Light*

clamp bolts. Install compartment top and secure with three cap screws and lock washers; install side plate and secure with four cap screws and lock washers.

### 154. HEADLIGHTS AND MARKER LIGHTS.

a. **Description.** Two sealed beam headlights with superimposed blackout marker lights are used on this vehicle (figs. 180 and 181). Both assemblies are demountable as an assembly. NOTE: *Installation of a blackout driving light and superimposed blackout marker light assembly can be made only on the left-hand side.*

TM 9-710
154

**BASIC HALF-TRACK VEHICLES (WHITE, AUTOCAR, and DIAMOND T)**

b. **Adjustment of Headlight and Blackout Driving Light.** To adjust the headlights for beam projection, shift the headlight body in its supporting bracket. Loosen three bracket to light body screws, shift light body as required for desired beam projection, and tighten mounting screws. Adjustment is provided for from four degrees below the horizontal center line of the light to two degrees above the horizontal center line.

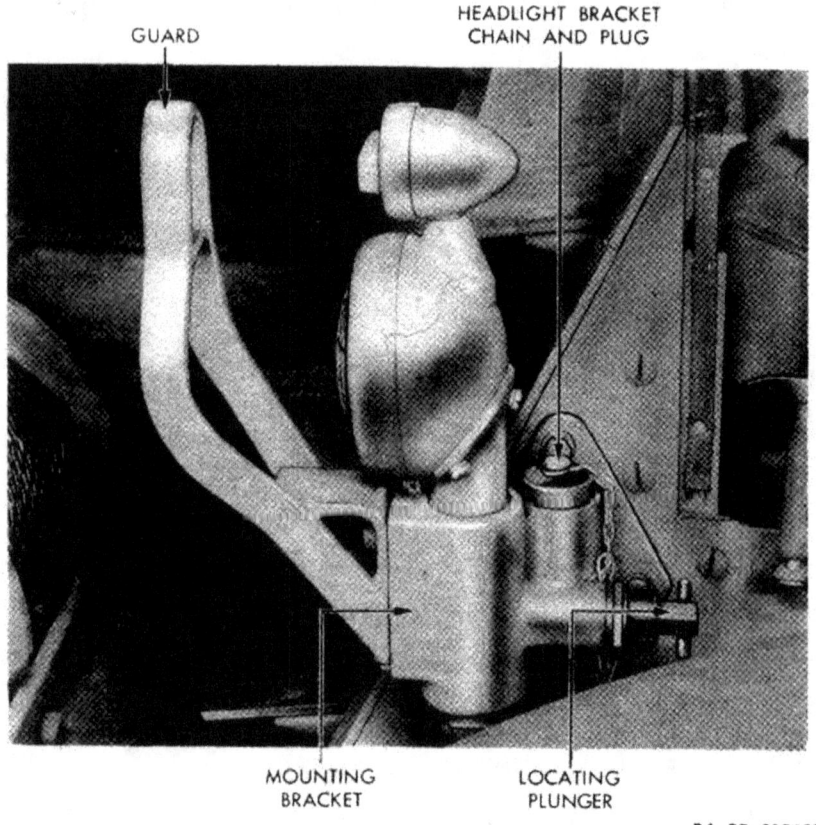

*Figure 181—Headlight Installed*

c. **Headlight Sealed Beam Lamp-unit Replacement.**

(1) REMOVAL. The optical portion of this light is of the sealed beam type requiring replacement of lens, reflector, and bulb assembly in case of failure of any part. To replace, remove the lower retaining screw from the moulding, remove the moulding and lens, and lift the sealed beam lamp-unit out of the body. Disconnect the wires at the connectors and remove assembly.

(2) INSTALLATION. Install new sealed beam lamp-unit and connect wires at the connectors. Install lens and moulding and secure with screw.

TM 9-710
154

## BATTERY AND LIGHTING SYSTEM

d. **Blackout Driving Light Sealed Beam Lamp-unit Replacement.**

(1) REMOVAL. The optical portion of this light is of the sealed beam type and is covered by a shield and hood assembly. Replace lens, reflector, and lamp-unit in case of failure of any one part. To remove sealed beam lamp-unit, remove the retaining screw at the base of the door and take off the door. Lift sealed beam lamp-unit with shield and hood out of the light body. Disconnect wires at connectors and remove unit. The shield and hood are integral with the optical portion of the light and must be replaced at the same time.

(2) INSTALLATION. Install sealed beam lamp-unit with shield and hood in light body. Connect wires at connectors. Install door and secure with retainer screw.

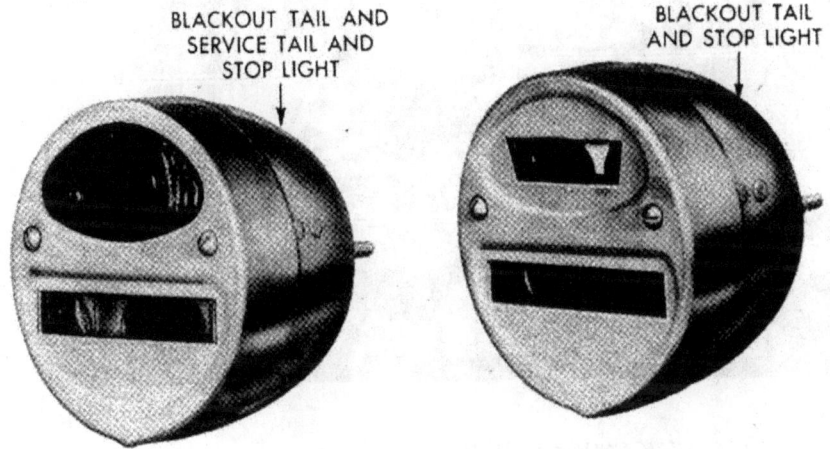

RA PD 18446

*Figure 182—Stop and Taillights*

e. **Blackout Marker Lights Lamp Replacement.**

(1) REMOVAL. Remove retainer screw which secures lens and door to bottom of light body and pull off door. Push lamp inward and counterclockwise until it is free of socket and remove.

(2) INSTALLATION. Place lamp in socket, force it inward and turn clockwise to secure in position. Place lens and door in position on light body and secure with retainer screw.

f. **Headlight Removal.** Remove headlight assemblies from their fender mounting bracket by screwing out on plunger which is mounted in the mounting bracket to release the locating pin from the light mounting shaft. Raise light assembly from mounting bracket.

g. **Headlight Installation.** Push light assembly to bottom of socket while locating pin is out. Screw locating plunger in to connect pin and hole in light shaft. NOTE: *A special chain-mounted headlight*

TM 9-710

**BASIC HALF-TRACK VEHICLES (WHITE, AUTOCAR, and DIAMOND T)**

A— LEAD TO LIGHT SWITCH TERMINAL "HT" (BLACK)
B— LEAD TO FUEL GAGE SWITCH (GREEN)
C— LEAD TO LIGHT SWITCH TERMINAL "S" (YELLOW BLACK TRACER)
D— LEAD TO BLACKOUT PARKING LIGHT CIRCUIT CONNECTOR (BROWN)
E— LEAD TO LIGHT SWITCH TERMINAL "BS" (BLUE)
F— LEAD TO BRAKE LOAD CONTROL RHEOSTAT (BLACK NAT. TRACER)
G— LEAD TO BRAKE LOAD CONTROL RHEOSTAT (YELLOW RED TRACER)
H— LEAD TO AMMETER COMMON TERMINAL (BROWN RED TRACER)
J— LEAD TO LIGHT SWITCH TERMINAL "SW" (ORANGE)
K— LEAD TO LIGHT SWITCH TERMINAL "SS" (BLACK RED TRACER)
L— LEAD TO STOP LIGHT SWITCH (BLACK RED TRACER)
M— LEAD TO STOP LIGHT SWITCH (ORANGE)
N— LEAD TO BRAKE CONTROLLER TERMINAL "BATTERY" (BROWN RED TRACER)
P— LEAD TO BRAKE CONTROLLER TERMINAL "BRAKE" (YELLOW RED TRACER)
Q— LEAD TO CONNECTOR SOCKET FOR TRAILER - TERMINAL "BRAKE 6 V." (BLACK NAT. TRACER)
R— LEAD TO CONNECTOR FOR BLACKOUT STOP LIGHTS (BLUE)
S— LEAD TO CONNECTOR FOR SERVICE TAIL LIGHT (BROWN)
T— LEAD TO SERVICE TAIL LIGHT (YELLOW BLACK TRACER)
U— LEAD TO LEFT FUEL TANK UNIT (GREEN)
V— LEAD TO TILT SWITCH (BLACK)
W— JUNCTION BLOCK ASSEMBLY, W/SCREW (3), NUT (3) AND LOCK-WASHER

RA PD 3578'8

**Figure 183—Terminal Block Installed**

## BATTERY AND LIGHTING SYSTEM

*bracket plug is attached to the headlight bracket.* It is used to close the headlight bracket opening when the lights are not in position.

### 155. TAILLIGHTS.
**a. Description.** The two taillights are of different types, but both contain sealed beam lamp-units. The left taillight is a combination blackout taillight (upper element) and a service taillight and stop light (lower element), and is mounted at the left rear of the vehicle (fig. 182). The right taillight is a combination blackout taillight (upper element) and a blackout stop light (lower element) and is mounted at the right rear of the vehicle.

**b. Sealed Beam Lamp-unit Replacement.**

(1) REMOVAL. Remove two retainer screws which secure light door to body and pull off door. Lift sealed beam lamp-units out of body.

(2) INSTALLATION. Place sealed beam lamp-units in light body so that lamp base fits into socket. Place light door in position on body and secure with two retainer screws.

**c. Light Replacement.**

(1) REMOVAL. Twist wire terminals clockwise and pull them out of lamp sockets. Remove two nuts and lock washers which secure light to vehicle and lift out light.

(2) INSTALLATION. Place light in position on vehicle and secure with two lock washers and nuts. Push wire terminals into lamp sockets and twist counterclockwise to secure them.

### 156. TERMINAL BLOCK.
**a. Description.** An insulated terminal block (fig. 183) with ten posts is provided in the engine compartment to facilitate testing of the forward wiring and connection to the instrument panel components. The block is secured to the dash by three screws, lock washers, and nuts below the ignition coil shielding box.

### 157. TERMINAL BOX.
**a. Description.** The radio terminal box is mounted on the floor at the center under the left-hand seat in the driver's compartment. The insulated terminal block has three terminals on it. The red wire terminal is marked $+$ 12V; the black wire $-$ 12V, and the center terminal is marked $+$ 8V.

### 158. FUSES AND CIRCUIT BREAKERS.
**a. Description.** Conventional automotive-type, glass-tube enclosed fuses are mounted on a fuse and junction block, which is secured behind the instrument panel within the shielding box. Access to the fuses is obtained by loosening the wing nuts below the box and removing the cover plate. A set of spare fuses must always be available. NOTE: *The later models have circuit breakers in place of the fuses.*

**TM 9-710**
158

**BASIC HALF-TRACK VEHICLES (WHITE, AUTOCAR, and DIAMOND T)**

RA PD 18281

*Figure 184—Horns Installed*

## BATTERY AND LIGHTING SYSTEM

b. **Maintenance.** Difficulty with blown fuses, as a result of rain or moisture collecting in the trouble lamp receptacle, is eliminated by pressing a cork of the correct size into the opening, when lamp is not in use.

### 159. HORNS.

a. **Description.** Dual type (high and low note) vibrator horns (fig. 184) are provided and mounted on the engine side of the dash below the air cleaner. A horn relay is also installed above the horn mounting. The center terminal is for the battery connection, the "S" terminal is for the button connection, and the "H" terminal is for the horn connections.

b. **Removal.** Disconnect cables from horns by unscrewing the top screw on each shell and removing shell; remove terminal screw and lock washer and remove cables. Remove two nuts and lock washers, holding each horn unit to bracket, and remove units.

c. **Installation.** Place horn units on support bracket and insert two mounting screws through holes in base and bracket and secure with two lock washers and nuts. Install cables to terminals and secure with lock washers and terminal screws. Install horn shells and secure with screw through top of shells.

# BASIC HALF-TRACK VEHICLES (WHITE, AUTOCAR, and DIAMOND T)

Section XXXII

## INSTRUMENTS AND GAGES

| | Paragraph |
|---|---|
| Description | 160 |
| Instrument cluster | 161 |
| Speedometer and cable | 162 |
| Tachometer and cable | 163 |
| Voltmeter | 164 |
| Compass | 165 |

## 160. DESCRIPTION.

**a. Instrument Panel** (fig. 185). The instruments and gages mounted on the instrument panel, consist of a four-unit instrument cluster, a speedometer, a voltmeter, and a tachometer. The speedometer is mounted in the center of the instrument panel and the voltmeter to the right of the speedometer. Attached to the back of the speedometer is a bracket which holds the socket and lamp for indirect lighting of both speedometer and instrument cluster. The instrument cluster is mounted to the left side of the speedometer. The tachometer is mounted in the left side of the panel and has a bracket attached to its case for holding the socket and bulb for indirect lighting of the dial.

## 161. INSTRUMENT CLUSTER.

**a. Description and Data.**

(1) DESCRIPTION. The gages of the cluster assembly are grouped in a circular case, with the ammeter at the top and the temperature gage at the bottom. At the right side is the oil pressure gage, and at the left is the fuel gage.

(2) DATA.

    Make ....................... Stewart-Warner
    Manufacturer's No. ................... 43,6004
    Ammeter ..................... electro-magnetic
    Temperature gage ............ fluid expanding
    Oil gage ............................ pressure
    Fuel gage ................... electro-magnetic

**b. Removal of Instrument Cluster.**

(1) REMOVE INSTRUMENT PANEL BOX COVER. Remove one thumb screw and lock washer from each end of box cover at bottom of box, and remove the cover.

(2) REMOVE ENGINE TEMPERATURE GAGE BULB. Loosen temperature gage adapter nut on cylinder-head and remove bulb from adapter. Pull bulb and tubing through grommets in dash.

(3) DISCONNECT OIL GAGE LINE AND ELECTRICAL WIRES. Un-

## INSTRUMENTS AND GAGES

screw flared tube nut on oil line connection to back of cluster case plate and disconnect line. Remove nuts and washers from the two ammeter terminals. Lift off wires and tag each wire so it can be connected to proper terminal when ammeter is reinstalled. Remove nuts and washers from two terminals on fuel gage and tag the three wires so they can be connected to the proper terminals when installed. Remove wires from terminals.

(4) REMOVE MOUNTING BRACKETS AND CLUSTER ASSEMBLY. Remove two mounting stud nuts and lock washers, lift off the two brackets and remove cluster from front side of panel.

c. **Installation of Instrument Cluster.**

(1) INSTALL CLUSTER ON INSTRUMENT PANEL. Place cluster assembly in from front of instrument panel to hole on panel. Install two mounting brackets on studs and secure brackets and cluster with two nuts and lock washers.

(2) INSTALL ENGINE TEMPERATURE GAGE BULB. Push temperature gage bulb through grommets in shielding box and dash. Install bulb in adapter on cylinder head and secure with adapter nut.

(3) INSTALL OIL GAGE LINE AND ELECTRICAL WIRES. Place oil line in fitting and secure by tightening inverted flared tube nut. Place wires on their proper terminal posts and secure with washers and nuts.

(4) INSTALL COVER OF INSTRUMENT PANEL BOX. Place cover of instrument panel box in position and secure with thumb screw and lock washer at each end.

## 162. SPEEDOMETER AND CABLE.

a. **Description and Data.**

(1) DESCRIPTION. The speedometer is the centrifugal magnetic type with a dial reading from 0 to 80 miles per hour. It also is equipped with an odometer unit for season and trip mileage. The odometer unit indicates total mileage up to 99,999.9 miles and trip mileage from 0 to 999.9 miles. The trip odometer is reset by pushing in the reset stem and turning it clockwise. The speedometer is driven by a flexible shaft and gear which meshes with a mating gear located on the rear of the front axle drive shaft in the transfer case.

(2) DATA.

| | |
|---|---|
| Make | Stewart-Warner |
| Manufacturer's No. | SW-585-AM |
| Type | centrifugal |

b. **Speedometer Removal.**

(1) REMOVE INSTRUMENT PANEL BOX COVER. Remove one thumb screw and lock washer from each end of box cover at bottom of box and remove the cover.

(2) REMOVE SPEEDOMETER. Unscrew round knurled nut from flexible shaft cable connection to back of speedometer and pull shaft from case. Remove screw and lock washer holding bracket to speedometer case and lift off bracket. Remove nut and lock washer from

# TM 9-710
## 162

**BASIC HALF-TRACK VEHICLES (WHITE, AUTOCAR, and DIAMOND T)**

two mounting bracket studs at rear of speedometer and remove brackets. Pull out speedometer assembly from front side of instrument panel.

c. **Speedometer Installation.**

(1) INSTALL SPEEDOMETER. Place speedometer in hole in instrument panel from front side of panel. Install the mounting brackets on the two studs at rear of speedometer and secure with lock washers and nuts. Install lamp bracket to rear of speedometer case and secure with screw and lock washer. Install speedometer flexible shaft cable connection to fitting at back of case and secure with round knurled connecting nut.

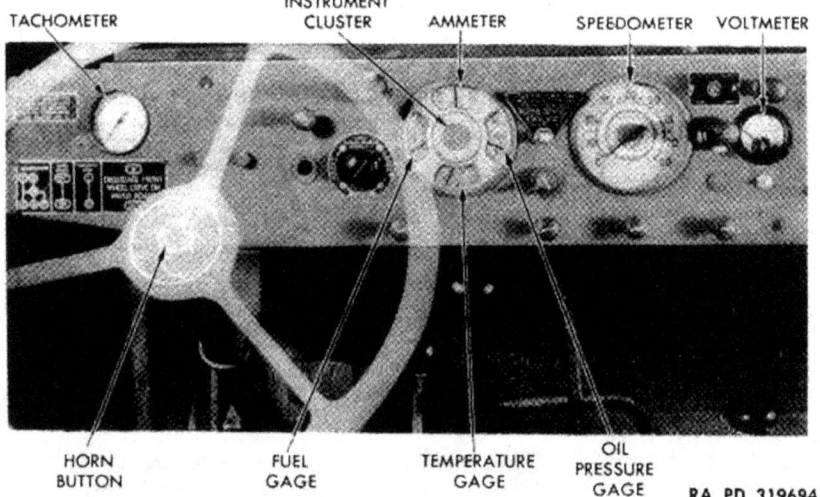

*Figure 185—Instrument Panel with Instruments and Gages*

(2) INSTALL COVER OF INSTRUMENT PANEL BOX. Place cover of instrument panel box in position, and secure with thumb screw and lock washer at each end.

d. **Speedometer Cable Removal.** Remove instrument panel box cover thumb screws and cover. Disconnect speedometer cable from the rear center of speedometer head by unscrewing the round knurled nut and pulling the drive shaft and cable free. Remove nut, lock washer, and bolt from clip on speedometer cable at cowl. Remove two cap screws, lock washers, and clips attaching the drive shaft flexible housing to the right-hand top side of transmission. Disconnect the speedometer cable at the rear right side of the transfer case by unscrewing the round knurled nut and pulling the cable free. Pull cable assembly through rear of instrument panel box and cowl after loosening grommets and remove cable.

e. **Speedometer Cable Installation.** Push speedometer head end of cable through cowl and instrument panel box holes. Insert tongue end of drive shaft into fitting at rear center of speedometer head and

## INSTRUMENTS AND GAGES

pull shaft housing into place against fitting. Secure assembly with round knurled coupling nut. Install grommets to cable holes in cowl and instrument panel box. Secure cable clip to cowl with bolt, lock washer, and nut. Place cable along right-hand side of transmission and fit tongue end of drive shaft into place at right rear of transfer case. Secure with round knurled nut. Attach cable housing to transmission case with two clips, lock washers, and cap screws making sure cable is positioned with no sharp bends. Install instrument panel box cover and secure with thumb screw and lock washer at each end.

### 163. TACHOMETER AND CABLE.

**a. Description and Data.**

(1) DESCRIPTION. The tachometer is a centrifugal-magnetic type, and indicates engine revolutions per minute from 0 to 3,500. It is driven by a flexible shaft connected to a spiral gear drive located just below the distributor in the tachometer adapter.

(2) DATA.

    Make .................... Stewart-Warner
    Manufacturer's Model No. .......... SW-598-Y
    Type ........................ centrifugal

**b. Tachometer Removal.** Pull socket and lamp assembly out of spring bracket attached to tachometer case. Unscrew round knurled nut from flexible drive shaft cable connection at rear of case and disconnect shaft. Remove two screws, lock washers, and nuts holding tachometer to panel, and remove tachometer from rear of panel.

**c. Tachometer Installation.** Insert tachometer in hole on instrument panel from back side of panel and insert screws through the panel and the ears on the tachometer case. Install lock washers and nuts and tighten. Install tachometer drive shaft to connection at rear of case and secure with round knurled nut. Insert socket and lamp assembly into spring bracket on tachometer case.

**d. Tachometer Cable Removal.** Loosen nut on screw holding tachometer cable clip to cowl, and slide cable from under clip. Unscrew round knurled nut, connecting tachometer cable to adapter just below distributor, and pull cable and drive shaft from adapter. Unscrew round knurled coupling nut connecting cable to rear of tachometer head and disconnect cable and drive shaft. Loosen grommet in cowl and pull cable through cowl from engine side of cowl.

**e. Tachometer Cable Installation.** Insert tachometer head end of cable and drive shaft through cowl and fit grommet into place. Install tachometer drive shaft tongue to tachometer head and secure cable to head with knurled coupling nut. Slip cable under clip on cowl and tighten nut and lock washer. Install tachometer drive shaft and cable to adapter at bottom of distributor and secure with coupling nut. NOTE: *Do not kink or sharply bend the flexible shaft.*

### 164. VOLTMETER.

**a. Description and Data.**

(1) DESCRIPTION. The voltmeter is graduated from 0 to 20 volts and reads direct current. It is not a substitute for a hydrometer in

# TM 9-710
164

**BASIC HALF-TRACK VEHICLES (WHITE, AUTOCAR, and DIAMOND T)**

determining the state of a battery's charge but is used to indicate, to some degree, the battery's condition in so far as current supply capacity is concerned. To operate voltmeter, press in push button until reading is completed, then release.

    (2) DATA.

        Make ........................ Sun Mfg. Co.
        Type ........................... electric
        Manufacturer's No. ..................... I-559

*Figure 186—Compass Mounting and Adjustment*

    b. Removal.

    (1) REMOVE INSTRUMENT PANEL SHIELDING BOX COVER. Remove one thumb screw and lock washer from each end of box bottom cover and remove cover.

    (2) REMOVE VOLTMETER. Remove two wire terminal nuts and washers. Remove wires from terminals and tag wires for proper identification when installing. Remove three sheet metal binder screws and speed nuts, which secure voltmeter to panel, and pull out voltmeter.

    c. Installation.

    (1) INSTALL VOLTMETER. Insert voltmeter in hole on instrument panel from front side of panel, lining up the three screw holes with the holes in panel. Insert the three screws in their speed nuts and care-

## INSTRUMENTS AND GAGES

fully tighten. Place the wires on their proper terminals and secure with nuts and washers.

(2) INSTALL COVER OF INSTRUMENT PANEL BOX. Place cover of instrument panel box in position and secure with thumb screw and lock washer at each end.

### 165. COMPASS.

**a. Description.** The compass and bracket (fig. 186) are mounted on the windshield divider strip facing driver and are secured in position by the third screw from the top of the divider strip.

**b. Compensation.** Check the vehicle compass against a known accurate compass and make any necessary adjustments as follows:

(1) Use a coin to adjust or compensate the compass, as a screwdriver may be magnetic and affect the setting.

(2) Point the vehicle north. (Determine directions by a reliable compass located outside the vehicle.) Turn the lower compensator screw slot (marked N-S) only as far as is necessary to make the dial read "NORTH" or "SOUTH," and no farther. (If the dial reads "SOUTH" instead of "NORTH", step (3) will correct it.)

(3) Point the vehicle east. Turn the upper compensator screw slot (marked E-W) just enough to make the dial read "EAST" and no farther.

(4) Point the vehicle south. If necessary, turn the lower compensator screw slot (marked N-S) slightly to make the dial read "SOUTH."

(5) Point the vehicle west. If necessary, turn the upper compensator screw slot (marked E-W) slightly to make the dial read "WEST." NOTE: *Close the body doors when adjusting compass and taking direction.* The engine should be running, or if practical, the vehicle should be in motion since the magnetic drives of the speedometer and tachometer affect compass readings. Drive straight ahead when making adjustments.

**c. Removal.** Remove screw in mounting bracket attaching compass to the windshield divider strip and lift off compass.

**d. Installation.** Mount the compass and bracket on the windshield divider strip, using the third screw from the top of the strip (fig. 186). Aline the compass horizontally and vertically with vehicle. Adjusting screw "A" (fig. 186), alines the compass vertically.

TM 9-710

**BASIC HALF-TRACK VEHICLES (WHITE, AUTOCAR, and DIAMOND T)**

Section XXXIII

## WINCH

|  | Paragraph |
|---|---|
| Description and tabulated data | 166 |
| Safety brake | 167 |
| Drag brake | 168 |
| Cable | 169 |
| Removal and installation of winch | 170 |

**166. DESCRIPTION AND TABULATED DATA.**

   a. **Description.** The winch (fig. 187) is mounted between the frame side rails at the front of the vehicle. It is driven by a propeller

A—SLIDING CLUTCH BLOCK
B—DRUM FLANGE DRAG BRAKE
C—CABLE
D—WINCH DRUM
E—TOW HOOK
F—MOUNTING BOLTS
G—JAM NUTS
H—SPRING EYEBOLT SPRING
I—HAND LEVER
J—CABLE HOOK
K—GUARD SHIELD

RA PD 319696

*Figure 187—Winch Assembly Installed*

## WINCH

shaft from the power take-off on the transfer case, and operates through a worm and worm gear. A universal joint, equipped with a shear pin, connects the propeller shaft to the worm shaft. The worm and gear are operated by power from the engine, both forward and reverse. A safety brake acts upon the worm shaft and holds the load at any position when the power is cut off from the winch. A drum flange drag brake bears against the flange of the drum to prevent the drum from overrunning the cable as the cable is pulled from the drum by hand.

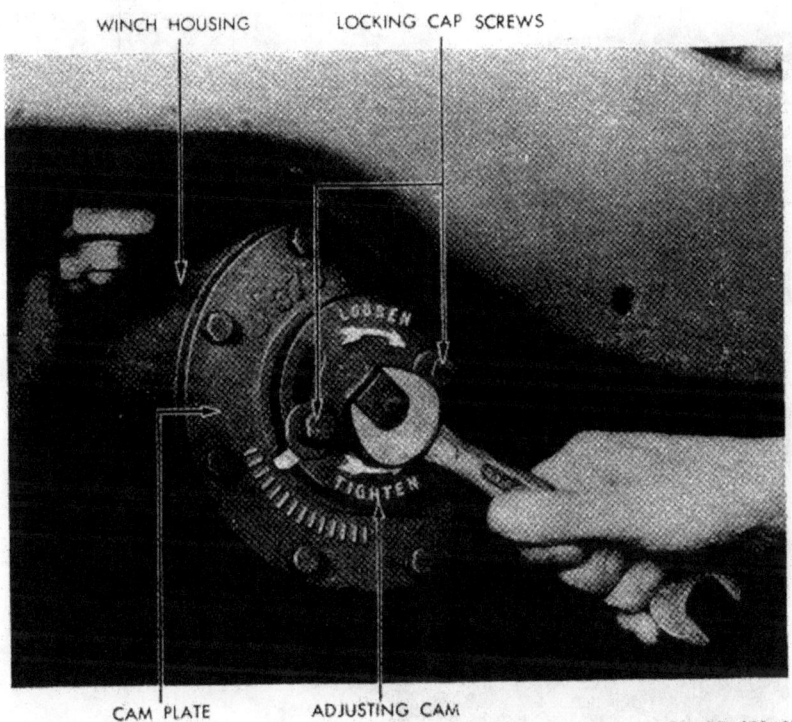

*Figure 188—Adjusting Safety Brake*

b. **Tabulated Data.**
```
Make .................................. Tulsa
Model No. ............................. 18 G
Type ............................. power driven
Location ................. front end of chassis
```

167. **SAFETY BRAKE.**

a. **Brake Band Adjustment.** Adjustment for the safety brake is made on the outer end of the safety brake housing located on the end of the worm gear case (fig. 188). If adjustment is necessary, the guard shield must first be taken off by removing four bolts, lock washers,

# TM 9-710
## 167
### BASIC HALF-TRACK VEHICLES (WHITE, AUTOCAR, and DIAMOND T)

and nuts. Loosen two cap screws in the slotted holes on the end of the worm brake housing and turn the adjusting cam to tighten or loosen as indicated by arrows on the housing. Turn two notches and test. (If new brake shoes are installed, set pointer on fourth notch.) Install and secure guard shield with four bolts, lock washers, and nuts.

b. **Brake Band Removal.** When all adjustment in the slotted holes has been taken up and the safety brake does not hold, replace

*Figure 189—Removing Brake Shoes*

the brake shoe assemblies (fig. 189). Remove eight cap screws and lock washers from the adjusting cam plate and remove plate. Lift out the two brake shoe assemblies.

c. **Brake Band Installation.** Replace the brake shoe assemblies and insert them into end of safety brake housing with their dividing line vertical. Loosen the two adjusting cam cap screws on the cam plate and turn adjusting cam back as far as slots will allow. Install adjusting cam and plate to brake shoes and housing, inserting fingers of cam

## WINCH

into proper position in brake shoes. Secure plate to housing with eight cap screws and lock washers and adjust brakes (par. 167 a). Install guard shield and secure with four bolts, lock washers, and nuts.

### 168. DRAG BRAKE.

**a. Drag Brake Shoe Adjustment.** The drag brake shoe requires adjustment whenever drum overruns the cable as cable is pulled from drum by hand. To increase the tension of the brake, remove the jam nut and adjusting nut on the spring eyebolt and remove the spring.

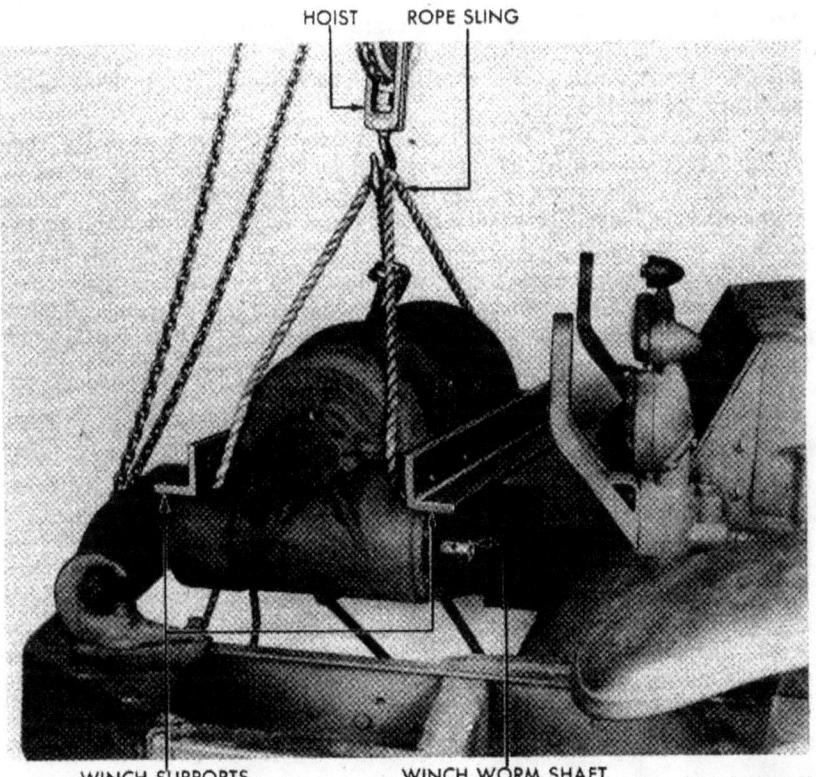

*Figure 190—Removing Winch Assembly*

Stretch the spring ¼ inch and reinstall. Disengage the drum clutch and determine if sufficient drag has been obtained. If not, stretch the spring farther until desired drag is obtained. Engage the drum clutch and set the adjusting nut so drag brake shoe clears the drum flange by ¼ inch. Secure setting of adjusting nut with the jam nut.

**b. Drag Brake Shoe Removal.** Engage the drum clutch and remove the jam nut and adjusting nut from the spring eyebolt. Disengage the drum clutch and pull cotter pin from bracket pin and punch out the bracket pin releasing drag brake shoe assembly. Pull cotter pin from brake shoe pin and remove pin, spring eyebolt pin, and spring.

**BASIC HALF-TRACK VEHICLES (WHITE, AUTOCAR, and DIAMOND T)**

c. **Drag Brake Shoe Installation.** Install spring eyebolt pin and spring to replacement brake shoe assembly, and secure with cotter pin. Install brake shoe assembly, placing spring eyebolt and spring in proper position to the knob lever and installing bracket pin to rear end of brake shoe assembly. Secure bracket pin with cotter pin and adjust drag brake shoe with adjusting nut and jam nut so brake clears drum ¼ inch when clutch is engaged.

### 169. CABLE.

a. **Removal.** Disengage drum clutch. Unhook chain from tow hook and pull cable straight out from winch by hand. Loosen two nuts on U-bolt ends which extend through drum flange. Pull cable end from under U-bolt.

b. **Maintenance.** Inspect winch cable for frayed or rusty condition. Apply engine oil to prevent rust on cable. Take care in securing cable to objects not to bend sharply or kink cable. When cable is found to be frayed or worn beyond point of being safe, replace the cable.

c. **Installation.** Attach the cable to drum by inserting cable end through U-bolt on drum flange. Tighten the two U-bolt nuts and wind cable on drum evenly and tightly, reeling cable on drum in the same manner as making a pull. (Refer to paragraph 9 e).

### 170. REMOVAL AND INSTALLATION OF WINCH (fig. 190).

a. **Removal.** Remove eight winch frame support mounting bolts, nuts, and lock washers (two at each corner). Pull cotter out of shear pin in hub of universal joint at winch drive shaft and remove shear pin. Lift winch from frame, using rope sling and hoist, slipping universal joint hub off winch drive shaft.

b. **Installation.** Install rope sling on winch. Lift winch with hoist and guide winch into position on frame of vehicle. Remove sling and insert universal joint hub and drive shaft over end of winch drive shaft. Line up the hole in shaft and hub, insert shear pin and secure with cotter pin. Secure winch assembly to frame support with eight bolts, lock washers, and nuts.

TM 9-710
171-172

Section XXXIV

## SHIPMENT AND TEMPORARY STORAGE

|  | Paragraph |
|---|---|
| General instructions | 171 |
| Preparation for temporary storage | 172 |
| Loading and blocking for rail shipment | 173 |

**171. GENERAL INSTRUCTIONS.**

a. Preparation for domestic shipment of the vehicles is the same, with the exception of minor added precautions, as preparation for temporary storage. Preparation for shipment by rail includes instructions for loading the vehicles, blocking necessary to secure the vehicles on freight cars, weight, and other information necessary to properly prepare the vehicles for domestic rail shipment. For more detailed information and for preparation for indefinite storage, refer to AR 850-18.

**172. PREPARATION FOR TEMPORARY STORAGE.**

a. Vehicles to be prepared for temporary storage are those ready for immediate service but not used for less than 30 days. If vehicles are to be indefinitely stored after shipment by rail, they will be prepared for such storage at their destination.

b. If the vehicles are to be temporarily stored or bivouacked, take the following precautions:

(1) LUBRICATION. Lubricate the vehicle completely.

(2) COOLING SYSTEM. If freezing temperature may normally be expected during the limited storage or shipment period, test the coolant with a hydometer and add the proper quantity of antifreeze compound to afford protection from freezing at the lowest temperature anticipated during the storage or shipping period. Completely inspect the cooling system for leaks.

(3) BATTERY. Check battery and terminals for corrosion, and if necessary, clean and thoroughly service battery (par. 153).

(4) TIRES. Clean, inspect, and properly inflate all tires, including spares. Replace with serviceable tires all tires requiring repairing or retreading. Do not store the vehicles on floors, cinders, or other surfaces which are soaked with oil or grease. Wash off immediately any oil, grease, gasoline, or kerosene which comes in contact with tires or tracks under any circumstances.

(5) ROAD TEST. The preparation for limited storage will include a road test, after the battery, cooling system, and lubrication service, to check on the general condition of the engine. Correct any defects noted in the vehicle operation before the vehicle is stored, or note on a tag attached to the steering levers, stating the repairs needed or describing the condition present. A written report of these items will then be made to the officer in charge.

(6) FUEL IN TANKS. It is not necessary to remove fuel from the vehicle tanks for shipment within the United States, nor to label the

**TM 9-710**
**172**

**BASIC HALF-TRACK VEHICLES (WHITE, AUTOCAR, and DIAMOND T)**

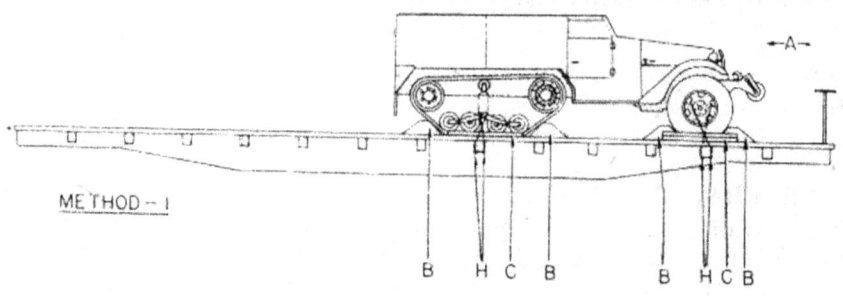

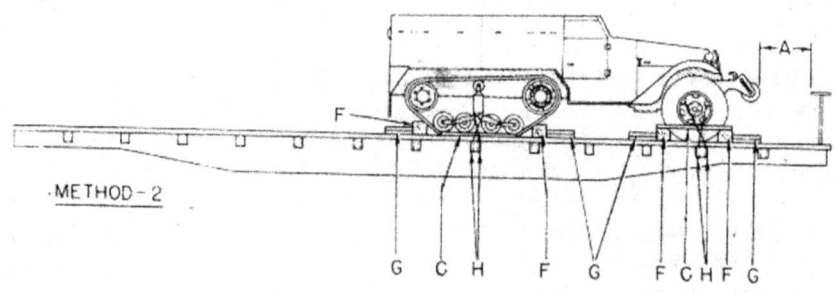

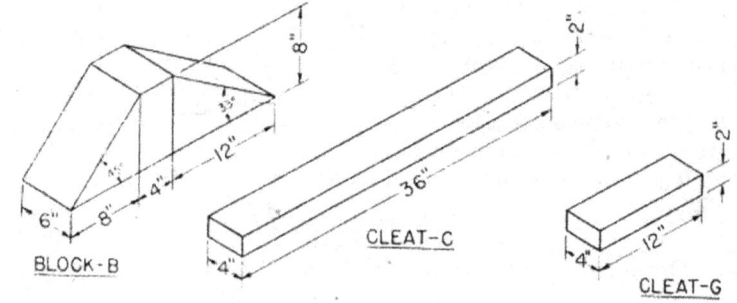

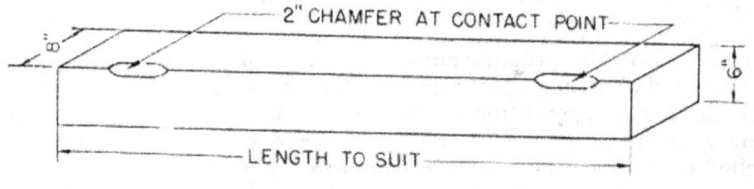

*Figure 191—Blocking Requirements for Securing Half-track Vehicles on Railroad Cars*

## SHIPMENT AND TEMPORARY STORAGE

tanks under Interstate Commerce Commission Regulations. Leave fuel in the tanks except when storing in locations where fire ordinances or other local regulations require removal of all gasoline before storage.

(7) EXTERIOR OF VEHICLE. Remove rust appearing on any part of the vehicle exterior with flint paper. Repaint painted surfaces whenever necessary to protect wood or metal. Coat exposed polished metal surfaces susceptible to rust, such as cables and chains, with medium grade preservative lubricating oil. Close firmly all doors, windows, and openings. Make sure paulins are in place and firmly secured. Leave rubber mats, when provided, in an unrolled position on the floor, not rolled or curled up. Equipment, such as Pioneer tools, track tools, and fire extinguishers, may remain in place on the vehicle.

(8) INSPECTION. Make a systematic inspection just before shipment or temporary storage, to make sure all above steps have been covered and that vehicle is ready for operation on call. Make a list of all missing or damaged items and attach it to the steering levers. Refer to Before-operation Service (par. 18).

(9) BRAKES. Release brakes and chock the wheels and tracks.

c. Inspections in Limited Storage. Inspect vehicles in limited storage weekly for condition of battery and, in case of anticipated freezing weather, cooling system. If water is added to the battery when freezing weather is anticipated, recharge the battery with a portable charger or remove the battery for charging. Do not attempt to charge the battery by running the engine. If freezing temperature is expected, add the proper quantity of antifreeze compound to cooling system to afford protection from freezing.

## 173. LOADING AND BLOCKING FOR RAIL SHIPMENT.

a. Preparation. In addition to the preparation described in paragraph 172, when ordnance vehicles are prepared for domestic shipment, the following preparations and precautions will be taken.

(1) EXTERIOR. Cover the body of the vehicle with the canvas cover supplied for such use during rail shipment.

(2) BATTERY. Disconnect the battery to prevent its discharge by vandalism or accident. This may be accomplished by disconnecting the positive lead, taping the end of the lead and tying it back away from the battery.

(3) BRAKES. The brakes must be applied and the transmission placed in low gear after the vehicle has been placed in position with a brake wheel clearance of at least 6 inches (fig. 191, "A"). Locate the vehicles on the car in such a manner as to prevent the car from carrying an unbalanced load.

(4) All cars containing ordnance vehicles must be placarded "DO NOT HUMP".

(5) Ordnance vehicles may be shipped on flat cars, end-door box cars, side-door box cars, or drop-end gondola cars, whichever type car is the most convenient.

b. Facilities for Loading. Whenever possible, load and unload vehicles from open cars under their own power, using permanent end

## BASIC HALF-TRACK VEHICLES (WHITE, AUTOCAR, and DIAMOND T)

ramps and spanning platforms. Movement from one flat car to another along the length of the train is made possible by cross-over plates or spanning platforms. If no permanent end ramp is available, an improvised ramp can be made from railroad ties. Vehicles may be loaded in gondola cars without drop-ends by using a crane. In case of shipment in side-door box cars, use a dolly-type jack to warp the vehicles into position within the car.

*c.* **Securing Vehicles.** In securing or blocking a vehicle, three motions—lengthwise, sidewise, and bouncing—must be prevented. Following are two methods involving the minimum allowed requirements for blocking medium tanks on freight cars (fig. 191).

(1) METHOD ONE. Place eight blocks "B", one at the front, and one at the rear, of each track and wheel. Nail the heel of each block to the car floor with five 40-penny nails. Toenail to the car floor, that portion of each block which is under the track or wheel. Locate three cleats "C" on each side of the vehicle, one against the outside of each track and two against the outside of each wheel. NOTE: *These cleats may be located against the inside of the tracks and wheels if conditions warrant.* Nail each cleat to the car floor with three 40-penny nails. Pass four strands, two wrappings, of No. 8 gage, black annealed wire ("H", fig. 191) over the bogie arms, back of the bogie frame brackets, and through a stake pocket. Pass four more strands of wire through each front wheel and then through a stake pocket. Tighten wires enough to remove slack. CAUTION: *When a box car is used, this strapping must be applied in similar fashion and attached to the car floor by the use of blocking or anchor plates. This strapping is not required when gondola cars are used.*

(2) METHOD TWO. Place four blocks "F", one at the front, and one at the rear, of the tracks; and one at the front, and one at the rear, of the wheels. NOTE: *Blocks "F" must be at least eight inches longer than the over-all width of the vehicle at the car floor.* Locate 16 cleats "G", 2 at front and 2 at rear, of each track and wheel. Nail the lower cleats to the car floor with three 40-penny nails. Nail the top cleat to the lower cleat with three 40-penny nails. Locate two cleats "C" on each side of the vehicle, one against the outside of each track, and one against the outside of each wheel (on blocks "F"). NOTE: *These cleats may be located against the inside of the tracks and wheels if conditions warrant.* Nail each end of cleats "C" to the car floor (or blocks "F") with three 40-penny nails. Pass four strands, two wrappings, of No. 8 gage, black annealed wire ("H", fig. 191) over the bogie arms, back of the bogie frames bracket, and through a stake pocket. Pass four more strands of wire through each front wheel and then through a stake pocket. Tighten wires enough to remove slack. CAUTION: *When a box car is used, this strapping must be applied in similar fashion and attached to the car floor by the use of blocking or anchor plates. This strapping is not required when gondola cars are used.*

*d.* **Shipping Data.** Data given below are for representative vehicles. Data on vehicles not shown are the same as, or very similar to, data given for a representative vehicle in the same general category.

TM 9-710
173

## SHIPMENT AND TEMPORARY STORAGE

(1) CAR M2.
Length, over-all (w/roller)............................19 ft 6 in.
Length, over-all (w/winch)............................20 ft 1 in.
Width, over-all.......................................7 ft 3 in.
Height, over-all......................................7 ft 5 in.
Shipping weight (approx.)............................19,195 lb
Approximate floor area occupied per vehicle (w/roller)..141.37 sq ft
Approximate floor area occupied per vehicle (w/winch)..145.58 sq ft
Approximate volume occupied per vehicle (w/roller)....1,049 cu ft
Approximate volume occupied per vehicle (w/winch)....1,080 cu ft

(2) PERSONNEL CARRIER M3.
Length, over-all (w/roller)...........................20 ft 2⅝ in.
Length, over-all (w/winch)............................20 ft 9⅝ in.
Width, over-all.......................................7 ft 3½ in.
Height, over-all......................................7 ft 5 in.
Shipping weight (approx.)............................17,165 lb
Approximate floor area occupied per vehicle (w/roller)..147.40 sq ft
Approximate floor area occupied per vehicle (w/winch)..151.63 sq ft
Approximate volume occupied per vehicle (w/roller)....1,094 cu ft
Approximate volume occupied per vehicle (w/winch)....1,125 cu ft

(3) 81-MM MORTAR CARRIER M4.
Length, over-all (w/roller)...........................20 ft 3⅞ in.
Length, over-all (w/winch)............................20 ft 10⅝ in.
Width, over-all.......................................6 ft 5½ in.
Height, over-all......................................7 ft 5⅜ in.
Shipping weight (approx.)............................17,350 lb
Approximate floor area occupied per vehicle (w/roller)..130.96 sq ft
Approximate floor area occupied per vehicle (w/winch)..134.67 sq ft
Approximate volume occupied per vehicle (w/roller).....974 cu ft
Approximate volume occupied per vehicle (w/winch)....1,002 cu ft

# TM 9-710

**BASIC HALF-TRACK VEHICLES (WHITE, AUTOCAR, and DIAMOND T)**

## PART THREE—VEHICLE ARMAMENT

Section XXXV

## ARMAMENT

| | Paragraph |
|---|---|
| Car M2. | 174 |
| Car M2A1. | 175 |
| Personnel carrier M3. | 176 |
| Personnel carrier M3A1. | 177 |
| 81-mm mortar motor carrier M4 and M4A1. | 178 |
| 75-mm gun motor carriage M3. | 179 |
| 75-mm gun motor carriage M3A1. | 180 |
| 75-mm howitzer motor carriage T30. | 181 |
| 105-mm howitzer motor carriage T19. | 182 |
| Multiple gun motor carriage M13. | 183 |
| Multiple gun motor carriage M15. | 184 |
| Multiple gun motor carriage M16. | 185 |

**174. CAR M2** (fig. 1).

   **a. References.**

    (1) FM 23-50, Browning Machine Gun, Cal. .30, H.B., M1919A4.

    (2) FM 23-60, Browning Machine Gun, Cal. .50, H.B., M2, Ground.

    (3) FM 23-65, Browning Machine Gun, Cal. .50, H.B., M2 (mounted in combat vehicles).

   **b. Basic Data.**

    (1) GENERAL.

Weight without armament, fuel and operator (approx. pounds) 16,800
Weight fully equipped (approx. pounds) . . . . . . . . . . . . . . . . . . 17,800
Over-all width (inches) . . . . . . . . . . . . . . . . . . . . . . . . . . . . . . . . 87½
Over-all height (guns fully elevated) . . . . . . . . . . . . . . . . 242⅝ in.
Over-all length (with winch) . . . . . . . . . . . . . . . . . . . . . . . 244⅝ in.

    (2) CREW.

Carries a crew of ten men.

    (3) MACHINE GUNS.

     (a) *1 Cal. .50 Browning Machine Gun M2, H.B. (flexible).*

Weight of gun (pounds) . . . . . . . . . . . . . . . . . . . . . . . . . . . . . . . . . . 82
Weight of barrel assembly (pounds) . . . . . . . . . . . . . . . . . . . . . . . . 28
Over-all length of gun (inches) . . . . . . . . . . . . . . . . . . . . . . . . . . 65⅜
Effective life of barrel (approx. rounds) . . . . . . . . . . . . . . . . . . 3,500
Number of grooves in barrel . . . . . . . . . . . . . . . . . . . . . . . . . . . . . . 8
Rate of automatic fire (rounds per minute) . . . . . . . . . . . . 400 to 500
Muzzle velocity (fps) . . . . . . . . . . . . . . . . . . . . . . . . . . . 2,500 to 3,000

## ARMAMENT

Maximum range (approx. yards)..........................7,200
Sight (graduated to yards)...............................2,600
Weight of ammunition chest, M2, empty (pounds)............29
Weight of ammunition chest, M2, loaded (pounds)...........89
Weight of 200 links, caliber .50 (pounds)..................8
Weight of 200 cartridges, caliber .50 (pounds)............52

    *(b)* *1 Cal. .30 Browning Machine Gun M1919A4 (flexible).*
Weight of gun (pounds)..................................31.5
Weight of barrel assembly (pounds)......................7.35
Over-all length of gun (inches).........................41.11
Effective life of barrel (approx. rounds)...........8-10,000
Number of grooves in barrel................................4
Rate of automatic fire (rounds per minute)..........400-550
Muzzle velocity (fps)...................................2700
Maximum range (approx. yards)
    M1 amm..............................................3,450
    M2 amm..............................................5,500
Sight (graduated to yards)..............................2,400
Weight of ammunition chest, M2, empty (pounds)............29
Weight of ammunition chest, M2, loaded (pounds)........42.31
Weight of 200 links, caliber .30 (pounds)..................2
Weight of 200 cartridges, caliber .30 (pounds).........11.31

    *c.* **Machine Gun Mounts.**
1 cal. .50 machine gun tripod mount M3.
1 cal. .30 machine gun tripod mount M2.

**175. CAR M2A1** (fig. 3).
    *a.* **References.**
    (1) FM 23-50, Browning Machine Gun, Cal. .30, H.B., M1919A4.
    (2) FM 23-65, Browning Machine Gun, Cal. .50, H.B., M2 (mounted in combat vehicles).
    *b.* **Basic Data.**
    (1) GENERAL.
Weight without armament, fuel and operator (approx. lb)....17,080
Weight fully equipped (approx. lb).....................18,080
Over-all width (inches)..................................87½
Over-all height (guns fully elevated, inches)...........242⅝
Over-all length (inches with winch).....................244⅝
    (2) CREW.
Carries a crew of ten men.
    (3) MACHINE GUNS.
    *(a)* *1 Cal. .50 Browning Machine Gun M2, H.B. (flexible) on Ring Mount, M49.*

## BASIC HALF-TRACK VEHICLES (WHITE, AUTOCAR, and DIAMOND T)

Weight of gun (pounds)...................................82
Weight of barrel assembly (pounds)......................28
Over-all length of gun (inches).........................65 3/8
Effective life of barrel (approx. rounds)..............3,500
Number of grooves in barrel..............................8
Rate of automatic fire (per minute)..............400 to 500
Muzzle velocity (fps)..........................2,500 to 3,000
Maximum range (approx. yards)........................7,200
Sight (graduated to yards)...........................2,600
Weight of ammunition chest, M2, empty (pounds)...........29
Weight of ammunition chest, M2, loaded (pounds)..........89
Weight of 200 links, caliber .50 (pounds)................8
Weight of 200 cartridges, caliber .50 (pounds)..........52

*(b) 1 Cal. .30 Browning Machine Gun M1919A4 (flexible).*
Weight of gun (pounds).................................31.5
Weight of barrel assembly (pounds).....................7.35
Over-all length of gun (inches).......................41.11
Effective life of barrel (approx. rounds)..........8-10,000
Number of grooves in barrel..............................4
Rate of automatic fire in rounds...................400-550
Muzzle velocity (fps).................................2,700
Maximum range (approx. yards)
  M1...................................................3,450
  M2...................................................5,500
Sight (graduated to yards)...........................2,400
Weight of ammunition chest, M2, empty (pounds)...........29
Weight of ammunition chest, M2, loaded (pounds).......42.31
Weight of 200 links, caliber .30 (pounds)................2
Weight of 200 cartridges, caliber .30 (pounds).......11.31

  **c. Machine Gun Mounts.**
1 cal. .50 machine gun tripod mount M3.
1 cal. .30 machine gun tripod mount M2.

**176. PERSONNEL CARRIER M3 (fig. 5).**
  **a. References.**
  (1) FM 23-50, Browning Machine Gun, Cal. .30, H.B., M1919A4.
  **b. Basic Data.**
  (1) GENERAL.
Weight without armament, fuel and operator (approx. pounds) 16,650
Weight fully equipped (approx. pounds).................17,650
Over-all width (inches)................................87 1/2
Over-all height (guns fully elevated) (inches)...........—
Over-all length (inches)..............................242 5/8

## ARMAMENT

(2) CREW.
Carries a crew of 13 men.

(3) MACHINE GUN.

(a) 1 Cal. .30 Browning Machine Gun M1919A4 (flexible) on Pedestal Mount M25.

Weight of gun (pounds)..................................31.5
Weight of barrel assembly (pounds)......................7.35
Over-all length of gun (inches).........................41.11
Effective life of barrel (approx. rounds)...............8-10,000
Number of grooves in barrel.............................4
Rate of automatic fire (rpm)............................400-550
Muzzle velocity (fps)...................................2,700
Maximum range (approx. yards)
  M1....................................................3,450
  M2....................................................5,500
Sight (graduated to yards)..............................2,400
Weight of ammunition chest, M2, empty (pounds)..........29
Weight of ammunition chest, M2, loaded (pounds).........42.31
Weight of 200 links, caliber .30 (pounds)...............2
Weight of 200 cartridges, caliber .30 (pounds)..........11.31

c. **Machine Gun Mount.**
1 cal. .30 machine gun tripod mount M2.

### 177. PERSONNEL CARRIER M3A1 (fig. 7).

a. **References.**

(1) FM 23-50, Browning Machine Gun, Cal. .30, H.B., M1919A4.

(2) FM 23-65, Browning, Machine Gun, Cal. .50, H.B. M2 (mounted in combat vehicles).

b. **Basic Data.**

(1) GENERAL.

Weight without armament, fuel and operator (approx. pounds) 17,425
Weight fully equipped (approx. pounds)..................18,425
Over-all width (inches).................................87½
Over-all height (guns fully elevated) (inches) .........—
Over-all length (inches)................................242⅝

(2) CREW.
Carries a crew of 13 men.

(3) MACHINE GUNS.

(a) 1 Cal. .50 Browning Machine Gun M2, H.B., (flexible) on Ring Mount M49.

Weight of gun (pounds)..................................82
Weight of barrel assembly (pounds)......................28
Over-all length of gun (inches).........................65⅜

# TM 9-710

## BASIC HALF-TRACK VEHICLES (WHITE, AUTOCAR, and DIAMOND T)

Effective life of barrel (approx. rounds)..................3,500
Number of grooves in barrel................................8
Rate of automatic fire (per minute)..............400 to 500
Muzzle velocity (fps)........................2,500 to 3,000
Maximum range (approx. yards)......................7,200
Sight (graduated to yards).........................2,600
Weight of ammunition chest, M2, empty (pounds)............29
Weight of ammunition chest, M2, loaded (pounds)...........89
Weight of 200 links, caliber .50 (pounds) ................8
Weight of 200 cartridges, caliber .50 (pounds)...........52

  (b) *1 Cal. .30 Browning Machine Gun M1919A4 (flexible).*
Weight of gun (pounds).........................31.5
Weight of barrel assembly (pounds)..............7.35
Over-all length of gun (inches)................41.11
Effective life of barrel (approx. rounds).........8-10,000
Number of grooves in barrel ......................4
Rate of automatic fire (rpm)..............400-550
Muzzle velocity (fps).....................2,700
Maximum range (approx. yards)
  M1 .......................................3,450
  M2 .......................................5,500
Sight (graduated to yards)....................2,400
Weight of ammunition chest, M2, empty (pounds)............29
Weight of ammunition chest, M2, loaded (pounds)..........42.31
Weight of 200 links, caliber .30 (pounds)..................2
Weight of 200 cartridges, caliber .30 (pounds)..........11.31

  c. **Machine Gun Mounts.**
1 cal. .50 machine gun tripod mount M3.
1 cal. .30 machine gun tripod mount M2.

## 178. 81-MM MORTAR MOTOR CARRIER M4 AND M4A1 (fig. 9).

  a. **References.** FM 23-90 and C1, 81-mm Mortar M1.
  b. **Basic Data.**

Weight of mortar and mount (pounds)..................136.0
Weight of base plate (pounds).........................45.0
Over-all length of mortar (inches)....................49.5
Elevations (approx. degrees).......................40 to 85
Traverse, right or left (approx. mils)..................65
One turn of handwheel (approx. mils)....................12
Rate of fire, rounds per minute:
  Maximum ........................................30 to 35
  Normal .............................................18

## ARMAMENT

Range (approx. yards):
  HE shell:
    6.87 pounds .................................. 100 to 3,290
    10.75 pounds ................................. 300 to 2,655
    15.05 pounds ................................. 100 to 1,275
  Chemical shell, 11.4 pounds..................... 300 to 2,470

**179. 75-MM GUN MOTOR CARRIAGE, M3** (fig. 11) (75-MM GUN M1897A4 AND 75-MM GUN MOUNT M3).

  a. **References.** TM 9-306.

  b. **Basic Data.**

Weight of barrel with breech mechanism (pounds)........... 1,035
Weight of breech mechanism (pounds)....................... 60
Weight of recoil mechanism (pounds)....................... 283
Life (average) (rounds) .................................. 10,000
Over-all length of barrel and breech mechanism (inches)... 110.6
Length of recoil (inches)................................. 41.5 to 46
Length of bore (cal)...................................... 34.5
Volume of powder chamber (cu in.)......................... 85.5
Caliber of gun (inches)................................... 2.95
Maximum pressure, per sq in., lb.......................... 36,000
Type of breech mechanism.................................. eccentric-screw
Type of firing mechanism.... percussion hammer; lanyard operated
Rifling:
  Uniform R.H. twist; one turn in 25.6 cal; No. of grooves 24; depth of grooves 0.02 in.
Rate of fire:
  Short bursts, per minute (rds)......................... 6
  Prolonged firing, per minute (rds)..................... 3
Weight of complete round H.E. (pounds).................... 19.3
Weight of projectile H.E. (pounds)........................ 14.6
Weight of powder charge (pounds).......................... 0.56 to 2.0
Muzzle velocity with HE shell M48 (ft per sec.):
  Supercharge ........................................... 1,950
  Normal charge ......................................... 1,500
  Reduced charge ........................................ 950
Elevation (max deg)....................................... +29
Depression (max deg)...................................... − 9
Traverse (total) in degrees............................... 40
  Right ................................................. 21
  Left .................................................. 19

## BASIC HALF-TRACK VEHICLES (WHITE, AUTOCAR, and DIAMOND T)

180. **75-MM GUN MOTOR CARRIAGE, M3A1** (fig. 11) (75-MM GUN M1897A4 AND 75-MM GUN MOUNT M5).

   a. **References.** TM 9-306.

   b. **Basic Data.**

Weight of barrel with breech mechanism (pounds)............1,035
Weight of breech mechanism (pounds).......................60
Weight of recoil mechanism (pounds).......................283
Life (average, rds).......................................10,000
Over-all length of barrel and breech mechanism (inches)......110.6
Length of recoil (inches)..............................41.5 to 46
Length of bore (cal).......................................34.5
Volume of powder chamber (cu in.).........................85.5
Caliber of gun (inches)....................................2.95
Maximum pressure, per sq in. (lb).........................36,000
Type of breech mechanism........................eccentric-screw
Type of firing mechanism.....percussion hammer; lanyard operated
Rifling:
   Uniform R.H. twist; one turn in 25.6 cal; No. of grooves 24; depth of grooves 0.02 in.
Rate of fire:
   Short bursts per minute (rds)...............................6
   Prolonged firing, per minute (rds).........................3
Weight of complete round H.E. (pounds)....................19.3
Weight of projectile H.E. (pounds).........................14.6
Weight of powder charge (pounds)....................0.56 to 2.0
Muzzle velocity with HE shell M48 (ft per sec.):
   Supercharge...........................................1,950
   Normal charge.........................................1,500
   Reduced charge........................................950
Elevation (max deg).......................................+29
Depression (max deg)......................................—6½
Traverse (total deg)......................................42
   Right..................................................21
   Left...................................................21

181. **75-MM HOWITZER MOTOR CARRIAGE, T30** (fig. 13) (75-MM PACK HOWITZER, M1A1 AND 75-MM HOWITZER MOUNT, T10).

   a. **References.** TM 9-321.

   b. **Basic Data.**

Weight of barrel and breech mechanism (pounds).............341
Weight of breech mechanism and firing mechanism (pounds)....45
Caliber of howitzer (inches)...............................2.95

## ARMAMENT

Life (average rds) .................................... 12,000
Length of recoil (inches) ........................... 32 to 35½
Construction of barrel, cold worked.
Over-all length of barrel and breech mechanism (inches) ...... 59.1
Length of bore (calibers) ............................. 15.9
Volume of powder chamber (cu in.) ..................... 57.3
Length of rifled portion (inches) ....................... 35.8
Maximum powder pressure, lb per sq in. ............... 26,000
Muzzle velocity (max ft per sec) ...................... 1,270
Muzzle velocity (min ft per sec) ...................... 700
Type of breech mechanism, horizontal sliding wedge
Type of firing mechanism, continuous pull
Rifling:
    Uniform R.H. twist; one turn in 20 cal; No. of grooves 28; depth of grooves, 0.03 in.
Rate of fire (rds per min) ............................ 6
Traverse (total deg) .................................. 45
    Right (deg) ..................................... 22½
    Left (deg) ...................................... 22½
Elevation (max deg) ................................. +22
Depression (max deg) ............................... − 9
Weight of complete round H.E. (pounds) .............. 18.25
Weight of projectile H.E. (pounds) ................... 14.4
Weight of powder charge (pounds) .................... 1.04

182. **105-MM HOWITZER MOTOR CARRIAGE, T19** (fig. 16) (105-MM HOWITZER M2A1 AND 105-MM HOWITZER MOUNT T2).

    a. **References.** TM 9-325.

    b. **Basic Data.**

Weight of barrel and breech mechanism (pounds) ........... 1,064
Weight of breech and firing mechanism (pounds) ............ 95
Weight of recoil mechanism (pounds) .................... 457
Caliber of howitzer (inches) ............................ 4.134
Life (average rds) .................................... 7,500
Length of recoil (inches) ............................. 42 to 44
Construction of barrel, cold worked
Over-all length of barrel and breech mechanism (inches) ...... 101.4
Length of bore (calibers) ............................. 22.5
Volume of powder chamber (cu in.) ..................... 153
Length of rifled portion (inches) ....................... 77.4
Maximum powder pressure, lb per sq in. ............... 28,000
Muzzle velocity (ft per sec) .......................... 1,550

**BASIC HALF-TRACK VEHICLES (WHITE, AUTOCAR, and DIAMOND T)**

Type of breech mechanism, horizontal sliding wedge
Type of firing mechanism, continuous pull
Rifling:
    Uniform R.H. twist; one turn in 20 cal; No. of grooves, 30; depth of grooves, 0.03 in.
Rate of fire (rds per min).............................................4
Elevation (max deg)................................................+35
Depression (max deg)................................................— 5
Traverse (total deg)...............................................40
    Right (deg) ..................................................20
    Left (deg) ...................................................20
Weight of complete round (pounds)...........................41.6
Weight of projectile (pounds)................................32.7
Weight of powder charge (pounds)............................2.8

**183. MULTIPLE GUN MOTOR CARRIAGE M13 (fig. 17).**
    **a. References.**
    (1) TM 9-223, Mount, Machine Gun, Twin Cal. .50, M33.
    (2) FM 23-65, Browning Machine Gun, Cal. .50, HB, M2 (mounted in combat vehicles).
    **b. Basic Data.**
    (1) GENERAL.
Weight without armament, fuel and operator (approx. pounds)..873
Weight fully equipped (approx. pounds)....................1,500
Over-all width (feet).........................................6
Over-all height (guns fully elevated) (inches)..............78½
Over-all length (inches).....................................72
    (2) POWER DRIVE.
Power drive................Maxson Variable Speed Drive Model 120A with electric motor, Style 441Q417, Emerson Corporation; 1 hp compound wound, 12V, 90 amp
Output torque..............13 in.-lb at 2,800 rpm approx. at either shaft, zero output at the other
    (Approximately twice this torque may be obtained with small speed loss)
Dimensions: height (inches)..................................11
        width (inches)..................................18½
        length (inches).................................25½
        weight (pounds).................................139
    (3) POWER CHARGER. Briggs and Stratton, Model 300, PC-1.
Watts (output) .............................................300
Volts (output) .............................................12

## ARMAMENT

Gasoline motor (4 cycle) .................................. cyl 1
Weight (with fuel and oil, pounds) ......................... 75

    (4) CREW.

One man in centrally located gunner's seat.

    (5) FUEL AND OIL.

Fuel capacity (quarts) ....................................... 2
Octane rating of fuel .................................... 68-72
Oil capacity (pints) ....................................... 1½
Oil rating ............................................. SAE No. 20
Oil capacity (per differential, cu cm (½₅ pt)) ............... 22
Oil, lubricating, preservative, light (Spec. AXS702)

    (6) PERFORMANCE.

Duty cycle (hours)
    (5 minutes off, 5 minutes on) ............................ 5
Azimuth speed (deg per sec) ........................... 0 to 55
Elevation speed (deg per sec) .......................... 0 to 55
Power charger speed (rpm) ....................... 2,600 to 4,000
Batteries (6V each) ......................................... 2
    Discharge capacity, 8-hr rate (amp-hr) ................. 133

    (7) MACHINE GUNS.

Weight of gun (flexible) without barrel (pounds) ............ 54
Weight of barrel, approximate pounds ........................ 30
Weight of ammunition, per 200 rounds (pounds) ............... 60
Capacity of ammunition chests (rounds) ..................... 200
Rate of fire (cyclic) ................................ 400 to 500
Muzzle velocity (ft per sec) ..................... 2,500 to 3,000
Sight (graduated to yards) ............................... 2,600

**184. MULTIPLE GUN MOTOR CARRIAGE M15** (fig. 18).

    **a. References.** TM 9-235 Rev.

    **b. Basic Data.**

    (1) 37-MM GUN M1A2.

Weight of gun, complete (pounds) ........................... 365
Length of gun, complete (inches) ........................... 104
Weight of tube (pounds) .................................... 119
Length of tube (inches) ..................................... 78
Length of bore (calibers) ................................ 53.53
Effective life of tube (approx rounds) ................... 2,000
Muzzle velocity (fps) .................................... 2,600
Rate of fire (rounds per min) .............................. 120
Type of breechblock, vertical sliding
Recoil mechanism, hydro-spring
Length of recoil (inches) ................................. 10¾

# TM 9-710
184-185

**BASIC HALF-TRACK VEHICLES (WHITE, AUTOCAR, and DIAMOND T)**

Recoil fluid, oil, recoil, light
Recoil fluid capacity (pt).....................................3½
Maximum vertical range (HE shell, yards)................6,200
Maximum horizontal range (HE shell, yards)............8,875
Vertical range, self-destroying (HE shell, yards)............3,960
Horizontal range, self-destroying (HE shell, yards)..........4,070
Weight of high-explosive projectile (pounds)................1.34
Weight of armor-piercing projectile (pounds)................1.9
Maximum number of rounds permitted to be fired before cooling..100
Weight of 1 round, Shell, HE, M54 (pounds)................2.62
Weight of 1 round, Shell, AP, M59 (pounds)...............3.12

    (2) CALIBER .50 BROWNING MACHINE GUN M2, HEAVY BARREL.
Weight of gun (pounds).......................................82
Weight of barrel assembly (pounds)..........................28
Over-all length of gun (inches)............................65⅜
Effective life of barrel (approx rounds)...................3,500
Number of grooves in barrel....................................8
Rate of automatic fire (per min).....................400 to 500
Muzzle velocity (fps)..............................2,500 to 3,000
Maximum range (approx. yards).............................7,200
Sight (graduated to yards).................................2,600
Weight of ammunition chest, M2, empty (pounds)..............29
Weight of ammunition chest, M2, loaded (pounds)............89
Weight of 200 links, caliber .50 (pounds).......................8
Weight of 200 cartridges, caliber .50 (pounds)................52

  **185. MULTIPLE GUN MOTOR CARRIAGE M16 (fig. 22).**
    *a. References.* TM 9-222, Multiple (4) Cal. .50 Machine Gun Mount M45.
    *b. Basic Data.*
    (1) GENERAL.
Weight, without armor, guns, ammunition chests, fuel
  and operator (pounds)..................................1,468
Weight, fully equipped, including gunner (approx. pounds)....2,396
Weight of armor (pounds)...................................132
Over-all width (inches)....................................81½
Over-all height (guns level, inches)..........................55
    (2) POWER DRIVE.
Power Drive...............Maxson Variable Speed Drive, Model 120 A with electric motor, Style 441Q417, Emerson Corporation, 1-hp, compound wound, 12-volt, 90-amp
Output torque.............13 in.-lb at 2,800 rpm approximately at either shaft, zero output at the other

346

## ARMAMENT

Dimensions, high (inches) .............................17
           wide (inches) ...........................18½
           long (inches) ...........................25½
           weight (lb)............................139

(3) POWER CHARGER.
Power Charger, Briggs and Stratton, Model 304, type 25592
Watts (output) ........................................300
Volts (output) ........................................15
Gasoline motor (4-cycle)..............................cyl 1
Weight (with fuel and oil, pounds)....................75

(4) CREW.
Number of men, one in centrally located gunner's seat

(5) FUEL AND OIL.
  (a) *Gasoline Power Charger.*
Fuel capacity (qt)....................................2
Octane rating of fuel.............................68 to 72
Oil, capacity (pt)....................................1

  (b) *Variable Speed Drive.*
Oil, lubricating, preservative, light (Spec. AXS-702)
Oil, capacity (cu cm (⅕ pt)) (per differential)................22

(6) PERFORMANCE.
Duty cycle (5 min off, 5 min on) (hours).....................5
Azimuth speed (deg per sec)............................0 to 60
Elevation speed (deg per sec)..........................0 to 60
Power charger speed (rpm).........................2,600 to 4,000
Batteries:
    Storage lead acid, 3-cell, 17 plates per cell (6 volts each).........2
    Discharge capacity (amp-hr) (8-hr rate)....................133

(7) MACHINE GUNS.
Weight of gun (flexible) without barrel (pounds)..............54
Weight of barrel (approx. pounds).........................30
Weight of ammunition, per 200 rounds (pounds).............60
Capacity of ammunition chests (rounds)....................200
Rate of fire (cyclic)..............................400 to 500
Muzzle velocity (ft per sec)........................2,500 to 3,000
Sight (graduated to yards)..............................2,600

# TM 9-710

## BASIC HALF-TRACK VEHICLES (WHITE, AUTOCAR, and DIAMOND T)

## REFERENCES

PUBLICATIONS INDEXES.

The following publications indexes should be consulted frequently for latest changes to, or revisions of the publications given in this list of references and for new publications relating to materiel covered in this manual.

| | |
|---|---|
| Introduction to ordnance catalog (explains SNL system) | ASF Cat. ORD-1 IOC |
| Ordnance publications for supply index (index to SNL's) | ASF Cat. ORD-2 OPSI |
| Index to ordnance publications (lists FM's, TM's, TC's, and TB's of interest to ordnance personnel, MWO's, BSD, OPSR's, S of SR's, OSSC's, and OFSB's. Includes alphabetical listing of ordnance major items with publications pertaining thereto) | OFSB 1-1 |
| List of publications for training (lists MR's, MTP's, T/BA's, TA's, FM's, TM's, and TR's concerning training) | FM 21-6 |
| List of training films, film strips, and film bulletins (lists TF's, FS's, and FB's by serial number and subject) | FM 21-7 |
| Military training aids (lists graphic training aids, models, devices, and displays) | FM 21-8 |

STANDARD NOMENCLATURE LISTS.
Vehicular.

| | |
|---|---|
| Car, half-track, M2 | SNL G-102 Vol. 1 |
| Car, half-track, M2A1 | SNL G-102 Vol. 2 |
| Carrier, personnel, half-track, M3 | SNL G-102 Vol. 3 |
| Carrier, personnel, half-track, M3A1 | SNL G-102 Vol. 4 |
| Carrier, 81-mm mortar, half-track, M4 | SNL G-102 Vol. 5 |
| Carrier, 81-mm mortar, half-track, M4A1 | SNL G-102 Vol. 6 |
| Carriage, motor, 57-mm gun, T48 | SNL G-102 Vol. 7 |
| Carriage, motor, 75-mm gun, M3 | SNL G-102 Vol. 8 |
| Carriage, motor, 75-mm gun, M3A1 | SNL G-102 Vol. 9 |
| Carriage, motor, 75-mm howitzer, T30 | SNL G-102 Vol. 10 |

## REFERENCES

| | |
|---|---|
| Carriage, motor, 105-mm howitzer, T19........... | SNL G-102 Vol. 11 |
| Carriage, motor, multiple gun, M13 (T1E4)....... | SNL G-102 Vol. 12 |
| Carriage, motor, multiple gun, M15 (T28E1)..... | SNL G-102 Vol. 13 |
| Carriage, motor, multiple gun, M15A1............ | SNL G-102 Vol. 16 |
| Carriage, motor, multiple gun, M16.............. | SNL G-102 Vol. 14 |
| Carrier, 81-mm mortar, half-track, M21.......... | SNL G-102 Vol. 15 |

### Ammunition and Armament.

| | |
|---|---|
| Ammunition, fixed and semifixed, all types, including subcaliber for pack, light and medium field artillery, including complete round date............... | SNL R-1 Part I Part II |
| Ammunition instruction material for pack, light and medium field artillery....................... | SNL R-6 |
| Gun, machine, cal. .30, Browning, M1919A4, fixed and flexible; M1919A5, fixed, and M1919A6, flexible.......................................... | SNL A-6 |
| Gun, machine, cal. .50, Browning, M2, heavy barrel, fixed and flexible................................ | SNL A-39 |
| Mortar and mount, 81-mm, M1.................. | SNL A-33 |
| Service fuzes and primers for pack, light and medium field artillery.................................... | SNL R-3 Part I, Part II |

### Maintenance.

| | |
|---|---|
| Cleaning, preserving and lubrication materials, special oils, and miscellaneous related items..... | SNL K-1 |
| Interchangeability chart of ordnance maintenance tools for combat vehicles....................... | SNL G-27 Vol. 2 |
| Soldering, brazing, and welding materials, gases and related items..................................... | SNL K-2 |
| Tools, maintenance, for repair of automatic guns and antiaircraft materiel, automatic and semiautomatic cannon and mortars; individual items and parts............................................... | SNL A-35 |
| Tools, maintenance, for repair of automotive vehicles........................................... | SNL G-27 Vol. 1 |
| Tools, maintenance, for repair of pack, light, and medium field artillery; and armament of these calibers for airplane and combat vehicles........ | SNL C-18 |
| Tool sets, motor transport...................... | SNL N-19 |

# TM 9-710

## BASIC HALF-TRACK VEHICLES (WHITE, AUTOCAR, and DIAMOND T)

EXPLANATORY PUBLICATIONS.

### Armament.

| | |
|---|---|
| Browning machine gun, caliber .30, HB, M1919A4 (mounted in combat vehicles) | FM 23-50 |
| Browning machine gun, caliber .50, HB, M2, ground | FM 23-60 |
| Browning machine gun, caliber .50, HB, M2 (mounted in combat vehicles) | FM 23-65 |
| Mount, machine gun, twin, cal. .50, M33 | TM 9-223 |
| Multiple cal. .50 machine gun mount M45 | TM 9-222 |
| 37-mm AA gun materiel | TM 9-235 |
| 81-mm mortar, M1 | FM 23-90 |
| 75-mm howitzer M1A1 (mounted in combat vehicles) | TM 9-321 |
| 75-mm gun M1897A4 (mounted in combat vehicles) | TM 9-306 |
| 105-mm howitzer M2 and M2A1 and 105-mm howitzer carriage M1A1 and M2 | TM 9-325 |

### Fundamental Principles.

| | |
|---|---|
| Automotive electricity | TM 10-580 |
| Ammunition, general | TM 9-1900 |
| Basic maintenance manual | TM 38-250 |
| Electric fundamentals | TM 1-455 |
| Military motor vehicles | AR 850-15 |
| Motor vehicle inspections and preventive maintenance services | TM 9-2810 |
| Precautions in handling gasoline | AR 850-20 |
| Standard military motor vehicles | TM 9-2800 |

### Maintenance and Repair.

| | |
|---|---|
| Cleaning, preserving, lubricating, and welding materials and similar items issued by the Ordnance Department | TM 9-850 |
| Cold weather lubrication and service of combat vehicles and automotive materiel | OFSB 6-11 |
| Ordnance maintenance: Power train (axles, transmission, and propeller shaft) for half-track vehicles (White, Autocar, Diamond T) | TM 9-1710 |
| Ordnance maintenance: Browning machine gun, cal. .50, all types | TM 9-1225 |
| Ordnance maintenance: Browning machine gun, cal. .30, all types; U. S. machine gun, cal. .22, and trainer, cal. .22, all types | TM 9-1205 |
| Ordnance maintenance: carburetors (Stromberg) | TM 9-1826B |

350

TM 9-710

## REFERENCES

| | |
|---|---|
| Ordnance maintenance: chassis and body for half-track vehicles (White, Autocar, Diamond T).... | TM 9-1710C |
| Ordnance maintenance: electrical equipment (Delco-Remy)................................ | TM 9-1825A |
| Ordnance maintenance: fuel pumps............... | TM 9-1828A |
| Ordnance maintenance: mortars, light field, and mounts, all types............................ | TM 9-1260 |
| Ordnance maintenance: twin cal. .50 machine gun mount M33 and multiple cal. .50 machine gun mount M45................................... | TM 9-1223 |
| Ordnance maintenance: White 160AX engine, half-track vehicles.................................. | TM 9-1711 |
| Ordnance maintenance: 37-mm AA gun materiel... | TM 9-1235 |
| Ordnance maintenance: 75-mm howitzer materiel.. | TM 9-1320 |
| Ordnance maintenance: 75-mm gun and carriage M1897, all types, and special field artillery vehicles..................................... | TM 9-1305 |
| Ordnance maintenance: 105-mm howitzer M2 and M2A1; carriage M1A1 and M2................ | TM 9-1325 |
| Tune-up and adjustment........................ | TM 10-530 |

### Protection of Materiel.

| | |
|---|---|
| Chemical decontamination, materials and equipment..................................... | TM 3-220 |
| Camouflage................................... | FM 5-20 |
| Decontamination of armored force vehicles........ | FM 17-59 |
| Defense against chemical attack................. | FM 21-40 |
| Explosives and demolitions...................... | FM 5-25 |

### Storage and Shipment.

| | |
|---|---|
| Ordnance storage and shipment chart, group G—Major items............................. | OSSC-G |
| Registration of motor vehicles................... | AR 850-10 |
| Rules governing the loading of mechanized and motorized army equipment, also major caliber guns, for the United States Army and Navy, on open top equipment published by Operations and Maintenance Department of Association of American Railroads. | |
| Storage of motor vehicle equipment.............. | AR 850-18 |

# TM 9-710
## BASIC HALF-TRACK VEHICLES (WHITE, AUTOCAR, and DIAMOND T)

# INDEX

### A

| | Page No. |
|---|---|
| Adjustment | |
|   carburetor | 166 |
|   clutch | 157 |
|   distributor | 191, 197 |
|   drag link | 302 |
|   drive sprocket bearing | 289 |
|   front axle | 220 |
|   headlight and blackout driving light | 314 |
|   pedal linkage | 259 |
|   service brake shoes | 277 |
|   steering gear | 298 |
|   tracks | 229 |
| Air cleaners | |
|   after-operation and weekly service | 51 |
|   at-halt service | 49 |
|   description | 168, 266 |
|   lubrication | 55 |
|   maintenance | 169, 266 |
|   removal and installation | 169 |
|   run-in test procedures | 96 |
|   tune-up | 136 |
| Ammeter | |
|   road test | 103 |
|   trouble shooting | 123 |
| Armament | |
|   car M2 | 336 |
|   car M2A1 | 337 |
|   81-mm mortar carrier M4 and M4A1 | 340 |
|   multiple gun motor carriage M13 | 344 |
|   multiple gun motor carriage M15 | 345 |
|   multiple gun motor carriage M16 | 346 |
|   105-mm howitzer motor carriage T19 | 343 |
|   personnel carrier M3 | 338 |
|   personnel carrier M3A1 | 339 |
|   75-mm gun motor carriage M3 | 341 |
|   75-mm howitzer motor carriage T30 | 342 |
| Auxiliary equipment controls and operation | |
|   winch cable operation | 32 |
|   winch controls | 32 |
| Axle, front | |
|   description and data | 218 |

| | Page No. |
|---|---|
|   front axle assembly | |
|     installation | 224 |
|     removal | 223 |
|   maintenance and adjustment | 218 |
|   preventive maintenance | 112 |
|   tie rod | 221 |
|   trouble shooting | 126 |
| Axle, rear (jackshaft) | |
|   description and data | 225 |
|   installation | 227 |
|     axle shaft | 225 |
|   removal | 226 |
|     axle shaft | 225 |
|   trouble shooting | 127 |

### B

| | Page No. |
|---|---|
| Batteries | |
|   after-operation and weekly service | 50 |
|   care after submersion | 41 |
|   care in extreme heat | 34 |
|   maintenance operations | 106 |
|   run-in test procedures | 96 |
| Battery and lighting system | |
|   battery | 310 |
|   description and data | 310 |
|   fuses and circuit breakers | 317 |
|   headlights and marker lights | 313 |
|   horns | 319 |
|   taillights | 317 |
|   terminal block | 317 |
|   terminal box | 317 |
| Blackout driving light sealed beam lamp-unit replacement | 315 |
| Body and frame | |
|   bumpers | 308 |
|   description | 303 |
|   floors, hood, doors, running boards, and mud guards | 303 |
|   frame | 308 |
|   pintle and tow hooks | 307 |
|   roller | 303 |
|   seats | 305 |
|   top and bows | 307 |
|   windshield and windshield wipers | 307 |
| Bogie | |
|   assembly | 242 |
|   bogie lower roller assembly | 237 |

**TM 9-710**

# INDEX

## B—Cont'd

| | Page No. |
|---|---|
| Bogie—Cont'd | |
|   bogie upper roller | 236 |
|   description | 235 |
|   preventive maintenance | 110 |
|   volute spring and crab | 241 |
| Bogie suspension and track | |
|   bogie | 235 |
|   description | 229 |
|   idler and adjustment mechanism | 246 |
|   track chains | 249 |
|   tracks | 229 |
| Brake booster | |
|   hydrovac | 263 |
|   vacuum | 261 |
| Brake drums, preventive maintenance | 109 |
| Brake master cylinder, preventive maintenance | 113 |
| Brake pedal and linkage | |
|   hydrovac | 262 |
|   vacuum booster | 259 |
| Brake shoes, preventive maintenance | 109 |
| Brake system | |
|   bleeding the hydraulic system | 256 |
|   brake booster | |
|     air cleaner | 266 |
|     check valve | 266 |
|     hydrovac | 263 |
|     vacuum | 261 |
|   brake pedal and linkage | |
|     hydrovac | 262 |
|     vacuum booster | 259 |
|   description and data | 251 |
|   electric trailer brake controller and linkage | 283 |
|   front and rear wheel cylinders | 269 |
|   hose, lines, and fittings | 271 |
|   master cylinder | 267 |
|   propeller shaft (parking) brake | 281 |
|   road test | 104 |
|   service brake shoes | 277 |
|   trouble shooting | 128 |
| Bumpers | |
|   description | 308 |
|   removal and installation | 309 |

## C

| | Page No. |
|---|---|
| Car M2 | 336 |
| Car M2A1 | 337 |
| Carbon, removal from engine | 139 |
| Carburetor | |
|   adjustment | 166 |
|   data | 161 |
|   description | 165 |
|   installation | 167 |
|   maintenance operations | 108 |
|   removal | 167 |
|   tune-up | 136 |
| Carriage, gun motor, 75-mm, M3 | 341 |
| Carriage, gun motor, 75-mm, M3A1 | 342 |
| Carriage, howitzer motor, 75-mm, T30 | 342 |
| Carriage, howitzer motor, 105-mm, T19 | 343 |
| Carriage, multiple gun motor, M13 | 344 |
| Carriage, multiple gun motor, M15 | 345 |
| Carriage, multiple gun motor, M16 | 346 |
| Carrier, motor, mortar, 81-mm, M4 and M4A1 | 340 |
| Carrier, personnel, M3 | 338 |
| Carrier, personnel, M3A1 | 339 |
| Check valve (brake booster) | |
|   description | 266 |
|   removal and installation | 267 |
| Cleaning oil pan and guard | 141 |
| Clutch | |
|   adjustment | 157 |
|   description and data | 157 |
|   during-operation service | 48 |
|   installation | 159 |
|   removal | 159 |
|   road test | 104 |
|   run-in test | 99 |
|   trouble shooting | 125 |
| Clutch pedal, preventive maintenance | 112 |
| Clutch pilot bearing, lubrication | 60 |
| Compass | |
|   compensation | 325 |
|   removal and installation | 325 |
| Cooling system | |
|   belts | 180 |
|   data | 175 |
|   description | 174 |
|   fan | 179 |

# TM 9-710
## BASIC HALF-TRACK VEHICLES (WHITE, AUTOCAR, and DIAMOND T)

### C—Cont'd

Cooling system—Cont'd
  operation
    care after fording streams or
      flood conditions............ 41
    extreme cold ............... 38
    extreme heat .............. 34
  radiator and shroud .......... 180
  surge tank .................. 183
  thermostat .................. 186
  trouble shooting ............. 121
  water pump.................. 175

Crankcase
  lubrication ................. 60
  maintenance operation........ 106

Crankcase ventilator
  description ................. 146
  maintenance ................ 147
  removal and installation....... 147

Cranking motor
  description ................. 200
  maintenance operation ........ 107
  removal and installation....... 200
  trouble shooting............. 122

Cylinder head and gasket
  installation ................. 139
  removal .................... 137

### D

Data
  basic half-track vehicles....... 20
  brake system ............... 251
  clutch ..................... 157
  cooling system.............. 175
  engine ..................... 133
  front axle................... 218
  fuel system ................. 160
  ignition system .............. 187
  instrument cluster............ 320
  oil filter ................... 145
  oil temperature regulator...... 143
  rear axle.................... 225
  starting and generating system.. 200
  winch ..................... 327

Description:
  armored half-track vehicles.... 6
  battery and lighting system.... 310
  body and frame.............. 303
  bogie suspension and track..... 229
  brake system................ 251
  clutch ..................... 157

cooling system............... 174
distributor ................. 191
engine ..................... 133
front axle................... 218
fuel system ................. 160
ignition system............... 187
intake and exhaust system..... 173
oil filter ................... 145
oil temperature regulator...... 142
rear axle ................... 225
starting and generating system.. 200
terminal block and terminal box 317
voltage regulator............. 203
winch ..................... 326

Differences among models of half-
  track vehicles................ 6

Differential, care in extreme cold.. 37

Drag brake
  installation of shoe........... 330
  removal of shoe.............. 329
  shoe adjustment ............. 329

Drag link
  adjustment ................. 302
  description and data.......... 302

Distributor
  adjustment ................. 197
  description ................. 191
  installation ................. 195
  lubrication ................. 60
  maintenance and adjustment... 191
  maintenance operation ........ 107
  removal ................... 195
  tune-up ................... 135

Driving axles, care in extreme heat 35

Driving controls and operation
  controls .................... 23
  operation of vehicles.......... 28
  towing the vehicle............ 31

### E

Electric trailer brake controller
  and linkage
  adjustment ................. 284
  description ................. 283
  removal of linkage........... 284

Electrical system operation
  care after fording streams or
    flood conditions............. 41
  extreme heat................ 34

# INDEX

## E—Cont'd

Engine
  data, maintenance, and adjustment in vehicle
    carbon removal............ 139
    crankcase ventilator........ 146
    cylinder head and gasket
      installation ............ 139
      removal ................ 137
    description and data........ 133
    oil filter .................. 145
    oil pan and guard.......... 141
    oil temperature regulator.... 142
    tune-up .................. 134
  installation ................ 153
  operation in extreme heat...... 34
  removal .................... 149
  road test.................... 104
  trouble shooting............. 118
Exhaust pipe, muffler, and tail pipe 173

## F

Fan
  description ................ 179
  maintenance .............. 179
Fire extinguisher
  before-operation service....... 45
  run-in test procedures......... 96
Fuel and vacuum pump
  data ....................... 160
  description and operation...... 163
  maintenance operation........ 108
  removal and installation....... 165
Fuel filters
  after-operation and weekly service ..................... 51
  data ....................... 161
  description and maintenance... 165
  run-in test procedures......... 96
  tune-up .................... 137
Fuel system
  air cleaner .................. 168
  carburetor .................. 165
  care after submersion......... 42
  care in extreme heat.......... 35
  description and data.......... 160
  fuel and vacuum pump., ...... 163
  fuel filter................... 165
  fuel tanks................... 161
  trouble shooting ............ 120
  tune-up .................... 136

Fuel tanks
  description ................ 161
  installation ................ 163
  maintenance .............. 163
  removal .................. 163
Fuses and circuit breakers
  description ................ 317
  maintenance .............. 319

## G

Gear cases, lubrication.......... 60
Generator
  description ................ 203
  installation ................ 203
  maintenance operation........ 107
  removal .................. 203
  trouble shooting............ 122

## H

Hand brake, preventive maintenance ..................... 112
Headlight sealed beam lamp-unit, replacement ................ 314
Headlights and marker lights..... 313
Horns, removal and installation... 319
Hose, lines and fittings
  description ................ 271
  installation ................ 275
  maintenance .............. 273
  removal .................. 273
Hubs and bearings
  description and data.......... 287
  drive sprocket hubs and bearings
    adjustment ............... 289
    removal and installation..... 290
  front wheel bearing adjustment. 287
  front wheel hubs and bearings
    installation .............. 288
    maintenance ............. 288
    removal ................. 287
Hydraulic system, bleeding...... 256

## I

Idler and adjusting mechanism
  description ................ 246
  idler and track tension mechanism
    installation .............. 248
    removal ................. 247

# TM 9-710
## BASIC HALF-TRACK VEHICLES (WHITE, AUTOCAR, and DIAMOND T)

### I—Cont'd  Page No.

Idler and adjusting mechanism
—Cont'd
  idler wheel and bearing
    installation .............. 247
    removal ................. 246
Ignition switch
  description ................ 187
  removal and installation....... 190
Ignition system
  description and data......... 187
    engine timing.............. 197
    ignition coil............... 190
    ignition switch............. 187
    ignition wiring and shielding. 198
    spark plugs................ 197
    trouble shooting ........... 121
    tune-up .................. 135
Inspection and preventive maintenance services
  after-operation and weekly
    service .................. 50
  at-halt service .............. 48
  before-operation service....... 45
  during-operation service....... 47
Instruments and gages
  compass ................. 325
  description ............... 320
  instrument cluster........... 320
  road test ................ 103
  speedometer and cable........ 321
  tachometer and cable......... 323
  voltmeter ................ 323
Intake and exhaust system
  description ............... 171
  exhaust pipe, muffler, and tail
    pipe .................... 173
  installation ............... 172
  maintenance .............. 171
  removal .................. 172

### J

Jackshaft, trouble shooting ...... 127
Jackshaft sprocket
  description ............... 286
  removal and installation....... 286

### L

Lighting and switches, trouble
  shooting .................. 131
Loading and blocking for rail
  shipment ................. 333
Lubrication guide.............. 54

### M  Page No.

Maintenance
  air cleaner ................ 169
  battery .................. 310
  brake booster (hydrovac)..... 265
  crankcase ventilator ......... 147
  distributor ................ 191
  front axle................. 218
  fuel tanks................. 163
  intake and exhaust system..... 171
  oil filter ................. 146
  radiator and shroud.......... 180
  shock absorbers and linkage.... 295
  tracks ................... 229
Manifolds, maintenance operation. 108
Master cylinder
  description ............... 267
  installation and removal....... 269
  maintenance .............. 268
MWO and major unit assembly
  replacement record........... 95

### O

Oil filters
  description and data......... 145
  installation on engine......... 154
  lubrication ............... 60
  maintenance .............. 146
  maintenance operation........ 106
  removal from engine......... 151
Oil pan and guard
  cleaning ................. 141
  installation ............... 142
    on engine ............... 155
  removal .................. 141
    from engine............. 150
Oil pressure gage, road test...... 103
Oil temperature regulator
  description and data......... 142
  installation ............... 144
  removal .................. 143
Oilcan points................ 61
Operation
  half-track vehicle ........... 28
  ignition system ............. 187
  surge tank ................ 183
  under unusual conditions
    extreme cold............. 35
    extreme heat ............. 34

# INDEX

## O—Cont'd

Operation—Cont'd
 fording streams or flood
  conditions .............. 41
 muddy terrain or deep snow.. 42
 rough terrain ............. 42
 sandy terrain ............. 40
 voltage regulator.......... 203
Organization preventive maintenance service ............... 101
Organization tools and equipment. 100

## P

Pintle and tow hooks, description. 307
Pitman arm replacement........ 299
Power take-off
 description and data........ 207
 installation ............... 211
 removal .................... 207
 road test................... 104
 trouble shooting ........... 126
Propeller shafts (and universal joints)
 power take-off to winch propeller shaft............. 216
 preventive maintenance ..... 112
 transfer case to front axle propeller shaft............. 214
 transfer case to rear axle propeller shaft.............. 215
Propeller shaft (parking) brake
 description and adjustment.... 281
 installation of brake shoe assembly ................. 282
 removal of brake shoe assembly. 281

## R

Radiator and shroud
 data ....................... 175
 description ................ 180
 installation ............... 183
 maintenance ................ 180
 maintenance operation....... 106
 removal .................... 181
Reports and records of lubrication. 66
Roller, removal and installation... 303
Run-in test, new vehicle
 correction of deficiencies...... 95
 test procedures ............ 96

## S

Safety brake
 adjustment of band.......... 327
 removal and installation of band 328
Service brake shoes
 description and adjustment.... 277
 removal and installation....... 278
Shipment and temporary storage
 loading and blocking for rail shipment .................. 333
 preparation for temporary storage .................... 331
Shock absorbers and links, preventive maintenance........... 111
Spark plugs
 description ................ 197
 maintenance ................ 197
 maintenance operations ..... 106
 removal and installation....... 197
 trouble shooting ........... 121
 tune-up .................... 135
Speedometer and cable
 description and data......... 321
 installation ............... 322
 removal ................321, 322
 run-in test ................. 98
Springs and shock absorbers
 shock absorbers and linkage.... 295
 springs and shackles......... 293
 trouble shooting ........... 129
Starting and generating system
 cranking motor ............. 200
 description and data......... 200
 generator .................. 203
 voltage regulator........... 203
Steering gear
 adjustment ................. 298
 data ....................... 298
 description ................ 296
 Pitman arm replacement ..... 299
Steering knuckles, preventive maintenance .................. 111
Steering system, trouble shooting. 130
Surge tank
 description and operation...... 183
 removal and installation......184

# TM 9-710
## BASIC HALF-TRACK VEHICLES (WHITE, AUTOCAR, and DIAMOND T)

### T

| | Page No. |
|---|---|
| Tachometer and cable | |
| description and data | 323 |
| removal and installation | 323 |
| Tachometer drive and adapter, maintenance operations | 108 |
| Taillights, description and replacement | 317 |
| Terminal block and terminal box, description | 317 |
| Thermostat | |
| data | 175 |
| description, removal, and installation | 186 |
| Throttle control button, description | 26 |
| Tie rod | |
| description | 221 |
| removal and installation | 221 |
| Tires and tubes | |
| data | 292 |
| description | 291 |
| operation in sandy terrain | 40 |
| removal and installation | 292 |
| Tools, special | 100 |
| Tools and equipment stowage on vehicle | |
| armament and ammunition | |
| M3A1 | 67 |
| M16 | 68 |
| gun tools and equipment | |
| M3A1 | 69 |
| M16 | 73 |
| vehicle accessories | |
| M3A1 | 77 |
| M16 | 80 |
| vehicle spare parts and tools | |
| M3A1 | 81 |
| M16 | 83 |
| Towing the vehicle | 31 |
| Track | |
| description | 229 |
| installation | 235 |
| maintenance and adjustment | 229 |
| removal | 233 |
| Track chains | |
| description and maintenance | 249 |
| installation and removal | 249 |
| Transfer case | |
| care in extreme cold | 37 |

| | Page No. |
|---|---|
| care in extreme heat | 35 |
| description and data | 207 |
| installation | 211 |
| removal | 207 |
| road test | 104 |
| preventive maintenance | 113 |
| trouble shooting | 126 |
| Transmission | |
| care in extreme cold | 37 |
| care in extreme heat | 35 |
| description and data | 207 |
| during-operation service | 48 |
| installation | 211 |
| preventive maintenance | 113 |
| removal | 207 |
| road test | 104 |
| trouble shooting | 125 |
| Trouble shooting | |
| brake system | 128 |
| clutch | 125 |
| cooling system | 121 |
| engine | 118 |
| front axle | 126 |
| fuel system | 119 |
| ignition system | 121 |
| lighting and switches | 131 |
| rear axle—jackshaft | 127 |
| springs | 129 |
| steering | 139 |
| transfer case and power take-off | 126 |
| transmission | 125 |
| wheels | 129 |
| windshield wipers (body and frame) | 131 |
| Tune-up of engine | 134 |

### U

| | |
|---|---|
| Universal joints, lubrication | 61 |

### V

| | |
|---|---|
| Vehicle accessories | |
| M3A1 | 77 |
| M16 | 80 |
| Vehicle tools and spare parts | |
| M3A1 | 81 |
| M16 | 83 |
| Voltage regulator | |
| description and operation | 203 |
| removal and installation | 206 |

## INDEX

| V—Cont'd | Page No. |
|---|---|
| Voltmeter | |
|   data | 324 |
|   description | 323 |
|   removal and installation | 324 |

### W

| | Page No. |
|---|---|
| Water pump | |
|   description | 175 |
|   installation | 177 |
|     on engine | 154 |
|   maintenance operation | 107 |
|   removal | 175 |
|     from engine | 151 |
| Wheel cylinders, front and rear | |
|   description | 269 |
|   installation | 270 |
|   removal | 269 |
| Wheels | |
|   description and data | 286 |
|   removal and installation | 286 |
|   trouble shooting | 129 |
| Winch | |
|   cable | 330 |
|     lubrication | 61 |
|     operation | 32 |
|   data | 327 |
|   description | 326 |
|   drag brake | 329 |
|   preventive maintenance | 114 |
|   removal and installation | 330 |
|   safety brake | 327 |
| Winch controls | 32 |
| Windshield wiper | |
|   removal and installation | 307 |
|   trouble shooting | 131 |

# IN HIGH DEFINITION NOW AVAILABLE!

**COMPLETE LINE OF WWII AIRCRAFT FLIGHT MANUALS**

## WWW.PERISCOPEFILM.COM

# Also Now Available!

**Visit us at:**

**www.PeriscopeFilm.com**

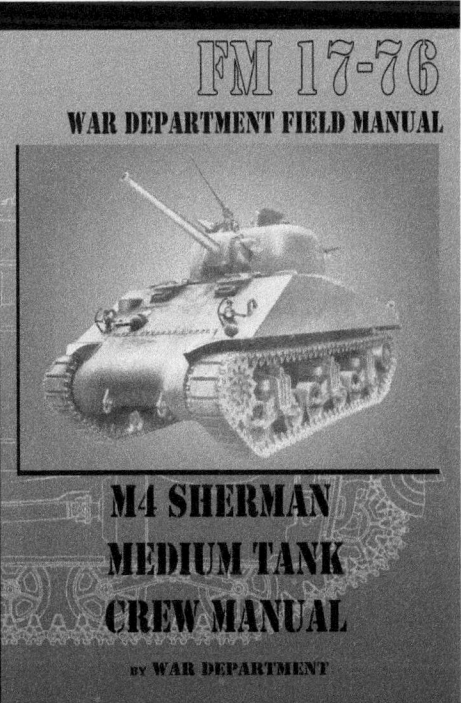

©2011 Periscope Film LLC
All Rights Reserved
ISBN# 978-1-937684-97-6

www.ingramcontent.com/pod-product-compliance
Lightning Source LLC
Chambersburg PA
CBHW050314170426
43202CB00011B/1890